The RegTech Book

This edition first published 2019
© 2019 Millennial Ltd

Registered office

John Wiley & Sons Ltd, The Atrium, Southern Gate, Chichester, West Sussex, PO19 8SQ, United Kingdom

For details of our global editorial offices, for customer services, and for information about how to apply for permission to reuse the copyright material in this book, please see our website at www.wiley.com.

Library of Congress Cataloging-in-Publication Data

Names: Barberis, Janos, editor. | Arner, Douglas W., editor. | Buckley, Ross P., editor.
Title: The regtech book : the financial technology handbook for investors, entrepreneurs and visionaries in regulation / edited by Janos Barberis, Prof. Douglas W. Arner, Prof. Ross P. Buckley.
Description: Chichester, West Sussex, United Kingdom : John Wiley & Sons, 2018. | Includes index. |
Identifiers: LCCN 2018043123 (print) | LCCN 2018044728 (ebook) | ISBN 9781119362166 (Adobe PDF) | ISBN 9781119362173 (ePub) | ISBN 9781119362142 (paperback)
Subjects: LCSH: Financial institutions—State supervision. | Finance—Technological innovations. | Trade regulation.
Classification: LCC HG173 (ebook) | LCC HG173 .R395 2018 (print) | DDC 332.068/1—dc23
LC record available at https://lccn.loc.gov/2018043123

A catalogue record for this book is available from the British Library.

ISBN 978-1-119-36214-2 (paperback)   ISBN 978-1-119-36216-6 (ePDF)
ISBN 978-1-119-36217-3 (ePub)   ISBN 978-1-119-36219-7 (WOL)

10 9 8 7 6 5 4 3 2 1

Cover Design: Wiley

Cover Image: © pkproject/Shutterstock

Set in 10/13pt Helvetica Lt Std by Aptara, New Delhi, India
Printed in Great Britain by TJ International Ltd, Padstow, Cornwall, UK

The RegTech Book

The Financial Technology Handbook for Investors, Entrepreneurs and Visionaries in Regulation

Edited by
Janos Barberis
Douglas W. Arner
Ross P. Buckley

Contents

6. RegTech for Authorized Institutions

7. RegTech from a Regulatory Perspective

8. Blockchain and AI in RegTech

9. RegTech Applicability Outside the Financial Services Industry

10. Social Impact and Regulation

11. The Future of RegTech

A FinTech and RegTech Overview:

Where We Have Come From and Where We Are Going

Douglas W. Arner
Kerry Holdings Professor in Law, Co-Founder, Asian Institute of International Financial Law, and Faculty Director, LLM in Compliance and Regulation, University of Hong Kong

Ross P. Buckley
KPMG Law – King & Wood Mallesons Chair of Innovative Disruption and Law, Scientia Professor, and Member, Centre for Law, Markets and Regulation, UNSW Sydney

and Janos Barberis
Senior Research Fellow, Asian Institute of International Financial Law, Faculty of Law, University of Hong Kong, and Founder, SuperCharger FinTech Accelerator and FinTech HK

Introduction

In this overview, we seek to set the scene for all that is to come by providing a brief history of FinTech and RegTech, and by giving our particular view on the truly transformative potential of RegTech. In doing so, we draw upon some of our major works in the field.[1]

Regulatory and technological developments are changing the nature of financial markets, services and institutions. Financial

technology, or FinTech, refers to the use of technology to deliver financial solutions, and regulatory technology, or RegTech, describes the use of technology in the context of regulatory monitoring, reporting and compliance. We argue that the true potential of RegTech lies in its ability to effect a profound transition from a Know Your Customer (KYC) to a Know Your Data (KYD) approach – one underpinned by efficient processes for the collection, formatting and analysis of reported data.

FinTech

The Evolution of FinTech

FinTech is not a new concept. The term 'FinTech' can be traced to the early 1990s,[2] and now refers to a rapidly developing evolutionary process across financial services.[3] The evolution of FinTech has unfolded in three stages, which we characterize as FinTech 1.0, 2.0 and 3.0.[4]

FinTech 1.0 (1866–1967)

Finance and technology have had a long history of mutual reinforcement, from early calculation technologies like the abacus, to the emergence of double entry accounting in the late Middle Ages and Renaissance. The late 1600s saw a European financial revolution featuring the rise of joint stock companies, insurance,

---

[1] D.W. Arner, J. Barberis and R.P. Buckley, 'FinTech, RegTech and the Reconceptualization of Financial Regulation', *Northwestern Journal of International Law and Business*, 37, no. 3 (2017): 371; and D.W. Arner, J. Barberis and R.P. Buckley, 'The Evolution of FinTech: A New Post-Crisis Paradigm?', *Georgetown Journal of International Law* 47, no. 4 (2016): 1271.

[2] Marc Hochstein, 'Fintech (the word, that is) evolves', *American Banker*, (2015), https://www.americanbanker.com/opinion/fintech-the-word-that-is-evolves

[3] Chloe Wang, 'Financial technology booms as digital wave hits banks, insurance firms', *Channel News Asia*, (2015), http://www.channelnewsasia.com/news/business/singapore/financial-technology/1875644.html

[4] D.W. Arner, J. Barberis and R.P. Buckley, 'The Evolution of FinTech: A New Post-Crisis Paradigm?', *Georgetown Journal of International Law* 47, no. 4 (2016): 1271.

and banking – all based on double entry accounting – which was essential to the Industrial Revolution.[5]

In the late 19th century, technologies such as the telegraph helped to forge cross-border financial connections.[6] This was followed by rapid post-World War II technological developments. By the end of this period, a global telex network had been implemented.[7]

FinTech 2.0 (1967–2008)

The late 1960s and 1970s saw rapid advances in electronic payment systems, including the establishment of the Inter-Bank Computer Bureau in the UK in 1968 and the US Clearing House Interbank Payments System in 1970. Reflecting the need to link domestic payments systems, the Society of Worldwide Interbank Financial Telecommunications (SWIFT) was established in 1973, followed shortly after by the 1974 collapse of Herstatt Bank – a crisis which served as the catalyst for the first major regulatory initiative, the establishment of the Basel Committee on Banking Supervision of the Bank for International Settlements in 1975.[8]

1987's 'Black Monday' saw stock markets crash globally; another reminder that global markets were technologically interlinked.[9] Advances in the mid-1990s underscored the initial risks with complex computerized risk management systems, with the collapse of Long-term Capital Management after the Asian and

Russian financial crises of 1997-98.[10] However, the emergence of the internet in the 1990s provided the foundational change that made FinTech 3.0 possible.

FinTech 3.0 (2008 – present)

A confluence of factors emerged between 2007 to 2008, which provided the impetus for FinTech 3.0 in developed countries. The brand image of banks was severely shaken. A 2015 survey reported that Americans trusted technology firms far more than banks.[11]

The GFC damaged bank profitability and the regulation that ensued drove compliance costs to record highs. The timing of the GFC also played a critical role in FinTech's development. This phase has required high levels of smartphone penetration and sophisticated application programming interfaces (APIs), which would not have existed had the GFC occurred five years earlier.[12]

The key differentiating factors of FinTech 3.0 have been the rapid rate of development and the changing identity of those who are providing financial services. Start-ups and technology firms have challenged established financial institutions by offering specific, niche services to consumers, businesses and incumbent financial institutions.

FinTech 3.0 has also been characterized by the rapid growth of companies from 'too-small-to-care' to 'too-large-to-ignore'

[5] Charles More, *Understanding the Industrial Revolution*, (Psychology Press, 2000): 36.

[6] Tom Standage, *The Victorian Internet: The Remarkable Story of the Telegraph and the Nineteenth Century's On-line Pioneers* (Bloombury, 1998).

[7] 'The history of fax: from 1843 to present day, Fax Authority, http://faxauthority.com/fax-history/

[8] History of the Basel Committee and its Membership, Bank for International Settlements, 2016, http://www.bis.org/bcbs/history.pdf

[9] Richard Bookstaber, *A Demon of Our Own Design* (John Wiley & Sons, 2007): 7–32.

[10] Philippe Jorion, 'Risk Management Lessons from Long-Term Management', European Financial Management, (2000), http://merage.uci.edu/~jorion/papers%5Cltcm.pdf

[11] 'Survey shows Americans trust technology firms more than banks and retailers', *Let's Talk Payments*, (2015), http://letstalkpayments.com/survey-shows-americans-trust-technology-firms-more-than-banks-and-retailers/

[12] We thank David Link for making the point that sophisticated APIs were necessary to underpin much FinTech 3.0 activity, at the Melbourne Money & Finance Conference, 18 July 2016.

and finally 'too-big-to-fail'. This landscape raises the important question for regulators of precisely *when* they should begin to focus on certain industry participants. This highlights why the evolution of FinTech requires similar developments in RegTech. A flexible, multi-level approach is necessary to impose regulatory requirements with differing intensity based on the size and risk of firms.

FinTech in developed and developing economies

Today, FinTech impacts every area of the financial system globally, with the most dramatic impact perhaps in China, where technology firms such as Alibaba have transformed finance. China's inefficient banking infrastructure and high technology penetration make it a fertile ground for FinTech. Emerging markets, particularly in Asia and Africa, have begun to experience what we characterize as Fintech 3.5 – an era of strong FinTech development supported by deliberate government policy choices in pursuit of economic development.

FinTech development in Africa has been led by telecommunications companies on the back of the rapid uptake of mobile telephones and the underdeveloped nature of banking services. Mobile money – the provision of basic transaction and savings services through e-money recorded on a mobile phone – has been particularly successful in Kenya and Tanzania.[13] Mobile money has significantly spurred economic development by enabling customers to securely save and transfer funds, pay bills and receive government payments. M-Pesa remains Africa's best-known success story.[14]

RegTech

RegTech refers to technological solutions that streamline and improve regulatory processes. In contrast to FinTech's inherently financial focus, RegTech has the potential to be applied in many regulatory contexts, both financial and otherwise. Further, while FinTech growth has been fueled by start-ups, RegTech has emerged in response to top-down institutional demand arising from the exponential growth of compliance costs.[15]

The Evolution of RegTech

RegTech 1.0

In the 1990s and 2000s, institutions encountered increasing regulatory challenges as they became more global, catalyzing the development of large compliance and risk management departments. By the 1980s, financial technology was being employed to facilitate risk management as finance itself became increasingly reliant on IT systems. Financial engineering and Value at Risk (VaR) systems became embedded in major financial institutions,[16] and would ultimately prove to be among the major contributing factors to the GFC.[17]

By the beginning of the 21st century, the financial industry as well as regulators suffered from overconfidence in their ability to apply a quantitative IT framework to manage and control risks.[18]

---

[13] CGAP, *Infographic: Tanzania's Mobile Money Revolution*, CGAP (2014), http://www.cgap.org/data/infographic-tanzanias-mobile-money-revolution

[14] Safaricom, *M-Pesa Timeline,* (2016) http://www.safaricom.co.ke/mpesa_timeline/timeline.html

[15] Institute of International Finance, *RegTech: Exploring Solutions for Regulatory Challenges 2*, no. 1 (2015).

[16] Joe Nocera, 'Risk Management – What Led to the Financial Meltdown', *New York Times*, (2009), http://www.nytimes.com/2009/01/04/magazine/04risk-t.html

[17] Andreas Krause, 'Exploring the Limitations of Value at Risk: How Good Is It in Practice?', *Journal of Risk Finance* 4, no. 2, (2003): 19.

[18] Felix Salmon, 'The Formula that Killed Wall Street', *Significance*, 9, no. 1, (2012): 16.

Regulator overconfidence manifested in the unduly heavy reliance of the Basel II Capital Accord on internal quantitative risk management systems of financial institutions.[19] This false sense of security was brutally exposed by the GFC, which ended the first iteration of RegTech, RegTech 1.0.

Another illustration of RegTech 1.0 is the monitoring of public securities markets. Regulators rely upon trade reporting systems maintained by securities exchanges to detect unusual behavior.[20] The GFC exposed the limitations of these systems – they cannot shed light on transactions that occur off the exchange.[21] Regulators around the world reacted by mandating the reporting of all transactions in listed securities, regardless of where they took place. Such reporting requirements will have to be met with enhanced regulator IT systems to analyse the reported information – an enhancement which is part of the next stage of RegTech's development.

Ultimately, RegTech 2.0 has emerged in response to post-GFC regulatory requirements. These waves of complex regulation have drastically increased compliance costs,[22] and regulatory fines and settlements have increased 45-fold.[23] Adding to

rising costs is the increasing fragmentation of the regulatory landscape. Despite attempts to establish similar post-crisis reforms, regulatory overlaps and contradictions between markets are not uncommon and financial institutions have unsurprisingly looked to RegTech to optimize their compliance management.[24]

RegTech 2.0

RegTech provides the foundation for a shift towards a proportionate, risk-based approach – a RegTech 2.0 – underpinned by efficient data management and market supervision. AI and deep learning are just two examples of new technologies that demonstrate the potential for automating consumer protection, market supervision and prudential regulation.[25]

RegTech 2.0 primarily concerns the digitization and datafication of regulatory compliance and reporting processes. Not only does it represent the natural response to the digitalization of finance and the fragmentation of its participants,[26] but it also has the potential to minimize the risks of the regulatory capture which occurred prior to the GFC.[27] Regulators in the US, UK, Australia and Singapore have already begun attempts to develop

[19] Staffs of the International Monetary Fund and The World Bank, *Implementation of Basel II – Implications for the World Bank and the IMF*, (2005), http://www.imf.org/external/np/pp/eng/2005/072205.htm#s2

[20] The Board of the International Organization of Securities Commissions, *Technological Challenges to Effective Market Surveillance Issues and Regulatory Tools: Consultation Report 14-15* (August 2012).

[21] United States SEC Commissioner Luis A. Aguilar, *Shedding Light on Dark Pools (Public Statement),* (18 November 2015), http://www.sec.gov/news/statement/shedding-light-on-dark-pools.html#_edn5

[22] Jeff Cox, *Misbehaving banks have now paid $204B in fines*, CNBC, (2015), http://www.cnbc.com/2015/10/30/misbehaving-banks-have-now-paid-204b-in-fines.html

[23] Piotr Kaminski and Kate Robu, *A Best-Practice Model for Bank Compliance*, McKinsey, (2016), http://www.mckinsey.com/business-functions/risk/our-insights/a-best-practice-model-for-bank-compliance

[24] Eleanor Hill, *Is RegTech the Answer to the Rising Cost of Compliance?*, (2016), FX-MM, http://www.fx-mm.com/50368/fx-mm-magazine/past-issues/june-2016/regtech-rising-cost-compliance/

[25] Maryam Najafabadi, Flavio Villanustre, Taghi M. Khoshgoftaar, Naeem Seliya, Randall Wald and Edin Muharemagic, 'Deep Learning Applications and Challenges in Big Data Analytics', *Journal of Big Data* 2, no. 1 (2015).

[26] Global Partnership for Financial Inclusion, *G20 High-Level Principles for Digital Financial Inclusion* 12, (2016), http://www.gpfi.org/publications/g20-high-level-principles-digital-financial-inclusion

[27] Douglas Arner and Janos Barberis, 'FinTech in China: From The Shadow?', *Journal of Financial Perspectives* 3, no. 3, (2015): 23.

a fresh regulatory approach that caters to the dynamics of the FinTech market.[28]

Examples of fertile areas for RegTech development include: (i) application of big data approaches, (ii) strengthening of cybersecurity and (iii) facilitation of macroprudential policy. With respect to big data, regulators are starting to consider technological solutions for the management of AML/KYC information produced by industry participants, notably suspicious transactions reports. Strong IT capabilities to analyse the data provided are paramount if regulators are to achieve the underlying objectives of such requirements.

Cybersecurity represents one of the most pressing issues faced by the financial services industry and further underscores the necessity of continued regulatory development.[29] The shift towards a data-based industry is inevitably accompanied by a rising threat of theft and fraud.

Macroprudential policy offers yet another promising ground for RegTech. It ultimately seeks to soften the severity of the financial cycle by utilizing large volumes of reported data to identify patterns and changes over time.[30] Central banks are making progress in identifying leading indicators of financial instability[31] in the form of data 'heat maps', which alert regulators to potential

problems identified through quantitative analysis and stress testing large volumes of data.[32]

These early efforts indicate the probable move of RegTech into macroprudential policy. This occurs against the backdrop of regulators continually identifying the need for ever more data.[33] The additional reporting requirements that this generates for institutions drives the need for refinement of RegTech processes and the establishment of centralized support services to manage not only the data, but the formats required. Risk data aggregation requirements have been established by the Basel Committee (in 'BCBS 239') which encourage institutions and regulators to focus on near real-time delivery and analysis.[34]

What's Next for RegTech: RegTech 3.0?

RegTech 3.0 is our term for the future of RegTech. The FinTech sector is shifting its focus from the digitization of money to the monetization of data, making it necessary for new frameworks to accommodate concepts such as data sovereignty and algorithm supervision.

The data-centricity underpinning the evolutions of both FinTech and RegTech represents the early stages of a profound paradigm shift from a KYC to a KYD approach. As this unfolds, regulators must invest heavily in the development of proportionate, data-driven regulation to deal effectively with innovation without compromising their mandate. One important aspect is the design

[28] ASIC, *Fintech: ASIC's Approach and Regulatory Issues* 10-12 (Paper submitted to the 21st Melbourne Money & Finance Conference, July 2016); ASIC, *Further Measures to Facilitate Innovation in Financial Services* (Consultation Paper No. 260, June 2016).

[29] Financial Stability Oversight Council, *FSOC 2016 Annual Report (2016)*.

[30] International Monetary Fund, Financial Stability Board and Bank for International Settlements, *Elements of Effective Macroprudential Policy*, (2016).

[31] BIS Committee on the Global Financial System, *Experiences with the Ex Ante Appraisal of Macro-Prudential Instruments*, CGFS, Paper No. 56, July 2016.

[32] International Monetary Fund, Financial Stability Board and Bank for International Settlements, *Elements of Effective Macroprudential Policy*, (2016).

[33] Financial Stability Board and International Monetary Fund, *The Financial Crisis and Information Gaps: Second Phase of the G-20 Data Gaps Initiative (DGI-2) – First Progress Report* (September 2016).

[34] The Basel Committee, *Principles for Effective Risk Data Aggregation and Risk Reporting*, (2013).

of core elements of financial ecosystems in order to leverage technology to achieve major regulatory objectives of financial stability, financial integrity, financial inclusion and balanced development – a path an increasing number of countries are choosing to follow.[35]

Conclusion

The longstanding marriage of technology and finance has been continuously evolving. In the near future, regulators will come under increasing pressure to adapt to the newly fragmented market comprising major banks, established tech firms and lean start-ups. RegTech can be employed to not only assist authorities to monitor and regulate industry participants, but to identify *when* to do so. In the wake of increased compliance burdens, regulators will need to work with FinTech and RegTech players to understand how data are being collected and processed, harmonize compliance requirements across markets, and enhance not only data sharing among regulators but the ways in which such data are used.

RegTech presents benefits to both industry and regulators by empowering financial institutions to effectively control costs and risks,[36] presenting new opportunities for FinTech start-ups and tech firms,[37] and allowing the development of continuous monitoring tools.[38]

RegTech's truly transformative potential lies in its capacity to enable the real time monitoring of financial markets. Markets are evolving to rely more on data. The institution with the most data will be best placed to assess the borrower's credit risk, and those institutions are increasingly likely to be large tech companies or retail conglomerates operating customer loyalty schemes, rather than banks.[39] The evolution of this new form of financial service provider will demand further evolution of RegTech as the market moves from relying on a 'know-your-customer' to a 'know-your-data' paradigm.

---

[35] See Douglas Arner, Ross Buckley and Dirk Zetzsche, *FinTech for Financial Inclusion: A Framework for Digital Financial Transformation* (Alliance for Financial Inclusion, September 2018).

[36] Citigroup, *Comment Letter on Regulatory Capital Rules*, 3 (2013), https://www.federalreserve.gov/SECRS/2013/October/20131030/R-1460/R-1460_102113_111420_579523237031_1.pdf

---

[37] Adrian Shedden and Gareth Malna, *Supporting the Development and Adoption of RegTech: No Better Time for a Call for Input*, Burges Salmon 2, (2016), https://www.burges-salmon.com/-/media/files/publications/open-access/supporting_the_development_and_adoption_of_regtech_no_better_time_for_a_call_for_input.pdf

[38] Daniel Gutierrez, 'Big Data for Finance – Security and Regulatory Compliance Considerations', *Inside Big Data*, (2014), http://insidebigdata.com/2014/10/20/big-data-finance-security-regulatory-compliance-considerations/

[39] D.A. Zetzsche, R.P. Buckley, D.W. Arner and J.N. Barberis, 'From FinTech to TechFin: The Regulatory Challenges of Data-Driven Finance', *New York University Journal of Law & Business* 14, no. 2, (2018): 393.

About the Editors

Janos Barberis

Janos Barberis is the Founder of SuperCharger and a Senior Research Fellow and PhD candidate at the University of Hong Kong. He has an established track record in the FinTech industry (32nd Most Powerful Dealmaker, *Institutional Investor*) and academia (13th legal scholar in the world, SSRN) and is driven to deliver actionable foresight. His areas of focus are FinTech regulation and RegTech developments and emerging trends. Academically, he developed the world's leading research that is directly used by regulators for policy design. Professionally, he has founded SuperCharger, Asia's leading FinTech accelerator sponsored by Tier 1 clients and a strong alumni network of 36 companies, which have raised in excess of US$370 million. Finally, he co-edited *The FinTech Book*, a global bestseller, covering 60 experts with more than 20,000 copies distributed in 106 countries and six languages. Two more titles, *The InsurTech Book* and *The WealthTech Book*, were released in 2018.

You can reach Janos on LinkedIn at www.linkedin.com/in/jbarberis/ and on Twitter via @jnbarberis.

Douglas W. Arner

Douglas W. Arner is the Kerry Holdings Professor in Law at the University of Hong Kong (HKU) and one of the world's leading experts on financial regulation, particularly the intersection of law, finance, and technology. He is Faculty Director of the Faculty of Law's LLM in Compliance and Regulation and LLM in Corporate and Financial Law, a member of the Hong Kong Financial Services Development Council, an Executive Committee Member of the Asia-Pacific Structured Finance Association, and a Senior Visiting Fellow of Melbourne Law School, University of Melbourne. Douglas served as Head of the HKU Department of Law from 2011 to 2014 and as Co-Director of the Duke University–HKU Asia-America Institute in Transnational Law from 2005 to 2016. From 2006 to 2011 he was the Director of HKU's Asian Institute of International Financial Law, which he cofounded in 1999.

He has published 15 books and more than 120 articles, chapters, and reports on international financial law and regulation, including most recently *Reconceptualising Global Finance and Its Regulation* (Cambridge University Press, 2016) (with Ross Buckley and Emilios Avgouleas). His recent papers are available on SSRN at https://papers.ssrn.com/sol3/cf_dev/AbsByAuth.cfm?per_id=524849, where he is among the top 300 authors in the world by total downloads. Douglas has served as a consultant with, among others, the World Bank, Asian Development Bank, Asia-Pacific Economic Cooperation (APEC), and the European Bank for Reconstruction and Development, and has lectured, co-organized conferences and seminars, and been involved with financial sector reform projects around the world.

He has been a visiting professor or fellow at Duke University, Harvard University, the Hong Kong Institute for Monetary Research, IDC Herzliya, McGill University, University of Melbourne, National University of Singapore, University of New South Wales, Shanghai University of Finance and Economics, and University of Zurich, among others.

You can reach Douglas at douglas.arner@hku.hk or on LinkedIn at www.linkedin.com/in/douglas-arner-91a678164/.

Ross P. Buckley

Ross P. Buckley is the KPMG Law – King & Wood Mallesons Professor of Disruptive Innovation, and a Scientia Professor, at the University of New South Wales in Sydney, Australia. His current research focus is FinTech, RegTech and blockchain.

He leads one of the largest Linkage grants ever awarded in law by the Australian Research Council into the enabling regulation of digital financial services in developing countries. He has previously led six other major, multi-year funded research projects, and is currently participating in major multi-year projects on FinTech related regulation in Hong Kong and Qatar.

He has written five books, edited a further five, and written over 140 book chapters and articles in leading journals in all major jurisdictions. His joint research on FinTech and RegTech has been downloaded from the Social Science Research Network more often than that of any other author.

He chairs the Digital Finance Advisory Panel of the Australian Securities and Investments Commission (ASIC), and consults frequently to the Asian Development Bank. He has previously consulted to government departments in ten countries, including Australia and the US; and twice been a Fulbright Scholar, at Yale and Duke.

You can reach Ross at ross.buckley@unsw.edu.au or on LinkedIn at www.linkedin.com/in/ross-buckley-06a00828/.

Acknowledgements

We would like to thank Dr Inna Amesheva, Ms Soumaya Bhyer, Ms Seyong Lee and the entire SuperCharger FinTech Accelerator team for all their assistance in the crowdsourcing process, Dr Cheng-Yun Tsang for his excellent assistance with editorial functions, and Ms Nechama Basserabie for her assistance with the manuscript. The authors would like to thank the Hong Kong Research Grants Council Research Impact Fund and the Australian Research Grants Council Linkage Grant for support.

Introduction

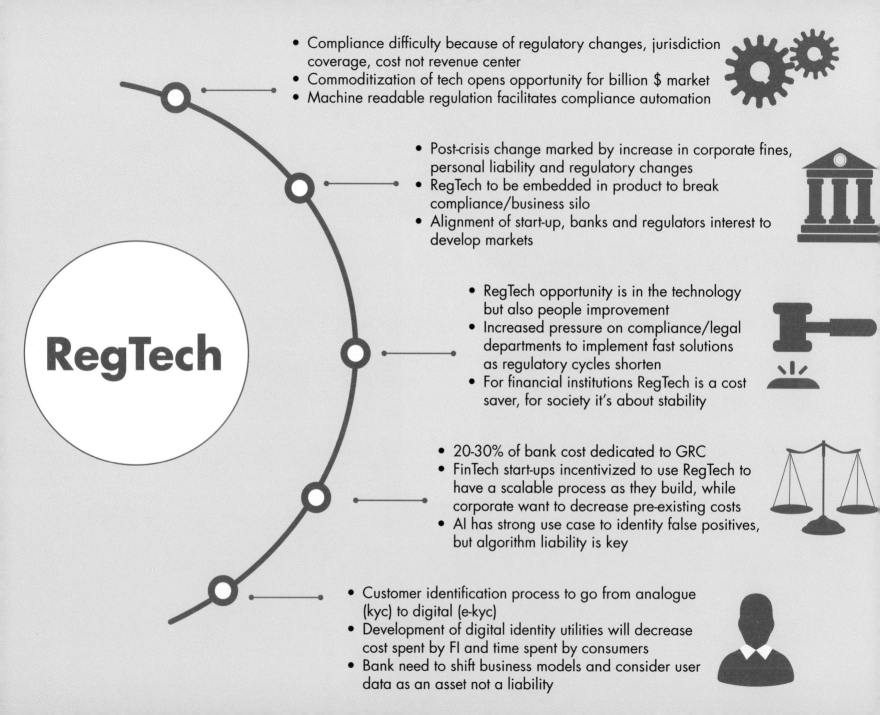

RegTech

- Compliance difficulty because of regulatory changes, jurisdiction coverage, cost not revenue center
- Commoditization of tech opens opportunity for billion $ market
- Machine readable regulation facilitates compliance automation

- Post-crisis change marked by increase in corporate fines, personal liability and regulatory changes
- RegTech to be embedded in product to break compliance/business silo
- Alignment of start-up, banks and regulators interest to develop markets

- RegTech opportunity is in the technology but also people improvement
- Increased pressure on compliance/legal departments to implement fast solutions as regulatory cycles shorten
- For financial institutions RegTech is a cost saver, for society it's about stability

- 20-30% of bank cost dedicated to GRC
- FinTech start-ups incentivized to use RegTech to have a scalable process as they build, while corporate want to decrease pre-existing costs
- AI has strong use case to identity false positives, but algorithm liability is key

- Customer identification process to go from analogue (kyc) to digital (e-kyc)
- Development of digital identity utilities will decrease cost spent by FI and time spent by consumers
- Bank need to shift business models and consider user data as an asset not a liability

This part sets out to provide an overview of the RegTech sector and its development.

By contextualizing the origin of the industry's growth generated by the post-financial crisis increase in fines and the acceleration of new regulation and personal liability, the following chapters highlight the opportunities RegTech offers. It is important to differentiate the RegTech opportunities as a market reform as opposed to a market reaction, to which FinTech is more akin. In addition, as will be elaborated upon in Part 9, RegTech applicability expands beyond the financial services industry. As a direct related matter, the US$20 billion in spending predicted to occur by 2020 is only for one industry.

The automation of regulatory obligations represents a transition from People, Process, Paper (3P) towards Automation, Real-Time, and Predictive (AIR). The obvious impact is in the decrease of compliance costs for financial institutions but also the improvement of the market supervision role for regulators and even customer experience for clients. A less immediate impact is that a well-implemented RegTech strategy can enable the multi-million-dollar digital transformation efforts being initiated by financial institutions globally.

As an industry in general, financial institutions perceive RegTech providers as cost-cutting options, with some systems benefiting from consortiums and network effects. As legal and compliance teams increase their understanding of the innovation potential of these start-ups and technologies, RegTech offers a competitive advantage in the market, from painless compliance procedures that enhance customer retention to the avoidance of large regulatory fines diverting capital away from new initiative.

Success will rely on corporates (see Part 6) and start-ups (see Part 5) addressing challenges such as how they can adapt solutions across jurisdictions, be future-proof against regulatory uncertainty, and convince clients of the opportunities despite a high risk of error.

What a RegTech Compliance Killer System Will Look Like

By Bernard Lunn
CEO, Daily FinTech

Compliance is a big, ugly problem, and it is getting worse, and nobody has nailed it yet. In short, compliance is a tremendous opportunity. Investors say: 'Show me compliance deals'. Bankers say: 'Show me a solution'. Financial technology (FinTech) companies say: 'We must spend our precious cash on lawyers and regulatory experts'.

Nobody loves compliance. Everybody hates compliance. That is why it is a massive opportunity. Like a cure for cancer or cheap and abundant renewable energy, the problem is easy to state, but the solution is far, far harder to build.

We have seen a lot of regulatory technology (RegTech) solutions, but we have yet to see the killer system. We see lots of lawyers and outsourcing firms willing to throw worker-hours at the problem. We also see lots of point solutions. These are, at best, putting bandages on the wound.

So far we haven't found a killer solution; however, we do know what a killer solution needs to look like. There are five attributes that we detail later, after presenting a requirements checklist.

Before detailing the checklist, here are the seven reasons why compliance is so hard.

1. *It is a moving target.* Since the financial crisis, we have had lots of new regulations and lots of new scandals (which trigger new regulation). At the same time, we have the emergence of bitcoin, which is entirely uncharted territory.
2. *It is a territorial hairball of complexity.* Finance is a global business, and 'bits do not stop at borders'. However, money does stop at borders, and each country has its own spin on regulation. There are even cross-border variants such as Islamic finance. Each is critical. Put them all together, and the result is seriously nasty and complex, and in a global economy, that is the reality we have to deal with.
3. *It is an easy lever for politicians to pull.* Beating up bankers is a natural vote catcher. The negatives from too much regulation are not so visible, and causation is unclear. So it will always be a moving target, and it will still get more complicated.
4. *It is a cross-cutting concern.* Like cyber security, compliance cuts across every system, including ones written before most of today's regulation was even a gleam in the eye.
5. *It does not have a revenue line attached.* Despite the massive risk posed by compliance failure, there is no revenue line from which a banker can grab budget.
6. *It is an existential threat.* Get it wrong, and you could be gone tomorrow. So, nobody loves spending money on compliance, but you have to spend money on it.
7. *It is functionally complex.* There are so many areas to understand, and each is complex on its own – money laundering (know your customer [KYC]), tax (Foreign Account Tax Compliance Act [FATCA]), consumer protection, data privacy, and systemic risk (Dodd-Frank Act). Add them all together, and it is a recipe for sleeping like a baby (waking every few hours screaming).

The following is the high-level five-point checklist for a great RegTech compliance solution:

1. *Real-time data in context.* Big data is just so-called digital landfill unless it is delivered just in time and in context. 'Just in time' means that the data is made available in real time even if it is not consumed in real time. It is not relevant until it is relevant in context (which is why it is not always consumed in real time). For example, consider a conflict of interest statement. The fact that a family member just moved into a conflict of interest position is

useful only if delivered within the context of a system where you need to declare any conflicts.

2. *Legacy integration.* Any solution that involves changing the legacy system is a showstopper. It is the weakest link issue. Just one legacy system that is not integrated could be your compliance nightmare. Combining 1 and 2 (real-time data in context plus legacy integration) is tough. Rewriting all apps to be compliant is expensive and takes too long. Doing integration according to the constraints of decades-old middleware and batch-based core systems is hard but essential.

3. *Understanding the risk/reward trade-off.* Perfect compliance is like perfect security. Designing an ideal compliance system is straightforward. Any bureaucrat can do that. The problem is that you will stop the business as all customer-facing processes grind to a halt, or you instead encourage people to ignore compliance rules and just pay the fines as a cost of doing business. In the real world, there is a trade-off between compliance and frictionless onboarding. When creating a compliance solution, you need marketing growth hackers on the team as well. You have to enable internal people, customers, and partners to all do their jobs without putting the business in great danger.

4. *Immutability.* A shared database where all parties can trust that nobody can change the data it contains is a big deal. This is where blockchain technology could be a breakthrough, although there is no need to use blockchain technology to get a distributed and immutable (append-only) database.

5. *Rules-based user interface for non-programmers.* Apart from death and taxes, we can be confident that compliance rules will change and grow in complexity. Unless a compliance person can 'code' these rules using legal language rather than programming code, any solution will quickly become obsolete.

There are two big reasons for optimism. The first is the perennial one that, with technology getting better, faster, and cheaper every day, some entrepreneur will create a compliance killer system that meets the aforementioned five attributes – the prize is certainly big enough. This is an article of faith, similar to saying that we will get a cure for cancer or cheap and abundant clean energy without knowing how we will get there.

The other reason for optimism is based more on the observable fact that the regulatory environment is getting easier.

Yes, you read that right. I wrote that the regulatory environment is getting easier.

The reason is that politicians, fearing citizen backlash, are starting to rein in the worst bureaucratic tendencies of regulators. For a long time, entrepreneurs faced competition, and regulators sent them the rule book. Regulators were government employees who thought about competition only in the abstract. Today, the environment is more fluid, as governments recognize the economic return on innovation regarding jobs and gross domestic product (GDP) growth. The regulators now face real competition because their political masters have to keep citizens happy, and citizens care about employment and GDP growth. With both FinTechs and global banks being increasingly mobile, jobs can disappear fast if regulators get it wrong. Plus, innovation is the primary driver of productivity, which drives GDP per capita.

Pity the poor regulator who must balance that with protecting citizens from fraud and abuse. This has led to two positive developments:

First, simpler and unbundled regulation in many countries. Unbundled regulation means you could get a payment license, or a deposit license, or a current account license.

Second, tech-smart regulation. Two examples are the second Payment Services Directive (PSD2) in Europe and payment bank licenses in India. This moves from 'throw the paper rule book at your compliance team of lawyers' to 'send standards docs and application programming interface (API) specs to your tech team'.

FinTechs and small and medium-size enterprises (SMEs) will drive change. Incumbents and corporate entities can throw lawyers and outsourcers at the problem. This is not an option for FinTechs and

SMEs. This is where tech-smart regulation is critical. Consider the eXtensible Business Reporting Language (XBRL).

Real-time Data Machine-readable Streams for Regulators

In the wake of the financial crisis in 2008, the US government mandated machine-readable financial reports via XBRL. That was a wonderfully progressive move that could dramatically change the efficiency and reliability of the capital markets by bringing financial reporting into the twenty-first century. Then came the backlash, with politicians claiming to save small businesses from the burden of regulatory compliance.

To understand why this is baloney, travel with a financial data item through the financial reporting process:

> Step 1. Start as an electronic bit in an accounting/enterprise resource planning (ERP) system. The data is now perfectly machine readable and gets aggregated and processed most efficiently.
>
> Step 2. The data is converted into a human-readable form for the Securities and Exchange Commission (SEC). For many companies, the only time their numbers are on actual paper is when they send their reports to the SEC.
>
> Step 3. Somebody extracts the data from a PDF or HTML file and turns it back into a machine-readable bit in XBRL format. That 'somebody' is probably working for an outsourcing firm that is being paid by the company doing the reporting because it has to comply with the SEC mandate.

Step 3 looks more like a burden that should be eliminated. However, the solution is *not* to eliminate Step 3. *The solution is to eliminate Step 2*. Technically this is simple.

Imagine the poor overloaded folks at the SEC surrounded by piles of paper. They are dedicated, smart, and hardworking. They will therefore have evolved a system that sort of works – poring over individual company filings and marking something odd about a data item in a footnote with a yellow pen, and then digging through a pile of documents to look on page 256 of another report (having cleverly marked the page) to correlate something odd on that other company's filing …

Imagine if all the data was in XBRL electronic format and they could let an algorithm do the grunt work so that they could do the higher-level work needed to catch the bad guys and maybe avoid a repeat of the financial system's 'cardiac arrest moment' in September 2008.

The algorithms could process thousands of companies to look for that anomaly, that weird thing that says, 'something looks fishy'. The data surfaced by the algorithms still require the higher-level cognitive and pattern-matching skills of humans. This is about empowering the SEC staffers to be more efficient. I imagine that they would vote for this change.

The work done by SEC staffers is impossible without better systems. The devil is in the details, or to put that in financial reporting language, the devil is in the footnotes (where a company buries that embarrassing fact it wants investors and regulators to gloss over).

Forward-looking regulations will eventually leave behind the cute constructs of the analogue age – paper and batch cycles – and demand data streams that they can parse as needed in real time. In the meantime, compliance has to deal with both the new real-time world and the legacy batch world, and history teaches us that legacy sticks around a lot longer than anybody anticipated.

Sharing the KYC Burden for Small Business Through Digital ID

Compliance is a pain for BigCo, but it is a manageable pain. It is impossible for SMEs, which do not have significant compliance departments. That is why we see change being driven by SME needs. This is starting to happen through partnerships. A natural fit could be a large telecommunications company partnering directly with a challenger bank. Telcos are hungry to diversify into new revenue streams amidst an increasingly digital landscape, and they are the natural repositories of digital identification (ID) (which is the key to KYC). Once the digital ID problem has been solved, the rest of RegTech is a lot easier. Digital ID remains a thorny issue, with societal-level problems around privacy, but these can be resolved with technology, and it is likely that forward-looking telcos will drive that change because the mobile phone is the key to digital ID.

Technology-Enabled Collaborative Compliance

By Zeeshan Rashid
Global Head – BF SI Risk and Compliance Practice,
Tata Consultancy Services Ltd

The tsunami of regulations that started from the financial crisis does not seem to have ceased, and the cost of non-compliance has become prohibitive. The quantum of fines that banks have had to pay over the past three to five years suggests that setting aside provisions will not suffice: non-compliance hits the top line and the bottom line directly. No wonder up to 70% of management's time is spent on managing compliance, which in any realm of the imagination is unacceptable.

The key challenges faced by the industry in managing compliance are the following:

Ever-increasing volume. New regulations just keep on coming. The Trump administration has said that for every new regulation introduced two old regulations have to go away. With the increasing complexity of businesses and risks, it is easier said than done. With Brexit, hundreds of laws and regulations will have to be drafted by the United Kingdom once it officially leaves the European Union.

Rising personal liability. There seems to be a direct correlation between the rise in regulations and the personal liability of compliance officers.

Growing staffing challenges. An immediate reaction to the rise of regulations is to hire more people to deal with them. There are two problems with this. First, skilled compliance personnel are always in short supply; second, hiring in a large number can at best be a tactical fix; the costs and complexities associated with mass hiring will bite in the long term.

There has always been a disconnect between the compliance department and the business lines, including risk management.

Traditionally compliance has been treated as the prime responsibility of the compliance department. Other departments handle it just as a tick in the box and focus only on their key performance indicators (KPIs). For example, for a trader, the key is to make money; for a salesperson, it is to increase turnover; and so on. In the process, compliance takes a backseat. If there is a compliance failure, the blame game starts, and in most cases the compliance department bears the brunt of it. There is a lack of collective or shared responsibility.

Technology-enabled collaborative compliance is the answer to the challenges faced by the stakeholders.

Collaboration in Compliance Is Key

Collaboration in any field or industry always has its positives. From a compliance perspective, partnerships can bring a lot of value to the organization and the industry.

Collaboration for compliance can be viewed on three fronts, as shown in Figure 1.

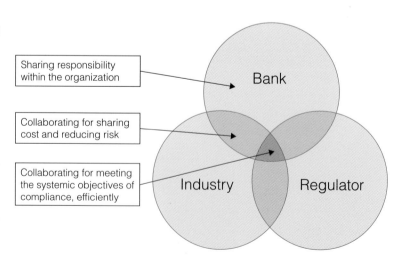

Sharing responsibility within the organization

Collaborating for sharing cost and reducing risk

Collaborating for meeting the systemic objectives of compliance, efficiently

Bank

Industry

Regulator

Figure 1: Areas for collaboration with FinTechs, customers and industry bodies

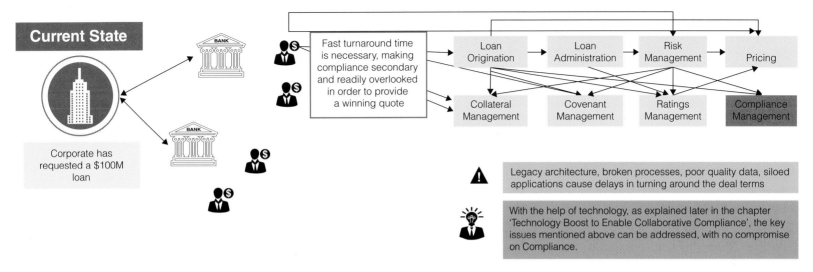

Figure 2: Examples of key challenges in the origination process

Let's consider each one of them in detail.

Sharing Responsibility Within the Organization

Compliance to a large extent is a centralized function within an organization. In this hypercompetitive world, all employees are driven by metrics they will be measured on, and compliance does not feature at the top of the list.

Figure 2 depicts the typical challenges in the case of a loan origination process.

Let's articulate a wish list for those personnel outside the compliance department. Compliance processes should not affect time to market, be an impediment to generating new business, or adversely impact the customer experience. Instead, compliance processes should have a high degree of automation, built-in circuit breakers, and early warning indicators, and should be demonstrable.

The key to collaboration, in this case, is to make compliance a part of the business processes with the help of technology. Key enablers (Figure 3) already exist within the organization. They just have to be channelled in the right direction.

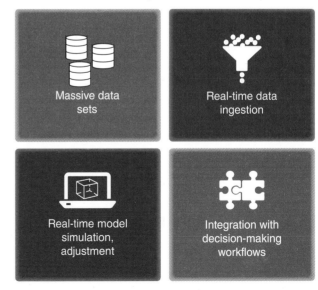

Figure 3: Key enablers for the wish list

Banks have massive data sets consisting of structured and unstructured data, which can be harnessed with the use of technology for multiple purposes, including compliance. Moving towards real-time data ingestion and real-time analytics models and simulation gives a shot in the arm to enable real-time compliance. There will be a need to scale up the infrastructure to manage the need for real-time data ingestion and analytics. Financial institutions understand the importance, and many are already running transformation programs to enable it. Last but not least is the integration of the real-time flows with decision-making work flows to complete the cycle and provide a well-rounded solution, helping everyone in the organization to feel responsible for compliance without feeling the burden of doing it.

In the case of the loan origination process as shown in Figure 2, a large multinational firm has invited banks to bid for a new $100 million multi-country credit line and needs to know the best deal in a very short turnaround time (TAT). Assuming our bank has a well-structured and real-time response for its sales needs and has baked in compliance as a part of the business processes, the sales staff will know that the numbers that will be given by the system would have ticked the boxes for all the compliance requirements. As a result, they can confidently give the numbers and other details to the customer. There is all-round collaboration within multiple divisions within the bank. If the competition tries to be aggressive without concern for compliance and churns out rates just to win the deal, our sales staff's tools will have circuit breakers that will not allow them to go beyond safe limits, in the process safeguarding the interests of the bank.

Collaborating Within the Industry

The basic reason for compliance is to 'provide protection to stakeholders and manage risks'. With this reasoning, compliance will not be considered a source of competitive advantage. Hence, there is a business case for collaboration within the industry to do the following:

- Bring down the cost of compliance.
- Reduce the risk of non-compliance.
- Enable real-time detection.
- Optimize usage of resources.

A collaboration would require agreement on a standardized information model, operational processes, data security and privacy, and the technology platform enabling the operations. Sharing services or utilities is an example of collaboration within an industry. The success of a utility depends on the critical mass (the number of organizations sharing the vision).

Know your customer (KYC) utilities have existed for some time now, providing the ability to assess the risk profiles of customers as part of onboarding as well as during the lifetime of engagement. Another example is in the area of operational risk.

Twelve member firms founded the Operational Riskdata eXchange Association (ORX);[1] membership has now grown to 93, with companies from 23 countries. ORX was set up as an organization that will help financial organizations collaborate to better manage operational risk by setting standards and sharing operational risk data, research, and tools to validate scenarios.

There is a buzz around creating utilities for transaction monitoring for anti–money laundering (AML) operations, large-scale reconciliation, regulatory reporting, and so on.

Blockchain is another exciting area for collaboration within the industry and also with the regulator. Blockchain, as we know,

---

[1] ORX – https://managingrisktogether.orx.org

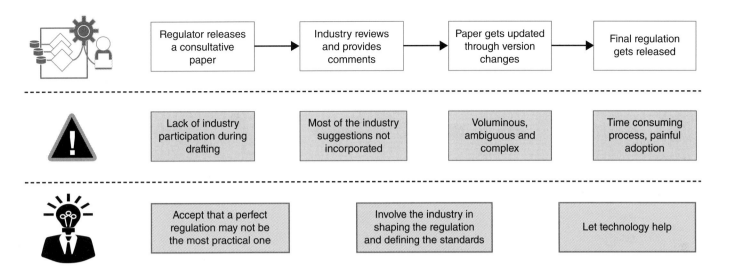

Figure 4: The genesis of compliance, issues in the current state, and ideas for improvement

creates records that are immutable. If a critical mass becomes available for a theme, e.g. for AML/KYC, blockchain can become the foundation for the utility. Digital identities and smart contracts can be further extensions to the concept.

Collaborating with the Regulators

Any discussion on compliance is incomplete without a mention of the regulator: it all starts and ends with the regulator. Until now, in many cases, the regulatory process has been a one-way street. Figure 4 maps out the current process a regulation goes through, the challenges in the current process, and what can be done to overcome the challenges.

The Technology Boost to Enable Collaborative Compliance

Through a technological lens, compliance can be seen largely as a logic program. This being the case, technology can be of immense help in all the three areas of collaboration discussed

previously. Figure 5 depicts the future state of a compliance journey, the technology boost, and the realization of the three areas of collaboration for compliance.

Let's analyse the key features and benefits of the new age compliance journey.

At the very beginning, when the regulator conceives a new regulation, it is important that there be industry participation during the design and drafting process. This will make compliance practical and easy to implement for the participants. There are five steps:

1. *Automated ingestion.* For the financial institution, the journey towards the new compliance starts with the ingestion of the regulation into its environment. Automated ingestion will reduce the need for manual processes, thereby reducing costs and risks and increasing efficiency.

2. *Data lake.* The regulation can be stored in the data lake in digital form, which should be the central repository for all data and

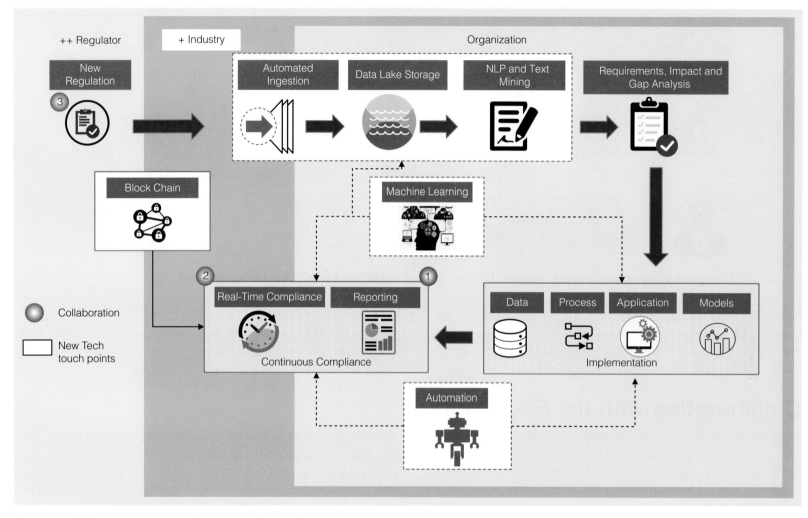

Figure 5: The next-generation compliance journey, powered by technology

regulations. The contents of the lake should be encrypted and have access control. Data lakes will act as a golden source of truth, ensuring safety and reduction of operational risks along with significantly reducing the total cost of ownership (TCO).

3. *Natural language processing (NLP) and text mining techniques.* NLP and text mining will read the information from the data lakes, define the taxonomy, and decode the compliance

into a machine-readable, objective format. They can also help decrease the ambiguity prevalent in most compliances by creating regulation models and mapping them to business, process, and data models.

4. *Requirements, impact and gap analysis.* Capture can then follow and the information be captured in digital form on work flow systems.

5. *Robotic process automation (RPA) and machine learning.*
The key selection criteria for RPA candidates are that they be repetitive, manual, voluminous, resource-intensive, and cost-ineffective processes. The following two components of the journey fulfil the selection criteria:

(i) *Implementation.* On the completion of steps 1–4, programs can be rolled out for the implementation of compliance. Data, processes, applications, and models, being the key components of the phase, can benefit immensely from RPA techniques. The data and processes can use RPA to increase efficiency and reduce manual interventions. The models and application can leverage machine learning to become dynamic and intelligent to capture business changes and reduce the number of false positives. In both cases, the TCO is expected to decrease significantly.

(ii) *Continuous compliance and reporting.* Machine learning and blockchain in addition to RPA will play a major role here.

- Because of its processes being voluminous, repetitive, and resource intensive, RPA will help in eliminating manual processes. From the wish list of the non-compliance personnel, as explained earlier, RPA can ensure that time to market is not impacted, automation increases, there is no impediment for new business, the system has built-in circuit breakers and early warning indicators, and there is no impact on the customer experience.

- Machine learning will infuse cognitive learning and help improve the efficiency of the logic designed and the RPA itself.

- This is the phase that will also facilitate the rise of industry utility models and adoption of blockchain, as was explained in the industry collaboration section.

Machine learning plays a key role across the value chain, as seen in Figure 5. With characteristics of feature learning, parameter optimization, and self-learning, it will aid in reducing risks and TAT, and efficient utilization of resources and TCO.

The Journey Has Just Begun

Collaboration in compliance with the help of technology has huge possibilities. We are just at the beginning of this exciting journey. With the right vision and collaboration models, costs can be brought down by 20–40%, management time can be freed up, and risk of non-compliance can be minimized. Technology is getting smarter by the day and is going to be a major contributor to facilitating collaborative compliance solutions.

The Age of RegTech Disruption to the Status Quo Is Here

By Jason Boud
Founder and CEO, RegTech Associates

and Mike Wilson
Co-Founder, RegTech Markets and RegTech Forum

Borrowing from Charles Dickens, in order to fully understand, appreciate, and anticipate the world of RegTech we need to take a journey with the ghosts of markets past, present, and future.

It is not by chance that today there is a concerted, albeit not fully coordinated, effort to atone for previous sins and ensure a cleaner bill of health for the financial markets. There is a clear line of history dating from the boom of the mid-1980s to the bust of Lehman Brothers. Hence, by default, we look back to look forward. We undertake an autopsy on the patient and determine what should have been done to avoid the grim reaper. Lessons learned.

However, can the problems of today, and proofing out for the future problems of tomorrow, really be solved through placing history under a microscope? Too often we bolt the gate long after the horse has already been dispatched for glue – only for a new area of weakness to be opened up for ill-gotten gains while our attention is elsewhere. For true 20/20 vision, do we also need a crystal ball?

Can the RegTech of today, through examining breaches that have already occurred, enable us to stay one step ahead in the future?

Strap yourselves in as we start with the ghosts of markets past.

What RegTech seeks to achieve is not new. The checks and balances for the financial markets to be safe and secure were thought to already have been in place. There was confidence that firms were following best practice, operating within the highest code of conduct, and adhering to the rules and regulations of the jurisdiction and markets they were operating in. That they were taking collective and individual responsibility for their actions, and delivering on the trust placed in them by their peers, shareholders, clients, employees, and wider society. We now know they were not.

Checks were missing, conduct was lacking, responsibility had been abandoned, and trust had broken down. Giants of the markets have since disappeared, bankers are being imprisoned, firms are being fined, and governments are bailing out banks.

Yet, RegTech is not tackling abstract theories – it is dealing with improper selling of financial products, insider dealing, tax evasion, money laundering, mispricing assets, manipulating benchmarks, and fixing rates. It is confronting wholesale corruption and abandonment of fiduciary responsibility. When the lines of ownership crossed between the wholesale market players and high-street banks, there was now a route for cheap international capital to be lent out to the public, fuelling a subprime mortgage catastrophe. The system was imbalanced in terms of risk, reward, and recognition – and by some, upon examination, set up purposely so.

Let's examine two contrasting roles: trader versus compliance officer. Trading desks of bulge-bracket firms were being paid millions in bonuses while constructing financial instruments and models so complicated that either their senior managers were too embarrassed to admit they did not understand them or in some cases they were happy to turn a blind eye as they were benefiting from the profits generated. Meanwhile, the compliance officers in place to oversee risk and financial regularity were by comparison poorly paid, poorly resourced, and with no voice or power to stop the practice. The process was never fit for purpose from the beginning. What did we expect would happen? The rest is history.

Jump to the ghost of markets present and the reversal of fortunes for the trader versus the compliance officer. If you joined a global bank after the financial crisis, you would not have expected a fast growth career considering the decline seen in profits and revenues over that same period. Yet, that is exactly what is happening. The regulatory, compliance, and legal professionals have seen their career prospects skyrocket during the same time period. In the past year as we researched this topic we saw:

- A head of compliance at a major international bank who saw his team grow from two to 70 in four years, while quietly professing that despite 20 years of experience in compliance, he did not fully understand most of the market his team covered.
- A highly qualified graduate who joined the front office in 2007 in the hope of being a banker and has only ever worked on regulatory projects.
- A program manager who complained that his much-needed regulatory architecture project was not approved because the 'regulatory change' category was five times oversubscribed ($2.5 billion worth of project submissions for a budget of $500 million).

The cost of regulatory compliance is unsustainable, and the industry now faces the task of ratcheting down costs and making the right decisions on which risks to carry and which burdensome processes to streamline. Welcome to the age of RegTech disruption.

So what is RegTech disruption? Well, it is not just about *technology* or tools to monitor, alert, and catch. Its *people* are at the heart of this solution – the *culture, rewards,* and *ethics* that will restore the trust in, and transparency and accountability of, financial markets. The bad guys are still here – and they are getting a lot smarter. The technology to expose them will need to be too.

RegTech may be a new label, but technology to reduce governance, risk, and compliance (GRC) is not. GRC is an industry segment expected to exceed $30 billion by 2020,[1] already including some well-established players such as IBM, RSA Archer,

Thomson Reuters, SAP, and Oracle. These companies exist alongside niche players such as NICE, Wolters Kluwer, SAI Global, and MetricStream.

The question is whether RegTech companies can truly challenge the established players. Alternatively, can they annoy the incumbents to the point of acquisition? The acquisition point could be analogous to the way that (FinTech) neobanks/digital banks have attacked the customer base of the large retail banks, as the RegTechs attack these established GRC players.

The RegTech start-up's DNA is often made up of deep industry expertise, coupled with the agility and hunger of new technology entrants. The practitioner experience within many RegTech companies allows them to realize that RegTech is not a single improved solution but a disruptor to a major part of the GRC market by collaboration, adaptability, and modern application design.

From our perspective, several factors are combining that will lead to disruption of the GRC market throughout 2019 and for the next few years. As of mid-2019, we have seen large players in the market acquisition hungry, online research[2] has shown both a growth in the total number of RegTech companies, but the beginning of a rationalization.

Regulatory Change Is No Longer a Project

In some respects, large financial institutions can be compared to mass production car manufacturing plants. Once set up, both are designed to operate in a certain way, regardless of the defects they produce. Both are difficult to change without large-scale retooling (or transformation projects), and both are in danger of becoming obsolete without large-scale changes.

---

[1] According to MarketsandMarkets Research Private Ltd.

[2] Research and Strategy firm RegTech Associates (https://rtassociates.co)

Figure 1: Simple process for regulatory change

In the regulatory arena, the pre-2007 compliance department could operate effectively like a 1940s Ford factory. The slow pace of regulatory change meant new regulations could be handled like a retooling exercise, with a project set up to study, interpret, and implement any changes required (system, process, and people). However, from 2008, we saw a steady increase in regulatory change and then a doubling of regulatory alerts per day from 2012 through 2015. Many analysts[3] predict these are yet to peak.

The result is that regulatory change can no longer be handled as a project (or a new car model). The process of regulatory change can be very complex; however, if we think about the simple steps involved they look something like Figure 1.

Identification. The process of monitoring regulatory notices, alerts, speeches, and enforcement actions enables identification of the main changes that are needed to move to the next phase.

Interpretation and analysis. When major regulatory events and rules have been identified, they must be interpreted and analysed by an organization. How do they affect the products and services the organization provides to its customers?

Change. When the previous phase indicates major changes, these are typically handled with a change or transformation project. Change projects are typically budgeted in the yearly cycle of change for the organization.

Run. Once the change or transformation project is implemented, the organization must run the systems and processes, and define people in roles to do so.

---

3 https://blogs.thomsonreuters.com/answerson/pace-regulatory-change

For large-scale regulatory changes, this is likely to be a process that lasts longer than 18 months per cycle. The cycle also requires many large organization overheads in areas such as program reporting, financial management, and hiring of appropriate experts to oversee all phases of the cycle. This cycle is no longer sustainable, and each heavily regulated company needs to work out the business as usual (BAU) process to manage such changes.

Step Forward RegTech

Defining an architecture that allows you to translate the (largely manual) steps of the process into a work flow and interfaces (APIs) that allow data to be exchanged between components is a necessary first step.

Modern API-based products, available from many RegTech start-ups, allow the regulated firm to choose a mix of new/best-of-breed RegTech companies and integrate them into their existing legacy systems. For example, RegTech is unlikely to result in the reengineering of bank product catalogues – but the list of which products exist in which markets is a key input into the risk decision making of the bank, as seen in Figure 2.

To the last stop on our travels – the ghost of markets future. What can we predict to be in store? In the same way that most of our kids will be working at jobs not currently invented, so too will the scammers continue to scam, the cheaters cheat, the takers take, and the fakers fake, but all in ways that do not exist today. We will not be getting misspelt emails from Nigeria asking for our bank details – and traders will not be setting fixed rates over telephones. Cryptocurrencies. Dark pools. Darker web. Identity. Mobility. Evasion. It is going to get more complicated, more sophisticated.

Figure 2: Example of high-level RegTech change architecture

Consequently, the RegTech foundations being laid down today to safeguard against the crimes of markets past require the foresight and vision to be extended to withstand the smarter wrongdoing of markets future. To stay ahead, regulators, regulated firms, and their technology providers will have to move faster, harder, and with sharper focus than the villains – constantly. And they will have to achieve all of this while not standing in the way of business, and while somehow making it more efficient. Regulation should not be viewed as a tax. Making money is okay. Though at times how some of it is made may be immoral, it is not illegal. Our communities are dependent on a safe, secure, and robust financial market. That is where the buck stops. So – RegTech. Yep. It is a pretty big deal. You can bet your house on that – literally.

RegTech and Financial Crime Prevention

By Jennifer Hanley-Giersch
Managing Partner, Berlin Risk Ltd

This chapter sets out the challenges facing the anti-financial crime (AFC) framework overall and the opportunities offered by the RegTech sector and their technology solutions. The chapter highlights the role that RegTech tools can play in supporting AFC and cybercrime prevention efforts, while adding value to the business in moving from a defensive risk avoidance mindset to a strategic risk management approach.[1] As with any advances in science, however, we must also take a critical stance and assess the risks that might emerge by adopting and implementing RegTech technologies.

Lack of ROI – Calling for a Framework Overhaul

Some 20–30% of banks' cost base globally can be attributed to governance, risk, and compliance costs. The British Bankers' Association estimated in 2016 that financial crime compliance costs its members some £5 billion a year, and is increasing yearly owing to changing regulatory requirements. Nonetheless, estimates suggest that well over a trillion dollars of illicit financing is raised and moved globally every year. Despite the significant funds invested, questions are being raised regarding the effectiveness of the procedures and AFC approaches, which have led to fines paid of some €300 billion,[2] in particular for crimes relating to money laundering and corruption, and in recent years for failing to prevent financial crime within their organizations.

Besides the question regarding the effectiveness of existing AFC frameworks, economic crime is seeking out new channels, and widening the landscape of financial crime, well beyond mere money laundering activities such as smurfing, Ponzi schemes, pump and dump, and the black market peso exchange, to name only a few, to include cybercrime involving a combination of social engineering (e.g. phishing, vishing, and pharming), the use of malware, advanced persistent threats, and distributed denial of service attacks using botnets. The cost of cybercrime is estimated at some €3 trillion, and, as noted in a draft report published by the European Parliament in January 2017, threatens financial institutions on a daily basis.

So one must ask what could be done better to tackle the financial and cybercrime risks, and the threat they bring to our societies and businesses. Regulators like the Financial Conduct Authority (FCA) recognize that technology could be used to make compliance processes more efficient with the help of machine learning, artificial intelligence (AI), and biometric identification. The dynamic emergence of RegTech tools and opportunities to harness these technology solutions in combating financial crime and cybercrime are not only of interest to financial institutions and corporations but also a chance for regulators to adapt their regulatory frameworks and the way they regulate.

Marrying and taking a proactive approach to using advancements in AI and data analytics and backing initiatives supporting the improvement of the financial crime prevention framework will also enable technology firms and others to find greater appreciation from regulators who are traditionally sceptical about these advancements.

A number of hurdles do, however, have to be overcome in order for financial institutions to be in a position to leverage the new

---

[1] https://www.theclearinghouse.org/research/2016/2016-q3-banking-perspectives/a-new-aml-system

[2] http://www.handelsblatt.com/finanzen/banken-versicherungen/nach-321-milliarden-dollar-strafe-banken-streichen-compliance-teams-zusammen/19567996.html

tool landscape. In its report published in March 2017 entitled 'Deploying RegTech against Financial Crime', the Institute of International Finance highlights how regulatory loopholes, data quality, and, not least, inhibitory procurement processes need to be amended in order for financial institutions to be able to harness the potentials of technology not only to strengthen AFC endeavours but also to introduce tools and technologies that can be adapted easily to a changing regulatory and criminal threat landscape.

Where We Stand Today – Manual, Manual, Manual

McKinsey published a study in February 2017[3] outlining the various inefficiencies it had identified in compliance teams, including fragmented efforts, manual processes, and mountains of data.

The study analysed the time spent on remediation at one global financial institution according to the importance (materiality) of the issue, in which the study identified that first- and second-line compliance staff were spending 80% of their time on issues of low or moderate materiality, and only 20% on critical high-risk issues. The results, which are usually representative of the situation within the industry as a whole, also found that the approach to compliance did not allow for an integrated view across the enterprise, as some risks were addressed by multiple assessments, and others not at all.

In addition, there was no consistent understanding of the material risks due to varying standards of materiality and testing, as well as

different teams applying different approaches, resulting in time-consuming efforts to reconcile the results.

Critically, despite the efforts of these teams and the numerous assessments, the study claimed that senior management was still not in a position to obtain a reliable view of either the institution's key compliance risks or the state of controls governing them.

Given this backdrop and the development of the RegTech space, there appear to be great benefits that organizations could derive from implementing some RegTech solutions.

Compliance teams are under pressure to innovate not only in order to effectively manage the increased day-to-day complexity of their expanded mandate, but, more importantly, in order to support their organizations in meeting the challenges financial institutions face in the wake of disruption by advances in technology. Those who succeed in this cycle of innovation will be those who harness the opportunities presented by tools and technology.

RegTech – A World of Opportunities?

RegTech uses digital technologies, including big data analytics, for early warnings coupled with ingestion technologies and unsupervised learning to facilitate AFC compliance, automate risk management, and support strategic planning.

Overall, RegTech solutions enable a more bespoke approach to regulatory and AFC issues. Given the very fragmented marketplace and the very different information technology (IT) legacies, it is recommendable to assess in detail which tools meet regulatory requirements and can be sufficiently flexible to the internal and external changes that might require the tools to be adapted.

---

[3] http://www.mckinsey.com/business-functions/risk/our-insights/sustainable-compliance-seven-steps-toward-effectiveness-and-efficiency?cid=eml-web

Figure 1 sets out an indicative overview of RegTech tools, which, although not claiming to be exhaustive, is relevant for financial and anti-cyber crime professionals. The chart draws from some excellent research reports, including Institute of International Finance (IIF)[4] and CB Insights reports,[5] as well as postings on social media by Jan-Maarten Mulder[6] and Fabian Westerheide.[7]

One of the key arguments is that technology can help cut costs and lower the error count (for example, in the case of false positives); help compliance and AFC professionals to improve their processes and procedures; and, finally, more effectively contribute to combating financial crime. Not only financial institutions but also corporations, including online retailers, can implement regulatory technology tools to assist in managing financial crime and environmental, social, and governance (ESG) risks throughout their supply chain. RegTech can also assist corporations in this area ensuring that they are ethically sourcing raw materials and avoiding being linked to human rights and environmental violations. RegTech tools should be used for those tasks that humans are less efficient at performing, freeing up resources to focus on the more complicated and high-risk situations, and providing insights and intelligence to add more value to the

business and provide a more solid risk management and security framework.

One of the areas that is drawing a significant amount of attention is the topic of know your customer (KYC) utilities and the use of distributed ledger technology (DLT) for the purpose of creating something of a KYC repository for storing digital identities and possibly also other documents.[8] By using DLT, the number and scope of KYC checks could be reduced and then made accessible, through a digital identity, to all those linked to the system. There would also be increased security and transparency through almost real-time distribution of information, which might also be of interest to regulators. Privacy, regulatory, liability, and security risks do, however, pose a series of constraints regarding the development of KYC utilities and the use of DLT.[9] Also, in the areas of fraud prevention and cyber security, a number of tools are emerging that can add value to the AFC professional's toolbox and assist organizations in meeting supervisory expectations for improved resilience plans and response planning for cyber breaches.

RegTech and FinTech

FinTech companies rising up the ranks to compete with more traditional banks are in a position to break new ground in the area of financial and cybercrime prevention. They can design a regulatory and risk management framework around their business and also secure great efficiencies by integrating financial and cybercrime prevention from the outset. FinTechs' ability to use emerging technologies to their advantage will in part define their success. If thought through smartly, their approach to financial crime prevention will enable them to succeed in establishing solid businesses that

[4] https://www.iif.com/system/files/regtech_in_financial_services_-_solutions_for_compliance_and_reporting.pdf and https://www.iif.com/press/regtech-can-help-industry-address-financial-crime-reporting

[5] https://www.cbinsights.com/blog/regtech-regulation-compliance-market-map/?utm_content=48771422&utm_medium=social&utm_source=linkedin and https://www.cbinsights.com/blog/periodic-table-cybersecurity-startups/?utm_source=CB+Insights+Newsletter&utm_campaign=3538cb0bef-ThursNL_3_23_2017&utm_medium=email&utm_term=0_9dc0513989-3538cb0bef-88537081

[6] https://www.linkedin.com/pulse/100-regtech-startups-follow-jan-maarten-mulder

[7] http://asgard.vc/the-german-artificial-intelligence-landscape

[8] https://www.ft.com/content/3da058a0-e268-11e6-8405-9e5580d6e5fb

[9] https://regtechfs.com/dlt-the-solution-to-kyc-inefficiencies

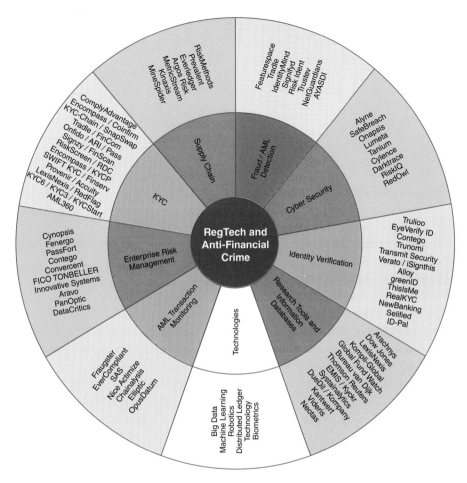

Figure 1: RegTech landscape

can use these adaptable tools via application programming interfaces (APIs). Not only will FinTech be able to meet the continuously evolving regulatory requirements, but it will also add real value to the businesses by leveraging the insights from anti–money laundering (AML) and fraud prevention to protect the organizations from cybercrime threats, an effort often lacking in more established organizations due to the fragmented development of the regulatory frameworks. FinTech companies and other technology-driven business models can free themselves from the traditional silo thinking, which is burdening traditional organizations that are caught in a structural time warp based on a foundation set some 30 years ago, and secure a competitive advantage. Given this, it is interesting to extend the thought further. Nasir Zubairi, a FinTech thought leader, calls for a RegTech offering that aggregates issues and provides a range of services. This is an innovative proposition, and it will be interesting to see who might spearhead such an initiative. It could be driven from within the FinTech sector, which might be more open to a collaborative approach.

Outlook

The European Union calls for a comprehensive and coherent regulatory and supervisory framework that sets standards for the exchange of best practices and major incident reporting. As many financial institutions have significant international exposure, the standards to be set should be in line with international standards.[10] The new technology-driven business models and changing criminal landscape also call for an integration of various AFC policies (AML, antifraud, cybercrime, anticorruption, tax evasion, human rights, environmental violations, and so forth) into a wider crime prevention policy framework that meets the requirements of an integrated global economy. RegTech solutions are versatile in this regard and can be used to deal with a number of financial crime threats jointly by dismantling a cost-intensive siloed approach to financial crime prevention. The resources freed up as a result of process optimization can be used to address the more serious risks facing organizations, which require more sophisticated management approaches. For example, Figure 2 shows how AML and cybercrime advisory fits as part of a RegTech implementation.

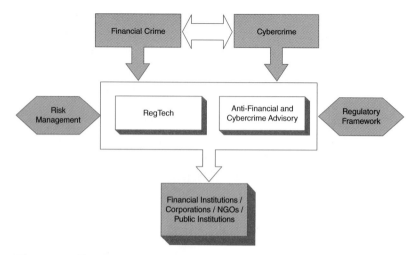

Figure 2: RegTech and anti–financial crime implementation

Although technology brings with it an enormous potential to increase the quality of AFC policies, risks attached to AI and its potential for exploitation should not be ignored, and measures to manage these risks must be considered. As noted in *The Guardian* recently, 'the moral economy of machines is not subject to oversight in the way that human bureaucracies are'.[11] The article referred to the issues linked to Microsoft's chatbot, Tay, and the vulnerability to discrimination and bad judgement. This highlights the importance of marrying the technology with sound management and governance frameworks in order to avoid instances of robotic intolerance and discrimination.

---

[10] http://www.europarl.europa.eu/sides/getDoc.do?pubRef=-//EP//NONSGML+COMPARL+PE-597.523+01+DOC+PDF+V0//EN&language=EN

[11] https://www.theguardian.com/commentisfree/2017/apr/20/robots-racist-sexist-people-machines-ai-language

The ongoing debates around data protection and ethics and the suggested limitations of RegTech solutions in the areas of risk management in assessing indirect compliance and regulatory risks and reputational risk exposure must also be taken into consideration when assessing the opportunities attached to RegTech solutions and their viability. Data privacy is a matter of key importance and an inherent societal value to be sustained. The topic, however, should not be considered in isolation but put in the wider context of the digital age and the transparency in which we already exist, as well as the risk attached to the ever-increasing threat of cybercrime.

Understanding the emerging RegTech solutions and using them wisely is part of a forward-looking approach to compliance, which, when linked to other areas such as risk management, will ensure the stability and security of businesses besides meeting regulatory and compliance requirements in the long term. However, given that statistical methods cannot substitute for intuition and long-term knowledge, and that algorithms are also not error-proof, the need for a risk-based discussion and human dialogue as well as critical thinking and good judgement in effectively managing organizations' exposure to financial, cyber, and other related crime continues to exist. Partnering this expertise with technological advancement is likely to be the recipe for sustained success in adding value and also in being prepared to deal with the fat tails, black swans, and hidden patterns of financial crime.

RegTech: Tackling Regulation with Innovation

By Jan-Maarten Mulder
Founder, Summer Capital

Certainly, RegTech is nothing new; incumbents and technology companies have invested in regulatory solutions for many years. However, RegTech as an interesting investment theme has emerged only in the last year and is now rapidly becoming mainstream. As opposed to FinTech, which is generally seen as early-stage companies looking to disrupt financial services companies, most RegTech companies solve problems faced by incumbents, which results in much greater willingness to engage in conversations and partnerships.

Removing the Bottlenecks to Innovation

It is hoped that RegTech entering the mainstream will speed up the delivery of solutions, which today are hampered for two key reasons. First, there is a limited amount of venture investment in the space. If you exclude investments made by incumbents and established technology providers (and focus only on RegTech within financial services), less than US$200 million per annum has been invested in early-stage RegTech start-ups. Second, the long sales cycle of selling a product to a financial services firm can be an inhibitor for start-ups. Probably as an unintended result of regulation, financial firms have become very conservative in working with new(er) external vendors. Here is where firms and regulators have a responsibility to catalyse innovation by collaborating with interesting solution providers at an early stage (and not subject them to countless procurement requirements; these can be addressed at a later stage). Also, financial firms should see the value of collaborating early with technology firms in terms of changing their own culture and should not hesitate to pay start-ups for pilot programs to ensure they are also motivated towards success.

Not Hibernating

The acquisition of Promontory by IBM shows that existing technology companies see RegTech as an interesting area. I have not spent much time writing about what major technology companies like Accenture, Bloomberg, or IBM offer (nor what incumbents are building themselves), but evidently they are not hibernating and are working on their own solutions.

Financial Services = Financial Technology

As leading FinTech investor Pascal Bouvier stated, we are currently in the second wave of the transformation of financial services firms into financial technology companies. While the first wave was concentrated on the potential of start-ups developing technology that would take down traditional banking models, the second wave has seen start-ups working with incumbents to provide viable solutions. Especially in RegTech, there are many examples of successful collaborations and partnerships between start-ups and incumbents.

Get ready for the third wave, which Bouvier believes is just around the corner, and which will show the application of emerging technologies such as artificial intelligence and robotics, and the likely entry into financial services of large tech companies like Facebook, Apple, and Amazon. I believe RegTech will play a major role here as well, both as a service provider to FinTech and as a catalyst for new products and services.

London and New York Dominate

The United Kingdom and United States still have the greatest number of different start-ups and diversity of problems being tackled. Given the UK's Financial Conduct Authority's proactive approach to innovation, it is no surprise that London is at the top of the list. As fellow RegTech investor Michael Meyer has said multiple times, regulators need to foster innovation and push financial firms to embrace working with early-stage innovators. I am surprised, though, at the relatively low number of start-ups in Asia.

Bright Future

For an industry that is transforming into a technology industry, the future is very bright. The application of emerging technologies will not only make processes more efficient, but also lead to new products and markets and may even allow previously unprofitable client segments (such as lending to small companies or self-employed individuals) to have (better) access to financial products. However, in order to get there, we will need regulators and incumbents to embrace change.

Key RegTech Trends

Market Surveillance

Any participant active in the global capital markets is looking for an advantage. Unfortunately, in some cases, such advantages are unlawful, such as insider trading or placing fake orders to manipulate prices (spoofing). New tools are being developed to monitor participants and to identify nefarious behaviour based on trading data and contextual information such as market information and news feeds, as well as chats and email. The most promising companies often combine advanced data analytics with behavioural science to provide faster and more efficient

ways to manage conduct. One of the hardest elements of market surveillance is to limit the number of false positives – nobody wants to analyse countless false notifications. As new regulations extend surveillance to more activities and asset classes, traditional technology and methods become prohibitively expensive. In addition, aggregating chat and voice communication by traders across multiple channels and converting it into usable data can be challenging. Machine learning could play a major role here too.

Owing to upcoming regulatory requirements, the greatest focus today is on surveillance for buy-side or sell-side firms. However, such tools are also going to be important for exchanges, clearing-houses, and regulators, as they need to meet new requirements more cost-effectively. In addition, another application of this technology is to assess the performance of traders based on the same multitude of data and potentially also deliver more analytics. By applying behavioural analytics, participants can be proactive in both surveillance and performance, opening up new ways to get a competitive advantage.

Regulatory Reporting

The amount and frequency of regulatory reporting have grown tremendously over the years. I recently spoke to the head of regulatory affairs from a major European bank, who said they regularly send reports of more than 50,000 pages every quarter to the European Central Bank. Apart from the usefulness of such reports, there are two important bottlenecks that RegTech companies are addressing.

First, extracting data from what are often legacy systems is a very difficult and error-prone process for financial firms. A number of RegTech companies have developed data aggregation tools that take information from different source databases and combine it into one complete data set. The tools often also provide feedback regarding any inconsistencies in the source information.

The second bottleneck relates to the actual reporting – regulation often changes and is described as published principles for which the firms need to interpret and create their own reporting. Given the staggering amount of regulation, firms often have multiple employees just to monitor required and ad hoc reporting. Fortunately, there are a number of RegTech firms that specialize in monitoring regulation and often provide an up-to-date reporting format. The next evolution is to move towards smart regulation using smart contract technology to create a form of dynamic oversight. This would allow regulators to change capital requirements live based on real market events instead of adjusting for historical events.

Stress Testing/Capital Planning

Stress testing of financial services firms' balance sheets is becoming a popular risk management and regulatory tool. When the European Banking Authority (EBA) recently took over supervision of banks from the national regulators, it performed a massive stress test of all the major European banks. Almost every bank had difficulties in delivering accurate and timely data. This was not surprising, given that data in banks is often contained in separate databases on outdated systems with often incomplete or wrong information.

In many cases, regulators have not provided specific instructions for how to complete tests. With new available technologies and data quality initiatives, a number of firms are building scenario and stress test platforms to manage risk and/or calculate capital requirements. Capital planning tools can also help reduce the capital ratios of banks by proving to regulators they have adequate reserves. This could significantly increase return on equity, a very difficult task for banks over the past eight years.

Fraud Detection

Closely related to know your customer (KYC), fraud detection includes solutions to protect against external and internal fraud. Solutions include identity verification and suspicious activity alerts.

Arguably, this extends well beyond RegTech and FinTech into e-commerce. However, some companies have a strong focus on financial services and use sophisticated analytics to monitor and detect all kinds of fraudulent activities during transactions.

Controls Automation

These technologies automate interpretation and application of regulatory rules and oversight of internal processes in order to flag potential issues. Many of the control functions at financial services companies are working with outdated, manual systems and cannot cope with the complexity of the financial services industry. So far, the response has been to set more controls and hire more people to manage these, as well as push controls towards the front office, which distracts salespeople or traders from what they are hired for. There is a huge opportunity to automate these controls, and several firms are working on smart solutions for different parts of the financial services industry.

Cyber Security/Data Privacy

With online becoming the main communication channel for financial services companies, the strength of cyber security and, in particular, data privacy is critical for business operation and trust. In addition, financial firms are increasingly working with external vendors that operate outside of the firm's firewall. Specific regulatory cyber security provisions and vendor obligations put the onus on financial institutions to secure their systems. RegTech companies have developed tools to qualify the cyber security protocols of vendors to financial services companies, which also can be used for insurance companies to assess cyber security insurance underwriting risks.

Risk Management

Traditional risk management in financial services is typically based on inflexible systems and is often front-end focused – trading limits, value at risk calculations, and so on. Advanced data analytics and visualization will reduce the time to analyse risk parameters, allowing firms to spend more time acting on insights. New tools will also allow firms to better analyse risk from middle and/or back office functions, which are often overlooked – including operational risks.

Client Due Diligence/Know Your Customer

One of the major challenges of new or ongoing client due diligence, in particular with small(er) companies, is that it is very difficult to accurately link names to bad press due to different spellings, local language, and so forth. This makes the onboarding and monitoring process slow and often incomplete. Unique identifiers or blockchain technology can play a role here but can result in data privacy discussions, which are further complicated by different approaches by regulators. Another approach is to mine open source information followed by human analysis. In any case, the RegTech tools that are currently being developed will make client acceptance more efficient and reduce the manual work this often entails. Any successful solution should be better than just a clever work flow tool, and should combine data from multiple sources and deploy strong analytics tools to come to decisions where human involvement is needed only for exceptions.

Communication Monitoring

Today's world of multichannel communication, including WhatsApp, Facebook Messenger, and more, leads to headaches for compliance officers owing to the difficulty of tracking all communications. Apart from ensuring that any communication is in line with internal guidelines, regulation increasingly requires firms to store all client communication. In order to satisfy such requirements, firms can either somehow integrate and monitor various communication channels or migrate account managers to controlled messaging environments. Some RegTech companies are building auditable communication tools to replace email with an instant messaging platform to allow for secure information exchange and transaction authentication. In addition, there are companies that focus on capturing voice communication. Applying technology that allows voice recordings to be transferred into searchable data would provide huge opportunities in various other RegTech areas, including market surveillance.

Other Developments

There are also emerging technologies not included in the previous categories addressing regulatory issues such as compliance training (very important for firms), model management, violation analytics, and internal auditing. Some help firms track regulatory enforcement activity across the industry and provide interesting tools to validate models and algorithms. RegTech will undoubtedly continue as a major area of innovation, and I expect much more investment as well as partnerships with incumbents in the next few years.

Identities, the RegTech Holy Grail

By Pascal Bouvier
Managing Partner, MiddleGame Ventures

and Dasha Cherepennikova
Product Manager

The Identity Problem

We are living in a digital age in which individuals and entities transact and exchange in ever-increasing degrees online. The digitization of services across industries is supposed to usher in an era of great benefit to users – the convenience of being able to access services on the go from just about anywhere in the world, the immediacy of not waiting for a physical location to open, and so forth.

However, a critical linchpin of enabling these seamless online experiences – the identity layer – is woefully inadequate for the digital world and in dire need of a reboot. An average consumer in a developed country may maintain relationships with more than 200 organizations. In fact, conservative estimates posit that there are currently 50–60 billion digital identities in existence for just people (not counting entities or machines). Yet, despite this proliferation, organizations across various industries face increasing costs in identifying someone or something to a high degree of trust. Without trust, transactions become much more difficult and costly to execute in the form of customer friction, as well as losses owing to both bad actors and the inability to let in would-be good users.

For example, in e-commerce, card not present fraud (using a stolen credit card) and account takeover (logging into someone else's account to spend that person's money) continue to grow at alarming rates. However, good user declines, or so-called false positives, are estimated to be at 10 times the size of fraud losses![1] Meanwhile, in financial services, the anti–money laundering (AML)/know your customer (KYC) solutions market is expected to continue to grow at a compound annual growth rate (CAGR) of 11% through 2021.[2] This narrative is playing out in almost every industry from e-commerce to healthcare, telecommunications, travel, and even government-provided services.

From the consumer standpoint, managing relationships with 200+ organizations means countless hours creating accounts, resetting passwords, and in some instances physically showing up with documents in hand to perform an in-person identity verification process. And if that was not enough, the looming threat of data breaches, identity theft, and misuse of private data continues to undermine customers' confidence and trust in using online services.

The explosive growth of the internet further exacerbates the inadequacy of the status quo. As more and more devices become connected, there is an imperative to reimagine how to scale and manage the complex network of identity relationships. Solutions that don't account for both human and device identities will ultimately leave a large vulnerability.

Simply put, today's existing identity schemes are fundamentally broken in the context of the modern economy. There is a clear multisided market that exists for a robust, reusable digital identity service. We contend that the financial services industry can and should be a central actor in building digital identity schemes that assure a high level of trust and bridge the gap between various problems ranging

---

[1] https://chargeback.com/false-positives-staggering-cnp-losses

[2] http://www.researchandmarkets.com/reports/4143977/global-anti-money-laundering-software-market-2017

from regulatory to privacy to legal, while delivering a much-needed retail and wholesale utility that will facilitate tomorrow's commerce for consumers and organizations alike.

Why Financial Services and RegTech?

The financial services industry specifically is faced with a set of intractable issues when it comes to provisioning identities, authenticating identities, and discharging their AML/KYC duties. We anticipate that regulatory pressure will continue to remain strong across the globe, thus continuing to keep KYC issues at the forefront and driving the need for identity management.

However, even if we suspend our disbelief and assume a loosening or elimination of regulation, the truth is that financial services providers will continue spending resources to verify and authenticate their customers to a high degree. Fundamentally, knowing the other side of a transaction continues to be vitally important not only to managing risk but also to unlocking opportunities to create value by matching customers to products they are likely to use. Lastly, whether you are a believer in the great unbundling Netflix trend or not, it is hard to imagine a bundling or unbundling of financial services into an offering where the need for an identity layer is absent.

The RegTech staples of automation, analytics, cloud computing, machine learning, and other technologies certainly hold promise to reduce the cost of performing and maintaining robust identity schemes. In the future, financial institutions will discharge their regulatory burden with a fraction of the number of employees needed today. However, given the aforementioned realities, we contend that there is a clear opportunity for financial services to fundamentally reimagine identity management from a regulatory burden into a new strategic business opportunity. Instead of just realizing internal cost savings, financial institutions can and should look to creating new products and services focused on the delivery and implementation of this identity layer into the broader marketplace.

The Race Is On

Given the pervasiveness of the digital identity problem, there are a large number and variety of stakeholders who have taken matters into their own hands. Governments, from the Nordics to India, have mandated or facilitated national digital identity schemes. India's Aadhaar program crossed the one billion enrolment mark in 2016. Would-be rival tech companies have shown unprecedented levels of cooperation in forming alliances and standards bodies to facilitate use. The GSM Association, the global telecommunications association, has launched Mobile Connect – a protocol for authentication using a mobile phone as well as a platform for identity data sharing. An impressively large cadre of start-ups is also attempting to storm the gates with solutions.

At a macro level, banks have been notably timid to date. The Nordics are a markedly progressive exception, with programs such as BankID in Norway starting to provide digital identity to users back in 2004. Financial institutions are also participants in government-driven strategies that marry the public and private sectors in providing digital identity services for citizens to access government services – for example, the United Kingdom's GOV.UK Verify or Estonia's e-ID program. However, at the global level, the number of users able to leverage their banking relationships for identity continues to be low.

The Path Forward

It is important to note that there are significant challenges to be solved. How can we build an architecture that supports the multifaceted data sets that comprise a holistic identity while accounting for the ability to use multiple context-specific personas? What is the commercial model for bringing such a system to market? Does such a system introduce new regulatory burdens or liability risks? How will consumer privacy be preserved? How does such a system scale?

In designing and implementing commercial solutions at scale, any implementation of digital identity needs to fundamentally reconcile that privacy lies at the heart of digital identity. Given the vast array of use cases and activities in today's digital world, consumers will need a framework that can let them share – or not share – personal information in very context-specific ways. They will need transparency in how their digital contrails can or cannot be aggregated, how data is retained or deleted, and mechanisms to have strongly authenticated transactions that are entirely decoupled from a real-life verifiable identity.

Banks do have most of the factors in place to be providers of identity digitally and overcome many of these hurdles.

The paradigm of banks being trusted custodians of customers' money can be extended to them being trusted custodians of customers' data. Paradoxically, in many markets, banks are not loved, but they are trusted – in contrast, the big tech companies (Google, Apple, Facebook, Amazon) are loved but not trusted, especially in the realm of personal data control. In addition, for all of the grumble about legacy and outdated technology, banks do have a history of creating and working in environments of interoperable systems and standards (SWIFT, etc.). A non-centralized identity model where multiple financial institutions, among other actors, provide utility in a federated way is likely one of the few viable options for scale.

Given that Nordic banks already provide identity as a service in their markets, it appears the question is not of technology but rather rooted in cultural and intent issues. Culturally, we have seen banks, especially in the United States and Europe, view customer data as a liability. While this viewpoint might be a positive force in pushing for safeguards, it has also engendered a reluctance to provide an identity service. The very fact that financial institutions have user data and consumer relationships that are valuable to the outside world inherently showcases the asset nature of the data. By embracing this asset nature and creating a mechanism to harness the data in a way that is transparent, gives control to end users, and provides a needed service, banks can create additional value in the ecosystem.

We do not expect, nor would we personally desire, the rise of a single centralized digital identity system. Furthermore, the need for both human and device identity foreshadows that collaboration between organizations that create and build relationships with each other will be necessary. Financial services will therefore not be the only piece of this complex puzzle. However, given the existing regulatory requirements driving financial institutions, we see a clear set of circumstances that positions them to become integral actors.

And for us, this is the true definition of the opportunity presented by RegTech.

The RegTech Landscape

2

- RegTech solutions are adjusting to market specificities, e.g. being sharia compliant
- Regulatory velocity and volume is calling for automation to stay compliant
- Automation is the first phase towards real time and predictive compliance

- RegTech can improve trust in financial markets and therefore increase economic growth
- RegTech short term impact: increase efficiency; long term impact: reform markets compliance and digitization efforts remaining a C-Level priority

- Post-crisis reform is asking for more frequent and granular data reporting

- Implement RegTech solution from start-ups because it is faster and cheaper than doing in-house
- Augmenting work flow of compliance officer to help identify false positives
- Future will move from dynamic reporting towards predictive risk analytics

- Data sovereignty is developing as a trend but is still looking for market wide acceptance
- Customer data base needs to become dynamic rather than following static models

- 300 million pages of documents to be processed post-crisis
- Implementation by RegTech solution can have an ROI in 3 years
- RegTech solution can impact customer journey and business IT Infrastructure

- Data volume and velocity requires automation
- Corporate to develop three lines of defense powered by tech
- RegTech product suite developed both by traditional providers and start-ups

This second part provides more detail on a market which is predicted to be one of the fastest growing areas of the financial sector.

The RegTech start-up eco-system has grown rapidly to match that expectation. Entrepreneurs are driven by the US$100 billion market opportunity that represents compliance spending. This has generated a market of over 300 start-ups (compared to 7000 FinTech start-ups), which is fuelled by a cumulative US$1 billion of investment by venture capital since 2012.

RegTech companies can be classified into three categories:

- **Regulatory Compliance**: learning about the impact of regulatory changes on the business logic of banks.
- **Risk Management**: identifying conduct risk to prevent another LIBOR scandal.
- **Financial Crime**: understanding the ultimate beneficiary behind a shell company.

Like FinTech companies, the majority of RegTech companies are B2B providers selling to financial institutions. While the demand from this client base is strong, it appears that that sales cycle remains long – on average 12 months – on par with what is seen in the FinTech industry. As this part will illustrate, there are certain noted exceptions particularly in the context of the regulatory deadline, such as MiFID II or GDPR which fast-track the sales cycle.

Additionally, RegTech start-ups can be found in two other areas: firstly regulators, which will be discussed more in Part 7 and the growing B2G space. Regulators globally are engaging RegTech start-ups via various channels, from hackathons to accelerators to find solutions to enhance their supervisory or regulatory function. Certain FinTech companies are directly adding regulatory compliance processes into their product. For example, in the context of wealth management, fund products are now being sold and marketed only to pre-qualified investors by using their data to access suitability, location, and investment profile.

Islamic RegTech

By Niclas Nilsson
Founder and CEO, Capnovum

and Inga Jovanovic
Managing Director, Capnovum

RegTech is battling large volumes of structured and unstructured information from dispersed regulators and supervisors. Frequently revised regulatory frameworks and compliance milestones add further complexity to already overlapping and sometimes contradicting requirements.

The volume of regulations and regulatory change already exceeds what can reasonably be processed without cognitive solutions. Reacting late results in duplication of effort, further cost, compliance risk, and ultimately sanctions. The rising cost of doing business has driven demand for advanced RegTech solutions that deal independently with discovery, understanding, and monitoring of regulations and obligations.

The similarities to the challenges faced by Islamic financial institutions are striking. Islamic finance has struggled with intersecting and often conflicting regulations and religious rulings since long before regulators went into overdrive in the wake of the financial crisis. RegTech solutions developed to meet global regulatory requirements therefore come with distinct benefits to Islamic financial institutions.

RegTech and artificial intelligence offer synergies for Islamic institutions by bringing together religious rulings with conventional regulatory frameworks, identifying associated obligations across regulations and jurisdictions. The additional transparency contributes to economies of scale, innovation, and Islamic institutions' ability to meet the demand for regionally targeted product offerings.

This chapter offers an introduction to the Islamic financial services industry (IFSI), Islamic financial regulation, and – building on common RegTech classifications[1] – a framework for addressing its specific complexities. Following the spread of Islamic finance in recent years, its relevance stretches far beyond traditionally Muslim countries.

The Industry

The IFSI incorporates three sectors: Islamic banking, Islamic capital markets, and Islamic insurance (*takaful*). This section provides an overview of these main sectors and their current status, drawing on the IFSI Stability Report 2017,[2] as well as major regional and jurisdictional differences that contribute to the diversity of the industry.

It also outlines key organizations for global cooperation and harmonization. These bodies define international standards for the industry, which are either directly adopted by or guiding central banks and regulatory authorities in member jurisdictions.

Islamic Banking

The most well-known difference between Islamic and conventional finance is that interest (*riba*) is prohibited by the Sharia. Wealth is created by putting money to work, rather than depositing it against interest. The Sharia considers money as a store of value and a medium of exchange, not a commodity to be traded. Islamic banking is thus structured to achieve profit sharing in transactions permissible under Islamic contract law.

---

[1] Douglas W. Arner, Janos Barberis, and Ross Buckley, *FinTech, RegTech and the Reconceptualization of Financial Regulation* (October 2016); Institute of International Finance, *RegTech in Financial Services: Technology Solutions for Compliance and Reporting* (March 2016).

[2] Islamic Financial Services Industry Stability Report 2017.

Total Islamic banking assets amounted to US$1.5 trillion[3] by mid-2016, with the Middle East and North Africa (MENA), including the Gulf Cooperation Council (GCC), making up 80% of that volume. Iran, with its all-Islamic financial system, accounts for 33% of the world's Islamic banking assets, followed by Saudi Arabia with approximately 21%.

Islamic banks increased their share of total banking assets in 18 countries – an indication of the growing acceptance in jurisdictions with dual financial systems – resulting in Islamic finance reaching systemic importance[4] in 12 domestic markets.

Islamic Capital Markets

Islamic capital markets (ICMs) incorporate the *sukuk* market, a Sharia-compliant listed equities market and Islamic funds market. Sukuk, commonly referred to as 'Islamic bonds', is the Sharia-compliant alternative to conventional fixed-income securities and the predominant sector of ICM. In 2016, the volume of Sukuk outstanding amounted to US$318.5 billion.[5]

Malaysia – one of the traditional Islamic finance strongholds and top-ranked in the Islamic Corporation for the Development of the Private Sector (ICD)–Thomson Reuters Islamic Finance Development Indicator (IFDI)[6] – has the largest domestic sukuk market and the third highest concentration of Islamic finance assets globally. Issuance by Malaysian obligors exceeded 50% of both sovereign and corporate universal sukuk volumes in 2016.[7]

---

[3] Ibid.

[4] Defined as jurisdictions where Islamic banking assets exceed 15% of total domestic banking assets.

[5] Islamic Financial Services Industry Stability Report 2017.

[6] ICD–Thomson Reuters Islamic Finance Development Report 2017.

[7] Islamic Financial Services Industry Stability Report 2017.

Islamic Insurance, or Takaful

Takaful implements the principle of risk sharing by concept of joint guarantee, where two or more parties agree to guarantee each other in the event of a loss. Commercial operations are structured on one or more Islamic contracts that determine the Sharia-compliant business model.

The global takaful and retakaful industry grew with a growth rate three times that of conventional insurance, albeit from a humble position. Total takaful contributions amounted to US$25.1 billion[8] at the end of 2015, with MENA (including GCC) again making up 80% of the volume. Saudi Arabia dominates the market with US$10 billion of contributions, followed by Iran with US$8 billion.

Islamic insurance in the GCC centres on medical/health, in some countries driven by new legislation introducing mandatory medical insurance, and motor takaful, while family takaful is most important in Southeast Asia. The insurance penetration is low in most Organisation of Islamic Cooperation (OIC) countries, which in combination with regional diversity often causes takaful undertakings to lack economies of scale.

International Standard-setting Organizations

The Islamic Financial Services Board (IFSB) issues global prudential standards and guiding principles for the Islamic banking capital markets, and insurance (takaful) sectors, with the objective to improve robustness and stability of the IFSI[9]

Supported by regulatory and government bodies, the International Islamic Financial Market (IIFM) drives transparency, harmonization and unification by issuing Sharia-compliant financial contracts and product templates for the capital markets, corporate, and trade

---

[8] Ibid.

[9] https://www.ifsb.org/

finance segments of IFSI. Its mission includes creating efficient Islamic financial markets.[10]

The Accounting and Auditing Organization for Islamic Financial Institutions (AAOIFI) issues global standards for Sharia-compliant accounting, auditing, ethics, and governance. Its standards are increasingly adopted, or used as a basis for national guidelines, by central banks and regulatory authorities, and followed by leading Islamic financial institutions around the world.[11]

The Opportunity

With the global Muslim population expected to grow twice as fast as the overall world population to 2050,[12] and total Islamic finance assets expected to increase to US$3.8 trillion by 2023,[13] it is uncontroversial to predict intensifying innovation in Sharia-compliant products.

The Islamic Development Bank Group (IsDB) and the World Bank Group[14] have outlined a potential for the risk-sharing principles underpinning Islamic finance to act as a stabilizing factor for the global economy, and the challenges faced by the industry that restrict effectiveness today.

Recent technological advances, underpinning the risk of FinTech and RegTech, provide infrastructure not previously available to execute on these opportunities. Smart contracts, distributed ledger technology (DLT) or blockchain, cryptocurrencies and crowdfunding, are seen by IsDB as "closer to the spirit of Islamic law of contracts, with an undiluted

---

[10] http://www.iifm.net/

[11] http://aaoifi.com/

[12] Pew Research Center, 'The Future of World Religions: Population Growth Projections, 2010–2050' (2 April 2015).

[13] Thomson Reuters and Dubai International Financial Centre, 'State of the Global Islamic Economy Report 2018/19'

[14] Global Report on Islamic Finance 2018 – 'Overview – The Role of Islamic Finance in Financing Long-term Investments'.

focus on cooperation, transparency, and avoidance of any kind of uncertainty regarding the settlement".[15]

The Challenges

However, regional and national variations in economic development, innovation and growth, and a diversity of approaches taken by regulators in different jurisdictions, are causing an increased focus on Islamic regulatory frameworks.

Islamic Financial Regulation

Islamic regulatory frameworks differ per country in their treatment of financial services. A few jurisdictions allow only Islamic finance institutions, whereas others either have specific laws for Islamic financial services or incorporate Islamic structures into a single set of financial services laws.

Some countries have adopted national-level Sharia boards, while others retain Sharia governance solely at the institutional level.

Standards and guidelines issued by international standard-setting organizations apply only to member institutions and jurisdictions, and only to the extent that they are adopted by each national regulatory authority.

Diverging Views and Interpretations

In the context of Islamic finance, Sharia scholars interpret and apply Islamic jurisprudence. Religious rulings – fatwas – are opinions issued by qualified scholars, and there are different schools of thought. It is possible that Sharia boards come to different interpretations, and standards may evolve over time to reflect changes in the environment. Prominent examples of this are the AAOIFI directive published in February 2008 in response to a prominent scholar having questioned the Sharia compliance of 85%

---

[15] Ibid.

of outstanding sukuk issues,[16] and the focus on asset-backed as opposed to the more common asset-based sukuk issues in the wake of high-profile sukuk defaults during the global financial crisis.[17]

FinTech and Emerging Issues

Similarly to conventional finance, start-ups are aiming to disrupt Islamic financial institutions by disintermediating the value chain. A common challenge for FinTechs is that they operate in a developing regulatory environment. Participating in regulatory sandboxes is sometimes the only way to anticipate how regulators will restrict innovaton in order to protect consumers and investors. Unanswered questions concerning the permissibility under Sharia law lead to further complexity and disadvantages for Islamic FinTechs relative to their conventional counterparts.

The IFSB highlights legal, regulatory, and Sharia issues with emerging Islamic FinTech products that require the attention of regulators and Sharia scholars.[18] Concerns include:

Should *cryptocurrencies* be exchanged according to the Sharia rules for commodities or for currencies? The answer to this question is likely to be derived from what constitutes a currency. It is not obvious that a cryptocurrency that is not widespread, is not regularly used for transactions, and is accepted by only a small number of merchants will at all be considered a currency. Transactions involving such tokens are akin to barter trade, and thus fall under the Sharia rules for commodities.

While the implementation of Islamic contracts as single *smart contracts* may not violate Sharia rules, interlinked smart contracts where one contract triggers the unstoppable execution of conditional contracts are more complicated. New types of collective investment vehicles without a corporate identity, with no legal personality and therefore potentially unlimited liability on its shareholders, and decision making by majority rule, are especially problematic. Although these sophisticated contractual arrangements, encoded through smart contracts, resemble *Musharaka* partnerships, the partners don't know each other, and majority voting contrasts with the ideal of consensus-based decisions and puts the minority at risk of mission drift.

Transparency is essential for Islamic *crowdfunding platforms*. Disclosure requirements for fund seekers and platform operators should reasonably include assuring Sharia compliance of contracts and projects, or ensuring that investors have sufficient information and expertise to assess the Sharia compliance themselves. These requirements remain throughout the investment period, since it is important for Islamic investors that the funded enterprise remains Sharia compliant. Non-compliant investments should ideally be liquidated or the income donated to charity. There is no equivalence to this requirement in conventional finance.

Other issues that need to be addressed are the enforceability of contracts in courts, tax neutrality, and Sharia governance. Treatment of contracts entered into while legislation and fatwas were still pending has become a growing pain for early adopters.

The Solution

In 2007, the Islamic Research and Training Institute (IRTA) and IFSB published a 10-year framework[19] to advance the Islamic financial services industry. The 10-year framework and the midterm review[20] set out recommendations around enablement,

---

[16] https://www.arabianbusiness.com/most-sukuk-not-islamic-body-claims-197156.html

[17] https://www.arabianbusiness.com/asset-backed-sukuk-scheme-may-lift-demand-372650.html

[18] Islamic Financial Services Industry Stability Report 2017.

---

[19] Islamic Research and Training Institute and the Islamic Financial Services Board, 'Islamic Financial Services Industry Development: Ten-Year Framework and Strategies', 2007.

[20] Islamic Research and Training Institute and the Islamic Financial Services Board, 'Islamic Financial Services Industry Development: Ten-Year Framework and Strategies – A MID-TERM REVIEW', 2014.

performance, and reach, with the ambition to further inclusive, free, fair, and transparent Islamic financial services markets.

It was recognized that an adequate legal, regulatory, and supervisory framework; international prudential, accounting, and auditing standards; effective corporate governance and tax neutrality are prerequisites, and that relationships and dependencies between different sectors of the IFSI needed to be better understood.

Standardization of products, transparency, and collaboration between international standard-setting organizations, and across Islamic finance jurisdictions, were encouraged. Innovative business models, new technology, and new delivery channels were to be embraced, and access to funding for small and medium-size enterprises (SMEs) and entrepreneurs improved.

At the time of the midterm review, progress had been made but not uniformly across jurisdictions, and challenges to growth largely remained. Views still differed as to whether countries should implement a specific legal framework for Islamic finance, adopt national-level Sharia boards, and allow conventional institutions to offer Islamic financial services.

The Global Report on Islamic Finance 2018[21] evaluates the results of the 10-year framework and draws on those findings to make further policy recommendations on how to better utilize Islamic finance in mobilizing funds for long-term investments. Many of the newly called-out recommendations are familiar. The report highlights that lack of transparency causes inefficiencies and financial exclusion. It emphasizes improving the financial system by developing a supportive legal, administrative, and regulatory environment, to provide unified Sharia, regulatory, and accounting treatments. It also recommends strengthening financial supervision and corporate governance to reinforce accountability, increasing

the availability of risk-sharing and asset-backed financing instruments, and incentivizing Islamic financial innovation driven by FinTech solutions.

Conventional RegTech offers solutions[22] for interpreting regulations, monitoring compliance and enable supervision, that can be immediately applied to Islamic finance. Combining regulatory data with non-regulatory information sources relevant to the IFSI can drive transparency and collaboration across communities.

Conclusions

Similar to waiting for conventional regulators and supervisors to agree and implement common regulatory standards, formats, and terminology, it is impractical to expect full convergence of Islamic finance regulations anytime soon. Whereas a supportive public policy stance is essential for enabling the industry to reach its full potential, countries have been successful with various models, and diversity is not the key challenge to overcome – opacity is.

Transparency drives understanding and reduction in perceived risk, thus increases the appetite for investing. Investments and economies of scale drive innovation and availability of financial products, which in turn drives financial inclusion. Utopia would be the passporting of Sharia-compliant financial contracts across the OIC member states, and beyond Islamic financial markets.

Regulatory technology developed to normalize regulations across jurisdictions, formats, and languages can help bring transparency to Islamic finance. Conventional RegTech is generally applicable to Islamic financial institutions, save for the necessity of recognizing restrictions under the Sharia and implementing Islamic contracts,

---

[21] Global Report on Islamic Finance 2018 – 'Overview – The Role of Islamic Finance in Financing Long-term Investments'.

[22] See e.g. https://fintech.global/regtech100/

while Islamic RegTech comprises two dimensions that are distinct from conventional RegTech:[23]

1. Intelligence and insights need to incorporate additional data sources, taking into account different schools of thought and fatwas by various scholars, to provide an effective foundation for predicting where regulations are heading.

2. Continuous monitoring of Sharia compliance is necessary throughout the duration of an investment, since income generated from non-compliant investments or activities is not permitted.

---

[23] Douglas W. Arner, Janos Barberis, and Ross Buckley, *FinTech, RegTech and the Reconceptualization of Financial Regulation* (October 2016); Institute of International Finance, *RegTech in Financial Services: Technology Solutions for Compliance and Reporting* (March 2016).

How RegTech Could Help Determine the Future of Financial Services

By Subas Roy
Partner, Oliver Wyman

Let's start with a true story, in which only the names are changed but the facts remain. The ringing of Esther's alarm clock woke her from a deep sleep. The noise of the alarm had been going on for some time while she was trying to continue sleeping. She got up from her bed trying to remember what had happened in the boardroom the night before; it all seemed to have left a sour aftertaste. Not only has she been asked to leave the bank immediately, but she is also very much aware of the amount of press and attention this will garner, adversely impacting her career and reputation, which she has been building meticulously over the past 25 years. Was it all worth it? Not at all.

Esther was a very successful senior executive; she was the Investment Banking CEO of Bank X, a global systemically important bank (G-SIB) with operations around the world. She had risen from front desks, across operations, to management, and had then been elected as the CEO of the investment bank three years ago. Among her many qualities, she was brilliantly persuasive with the very strong commercial skills of a frontline sales executive. I interviewed Esther in November 2016 while preparing for my RegTech book and also this very chapter. She is a real person, but I have taken the liberty of changing her name and identity for these writings. The message will remain unaltered.

Where It All Started

In the early 1990s, financial services and, most importantly, banking and capital markets to which we now refer were in their early days. Trades and deals were agreed and recorded at a much slower pace, allowing the risk and compliance functions to play a more integrated business partner function. The number of countries that could be involved in large, global transactions was only a few, which helped to create a small group of traders and bankers to place bets, forwards, and swaps with one another. That is where the so-called investment banking started.

Then came the internet (dot-com) boom and suddenly we realized that a whole lot of new information (data) could be made available that was integral to business and economic growth. For instance, more information about the industries or agriculture in a country in East Asia or Latin America would mean more possibilities to enter into new contracts, options, and forwards; more money the financial services could make; and faster economic growth the countries could achieve. It all makes sense, doesn't it?

Growth seemed the easiest of all over the next 10 years (1995–2005). We created data analytics, customers and sales analytics, and econometrics to measure and predict growth. Governments and central banks now employed more analysts than ever before to predict further growth, markets of untapped potential, and commodities that could make more money through forwards, estimates, and cross-border trades.

And so they did too. Between 1990 and 2005, the world's gross domestic product (GDP) rose from US$27.5 trillion to US$43 trillion, i.e. by almost 60%, which is still an all-time record, as the next 10 years from 2005 on have shown a very mixed response.

So, what did we forget or, rather, overlook? Before the 1980s, all the great economic depressions that humanity had experienced had been linked to either a great war or a famine. It was only after the 1980s that we started seeing depressions linked to duped financial systems and/or our banking and lending environments. What do we learn from this fact?

Let's go back to our story with Esther. She was a determined leader who achieved double-digit growth over a continuous five-year period during her time as CEO, a very sound appointment indeed. She, however, overlooked the importance of the business partnership with controls, i.e. the so-called risk and compliance functions in the 1980s and 1990s, that worked alongside the front desks and operations and participated in major decisions, such as which cross-border trade to book, which loan to approve, and/or which deal to sign off on.

Under Esther's leadership, targets were set to increase the market share, grow top-line revenues and eventually bottom-line revenues too, reduce overheads, and embed an offshore/onshore business support and utility-based operating model. Sound all too familiar? It is because every other large financial institution has similar strategies, and even a great number of small to medium-size enterprises (SMEs), too, have followed their lead. Growth was the boardroom's agenda, and everyone focused on making every last possible penny.

That was an incorrect, shortsighted move by Esther, and by many other business leaders like her. History had to be repeated, and so it was in 2008. We were back in depression, one of the largest economic recessions humankind has ever seen. In the United Kingdom alone, the government needed to provide for an additional £850 billion (one-third the size of the UK economy), which would take at least the next 20 years to balance, creating budget strains on much-needed areas like health and other public services, safety and security of UK citizens, roads and transportation.

$$Growth = Opportunity + Trust$$

Growth is the sum of opportunity and trust. In simple terms, for growth to be sustainable it is equally important to create a trusted business environment while working through new opportunities. Otherwise, there is a very real risk of decline or even termination. What happened with the financial services between 1990 and 2008 reflects exactly that. They rose to new heights and then came crashing down to a record low level because of eroding trust. The investigations, fines, and penalties are all part of the aftermath that we are still experiencing and that will continue over the next decade or so.

Esther recalled the amount of mistrust and unease in the work environment amongst members of her senior management team. Because their revenue index measured almost everyone, the support functions, including the second and third lines of defense, did not have much face value. There was a time when they became almost an auxiliary function, called for when needed but otherwise kept at bay. Innovations in risk management and compliance between the years 2000 and 2008 were at a low, with most projects spending on new utility operating models and operating systems, which provided faster turnaround and better access to and analytics of customers' data (particularly of the untapped markets and developing economies). She mentioned to me that one of the key reasons the board wanted her to leave was to be able to bring changes to this working style and culture that had evolved during her time as CEO, and to consider what had been done right in the 1980s. Did we build a solid foundation of a trusted banking environment, and was it possible to instill some of that in today's global trade and transactions environment? Esther welcomed the board's decision but will still be subject to three remaining investigations with the regulators and the governments on both sides of the Atlantic, so it is not all the end for her, sadly.

Could It Have Been Different for Esther?

Yes, very much so, she opined. She thought that, as the CEO and part of the board, she could have played a more active role as the custodian of the sound old practices of consultation and reviews before decisions were taken, and she could perhaps have instructed the business executives to remain personally accountable for any problems, and to trickle the same message downwards. The so-called free access to trade and the single market could have been enlivened by her firm, allowing greater competition and setting some positive trends for her peer firms too. Rather than engaging with the regulators only at year-end review meetings, she could perhaps have spent more time building relationships, demonstrating her intent as the CEO to her own management team.

Advent of RegTech and Innovation in Trust

Let us now take a look at RegTech and innovation in trust and try to recoup some of the points that Esther has mentioned. We will then turn to the 'trust' agenda to see how this can help to shape the future of financial services and, most important, the opportunity it provides to all of us.

Technology and Regulation

Smart and disruptive methods of risk and regulatory compliance mean using new technologies with the same principles that date back to the pre-1990s, i.e. to bring a business partnering relationship between the operations and controls, thereby reducing the time gap between a business process, a business decision, and the necessary tests that it needs to endure to prove its prudence. There are emerging regulatory technologies – e.g. artificial intelligence (AI) and cognitive learning – which are capable of taking this to the next level, i.e. to continually learn from these tests and apply the learning with stronger, more accurate predictions so that not all the basic, routine tests need to be carried out on every occasion. This could save precious time and effort, and also help to bring the risk and compliance functions closer to the business, to integrally align them. It is important to note that some of these technologies are still in their early days, so we all need more prototypes and proof of concepts to ensure these get embedded adequately.

Analytics, AI, and APIs

Some of us do think that RegTech is predominantly about application of faster and more innovative analytics; pattern recognition to prevent fraud and understand our customers' behaviour better; improving conduct through better, real-time surveillance of conversations; and utilizing application programming interfaces (APIs) to connect and reconnect various data and technology platforms to achieve the end goal. Whilst all of these are true, the very essence of RegTech lies in its ability to help us innovate for generating trust: trust for our digital financial services, trust for our consumers, and trust for the societies and the next generations who will be our customers of the future.

This is a classic difference between macro and micro outlooks, the so-called strategy vis-à-vis purpose paradigm. Let's have a look at this from both angles and prove that the two are indeed intertwined.

The comparison in Table 1 provides us with a useful set of information and confirms that both macro and micro objectives are quite integral to each other. For instance, applying regulatory technology to reduce manual intervention and to select better samples for compliance reviews ultimately assists in bringing risk and compliance functions closer to the business process operations. It also helps to reduce time gaps between actual performance and post-reviews. In addition, it enables the application of resources where they should be, i.e. applying more analytics into the root cause of the issues and less into preparing the data sets.

I see the advent of RegTech over the next five years to focusing predominantly on the micro issues, i.e. how we reduce compliance costs, gain better insights from data analytics, and create a more intelligent, yet simpler data architecture by using some of the new technologies, enabling the creation of a second layer of data architecture in parallel to the traditional one built over the last 10–20 years. It is, however, for the financial services leaders,

Table 1: RegTech macro and micro objectives comparison

Innovation in trust	Cost reduction, analytics, AI, and APIs
• Resembles applying a by-design principle of risk and regulatory compliance to the future of financial services.	• RegTech is used to identify areas of risk and compliance functions and processes that are currently being performed manually, e.g. routine compliance checks, documentation reviews, and research on new or revised regulations and ideas on how to use robotics and process automation to reduce or even eliminate human intervention.
• Regulations and rules are built into business processes and decisions. For instance, stress testing of capital ratios is automated and anomalies sighted and addressed in real time. Regulators are also informed with increased frequency (e.g. 72-hour frequency as currently exists under the data protection regulations). The same principle applies to risks related to conduct or fraud and financial crime.	• How can AI be used to scan through terabytes of data or even more at lightning speed to improve accuracy of findings, select better samples for review of compliance, reduce false positives, and ensure compliance officers are looking into potential risks rather than trying to find needles in haystacks?
• Risk and compliance teams within the financial services organization review and approve any new or revised products and/or services before being offered to the market and consumers.	• How could APIs be used as a potential response to ill-equipped, complex data architecture? Can various sources be linked through APIs to create a data lake and then apply smart analytics to extract real data out of many signals?
• Data analytics is used not only for understanding customers' behaviour but also for discovering any potential non-compliance by linking various pieces of data. Records are maintained and shared with regulators and peer firms.	

regulators, and governments to set the right priorities and macro strategies, as we all know that financial services are key to the economic stability of the world, and, in fact, innovation in trust is key to providing future sustainability and stability to financial services, as Figure 1 explains.

Figure 1: RegTech and innovation in trust for the future of financial services

View from the Top – Feedback Received from Interviews of 120+ CEOs and Board Members

Let us now look at some of the feedback I received while either discussing RegTech and the importance of innovation in trust in organizations or conducting interviews on this very topic with some of the CEOs and other key C-suite members. More details will be contained in my RegTech book, but for this chapter, here is a summarized view.

In Figure 2, we see the innovation focus areas of CEOs and other key members of the C-suite in the years 2006–2016. Predominantly, digitization of business processes and channels has taken precedence, including new function formation, deployment of strategic resources, and implementation of new technologies. This goes hand in hand with what Esther had told us about her organization.

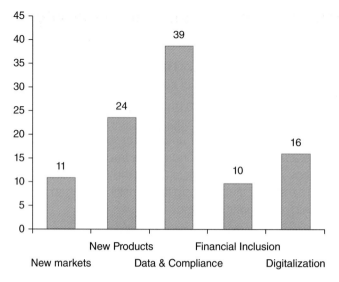

Figure 3: **Innovation focus areas 2016–2025 – priorities (%)**

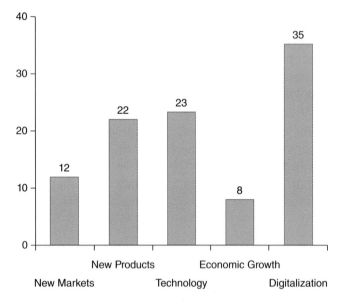

Figure 2: **Innovation focus areas 2006–2016 – priorities (%)**

Figure 3, on the other hand, shows the predicted areas of focus by the same CEOs and senior leaders of the G-SIBs and other large financial institutions. Financial inclusion and data and compliance replace economic growth and technology as the key focus areas, with data and compliance taking a 35% priority towards new programmes of initiative and new directions, followed by new products at 24%.

These observations are not surprising and are timely too. With the mounting legal battles, fines, and penalties, the most important and pressing points of debate at board meetings are how to secure the future of the financial institution and what relevant actions need to be taken, which might include appointing a CEO whose mindset is pro-compliance and to 'play by the book whilst also inventing new revenue channels'. In addition, these findings are in line with the macroeconomic and microeconomic senses of RegTech and innovation in trust. Most of the CEOs now look at this as having increased importance, as well as a number of chief risk officers (CROs) and chief compliance officers (CCOs) tasked with increasing utilization of regulatory technology and innovations in their functions. These are integral steps towards achieving sustainable business growth. We now turn to business cases.

Use Cases

Let us also look at a couple of examples where financial institutions are innovating with RegTech for a number of strategic benefits.

Blockchain Proof of Concept for a Globally Integrated Regulatory Intelligence and Reporting Function (Banking)

A major global bank just completed phase 1 of its proof of concept to create a blockchain-based solution for integrated regulatory intelligence sharing and reporting across its 54 different legal entities. The initial work involved creating a data-sharing forum on a blockchain with particular users designed as different legal entities, which then shared intelligence and information from their own jurisdictional review of upcoming regulations and the impact on their local business units. Each of them was part of the distributed ledger who could access and reciprocate with the information of other legal entities in real time. The blockchain also assessed the regulatory risks against a set of defined parameters for each of the legal entities and provided a combined weighted average risk score to the whole block as well as the individual member entity.

Findings so far have been positive and will now be utilized by the group compliance and innovation team in this bank to implement the initiative further. The initial estimate shows 60% elimination of manual reviews and information sharing through emails and SharePoint sites, and approximately 40% reduction in costs along with improved accuracy and timeliness of information sharing.

Applying Robotics with AI for Processing of Insurance Claims and Claimant Data, Identifying and Addressing Risks and False Claims (Insurance)

A global insurance enterprise headquartered in Europe has started using a combination of robots and AI solutions to process data relating to new insurance claims from its riskier markets

with histories of large claims linked to motor and building insurance. First, six months of tests have produced some really interesting results with extrapolation of the types of customers with disproportionate claims histories compared to others. This has helped the organization to look at its sales and premium calculation models, enabling the insurer to provide well-calculated, risk-weighted, price-competitive insurance products. The organization is now looking to expand the use of RegTech in other parts of its businesses and for more activities.

There are many more examples that can be used, but as a rule consider these five factors when adopting a RegTech solution.

Key considering factors for adopting RegTech: issues and challenges to overcome:

1. *A clear view of the existing regulatory compliance risks and associated complexities.* Before investing, it is key to have clarity on the compliance risks and resulting requirements.

2. *A centralized regulatory compliance monitoring and reporting framework.* The design and delivery of an integrated framework are fundamental for a standardized taxonomy and rule mapping.

3. *A set of RegTech innovation standards that are appropriate to the organization.* It is important to define the macroeconomic and microeconomic purposes of RegTech in the organization and thereby shape the strategy for innovation and further investments.

4. *Skilled resources.* Determine that you have skilled people around you to take you through the journey.

5. *Pilot and proof of concept.* Always commence with a pilot project to test the concept and underlying benefits.

Network and collaborate with the RegTech ecosystem – proactively approach your network and ask questions about what others are doing and why.

Introducing the RegTech Quality Compass: The Five Factors of RegTech Quality

By Tobias Houdek
Senior Product and Marketing Manager, Investment Navigator

Regulatory and commercial pressure has significantly increased over the past decade, providing ground for fundamental changes in the financial services landscape and the emergence of the RegTech space. In such a thriving environment, why focus on quality from the very beginning? Because quality is a decisive basis for sustainable long-term success. Quality is directly linked to customer satisfaction, which in turn supports loyalty, pricing power, and the probability of lower costs, as well as ultimately improved company profitability.[1]

According to the American Society for Quality (2017), 'quality' can refer to a products or services ability of either being free of deficiencies or fulfilling needs through performance or features as promised or implied.[2]

The SERVQUAL Dimensions in Brief

To assess service quality, Parasuraman et al. published in 1988[3] the concept of SERVQUAL as a diagnostic tool to identify a company's strengths and weaknesses in five service quality dimensions:

1. *Responsiveness.* Management of and adherence to time- and speed-related expectations.
2. *Empathy.* Ability to predict customer demands.
3. *Assurance.* Demonstrating politeness, skills, and avoidance of physical, financial, or social risks.
4. *Reliability.* Homogeneity of service performance.
5. *Tangibles.* Standard of the look and feel of facilities, staff, or marketing collaterals.

Within these five dimensions, SERVQUAL compares customer perceptions to what customers can expect from a high standard of quality in service delivery.

The SERVQUAL dimensions serve as the starting point for a new quality concept for the emerging RegTech sector.

Developing a Quality Framework for the Digital RegTech World

The essential idea behind the RegTech quality compass is to create a holistic quality framework for this young and upcoming digital industry that is useful for the providers and consumers of RegTech solutions.

A major reason for referencing an established service quality criterion framework is based on acknowledging the fact that RegTech solutions have a lot in common with traditional service businesses. Typical characteristics of services are:[4]

- Intangibility
- Inseparability

---

[1] P. Kotler and K.L. Keller, *Marketing Management*, 14th ed. (Harlow, UK: Pearson Education Limited, 2012).

[2] American Society for Quality, *Quality Glossary*. Available at https://asq.org/quality-resources/quality-glossary/q (accessed 15 April 2017).

[3] A. Parasuraman, L.L. Berry, and V.A. Zeithaml, 'SERVQUAL: A Multiple-Item Scale for Measuring Customer Perceptions of Service Quality', *Journal of Retailing* 64, no. 1 (1988): 12–40.

[4] K.D. Hoffman, J.E. Bateson, G. Elliott, and D. Birch, *Services Marketing – Concepts, Strategies and Cases*, first Asia-Pacific ed. (South Melbourne: Cengage Learning Astralia Pty Limited, 2010).

- Heterogeneity
- Perishability

Undoubtedly, RegTech solutions are predominantly intangible. Most RegTech outputs are also inseparably connected to the customer entity, for example through the provision of internal data or by means of accurate application handling.

On the other hand, thanks to digitization and automated processing, the typical service problems of perishability and heterogeneity seem not to be relevant.

Another reason to make the comparison to classic service businesses is revealed by looking at the value-generation cores or major purposes of RegTechs. These are typical service processes like advising, monitoring, screening, or alerting. While the execution format has changed from personal to digital, it is fair to assume that the types of expectations from (potential) customers remain unchanged whereby the level of expectations even increases.

Any valid framework needs to take into account the digital environment of RegTech solutions and should aim to respect the expectations of different stakeholders to holistically appraise a RegTech application. Relevant stakeholders include but are not limited to a solution buyer's executive management, end users, the buyers' shareholders, regulators, and the public. The framework should help RegTech entrepreneurs, product managers, and marketers to identify areas of differentiation for their products and to develop strategies to exploit strengths and minimize risks from weaknesses.

The Directions of the RegTech Quality Compass

For this new model, the following five factors are proposed as influential to the perceived performance quality of RegTech solutions:

1. Efficiency

2. Intelligence

3. Assurance

4. Availability

5. Enjoyment

Using these five factors, assessments revealing strengths and weaknesses in these areas should provide strategic and tactical directions for RegTech solution providers – hence the framework is named a quality compass. In the following sections, each direction is concisely described. Assessment questions and scales to score these directions are suggested in the tables without being limited to them. A high score indicates high quality in the respective criterion. It is suitable for comparative and individual appraisals.

Efficiency

Efficiency refers to all forms of costs, including time and psychological efforts associated with a solution in daily business. High monetary costs signalling high quality automatically lead to higher expectations in a product or service.[5] Consequently, the bar of customer satisfaction is raised and more challenging to achieve. See Table 1.

Intelligence

Generating additional value beyond expectations is the core idea of the intelligence factor. A RegTech solution must do more than create reports and ex post alerts. It must recognize and reveal patterns, combine input data logically, and differentiate between causality and coincidence. See Table 2.

---

[5] Kotler and Keller, *Marketing Management.*

Table 1: Questions to score the efficiency direction

Over a medium-term horizon, does the solution reduce effective monetary costs?			
Cost increase (0)	Cost neutral (1)	Minor cost reductions (2)	Substantial cost reductions (3)
Does the solution reduce time and/or psychological effort levels from employees?			
Effort increase (0)	Effort neutral (1)	Minor effort reductions (2)	Substantial effort reductions (3)

Table 2: Questions to score the intelligence direction

Does the solution bring additional relevant knowledge into the buyer's company?		
No (0)	Some additional knowledge (1.5)	Substantial additional knowledge (3)
Does the solution differ between causality and coincidence (if applicable)?		
No (0)	Not applicable to the solution (1.5)	Yes (3)

Table 3: Questions to score the assurance direction

Do the key personnel of the RegTech company have relevant experience and knowledge?	
No (0)	Yes (3)
Does the solution provider have partners with high reputations?	
No (0)	Yes (3)

Assurance

The inherent need for security must be satisfied through competence, knowledge, and skills embedded in the RegTech solution, making up the assurance dimension. Assurance includes also reducing a buyer's post-purchase cognitive dissonance – resolving concerns after having taken a major purchase decision by providing confirming clues (Schiffman and Kanuk 2010).[6] See Table 3.

---

[6] L.G. Schiffman and L.L. Kanuk, 'Consumer Decision-Making Processes', in *Advertising and Consumer Behaviour*, ed. N. Robertson (Sydney: Pearson Australia, 2010), 2–33.

Availability

Availability expectations include not only the core application functionalities but also all support and service components. Nowadays, service disruptions and unavailable support are hardly tolerated. See Table 4.

Enjoyment

Last but not least, and arguably the most controversial dimension, is enjoyment. Compliance and risk management have been perceived for too long as fun-free zones. Working with a RegTech solution should be a pleasurable, motivating, and rewarding experience. See Table 5.

Table 4: Questions to score the availability direction

Can users access human support in a reasonable time?	
No (0)	Yes (3)
Is a 24/7 self-help support remedy available (e.g. chatbot, instructional videos)?	
No (0)	Yes (3)

Table 5: Questions to score the enjoyment direction

If the solution is an application with a user interface, is it visually pleasant?			
Unpleasant (0)	Neutral (1)	Mildly pleasant (2)	Very pleasant (3)
Does the solution provide a sort of gratification for completed tasks?			
No (0)		Yes (3)	

Quality Drives Satisfaction Drives Profitability

As initially stated, quality could be directly linked to customer satisfaction, which ultimately supports company profitability through the means of increased loyalty, pricing power, and probably lower costs.[7] Figure 1 visualizes the influence of the RegTech quality compass directions on satisfaction and possible outcomes like loyalty and profitability.

Benefits of Working with the RegTech Quality Compass Framework

One criticism about the RegTech quality compass may be that some factors and the related measurements feature highly subjective and even emotional elements, whereas the typical

RegTech target market is a professional business-to-business affair. However, it might be necessary to acknowledge that corporations are the sum of their employees with all their individual knowledge, experiences, perceptions, expectations, and human feelings. Ultimately, purchase decisions by humans will never be completely rational. The proposed quality compass can provide guidance for strategic and tactical decisions of RegTech companies and be used as a self-assessment tool to determine resource allocation and identify unique selling propositions.

Paired with a reasonable value proposition or core idea (critical question: does my solution really solve a relevant problem?) and an innovative product pipeline, as well as sound financial and human resources, RegTech companies scoring high in all five dimensions of the introduced quality compass should be in the pole position to gain ambassadors, convince clients, and sustain long-term success. Last but not least, a proprietary service quality DNA in factors like those outlined in the quality compass is a competitive advantage. A distinct quality profile is much harder to copy or to be matched by competitors than any technologies or processes.

---

[7] Kotler and Keller, *Marketing Management*.

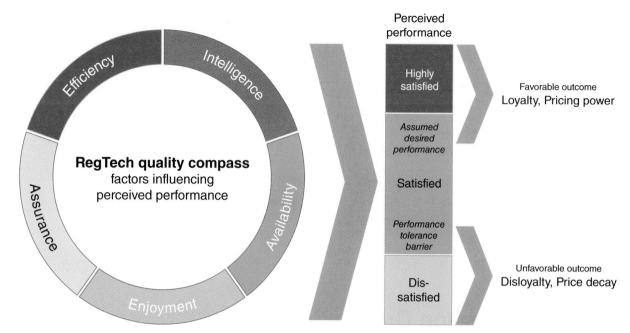

Figure 1: Influence of the RegTech quality compass

How Banks Are Managing Their Risk Through Technology and Market Infrastructure

By Kinsuk Mitra
Global Director and Head of RegTech, Risk and Compliance, HCL Technologies

With the regulatory technology (RegTech) landscape set to change dramatically over the next few years, you will have winners and losers. This is what the following chapter will explore, as we explain how RegTech will impact banks' daily business, service levels, and operating models.

Following Lehman Brothers' default in 2008, which was triggered by significant exposure to over-the-counter (OTC) derivatives, governments and regulators have continued to take steps to derisk the OTC market. The common goal has been to reduce the threat of counterparty failure and to avert another financial crash.

The Markets Post Lehman Brothers

The reformation of the financial markets following the global financial crisis has had a deep effect on how collateral is used and managed, with restructuring of the market not yet complete.

Questions that need to be answered are: will collateral fall short in the future? What is the future of collateral management? What changes can participants make to their existing infrastructure, information technology (IT), and services? What will be the role of third-party service providers?

Basel III

In a post-Basel III world, banks have been reassessing how they manage liquidity and working capital in order to comply with a plethora of liquidity monitoring requirements. The key ratios include the short-term liquidity coverage ratio (LCR), which assesses the bank's reserve of high-quality collateral in proportion to its net liquidity outflows over a 30-day period, and the net stable funding ratio (NSFR), a longer-term structural ratio that measures the required and available funding beyond a one-year horizon. The leverage ratio is a capital ratio that looks at tier 1 capital supporting a bank's exposure to be maintained at a minimum of 3%.

Dodd-Frank, EMIR, and Liquidity

The Dodd-Frank Act regulations in the United States and the European Market Infrastructure Regulation (EMIR) in Europe were introduced to take mitigating actions in the event of future counterparty defaults. The rules allow regulators to transfer the OTC derivatives positions – used mainly to mitigate foreign exchange and interest rate risk – smoothly to an applicable market participant, thereby averting another systemic crisis. These regulations require increased transparency over the derivatives market and high-grade liquid securities and/or cash to be set aside.

Trades need to be sufficiently collateralized to meet the initial and variation margin payment requirements that ensure a trade is correctly financed with future levels of collateral and liquidity available to derivatives users that are impacted. Scrutiny over these risk management practices means banks need to plan their trading strategies effectively and ensure they are well-positioned to guarantee future regulatory compliance.

As the leverage ratio ignores the risk-reducing benefits of collateral, it has had a major impact on multitrillion-dollar repo and securities financing markets, resulting in some cases in substantially higher capital requirements for what is usually a low-margin business. Before the new rules, use of high-quality collateral allowed an efficient distribution of liquidity and collateral around the financial system and minimal capital requirements.

Market players will therefore need to consider the impact of the leverage ratio on both their business model and those of their key counterparties. The structure, collateralization, and pricing of securities financing transactions will need to be adjusted to achieve capital efficiency relative to both risk-weighted and leverage-driven regulatory capital requirements, with some products consequently phased out.

BCBS 248

With Basel Committee on Banking Supervision (BCBS) 248 covering intraday liquidity monitoring, the rules set higher granularity requirements for banks usually segregated for each clearing and settlement infrastructure. While aggregated data is readily available at the central bank and direct participant level, there are benefits to banks of not limiting the calculation of liquidity buffers to 30 days, but rather in providing the aggregation of such data by increasing the current analytics and calculating on an intraday basis.

Banks need to invest considerably in order to efficiently manage their liquidity on an intraday basis, and their operational model is moving rapidly towards the centralized and integrated management of liquidity and collateral.

Market research shows bank treasuries need visibility of their payment flows and collection of data with little manual intervention. The desire is to improve current IT infrastructures in order to produce detailed and reliable forecasting on a short-, medium-, or long-term basis.

EMIR, Dodd-Frank, and MiFID II – More Players, More Competition

The succession of EMIR, Dodd-Frank, and second Markets in Financial Instruments Directive (MiFID II) regulations that tackle the risks of OTC derivatives products has resulted in a global market with greater competition expected from service providers such as custodians and triparty agents, and also new market infrastructure providers such as central securities depositories (CSDs) and central clearing parties (CCPs) offering new services. It is worth noting that while MiFID II is an EU-centric regulation, it specifies comparable standards of access to equivalent third-country markets located outside the European Union. Under MiFID II, for derivatives trade execution there is a list of eligible derivatives subject to mandatory trading and clearing obligations. Furthermore, newly created swap execution facilities (SEFs) in the United States and organized trade facilities (OTFs) in Europe's respective electronic trading platforms are planned to be migrated from traditional voice-brokered dealing facilities. SEFs and OTFs will offer pretrade information, e.g. bid and offer quotes, and bring greater transparency to the pricing and trading of derivatives. OTFs will focus on non-equities derivatives and cash bond markets. New trade repositories are another requirement, and will be used to receive, store, and disseminate trade data from a variety of sources, including trade counterparties, derivatives clearing organizations, and trading platforms, which will facilitate market transparency.

With specific regulations targeting the OTC derivative market, participants will be required to collateralize increased volumes of transactions. This means the right collateral could become scarce under initial and variation margin requirements. As a result, participants will need to make sure they have access to the right collateral at the right time to support successful credit risk strategies.

To be efficient, it is envisaged that a single pool of collateral inventory will be needed on a physical basis, or virtually. Ultimately a centralized independent collateral function with the authority to manage the whole firm's collateral and management information that tracks regulatory compliance is envisaged. The key task will be having the right infrastructure in place, leading to a complete and transparent view of a firm's collateral usage.

Role of Clearing-houses and Related Infrastructure

With the role of clearing-houses having changed under EMIR, central clearing-houses act as central counterparties for the majority of derivatives transactions. In the future, clearing will become mandatory for the various categories of investors and instruments, and all market participants trading OTC derivatives will be subject to the same rules.

The key market impact is that new infrastructure is needed to manage the new process of central clearing. When making a trade, assets affected by the regulations must be cleared by an authorized clearing member responsible for the clearing, matching, and settlement of the trade and the collection and delivery of initial margin payment.

A new derivative CCP will have the responsibility to safeguard the initial margin, the valuation of all of the derivatives trades that it holds, and the 'calling' and management of variation margin. Both sides of the cleared derivative trades must provide details of all open positions to a trade repository. This will enable monitoring of market exposure and allow regulators to act if they decide the market is at risk due to the exposures being taken by market participants.

Management of Collateral Requirements by CCPs

With increased collateral requirements, investors using derivatives will put aside capital to ensure initial margin requirements can be met. Consequently, owing to global regulations, a move to a

cleared environment is predicted to create additional demand for collateral of around $4 trillion.

Expectations are that new regulations will also require bilateral trades to be fully collateralized, and the need for collateral will increase even further. Brexit uncertainty has also forced a review of future bilateral margin requirements in the event derivatives contracts will be novated by replacement of an existing UK counterparty with an EU counterparty. Such a scenario would normally trigger clearing obligations and costs. To maintain financial stability and an orderly market, ESMA will not trigger this procedure with a 12 month exemption granted in a no deal scenario.

The initial margin will need to be in the form of high-quality, liquid assets such as government bonds, gold, cash, and bonds issued by some government agencies. Having a potential shortfall in these eligible assets is therefore an issue for market participants.

Transparency requirements for the initial margin will see banks deploying much more collateral against more counterparties and transactions. This has raised the question about the safety of assets as they move through the clearing cycle. Participants will review the transparency of their assets at every stage of the clearing cycle to check where collateral is held safely. Custodians and asset services will need to offer downstream asset segregation up to the central clearing-house.

There will be increased costs to those trading and owning derivatives to support the maintenance of the centrally cleared structure. These costs will include clearing-house and clearing member fees, collateral conversion costs, liquidity access, default fund contributions, administration, and IT setup costs. The incremental cost per trade is expected to be significantly higher than those for bilateral trades. Evidently, with such high costs, new technologies such as blockchain are recognized as attractive solutions for CCPs in the future.

RegTech and the Science of Regulation

By Shirish Netke
CEO, Amberoon Inc

Science Fiction and Banking Reality

In the movie *Minority Report*, John Anderton is a law enforcement officer and chief of pre-crime in the year 2054 in Washington, DC. In an opening scene, the chief, played by Tom Cruise, arrests a man for murder – a crime he had planned to commit later that day. The premise of the story is that the future could be seen with enough certainty that a criminal could be arrested for a crime even before committing it.

The movie is science fiction. However, the state of the art of data science in predicting the future is not too far behind. A few years ago, Netflix analysed 70,000 attributes of TV shows to predict the success of its series *House of Cards*. Target analysed shopping patterns to infer a woman was pregnant before her family knew about it. Doctors at the University of Ontario analysed data that could save the lives of premature babies in the ICU by predicting the onset of an infection.

Managing risk in banking is about predicting the future. The banking challenge is to measure, monitor, and analyse data that can be used to predict regulatory risk. Banks use quantitative analysis extensively to predict their exposure to credit risk and market risk. Compliance and regulatory risk, which is a part of operational risk, have traditionally been harder to quantify and to predict. The advent of new technology has the potential to change that.

Modern technology brings the ability to connect the dots between the approach one uses to predict TV show preference, consumer behaviour, and infections to managing a bank's regulatory risk. Predicting a bank's exposure to bad actors that are laundering money is one step in mitigating compliance risk for the bank. The requirement to combat money laundering and the financing of terrorism drives regulatory compliance. The United Nations Office on Drugs and Crime estimated that 2.7% of global gross domestic product (GDP) is laundered through the global financial system. Based on 2016 GDP numbers, the money laundered through banks could be more than $2 trillion a year. Mitigating a bank's risk in anti–money laundering (AML) and combating the financing of terrorism (CFT) is one of the largest business opportunities for RegTech.

Managing Risk – The Holy Grail of Banking

A bank's ability to manage operational risk has a direct bearing on its performance as a financial institution. Regulators use this metric to measure the health of a bank. In the past 10 years, a few things have changed for banks that are supervised by regulatory bodies.

First, in the current environment, bankers are responsible for what they know as well as for what they do not know about criminal activity that happens within their bank. In many ways, they are deemed to be an extension of law enforcement to investigate and prevent criminal activity. Fines levied by regulators on banks for compliance violations in the last 10 years have been estimated to exceed $200 billion. These fines had a material impact on the profitability of affected banks. Given this situation, most banks consider that prioritizing compliance activity is mandatory and no longer optional.

Second, bad actors have become smarter. Laundering $2 trillion through the global banking system has attracted a lot of sophisticated players. It strongly incentivizes criminals to update their methods and deploy state-of-the-art technology to accomplish their goals. In a sense, banks are competing with bad actors on technological innovation. Who remains ahead will determine the proliferation or containment of money laundering activity.

Third, current bank technology is not geared towards criminal investigation. Over the decades, banks invested extensively in automation and sophisticated technologies for core banking activities. However, these information systems were not designed to provide insight on potential criminal activities. Retrofitting them to perform this function is a nontrivial undertaking.

RegTech and the Regulatory Framework

The regulatory framework for banking in the United States is also under pressure to reform, specifically as it relates to AML/CFT. The Clearing House, a banking association owned by 25 leading US banks, published a report in 2017 entitled 'A New Paradigm: Redesigning the US AML/CFT Framework to Protect National Security and Aid Law Enforcement'. This report calls for a complete overhaul of the current regulatory framework to update it and align it with the current goals of regulators. The report highlights that the AML/CFT goals of regulators depend on the quality of insights received from information collected through the banking system. However, the most common current practice of bank examiners focuses on examining auditable processes rather than investigating criminal activity. Meeting AML/CFT goals requires an alternative approach.

On the banking side, safety and soundness best practices depend on information systems that have been built over several decades.

These are systems of record such as a core banking system, systems of engagement such as an online banking system, and systems of automation such as a loan origination system. While these systems are effective in measuring, monitoring, and running a bank, they do not provide quality insights into the various risks associated with today's banking environment.

Modern technology such as predictive analytics, big data systems, and machine learning can create advanced systems of insight. These systems straddle all three types of legacy banking systems and can shine a light on all aspects of customer activity within a bank. Such systems are required to assess various forms of operational risk. For example, a system of insight can flag the activities of bad actors based on their transaction patterns. It can also provide insights into what they are likely to do next and prevent them from doing it – much like Tom Cruise in the movie *Minority Report*.

RegTech and Modern Technology

A Bain & Company report, 'Banking RegTechs to the Rescue?' estimates that costs for governance, risk, and compliance (GRC) account for 40% of banks' budgets for building new systems. The foundation of these updated systems will be based on a system of insight that uses data from disparate data sources. The technologies used to build these systems will take advantage of the latest advances in technology.

Modern technologies will enable banks to manage their operational risks in ways that were impossible 10 years ago. Moore's law, which refers to the speed of technology's evolution, states that processing power doubles every 18 months. Indeed, we can speculate that if the automobile industry evolved as quickly as the computer industry, we would have cars that cost $500 and could run a million miles on a tank of gas. The efficacy gains in the banking industry are not as dramatic but are nevertheless significant. The Bain & Company report cites an example of how major banks could take $10 million and two years to implement a customer onboarding solution using legacy technology. A more technology-savvy bank could implement the same solution for $300,000 in three months.

Human-Factors Impact of RegTech

The pace of adoption of RegTech will be affected by the people responsible for implementing operational changes. The human-factors dependency on RegTech is accentuated by the fact that implementing regulatory requirements is currently a very labour-intensive operation for banks and regulators alike. RegTech has the capacity to make fundamental changes in how day-to-day activities are conducted by people running the operations of a bank as well as for regulators who supervise them. RegTech would cause many banks and regulatory bodies alike to reexamine job descriptions and the type of people who can be most effective in them.

The human-factors impact is evident in an area such as AML/CFT. In a typical bank, 9 out of 10 alerts generated by traditional AML monitoring systems are false alarms. These alerts are manually scrutinized to find one that requires a suspicious activity report (SAR). Reviewing large numbers of alerts to find a few bad actors increases operational expense. Fatigue from performing repetitive tasks also can lead to human errors, which can potentially increase risk for a bank. RegTech has the potential to increase the productivity of compliance teams by as much as 100% while measurably reducing risk for a bank.

Productivity improvements are not new to other areas of financial services. Ten years ago, the UBS trading floor in Stamford, Connecticut, which housed traders in one pillarless hall, was the size of 20 basketball courts and considered the largest in the world. It is now largely empty, as these jobs were eliminated or moved to other locations. Goldman Sachs went from 600 cash equity traders down to two traders over the past 15 years as it added computer scientists and automated trading programs.

With the current state of technology, some jobs can be done only by human beings. The right answer to using technology in financial services is, and always has been, a judicious combination of human intelligence and machine intelligence. The hard part about making a choice between the two is an understanding of the trade-offs.

The consequences of not understanding the dividing line between man and machine can be disastrous. A few years ago, a car using a semi-autonomous driving feature led to a fatal accident. The car manufacturer recommended that even though the car was automated with advanced machine-learning technologies, drivers are required to stay alert and keep their hands on the wheel. It was also reported that the driver was engrossed in watching a TV show while driving. The difference between delegation and abdication of duties in using machine intelligence meant the difference between life and death for the pedestrian struck by the automated car. For an automated RegTech system, the right allocation of responsibilities between humans and machines can mean the difference between success and failure of the system.

Preparing for RegTech – Technologists and Bankers

While there are several initiatives to change banking regulations, some regulatory aspects are inherently embedded in the economics of the banking industry. A simplified way of describing the banking business model is that banks borrow money from depositors who can withdraw their money at any time, and lend it to borrowers who will return it on a predefined schedule. If the bank deposits are insured by the government, depositors are less likely to withdraw their deposits on a whim. Deposit insurance to prevent a run on the bank is essential for the successful execution of the banking business model. In return for insurance, the bank is subject to regulation from a supervisory body. Eliminating regulation is not desirable if it means eliminating deposit insurance, as it would mean changing the fundamental banking business model.

Technologists are well served in recognizing that regulation is a feature of banking and not a bug. This will help the next generation of technological innovators address risk management and regulation for financial institutions. These include solutions that help banks make better risk decisions at lower cost and in compliance with regulations. Emerging technologies such as cognitive analytics, big data systems, machine learning, and predictive analytics offer a lot of options for companies to manage their regulatory compliance risk in a dynamic manner. Some of these technologies did not exist for commercial deployment 10 years ago. The future of RegTech will be incorporating technology in the process of running a bank.

In the coming years, RegTech will evolve through an unprecedented partnership of banks, regulators, and technologists. In an ideal world, we would like to see the confluence of efforts between the disruptors and incumbents into a newly defined ecosystem. Realistically, we should expect a chaotic learning curve for all concerned for the next five years. Companies that can straddle these multiple ecosystems in building value-added solutions will be the dominant players of RegTech in the future.

GDPR and PSD2: Self-Sovereign Identity, Privacy, and Innovation

By Paul Ferris
CEO, ObjectTech Group

The years 2017 and 2018 have seen two of the biggest regulatory changes in banking and in the technology that underpins our modern system – but these two pieces of European legislation can, on their face, seem to be at odds with each other in certain respects.

PSD2 – the second Payments Services Directive – is a piece of European law that effectively forces banks to open up their customer databases and allow third parties to use this data and put it to work through new services, rather than it just sitting in a silo inside a bank. It seeks to create interoperability between banks and their customers via standardized open application programming interfaces (APIs).

The vision is that services like comparison websites will be able to aggregate account information and advise users if they would be better off moving their money into an account with an alternative bank. These are account information service providers (AISPs) under the Directive. Or social media platforms will be able to instruct that payments from users' bank accounts be sent to their friends – payment initiation service providers (PISPs).

Online banking, in general, will cease being something one does solely through clunky banking apps, but will instead be delivered via an innovation-driven market. It is the baseline on which a new generation of financial technology (FinTech) companies and services will proliferate.

A Market in Data-led Services

The incentive that fuels this innovative new market is the ability to monetize insights from the personal data of the customers who choose to use these new third-party applications. To use the example of comparison websites – rather than matching form-filled requests from customers with the offers and parameters of their member companies and then running credit checks where necessary, comparison services will be able to access live information on balances, transactions, and what services they are currently accessing. This can then form part of a more automated process of selling tailored services, based on richer data.

This is where the second important piece of legislation comes into play.

The General Data Protection Regulation (GDPR) updates 20-year-old European data privacy legislation, and requires nuance when added to many of the assumptions of how the FinTech market will develop post-PSD2. One forces banks to open up their systems to third parties via APIs; the other imposes punitive financial sanctions for the misuse and mishandling of this data – €20 million or 4% of global turnover in extreme scenarios.

The most important aspect of the GDPR here is the requirement for companies that store customer data to have *specific, informed, freely given* consent from their customers, and that the consent forms an *unambiguous indication of their customers' wishes*.

This means affirmative action; it does not mean a customer who does not untick a box, or scrolls past a statement of consent – the flip side of this is that the individual also has the right to withdraw that consent. Article 17 of the Regulation requires data controllers to delete any personal data 'without undue delay' if the data subject objects to it being held – though this is to be balanced against freedom of expression rights.

Finally, there must be a means of verifying the consent given, in the form of a record of how and when (specific, informed, freely given, and unambiguous) consent was given by customers for storage, processing, and sharing of their data.

PSD2 has from the outset had the intention of empowering customers, of allowing them to bring their data to market, but because it also brings into play third-party companies that are in the business of processing and sharing data, making sure the privacy protections are in place from the outset is in everyone's interest.

For these pieces of legislation to work in harmony, and for service providers and customers to experience the positive spirit and literal intentions of both of these pieces of statute, we need new thinking and, I would argue, the use of new technology.

The Need for a More Nuanced and Better Understood Working Definition of Privacy

The purpose of PSD2 is to give customers the opportunity to access services they previously could not, essentially in exchange for allowing third parties to monetize insights from their data. The customer's decision is central here.

Given that there is an almost explicit transactional element to this arrangement, and the fact that the insight that can be gleaned from an individual's spending history and behaviours is arguably much more useful (and thus intrusive) than click-throughs on social media sites (given that by nature it is accurate information on completed purchases and a user's financial position), it is vital that we think about privacy in a way that reflects this transactional fact.

Therefore privacy must not be understood just from the service providers' perspective as the rules by which they agree to use

(and not use) data, but it must also be understood from the perspective of the clients' interests, as something over which they have explicit and real-time control.

Privacy Is Not Just About Withholding Information from Others; It Is About the Individual Having Control Over Who Has Access to It

In many countries, privacy is a (qualified) human right enshrined in constitutional law. This is reason enough for the principle to be protected and deferred to – it has intrinsic value in and of itself. But more than that, data privacy protects us from both the malicious intent and the incompetence of others. It has an instrumental, functional value also. This is where technical as well as legal capabilities are needed.

If any individuals believe that the third-party service provider, which they have entrusted with some of their most important data, is no longer deserving of that trust, then they should be able to revoke access in real time and close the exposure to that risk. Having one's spending history or bank balance potentially exposed to the world is not a risk that anyone wants to increase the likelihood of, and something an individual should have total control over.

This is the other side of the data transaction.

Users can access aggregated banking (account information service providers) in exchange for giving access to the data on which these service providers then profit. But if the price of this exchange becomes too high to bear because, for instance, users have concerns over data storage and vulnerability to hacking, or because of fears that a service provider is sharing data with others without their consent, then they should be able to completely pull the plug, no longer allowing the service provider to access their data, and ensure the full deletion of any data held.

How Can Technology Help Implement These Principles and the Intention of GDPR?

Creating this new market in data, and ensuring it is a fair market where individuals are empowered on their side of the transaction, requires not just newer thinking on privacy, but a better practical means of implementing it.

It is in giving individuals control of their data that you find harmony between usability (PSD2) and privacy (GDPR). Self-sovereign identity (and self-sovereign data control) means giving individuals legal ownership and functional control over their data – rather than them granting permission for access between one database and a third party.

This is something that has recently been made possible through the advent of blockchain technology. I will not go into detail on the technical means of achieving this here, but at its heart, blockchain technology allows us to create a secure data store, which is immutably linked to an individual, and over which the individual has total control.

When the individual holds data, the consumer is empowered in a way that allows market innovation, with control remaining in thei consumer's hands. In effect, individuals can be their own aggregators, in the language of PSD2.

The best means of unambiguously ensuring privacy, consent, and control is to make sure that individuals have the ability to turn the tap off on access to that data because they ultimately hold

it. Consent is direct and comes unambiguously from the data source – the customer.

Self-sovereign identity brings a vast number of benefits that are relevant to the better realization of the innovative and market-led approach envisaged by PSD2, and the control and consent required by GDPR.

Service providers (such as PSD2 aggregators) no longer need to retain data; they just need ongoing access to it. Rather than an API between a service provider and a customer's bank, data aggregation can be done by the individual. By opening a smart contract between their own data and the service provider, users ensure that the actual data remains solely in their own hands. They, in turn, can permit access to third parties who offer additional services.

This, in turn, means that individuals can turn off the 'data tap' if they lose faith in how their data is being used. Moreover, they can be assured that there is no remnant data footprint held by the aggregator because there was no need for it to ever have been held by the aggregator in the first instance.

Furthermore, because they have verified data (particularly their identity), users in control of their data can quickly switch to a competing service provider, and onboard instantly. This serves the real market-making intention of open banking, allowing individuals to put their valuable data to use, and creating competition for access to the bank's data and customers.

The fact that data is not being held, in yet another static iteration, on yet another database means there is one less honeypot of data putting you at risk of having your data exposed by hacking. As well as a direct security measure in the interests of the user, this in itself reduces the liability for data storage on the part of the third party. Given the nature and value of this kind of data, this is something that should be seriously borne in mind by all parties in this market.

Self-sovereign data control effectively brings the terms and conditions (T&Cs) of banking into the present tense and makes them a real, tangible set of principles with which a user can interact.

Rather than being something they sign off on and forget about, a privacy policy should be something that has real meaning in the way individuals conduct banking and commerce online. Self-sovereign identity is the means of facilitating this.

The Future: Privacy and Innovative Markets Both Better Served by Self-Sovereign Identity

PSD2 and the open banking revolution will undoubtedly bring great benefits to consumers, but privacy-centric technologies are a seeming necessity to meet the full intention and potential of this market-driving legislation.

The clear direction of travel of PSD2 and GDPR – and one that should be welcomed – is the fact that individuals are being empowered within a framework of better data protection. However, self-sovereign identity is the next step in this direction, as it puts individuals in real-time control of access to their data.

Technology moves very fast, and regulation moves very slowly, so while individual control of data may not have been a possible solution when PSD2 was first being dreamt up, it may eventually be recognized under a future PSD3.

However, the technical architecture exists so that it is now possible to allow the core data store and the control over access (and thus the guarantee of privacy) to become one and the same.

Privacy legislation places duties on companies, but it will require new technologies such as self-sovereign models of data control and ownership to better allow individuals to exercise control over their data.

Rise of RegTech in the German Market

By Dr Matthias Lange
Managing Partner, FinLeap

Selcuk Kuram
Consultant, Berlin Hyp AG

and Christina Fellner
Head of Unit B2C, Fidor Bank AG

Let the numbers speak for themselves: according to the *Financial Times*, the big banks spend well above US$1 billion per annum on meeting compliance regulations. The annual volume of regulation went up by 492% from 2008 to 2015 according to Thomson Reuters. Recent estimates suggest that more than 300 million pages of additional regulatory documents will be published by 2020.

The financial services industry increasingly complains about the amount and intensity of rules to be adhered to, mostly because financial institutions' information technology (IT) infrastructures are often not yet capable of implementing the demands into their legacy infrastructures. IT systems are old-fashioned and silo-based, which leads to inefficient, slow, and cost-intensive work-arounds – often dependent on manual inputs. This will result in even more complex, opaque, and inflexible IT environments in the future, and market players realize more and more that this will become an additional problem – one that's negatively impacting and decelerating the needed innovation cycles.

So financial institutions, as well as the regulators themselves, started to search for ways to implement processes more efficiently by applying new technological solutions. In parallel, the FinTech area evolved with new, innovative business models, but is faced with the same obstacles and problems as traditional financial institutions. Hence, innovative ways need to be explored, and FinTech companies are starting to also focus on this segment – often referred to as RegTech.

The government of Singapore, an important hub for the industry, has started promoting 'smart nation', which means that the Monetary Authority of Singapore is shifting towards an application programming interface (API)-driven architecture to enable improved collaboration between financial institutions and the regulators. This, of course, gives RegTechs the possibility to use it as an opportunity to develop their models in strong alignment with market needs. Other jurisdictions like the United Kingdom and Australia have also started to see the benefits of RegTech and have developed supporting measures themselves.

RegTech has a huge market potential, as it can significantly lower the effort in terms of investment and labour intensity. For example, experts suggest that investments in RegTech could have a payback period of only three years and a high impact on the return on investment (ROI). In addition, customers benefit from leaner and more convenient processes. On average, a customer nowadays is contacted four or five times within a timeframe of 26 days to execute a correct onboarding process with the necessary documentation. By applying innovative solutions like video identification, this number can be lowered considerably.

Overview of RegTech Business Models in Germany

The RegTech landscape develops very differently throughout Europe. The United Kingdom, with more than 30% of all RegTechs worldwide, is one of the innovation hubs, while countries like Germany lag behind in terms of speed and variety. On closer examination, despite the fact that Germany is one of the most heavily regulated markets in the world with very complex rules to be applied, RegTechs still have significant potential. The investments are growing, and the development is starting to accelerate. Right now, only a few solutions can be identified along the value chain. Grouped broadly into three areas, the market evolution path shown in Figure 1 can be identified: customer journeys, business-related rules, and IT infrastructures.

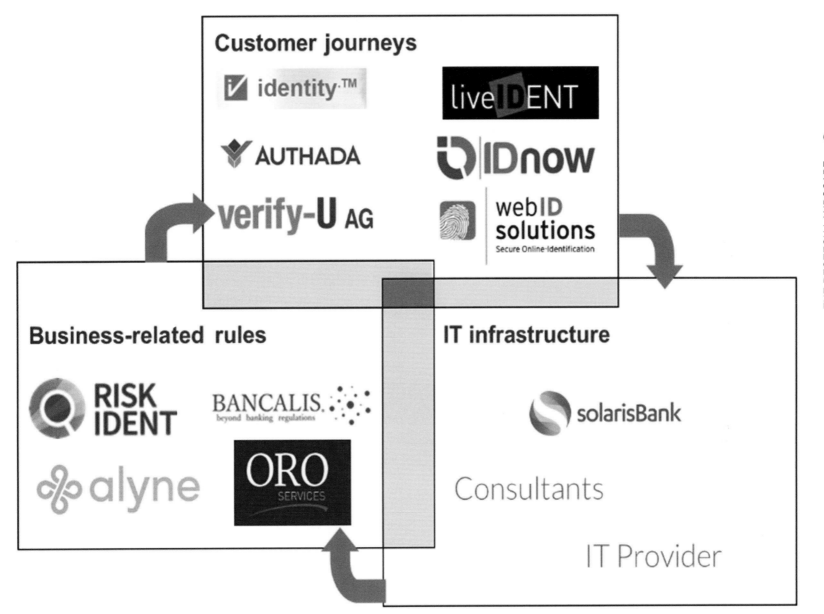

Figure 1: Market evaluation path

Customer Journeys

Most RegTechs in Germany are active in the field of customer journeys. So far, the business models have concentrated on innovations related to know your customer (KYC) and anti–money laundering (AML). This acceleration is driven by the permission of the German Federal Financial Supervisory Authority (BaFin) in 2014 to establish a banking relationship also via video legitimation and leveraging the positive development of the FinTech industry. Further opportunities exist in financial advice-related regulation and customer services. Successful use cases deal with optimizing customer due diligence for individuals and small companies. The venture ID, for instance, now offers a secure and legally compliant AML solution for online identification via video chat, thus enabling faster customer onboarding without a breach of the customer contract.

Business-Related Rules

Especially, the vast majority of business-related rules and required reportings give financial services a hard time. RegTechs in this sector are focusing on regulatory intelligence, meaning the aggregation and analysis of data, transparent compliance processes, regulatory reporting, and innovative risk management models. Interesting German ventures are Alyne and Risk Ident. Alyne offers a software as a service platform that supports organizations in implementing legal and regulatory requirements, determining maturity, aligning with industry standards, and sharing subject-matter expertise. Risk Ident has developed software for intelligent fraud detection.

IT Infrastructure

Having flexible and transparent IT infrastructures is crucial to meet regulatory demands. In addition, due to the strong evolution of the financial services industry, new and innovative IT infrastructures are needed. This field is shaped not only by start-ups but also by consultancies and IT providers, such as GFT Technologies, zeb. rolfes.schierenbeck.associates GmbH, and BearingPoint. One innovative approach to leveraging existing compliant IT systems is offering the existing compliant IT infrastructure to others, e.g. digital companies, to enable faster compliant financial services business models. One important example of this in IT infrastructure is the FinLeap venture solarisBank.

Use Case: SolarisBank

Offering financial services in Germany requires approval by BaFin according to the Banking Act. In addition, it is necessary to meet the regulatory and transparency requirements. Two separate ways evolved for FinTechs to get into business: either partnering up with a fully licensed traditional bank or applying for their own licenses. Until recently, FinTechs mainly partnered up with traditional banks, but found that this is often not yet suitable for the early start-up stages and is too cost intensive. About a year ago, FinLeap developed the venture solarisBank, a fully licensed banking platform that enables digital companies to create solutions tailored to their financial needs. In contrast to challenger banks like N26, Atom, and Tandem, solarisBank is focused on providing infrastructure services for the digital economy under a full regulatory umbrella. The company has a partnership-centred approach, offering an innovative technological infrastructure for the needs of the digital economy. SolarisBank has developed what is described as a modular-based banking toolkit, including, crucially, various modern banking application programming interfaces (APIs). This means that it's able to offer other FinTech businesses numerous services that, in turn, they can offer to their own customers. It provides the opportunity to develop individual banking solutions in a faster and more convenient manner. With this approach, solarisBank gives digital companies the opportunity and the freedom to develop banking solutions while working in a fully regulated environment and complying with the requirements BaFin has set.

How RegTech Will Evolve

The RegTech development cannot be seen independently from FinTech, digitization, and the ongoing change in financial institutions' business models. For financial institutions, the need for flexible IT solutions is increasing. They still have very individual and complex IT environments that work with different legacy systems, making it difficult to implement a standardized solution. In addition, for companies selecting a technology provider to improve processes, the assessment of third-party risk is quite intense, especially when it comes to dealing with regulation. RegTechs need to establish and maintain a strong brand and proof of their stability to be accepted by larger players as they get access to sensitive information and deal with critical tasks. Young RegTechs with short track records experience difficulties in meeting these demands. Hence, collaboration with partners from the beginning on will be the key to success. Therefore, RegTechs have different possibilities to evolve: they can start by targeting mainly smaller players and enlarging the business to bigger players depending on business growth, gathered experience, and market position. Another possibility is to concentrate on small parts of the value chain and enlarge the business model along the defined position within the value chain. Apart from these approaches, ventures can innovate existing processes, demonstrating that results are stable, and then phase out old process components, e.g. for compliance detection with artificial intelligence.

In the short term, we expect further traction in companies addressing single regulatory topics, especially pertaining to compliance monitoring and smart data analysis involving multiple complex regulatory frameworks. In the medium to long term, we expect holistic and institution-agnostic solutions to emerge in the areas we have mentioned, namely customer journeys, regulatory business intelligence, and IT infrastructure.

RegTech is the consequent development of the financial services industry – moving away from the customer front end to the back end by applying technology to innovate.

The real benefit from RegTech will come when this cost centre is turned into revenue that benefits companies as well as customers.

The Power of RegTech to Drive Cultural Change and Enhance Conduct Risk Management Across Banking

By Susanne Chishti
CEO and Founder, FINTECH Circle and FINTECH Circle Institute
Bestselling Co-Editor of The FinTech Book, The WealthTech Book
and The InsurTech Book

The complexity of financial services such as trading activities and the amount of data (both structured and unstructured) involved in trade surveillance, market abuse monitoring, and compliance management overall requires cutting-edge technologies. In today's world, compliance without technology to support it is ineffective and costly – a small error of oversight can have catastrophic effects if regulatory breaches cannot be prevented.[1]

Since the financial crisis, the world's biggest banks have been fined $321 billion, according to data from the Boston Consulting Group (BCG). These fines were the result of numerous failings from money laundering to market manipulation since 2008. Regulatory requirements continue to increase. The number of rule changes that banks must track on a daily basis has tripled since 2011, to an average of 200 revisions a day based on BCG's report.[2]

However, senior managers (not only across financial services) continue to fail to set the right tone from the top on business ethics, EY's 'Fraud Survey 2017' found. Of board members or senior managers, 77% said they could justify unethical behaviour to help a business survive, with one in three willing to offer cash payments to win or retain business.[3]

Regulatory technology (RegTech) can meet the growing demand from heads of compliance and risk who are tasked to protect their firm's reputation by complying with the constantly increasing regulatory requirements globally. The regulatory focus has shifted from focusing on systems and controls to outcomes such as better behaviour, culture, and governance.

Culture Determines What You Do When No-one Is Looking

Integrity and ethical behaviours are central in determining how customers and investors are treated. Bad culture is leading to good people standing by and doing nothing to prevent misconduct. One benefit of good culture is the clear guidance on how to manage complex conflicts of interest. Conflicts exist because individuals have economic incentives to make certain judgements and also as a result of cognitive biases that determine how we interpret and manage information leading to unconscious conflicts. Conflicts of interest can also be the result of opposing short-term and long-term goals.

Conduct risk is the gap between how a financial services firm wants its staff to behave and how they actually do. Global players have implemented conduct programs, often with a focus on how customers are treated, to improve the moral compass, comply with the latest conduct regulations, and avoid large fines.

[1] Aite Group, 'Trade Surveillance and Compliance Technology: 2017 Spending Update'; http://aitegroup.com/report/trade-surveillance-and-compliance-technology-2017-spending-update

[2] Boston Consulting Group (BCG), 'Global Risk 2017: Staying the Course in Banking' (March 2017), https://www.bcg.com/publications/2017/financial-institutions-growth-global-risk-2017-staying-course-banking.aspx; Gavin Finch, 'World's Biggest Banks Fined $321 Billion Since Financial Crisis' *Bloomberg* (March 2017), https://www.bloomberg.com/news/articles/2017-03-02/world-s-biggest-banks-fined-321-billion-since-financial-crisis

[3] EY, 'Fraud Survey 2017' and 'EMEIA Fraud Survey' (March 2017); http://fraudsurveys.ey.com/2017/executive-summary

For me good culture is 'what you do when no-one is looking'.[4] In the United Kingdom, the Financial Conduct Authority (FCA) applies behavioural economics and concludes that 'people do not always make choices in a rational and calculated way. In fact, most human decision-making uses thought processes that are intuitive and automatic rather than deliberative and controlled.'[5]

Rewards and the environment in banking in the past did not encourage good behaviour of traders, for example, wanting to be part of a group of like-minded, successful traders across different banks. Success was measured in personal wealth and achievement of high targets rationalizing bad behaviour due to perverse incentives. 'If I breach the code of conduct, I may or may not get caught, but if I miss my numbers for two quarters, I will be fired.'[6] Thus, the cultural environment effectively reinforced their wrong actions by failing to stop their incorrect behaviour, as red flags to supervisors were ignored and the activity became normal when their team, including the line manager, continued to reward increased profit with no checking of such behaviour.

Significant focus has now been put on individual accountability and personal behaviour. The reason why regulators focus on the conduct of individual executives is because prosecuting individuals helps deter fraud, bribery, and corruption. In the United Kingdom, conduct standards for senior management were installed in 2016 (Senior Management Regime), leaving senior banking executives open to penalties up to and including jail for misconduct of their team or business unit. Regulators have started to name and shame both companies and individuals. The FCA's website where individual fines are presented provides great case study material on how not to behave.[7]

Governance Framework: Three Lines of Defence Powered by RegTech

Since the financial crisis, strong risk and governance frameworks have been implemented around three lines of defence (LODs). The board provides direction to senior management and sets the bank's risk appetite. The board then delegates to the CEO and senior management ownership and responsibility for operating risk management and controls, and thus needs to rely on adequate line functions, which are accountable for monitoring and assurance within the bank. The three LODs model explains the relationship within these functions and provides a guide to how responsibilities should be divided.[8]

In the past, the three LODs model was challenged due to the lack of available technology, data management, and analytics to allow

---

[4] First FinTech Academy Africa designed by FinTech Circle and the Cape Innovation and Technology Initiative focused on latest innovation across FinTech, WealthTech, InsurTech, and RegTech. Presentation on RegTech Trends by Patrick Butler, RegTech expert, in April 2017; http://www.fintechacademyafrica.com

[5] 'FCA: Applying Behavioural Economics at the Financial Conduct Authority', Occasional Paper 1 by Kristine Erta, Stefan Hunt, Zanna Iscenko, and Will Brambley (April 2013); www.fca.org.uk/publication/occasional-papers/occasional-paper-1.pdf

[6] First FinTech Academy Africa designed by FinTech Circle and the Cape Innovation and Technology Initiative focused on latest innovation across FinTech, WealthTech, InsurTech, and RegTech. Presentation on RegTech Trends by Patrick Butler, RegTech expert, in April 2017; http://www.fintechacademyafrica.com

[7] 'FCA: 2017 Fines', www.fca.org.uk/news/news-stories/2017-fines; 'FCA Fines Former Investment Banker for Sharing Confidential Information over WhatsApp' (March 2017); www.fca.org.uk/news/press-releases/fine-former-investment-banker-sharing-confidential-information-whatsapp

[8] Chartered Institute of Internal Auditors, 'Governance of Risk: Three Lines of Defence' (last accessed on 6 May 2017); www.iia.org.uk/resources/audit-committees/governance-of-risk-three-lines-of-defence

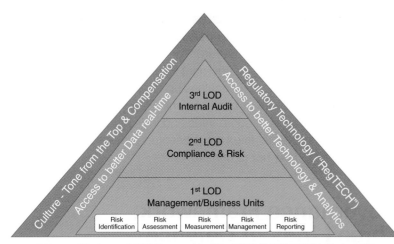

3 Lines of Defence (LOD) Powered by "RegTECH" ©FINTECH Circle 2017

Figure 1: Three lines of defence (LODs)

employees to properly own risk as they had no tools to effectively monitor their areas of responsibility.[9]

Therefore, we developed a three LODs governance model powered by data and technology, as Figure 1 shows:

1. The first line of control is the business units (including the front office functions that own and manage risk).

2. The second line of control includes the compliance and risk divisions, which oversee and are specialists in risk management.

3. The third line of defence is internal auditing to provide independent assurance.

All levels are empowered by access to better data and better technology and analytical tools offered by the wide range of FinTech and RegTech companies and available today. This is

embedded in a culture of clear leadership (tone from the top/walk the talk) and a compensation strategy that incentivizes employees to do the right thing. Training can play an important role to help individuals understand how to manage conflicts of interest and the consequences of misconduct.

Data and New Skills as Strategic Assets

Conduct risk and financial crime are at the top of regulators' agendas. As illustrated in the three LODs model, there is a clear shift to make the front office take over risk management responsibilities, as business units need to own their risks. This requires that technology, data, and analytics can empower management to access the right information at the right time. This shows the dependency on technology to effectively implement and manage controls. There is no doubt that poor data is still the biggest obstacle to a financial services company's success and may contribute to misconduct going undetected. In fact, Chartis Research shows that in 'a typical risk system project, about 80% of the total project lifecycle costs will be spent on getting the data ready, making aggregation the natural home for reducing costs and rationalising data'.[10]

In financial crime, new risks appear constantly while the old risks, unfortunately, do not go away. New risks are linked to the management of increasing amounts of data and a lack of people who understand both compliance/risk and data/technology. Excel spreadsheets are obviously not enough anymore to counter fraud, and new skill sets are required for financial services employees who understand risk/compliance, coding, data science, and advanced analytics based on mathematical and statistical training.

---

[9] PwC, 'The Three Lines of Defence Model of Tomorrow – PwC' (September 2016); https://www.pwc.com/ca/en/banking.../pwc-three-lines-of-defence-2016-09-en.pdf

[10] Chartis Research, 'Global Risk IT Expenditure in Financial Services 2017'; http://www.chartis-research.com/research/reports/global-risk-it-expenditure-in-financial-services-2017

Technology to the Rescue

Client onboarding, including know your customer (KYC) and anti–money laundering (AML) requirements, poses a huge risk for banks. Manual checks and processes are not only slow and costly but also ineffective in preventing non-compliant actions, resulting in huge fines. FinTech solutions allow the automatic authentication of customers' identities, rate their credit risk, and provide ongoing due diligence and monitoring functionalities to identify illegal activity. FinTech and RegTech companies often apply artificial intelligence (AI), machine learning, advanced natural language processing, big data analytics, and robotic process automation to solve these complex compliance challenges.

Chatbots based on AI, for example, can help customers during the onboarding process or support compliance staff checking AML/KYC requirements. It is important to ensure that any AI system is not a black box but can be explained and documented so that controls can be incorporated to avoid any unintended consequences (i.e. an AI-based chatbot could be accused of misselling).[11] As a consequence, regulatory oversight should also be extended to tech giants such as Apple, Facebook, Amazon, Google, Ant Financial (owned by Alibaba), Samsung, Tencent, and Uber, who not only control lots of our personal data but also have started to offer various forms of payment, lending, and/or other financial services. There is a strong call for regulators to address the regulatory challenge of data-driven finance by these tech giants to avoid false predictions, discriminatory practices towards the public, and denial of service and search results based on 'pay for display' instead of objective selection based on quality or price. The tech giants are 'neither subject to client/customer/ investor protection rules nor subject to measures that ensure

the functioning of financial markets and prevent the build-up of systemic risk – these being the three pillars of modern financial regulation'.[12]

Compliance Spending

In 2017, *Bloomberg* reported thousands of job cuts as a significant amount of monitoring and surveillance activity could be automated going forward.[13] Smaller profit margins require the use of technology to control costs. It is expected that compliance spending plateaued in 2017 as compliance budgets had been increasing steadily over the prior few years.[14] Yet, a Nasdaq/Aite survey found that less than 20% of financial services firms believed they were 'completely prepared' for new regulatory changes.[15] Although the strong growth of compliance departments within banks will come to an end, investment in automated compliance solutions offered by FinTech, RegTech, WealthTech, and InsurTech companies will continue, as this is a more scalable and cost-effective approach in the long term. Still, in absolute terms, compliance costs are huge: for example, HSBC Holdings PLC expected the spending on regulatory programs and compliance to

---

[11] Global Risk Regulator, a service from *The Banker*. 'Regtech's Deepening Role Likely to Spark Greater Regulatory Scrutiny' by Justin Pugsley (April 2017); https://www.globalriskregulator.com/Subjects/ Reporting-and-Governance/Regtech-s-deepening-role-likely-to-spark-greater-regulatory-scrutiny

[12] 'From FinTech to TechFin: The Regulatory Challenges of Data-Driven Finance', European Banking Institute Working Paper Series 2017 – No. 6 by Dirk A. Zetzsche, Ross P. Buckley, Douglas W. Arner, and Janos N. Barberis, page 27; https://papers.ssrn.com/sol3/papers.cfm?abstract_ id=2959925

[13] Richard Partington, 'Banks Trimming Compliance Staff as $321 Billion in Fines Abate', *Bloomberg* (23 March 2017); https://www.bloomberg.com/ news/articles/2017-03-23/banks-trimming-compliance-staff-as-321-billion-in-fines-abate

[14] Fn/Financial News, 'Banks' Compliance Spending to "Plateau" in 2017' by Lucy McNulty (19 December 2016); https://www.fnlondon.com/articles/ banks-compliance-spending-to-plateau-in-2017-20161219

[15] Aite Group, 'Global Challenges for Regulatory Compliance: The Rise of RegTech' (December 2016); http://aitegroup.com/report/global-challeng-es-regulatory-compliance-rise-regtech

peak at about $3.3 billion in 2017 as improved IT systems help the bank to grow without adding new costs.[16]

FinTech and RegTech Solutions

The offerings by FinTech companies are varied, and many great RegTech companies are represented in this book. Compliance IT vendor and RegTech rankings are published regularly. Tech firms range from global IT giants such as IBM, Oracle, FIS Global, and SAS to more specialized FinTech and RegTech companies. They often offer cloud-based risk and compliance solutions and the use of big data analytics and artificial intelligence/machine learning capabilities. As part of the Chartis 'RiskTech 100 Report' in 2017,[17] the following companies were selected as category winners:

- *Financial crime – NICE Actimize* (detect, prevent, and investigate money laundering, fraud, and compliance violations with a holistic view of risk across the organization).[18]

- *Regulatory reporting – Wolters Kluwer* (solutions will help legal, finance, risk, and compliance professionals and small business owners better manage governance, risk, and compliance challenges in dynamic markets).[19]

- *Artificial intelligence – Ayasdi* (deploy a fast and effective process to put models in place that can accurately measure and control risk, proactively detect and prevent fraud, and effectively evaluate capital reserve adequacy).[20]

- *Data integrity and control – Gresham* (data integrity platform offering regulatory compliance, internal risk control, financial control, and transition management solutions).[21]

- *Innovation – Digital Reasoning* (using cognitive computing, its solution is driving competitive advantage, mitigating threats and risk, and discovering new revenue opportunities across the enterprise).[22]

AIM Software has also been selected among the top 100 RiskTech companies, as the largest independent provider of enterprise data management solutions focused on investment management, asset servicing, and private banking/wealth management to solve data quality challenges.[23]

Another ranking called 'The RegTech Top 100 Power List'[24] includes influential RegTech companies. Among the top companies are:

- *Temenos*. Market-leading provider of banking software solutions to financial institutions.[25]

- *Qumram*. Ensures compliance, detects online fraud, and improves customer experience by recording every digital interaction and replaying it on demand.[26]

- *Trulioo*. Leading global identity verification provider helping businesses meet AML and KYC requirements and mitigate fraud and risk.[27]

---

[16] Fn/Financial News, 'Banks' Compliance Spending to "Plateau" in 2017' by Lucy McNulty (19 December 2016); https://www.fnlondon.com/articles/banks-compliance-spending-to-plateau-in-2017-20161219

[17] Chartis, 'RiskTech100 Report 2017'; http://www.chartis-research.com/research/reports/risktech100-2017

[18] http://www.niceactimize.com

[19] http://wolterskluwer.com

[20] https://www.ayasdi.com

[21] https://www.greshamtech.com

[22] http://www.digitalreasoning.com

[23] https://www.aimsoftware.com

[24] Planet Compliance, 'The RegTech Top 100 Power List: The Most Influential RegTech Firms' (last updated in March 2017). http://www.planetcompliance.com/2017/03/21/regtech-top-100-power-list-influential-regtech-firms

[25] https://www.temenos.com

[26] http://www.qumram.com

[27] https://www.trulioo.com

To summarize, we believe that technology can play a role in cultural change as an enabler and catalyst.[28] RegTech helps to automate and improve tasks by considering more data and information.

RegTech can provide intelligent support solutions for human experts. Long-term 'compliance robo-advisors' will exist to support the risk and compliance function, carrying out thousands of standard checks resulting in significant cost savings. In addition, these 'compliance robots' could support the business units and the front office directly by providing the right data at the right time. The WealthTech Book[29] explains the critical requirements for financial institutions using robots:

• risk profiling methodology

• consistent language of risk

• explanations of risk.

RegTech innovation can identify and monitor leading indicators of poor behaviour and encourage good conduct. It will also improve decision making by providing more adequate data to all three LODs in addition to the regulators themselves. This will lead to increased trust in the industry. To conclude, financial institutions will benefit from new RegTech, FinTech, WealthTech, and InsurTech technologies. These companies have developed cutting-edge capabilities and solutions to help established players increase revenue, cut costs, and be compliant across banking, investment management/private banking, and insurance. The impact of RegTech to drive cultural change and lead to a more robust corporate governance framework should not be underestimated.

[28] FINTECH Circle and FINTECH Circle Institute; https://fintechcircle.com

[29] *The WealthTech Book* by Susanne Chishti and Thomas Puschmann, published by Wiley, 2018. Chapter 'How to give "Sleep-Tight" Robo-Advice' by Paul Resnik, p62-64.

Regulatory Innovation and Sandboxes

3

- Big data to break information silos in organizations
- From T+20 reporting to "streaming monitoring"
- Current data processing method does not meet customer expectations or technological capacities

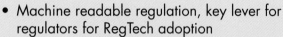

- Machine readable regulation, key lever for regulators for RegTech adoption
- Technical standards to be adopted, especially in EU context
- Move from regulatory interpretation towards regulatory execution to allow automation

- Open banking enhances monitoring obligations of 3rd party providers
- GDPR/PSD2 developed in parallel but without co-ordination
- 4th party service provider opens-up liability issue in product distribution chain

- Regulatory sandbox deployment subject to a country's regulatory architecture heritage
- Tech companies have interest in cross-federal rules for providing financial services
- RegTech cost savings makes low margin markets (SME lending) economically viable again

- Regulatory sandbox trade off: licensing obligations impose limits on business model
- Sandboxes offer a flagging exercise for start-ups but environment is timebound and exit needs to be prepared
- Eligibility criteria vary across jurisdiction especially on applicant background (i.e. start-up vs incumbent or both)

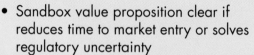
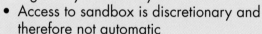

- Sandbox value proposition clear if reduces time to market entry or solves regulatory uncertainty
- Access to sandbox is discretionary and therefore not automatic

- Innovation in compliance space can be divided as RegTech solutions for supervised firms and SupTech solutions for regulators
- Sandbox strengthen financial center status by showing market dynamism and readiness for competition

Part 3 looks at how innovation has been (re)introduced following the 2008 financial crisis. In an industry that is highly supervised, tolerance for error is almost inexistent. In the meantime, regulators, after a decade of post-crisis reform, are starting to look forward.

Regulatory innovation can be seen at two levels. RegTech solutions enable a series of objectives, reducing silos created by product or corporate ownership structures. Further, the speed at which data is processed is moving away from T+20 reporting and instead closer to "supervisory streaming", which allows for real-time identifications of risks. The net effect will be overall cost reductions in the compliance function, which increases profitability but also makes viable banking in certain customers segments that would otherwise be unprofitable.

While the commoditization of certain technical capacities has driven these innovations, the regulators are playing a key role in the adoption and standardization of RegTech solutions. Indeed, the methods of how new regulations are issued, their end impact and how they are drafted, all have a role to play in developing a modern regulatory framework.

The move towards machine-readable regulation will allow for faster implementation of new obligations in banks' internal processes. Reforms such as GDPR and PSD2 are opening up and giving ownership of the data to consumers, increasing information granularity for banks. Finally, the development of new regulatory policy to support the development of business models or companies that previously didn't exist goes a long way to showing the recent flexibility in governments to adjust regulation to allow for better competition in the market, having end-user benefits in mind.

This last example has now been formalized as a process, with the creation of regulatory sandboxes. In effect, sandboxes are a controlled environment for experimentation made possible by trading off lighter regulatory obligations against limitation of participant business models. Their emergence across the globe in recent years illustrates the realization by regulators that technological neutrality is no longer sustainable. Therefore, the sandbox also provides a learning opportunity for regulators to perform their role better, as they are exposed to new business models.

However, sandboxes, while positive, are not a pre-requisite to be a modern regulator nor a FinTech leader. China and the USA are two prominent examples of countries missing a regulatory sandbox, explained by another approach to social experimentation in the case of the former and the heritage of a regulatory architecture in the case of the latter.

The final chapter in this part will further explore the forms regulatory innovation takes in different jurisdictions and the opportunity created by sandboxes.

Discover the Innovative Technology Behind RegTech Leaders

By Pierre Bittner
CEO, WeeFin

Nowadays, banking regulations have become so complex that it is no longer possible to implement them by using existing tools or methods. The granularity of reported data, the increase of frequency, and the completeness of information leave no part of the organization untouched.

Those new regulations, as seen by authorities, are one of the pillars of good economic health because they help to restore confidence in the monetary system. However, their representatives understand that the complexity is a real challenge for banks. The smaller actors or those who have retained practices based on manual processes could not conform to the requirements of granularity, risk aggregation, or traceability.

The ongoing digitization of the sector, accelerated by the arrival of FinTech, is another pillar of the return of growth, as it will improve customer relationships and create new opportunities.

Banks must start to change their strategy and their culture and base them on collaboration amongst actors. They need to shift from project- and product-based organization to agile organization that delivers digital services and customer experience. However, without introducing major innovations to support this transformation, many players, limited by their investment capacity, will not be able to come through this period.

Many new technologies have been created by 'digital native' companies to build a huge market based on a partnership ecosystem while maintaining their ability to innovate and answer customer expectations. The same technologies also empower RegTech leaders to successfully implement regulations and accelerate the digital transformation.

With the emergence of 'banking as a service', finance is becoming a technology. All bank executives must understand the impact of digitization and align their organization with new core capabilities.

In this chapter, we will go through the technologies that are shaking the banking industry and explain the necessity for banks to adopt them to complete their regulatory compliance program.

First, we will go through compliance processes for a regulatory directive roll-out to show how data has become a major issue for banks. Next, we will explain how new big data architecture and event-driven IT create scalable organizations and enable business agility. Finally, we will look at how managed services from cloud leaders free up IT teams from operational burdens securely and cost-effectively.

The Regulatory Quest

Rolling out a new regulatory compliance program is laborious, and data is the core issue.

To roll out a new directive, compliance must understand how it impacts the organization, model the changes requested by the authority on every business function, and deploy them across the organization. Finally, reports that aggregate information from all concerned IT systems must be produced to demonstrate that the regulation has been properly implemented. If all business data were easily accessible, mapped, and documented, this would ease the task.

To produce the report, the compliance team must identify all system records where data should be collected. As ad hoc reports are used, new extracts need to be specified, implemented, and deployed from all IT applications for every single new directive. To accelerate the step of collecting for various projects, trade repositories have been created. Historically, compliance reports have been produced from accounting systems on a monthly basis. The recent directive requires new data sets and daily reporting from front-office systems, which makes most of those compliance data warehouses and processes irrelevant. Collecting and storing data in a central repository is of course very time-consuming and costly, as a common dictionary and structure need to be defined and validated by all contributors. Recent directives, such as MiFID2, have such high requirements for granularity and data completeness that it is very difficult if not impossible to reuse existing development.

As traceability expectations from authorities are high, once the directive is rolled out, every change must be tracked and justified. With many data quality issues, due to modelling gap or operational error, it is not unusual that manual correction must be realized to remove discrepancies in reporting. In the very near future, all manual intervention will become impossible due to the size and granularity of the report to be produced. Compliance teams cannot grow indefinitely and should focus on analysis and guidance.

Big Data

New big data solutions could free up compliance by giving transparent and easy access to data to all business functions.

How do cloud-native companies create so much value from huge, unstructured, or semistructured data sets that flow continuously from websites, social networks, or mobile applications?

Those companies have positioned data as their core asset, which is centrally accessible to the whole organization. This central role of data is best demonstrated by their decision-making process, which is based on facts collected from experimentation on every feature they release. Digital native organizations have developed a so-called data-driven decision culture.

Obviously, we cannot expect banks to process zettabytes of unstructured data. Most banks don't even have big data issues, although we could expect more from them on how they manage what could be their most valuable asset. It is in the transverse functions like conformity where we observe most of this disability on data.

Web giants and digital natives have the methodology and technology to be agile with data. Even more so, they get their agility from data. Banks should take inspiration from those who have brought the data to the core of their business. It is the only way for them to face the challenge of the complexity of new compliance directives.

Event-driven Business

The methodology of digital native enterprises is not an unreachable goal for financial actors. As big data technology has become mature, new software architecture patterns have emerged. This is based on streaming business or system events, described as an append-only immutable log. Those events represent the facts that have occurred in any place of the organization. Companies can build a global data hub to create a real-time data pipeline that gives free access to business events in a fast, secure, resilient, and fault-tolerant manner. Data can be shared between business silos, legacy systems, or transversal functions such as compliance. This new design is a perfect match for bank IT systems. It would empower business functions with data and help the roll-out of new regulatory directives.

Banks' core internal business models are orders, transactions, market data updates, and other corporate events. With market access, electronic trading platforms, and order management systems, most bank IT platforms have events in their core design. On the other hand, regulatory and risk platforms are based on business intelligence tools and data warehouses that are fed with batches of flattened data extracts. The modern data architecture creates a great opportunity to reinvent the design of regulatory compliance systems and accelerate the digital transformation by easily collecting business events from front-office sources.

Modern Big Data Architecture

Early big data solutions were either batch or streaming. Batch is used when data completeness is required from businesses. Streaming solutions are used for real-time alerting or intraday decision making. Most of the time, streaming applications have not reached expectations of consistency, reliability, flexibility, and ease of use. On the other side, the data set has become so huge that it is more efficient to spread the workload evenly over time.

A new big data architecture, called kappa, has developed rapidly during the past few years as it allows real-time acquisition and distribution of data, while being able to construct accurate reporting on the flows of information.

In kappa architecture, it is not a set of records grouped by files that are distributed across applications, but an immutable log of facts that are captured instantly when they occur. The log tracks everything that happens in IT systems from technical to business events. This sequence of application log, collected from a system of records or operational databases, feeds organizational layers in a reliable and real-time way to allow the construction of scalable and fast data architecture.

The platform behind this architecture is Kafka, an open source framework from Apache Foundation. Kafka was created in LinkedIn to stream user activity to various products such as Newsfeed and LinkedIn Today. Apache Kafka is commercially supported by Confluent.io and now powers most web giants like Twitter, Uber, and Netflix, by supporting their data pipelines. Major financial actors and FinTechs such as Goldman Sachs, Capital One, Square, and PayPal are also using Apache Kafka for core activities such as real-time risk management and fraud detection.

With a simpler representation (log of events), many sources can be injected into the flow of data and widely spread to other business functions and systems. Data can be easily shared across organizations, which can construct their own dedicated data repositories. This mechanism avoids the complexity of building a unique shared data lake. Kafka is used as the backbone of real-time data distribution to a federation of business data repositories.

Unified Data Processing

Now that we can collect and share everything that happens in the organization as a stream of facts, many engines are competing in processing the unbounded stream of data to extract information and insights. Frameworks used to be categorized into two domains: batch-only frameworks (Hadoop MapReduce) and stream-only frameworks (Apache Storm). Today, modern solutions such as open source Apache Spark and Apache Flink have a hybrid model that allows using the same code to be executed on historical batches or streams of data. While Spark enjoys a vibrant user community and a larger customer base, Flink has recently acquired strong references like Alibaba or Capital One. They cover the same set of features such as machine learning, graph processing, and stream SQL, and allow in-memory processing of large sets of data with very high output and low latency.

As seen earlier, data structure management is a core issue in large corporations. This problem is managed by big data platforms that can store historical data for a very long time. A data schema is not handled by persistence layers as in relational database management systems (RDBMSs), but is delegated to application layers. This allows fast storage and avoids complex maintenance for a schema upgrade. A serialization format like Apache Avro has a dynamic data schema built in so that an upgrade of the schema is handled in a transparent way that secures the application from interruption due to incorrect data.

Alerting and Other Complex Real-time Processing

Some compliance control requires more complex data processing like real-time alerting for market abuse or fraud detection. In this case, the streaming model can fall short. Those use cases require the keeping and sharing of results across concurrent distributed processes. To manage this complexity, a programming model called Actor can be used for building highly concurrent applications. Akka framework is the most famous toolkit based on Actor. Its message-driven nature makes it operate with Kafka very easily. It is used internally by streaming frameworks like Spark or Flink. PayPal is using Akka for low-latency payment delivery and has built its own framework over it.

Serving Layer

The role of the serving layer is to give optimized access to data to end users or external applications. The data output is stored in dedicated views for efficient responses to the various access patterns. The landscape of the serving layer is large, so we will enumerate only the biggest family. It is very important to remember that every category has its own purpose, and, unlike previous generations of programs where RDBMSs could respond to different data-access patterns, architects should select carefully the solution that best matches their requirements. The beauty of modern data architecture is that it is not a problem to feed distinct data layers in a resilient and secure way.

NoSQL for Fast Read-write Access

The first category of data store is NoSQL. NoSQL allows fast storage and retrieval of unitary data. Those features ensure high output and low latency, and those systems, as for most big data solutions, are natively distributed with a scale-out architecture. NoSQL ensures data distribution and has replication built in for fault tolerance.

Full-Text Search

Giving fast and reliable access to data is a very important feature for audit and investigation. Special-purpose databases for full-text search can be a lifesaver when added to a compliance data platform.

By constructing data pipelines that feed a functional data lake, companies ensure fast data distribution to a dedicated system that will permit live alerting, reporting, and decision making as well as deep analysis.

Embrace Cloud to Accelerate Transformation

With enterprise data hubs, banks could create a data-centric architecture to support the long-term vision of their information system.

Although big data is a real technological breakthrough, with converged and distributed architecture, it requires new technical skills and can have major impacts on IT infrastructure and operations. Network layers and obsolete security strategy are not compatible with the implementation of data lake or data hub services. Also, the operating model and functional responsibilities required by big data are orthogonal to those commonly in place.

Big data is a cloud-native solution. RegTech leaders take advantage of the transition to data-centric architecture to move to the cloud. This smart move lets IT teams focus on building a new functional stack, and a dedicated budget can be defined for those strategic and transformative projects.

Capital One and major regulatory authorities like the Financial Industry Regulatory Authority (FINRA) or Financial Conduct Authority (FCA) are some of the early adopters of the cloud for their core banking systems and market monitoring solutions.

Cloud providers assure a high level of proactive security that is unaffordable for most banks. One of the best examples is the numerous encryption strategies proposed by server-side encryption that protects data at rest. Coupled with fine-grained access control, only authorized users and programs can read stored data.

Another key factor for cloud adoption is the enablement of managed services. The life cycle of core infrastructure can be entirely operated by the cloud provider in a transparent and scalable way. Delegating common activities like change requests, supervision, backup, and active security reduces operational overheads and risk.

Most big data frameworks can find their alter egos as managed services: Amazon Kinesis for data streaming; Amazon DynamoDB and Google BigTable for NoSQL; Amazon EMR, Google DataProc, and Azure HDInsight for distributed computation; and Amazon QuickSight and Microsoft PowerBI for business intelligence.

An illustration of this to make services as transparent and cost-effective as possible is the move to being serverless that requires no infrastructure to provide. A good example of this new paradigm is Amazon Athena, an interactive query solution for which the user is charged only for the data scanned.

By adopting cloud computing, banks can accelerate their transition to agile and data-driven business while enjoying the innovation capacity of technology giants.

Conclusion

To face the complexity of new regulations, banks must embrace modern big data architecture. By implementing data hubs, incumbents will create a collaborative data platform inside their organization to establish a data-driven culture and face future regulatory compliance challenges.

With big data technology such as Apache Kafka and a modern computation framework that unifies historical and stream processing, banks can create data pipelines that will extend core functions to build innovative digital services. The transition will simultaneously facilitate the modernization of bank front-office solutions that rely on business events. Finally, banks can expect leverage from the cloud to accelerate the transition, as managed services will avoid major infrastructure upgrades while reducing the total cost of ownership.

Enabling RegTech Up Front: Unambiguous Machine-readable Regulation

By Marcel Fröhlich
Director Services, Eccenca GmbH

and Donald Chapin
Principal Consultant, Business Semantics Ltd

RegTech functionality ranges from data collection technologies to complex decision automation and behavioural analysis. Some tools have an obvious task, e.g. 'record customer dialogues', whereas others try to apply various artificial intelligence (AI) approaches to extract definitions and rules out of regulatory documents to automate complex checks.

Our focus is on the latter type of RegTech solutions, which are especially relevant for large regulated organizations like banks operating in multiple jurisdictions. This chapter does not describe a new method of information extraction but rather turns the challenge upside down and tries to answer the question: 'What can the regulators do to enable RegTech?' Regulators are the owners of regulatory instruments, typically rules and definitions provided in a hierarchically structured textual form (e.g. the FCA Handbook).[1]

Regulations are often a mix of principles-based (outcome-oriented) and rules-based (ticking checkboxes) approaches to define compliance. In general, clear rules are more accessible for automation, but in both cases the key hurdle for automation is clarity of meaning with ambiguity removed. Without unambiguous, easily understood defined meanings for the terms used in regulatory rules, automation is useless because meaningful logical conclusions are impossible as long as the meaning of constituent parts is unclear. The automated output will be disconnected from the legal requirements.

Some RegTech companies believe that they can beat ambiguity with statistical black-box algorithms like deep learning instead of logical reasoning. The problem with this approach is that there is no way to know whether the result is correct, because there is no verifiable substantiation (reason why) behind the type of automated conclusions or decisions available.

Another idea is to agree on shortcuts, bypassing all the written rules and engaging the regulators in a dialogue to ultimately sanction certain technologies.[2] However, this is a slippery slope that could easily collide with regulatory instruments in place and hinder further innovation.

Our approach, in contrast, is to refine and support the regulators' editorial process of regulatory texts, and create regulation as unambiguous as possible using an Object Management Group (OMG) standard designed to remove ambiguity from governance documentation, especially regulatory rules and business policies: Semantics of Business Vocabulary and Rules™ (SBVR).[3] Without regulatory rules that are unambiguous both to people from the regulatory text and to computers from the machine-readable version of the visual text, the whole compliance process is built on quicksand.

Publishing Machine-readable Regulation on the Web

A key change we propose is to move from regulation distributed as XML files to hyperlinked HTML documents on the web. The data and metadata embedded in the XML files can be included today by embedding structured data using Resource Description Framewok (RDF) technology.[4] The data can both define the

---

[1] https://www.handbook.fca.org.uk/handbook

[2] https://regtechfs.com/its-unanimous-we-need-a-regtech-council

[3] http://www.omg.org/spec/SBVR

[4] https://www.w3.org/TR/2014/NOTE-rdf11-primer-20 140 225/

meaning of textual elements with semantic web vocabularies like legal extensions to schema.org[5] and add related metadata.

Fusing text with structured, machine-readable data creates an artefact that is both human-readable and machine-readable. The web feature of linking between items can be applied not only to web pages but likewise to structured data elements. This creates an open web of data that can be interpreted as a global database.

Putting semantically enriched documents directly on the web allows for distributed services that are remarkable and could serve as a powerful pattern for new RegTech services. An example of such a service is dokieli[6] for decentralized authoring, annotations, and notifications in the domain of research documents.

Unique Identifiers for All Parts of the Regulation Minted by Regulators

A global database requires globally unique identifiers for data points and text segments down to single sentences. There are standards for such identifiers on the web called Unique Resource Identifiers (URIs)[7] and Internationalized Resource Identifiers (IRIs)[8] for the internationalized Unicode-based version. For legal texts, there is even a specific recommendation for how to create URIs to identify pieces of law or regulations called the European Legislation Identifier (ELI).[9]

The ELI standard defines how a URI in the legal domain should be structured, and that it should be based on linked open data[10] principles.

In the target state, a regulator will provide official URIs for each element of the published regulatory text down to single sentences, including versioning/validity period information to represent change processes.

Using those identifiers, different RegTech providers can create machine-readable formal knowledge bases on the web with additional insights that can be easily reconciled and consumed because they all refer to the same identified things.

A market for RegTech data and services could be ignited with this approach.

Adding Metadata to Regulatory Text via Its ELI

Metadata is additional contextual data. This could be data provided by the regulator, e.g. the date when a regulation comes into effect. It could be internal data, e.g. to which legal entities within a group or to which processes a piece of regulation is relevant. It could be third-party data, e.g. a screening of enforcement actions that puts a price tag or a risk level to a specific regulatory rule provided by a third-party RegTech firm on the web. Any such data can be attached to the respective ELI using semantic web technology.

Maintaining Regulatory Meaning End-to-End

Today in big regulated firms, new regulation is evaluated by experts and interpreted with respect to the specific role and

[5] http://legal.eli-legislation-schemaorg.appspot.com

[6] http://csarven.ca/dokieli-rww

[7] https://tools.ietf.org/html/rfc3986

[8] https://tools.ietf.org/html/rfc3987

[9] http://publications.europa.eu/documents/2050822/2138819/ELI + Implementation+Methodology.pdf/

[10] https://www.w3.org/standards/semanticweb/data

situation of a firm. This interpretation is used to manually identify necessary changes in the firm's internal controls (business policies). Again, those business policies are currently plain text and need to have ambiguity removed just as much as the regulatory rules do.

Our vision is that the principle of URI identification should be applied to all relevant artefacts in all stages of the chain we have described and machine-readable links be created between dependent items: e.g. between a regulatory update, the affected business policy, and subsequent operational processes and data items as illustrated in the OMG's Business Motivation Model (BMM) standard.[11]

The resulting structure is a knowledge graph of the firms' regulatory compliance regime.

With dependencies explicitly represented as linked data, those chains can be automatically traversed in both directions by software. They can be automatically traversed, starting with a regulatory update, to understand the impact of a change by discovering all affected processes and data elements. Moreover, they can be traversed vice versa to understand which regulations shape and influence a specific process or data element.

Our Proof of Concept at FCA TechSprint

In November 2016, this method was demonstrated for a small part of section SUP 16 of the FCA Handbook. We combined the SBVR authoring tool from Business Semantics with the semantic data management software from eccenca to demonstrate all aspects of our approach.

---

[11] http://www.omg.org/spec/BMM

Balancing the Trade-off Between Precision and Ambiguity

Amazingly, there is much potential in clarifying regulatory texts. Unlike law, where uncertainty and fuzziness are important features of the consensus process of legislation, regulation needs to be clear so that it can be well complied with.

In an example regulatory rule from the FCA Handbook detailing reporting duties for funds that is less than 50 words long, we identified 10 ambiguities that we were able to resolve in consultation with the authors from the FCA policy team at the FCA TechSprint event.

In other words, the sense of meaning was in their heads, but was not as clear in the official text. The clarification comprises both the logical structure of the rule sentence and the coverage and clarity of glossary definitions.

Original sentence from SUP 16.11.8.A (underscore means that there exists a glossary definition – not shown here):

> Where the manager of an authorized AIF or a UCITS scheme receives business from a firm which operates a nominee account, the sales data report in respect of those transactions submitted by the manager should treat those transactions as transactions undertaken by the manager with the firm.

Proposal of a revised disambiguated version (some disambiguation required additional glossary entries, including verb phrases):

> Each sales data report for transactions that is submitted by the manager of an authorized AIF or a UCITS scheme who undertakes a transaction with a firm which operates a nominee account should report that transaction as a transaction with the firm, rather than with the client of the firm with which the transaction was undertaken.

There is no need to remove all ambiguities. Sometimes a rule needs to be kept verbatim because it is copied from a law.

The revised sentence uses well-defined SBVR constructs that translate to a formalized interpretation based on ISO 24707 common logic.

Note that the revised version is still a proper English sentence. There is no need to learn a formal notation or any new grammar rules. Refining or creating text with SBVR elements can be supported by an authoring tool normally used by authors of legal texts.

In perspective, the resulting formalization can be used for fine-grained machine interpretation using ontologies to automatically reason about certain aspects of regulations.

Understanding SBVR

SBVR, currently an OMG standard, will become an ISO TC 37 (terminology and other language and content resources) standard. It is designed to remove ambiguity in governance documents. The level addressed is business communication and concepts, not information systems or data. The model of SBVR comprises a terminological dictionary (extending ISO 704/1087) and behavioural guidance (rules). It is fully multilingual and can handle multiple terminologies in parallel.

Improved Regulation

This unambiguous, machine-readable regulatory text approach enables regulators to write their regulatory rules and glossaries in unambiguous natural language for human understanding and to publish them as RDF-linked data that preserves the natural language meaning in formal logic for AI-based processing, thus enabling vendors to add value in a holistic way. It moves the entire regulatory compliance process onto a bedrock semantic foundation of human legal meaning. Without this innovative approach, the only foundation the entire regulatory compliance process can build on is one where everyone must interpret the regulations for themselves and where the interpretation is still natural language text that can't be processed with semantic accuracy by computers.

At every stage along the regulatory compliance process, this new semantic foundation of machine-processable human legal meaning dramatically improves the accuracy and reliability of outputs, and opens up a whole range of possibilities for new automated capabilities, while still keeping people in control of what happens.

Impact for Regulated Firms and Consumers

Some key benefits to regulated firms of the new capabilities are a drastic reduction in the costs of interpreting regulations; a dramatic decrease in the time to put new and changed compliance procedures in place, resulting in a much quicker time to market for new and improved products and services, and an increased ability to demonstrate an in-place compliance regime to the regulators; significantly reduced costs of regulatory reporting; and the ability to gain improvements in the business from the same costs required for regulatory compliance.

Consumers will benefit from higher protection because it is easier to both comply with, and to enforce compliance with, the regulations. They will also benefit from the new and improved products and services made possible by the decreased cost and time to market this approach enables.

Align Open Banking and Future-Proof RegTech for Regulators and Third-Party Providers to Deliver the Optimal Consumer Convenience and Protection

By B.J. Perng
CEO, NiveauUp Inc

This chapter explores the application of a transaction model that will pose a picture-perfect scenario of open banking for most consumers or small-scale merchants,[1] upon the second Payment Services Directive (PSD2) and General Data Protection Regulation (GDPR) entering into effect. The transaction model itself operates between well-segregated metadata and communication data, providing an advantage for GDPR compliance. Then, the chapter highlights how online know your customer (KYC) derivatives on their own advancing path may enhance the transaction model. Should a fully automated, end-to-end monitoring process be necessary for consumer protection, a future-proof and purposed RegTech enabling tool can be provided for payment service providers (PSPs), third-party providers (TPPs), or regulators, by coupling secure mechanism to collect and store metadata with advanced KYC derivatives.

[1] Small-scale merchants are to benefit as much as consumers from the propositions raised in this chapter; however, elaboration has to be truncated due to the total text limits per chapter.

Transaction Model (for a Picture-perfect Open Banking Scenario)

We believe aggregating each individual consumer's (or small-scale merchant's) access to and control of all possible payment services to a personalized mobile application or web service will offer an overall better usability than letting consumers install, engage, and cross-manage PSPs' or banks' applications serving either familiar or different needs, as we all do now.

What are 'all possible payment services'? The following four categories suffice to cover most applicable client requirements, together with the support of non-financial transactions on PSPs' apps, such as banking registration, one-time password (OTP), PIN setup/reset, and transaction status check:

1. *Physical stores/merchants payments*: from street vendors, grocery stores, taxi/car/bus/train/air or toll station fares, or restaurants/shops/petrol pumps to trust or non-governmental organization (NGO) donations.
2. *Utility payments*: from electricity, water, telephone, rent, credit card, or insurance premiums to loan instalment payments.
3. *Online merchants/e-commerce*: COD payments, in-app payments, online trading, mobile recharge from online or offline advertisements using 'scan to pay', e-commerce (collection/pull) checkout, ticket booking, and more.
4. *Peer to peer*: remittance (both push and pull), payment to friends (IOU), sharing of bills with friends, or salary paid to temporary workers to inward remittances to another bank account.

Per PSD2, competition is encouraged by allowing TPPs to have access to account information to provide payment initiation services (PISs) and account information services (AISs). A user-agent style of application API, with its programming plug-ins/extensions initialized from banks' core banking systems, however, would interoperate with a universal application to handle multiparty, multichannel transactions to deliver the 'all possible payment services'.

This universal application powers multiple bank accounts into a single mobile application or web service, merging several banking features, seamless fund routing, and merchant payments under one hood, and it also caters to the peer-to-peer collect request, which can be scheduled and paid as per configurable setups and convenience. There are two main financial transaction types to construct this transaction model:

1. *Pay request.* A pay request is a transaction where the initiating customer is pushing funds to the intended beneficiary. Payment addresses may include mobile number, ID number, account number, or virtual address.

2. *Collect request.* A collect request is a transaction where the customer is pulling funds from the intended remitter by using a virtual address. Payment address includes virtual address only.

The model is designed so all transactions are conducted over virtual IDs and virtual addresses of the customer for both pull and push, thus adding incremental security by restricting customers from submitting sensitive details such as card numbers or account numbers; the use of virtual IDs is applied so as to minimize risks of credential sharing.

(Customer) Metadata

Customer metadata can be generalized to be those data per the European Union's new GDPR to regulate,[2] which are to be aligned

with rules for electronic communications and transactions. These new rules require businesses to store customer data, mandating them to acknowledge unambiguous customer consent before sharing or processing customers' data.

Given that banks would channel account information, personal sensitive data, consent interactions, and other communication data on those existing user-agent APIs, some early debates surfaced about how the initial promise by PSD2 may be offset by GDPR entering into effect at an overlapping timeframe. Conventional banking apps had delivered meaningful, proven user traction, and therefore whether the open banking deployment, by following a track similar to that of the traditional development of APIs, can be scaled to mass adoption is subject to some early-day uncertainty.

The proposed transaction model provides an architectural advantage for TPPs to build up each consumer's personalized metadata without overlaying it with communication data, and flexible consent management by channeling clients to interact with their own metadata – achieving an overall consumer-centric approach to data rights management, and paving a solid groundwork with both regulatory lawfulness and consumer protection committed in the core, base transaction model, for a highly anticipated sharing economy.

Also, this metadata buildup for the PSD2 and GDPR era can be business-process agnostic and lighter weight than its predecessors' offerings.

(Online) KYC Derivatives

Various standardization efforts are in development, which will strengthen KYC and strong customer authentication (SCA) to advance beyond the status quo. Smartphone payment aggregators such as Apple, Samsung, and Android have

---

[2] Metadata may have different implications otherwise. In most cases, it's the data demanded by a specific regulatory compliance to be protected from a breach or a leak.

popularized the use of authenticating users via biometric sensing interacting with private key management[3] in the device.

The author proposes to collectively classify such online authentication technology, in leveraging components integrating private key management and biometric sensors, as KYC derivatives, whereas some people call the technology KYT (with T standing for things on users' devices).

A good KYC derivative matching for open banking will be the FIDO Alliance, which the UK government recently endorsed.[4] 'Identity on Blockchain' is another alternative pursued by a W3C working group,[5] evolving along the KYC derivative structure,[6] with blockchain's crypto operations to include KYC derivatives by signing a multitude of transactions generated by web applications.

With the provision of personalized metadata and KYC derivatives, we show how a regulator could shift liability[7] in a triangular transaction model amongst the merchant, the issuing bank,

and the payment bank in a credit card settlement scheme, by combining SCA and our proposed transaction model for PSD2. We identify the potential to transplant a credit-card-like or equivalent use case to an open banking use case, and demonstrate a future-proof RegTech enabling tool purposed for the picture-perfect open banking scenario.

RegTech Enabling Tool

An example of a RegTech application is its ability to assist answering regulations requiring complicated quantitative calculations such as forecasting of interest rate risk and credit risks, which extends to deploying more solutions by leveraging the power of artificial intelligence (AI) or machine learning, reaching possibly each individual consumer, as some chapters in this book envision.

With RegTech, regulators encourage information gathering to help them learn what should be monitored and how. Regulators are positive that PSPs and TPPs take seriously how they apply technology to their own compliance questions. Ultimately, RegTech risks (by not being compliant with changing regulatory requirements) are still PSPs' and TPPs' responsibilities.[8]

RegTech that directs those tasks which banks or PSPs have to comply with in satisfying consumers can win consumers' trust: in this chapter, we propose a transaction model for the open banking (PSD2) implementation and, by interoperating with its inherent metadata aggregating capability, to ease GDPR compliance and the KYC derivatives, supporting SCA's

---

[3] Private key under the public key infrastructure (PKI) is an essential concept to be acquired for readers who have not done so. Plenty of information can be found online.

[4] http://findbiometrics.com/uk-government-fido-311074

[5] https://http://www.w3.org/2016/04/Blockchain-workshop/report.html#identity

[6] This is one example paper from the W3C working group to approach 'Identity on Blockchain' with KYC derivative structure: https://docs.google.com/document/d/1zSWyXpAwCbQwkCgmbfxjpZ-QPYEwpxNfyt6mnos-gNAU/edit?pref=2&pli=1

[7] The author has drawn this conclusion based on live implementation elsewhere. In PSD2, 'EPC regrets that the draft RTS do not propose exemptions based on a transaction-risk analysis performed by the PSP', as quoted from page 2 of the following publication under 'Exemptions from strong customer authentication': http://www.europeanpaymentscouncil.eu/pdf/EPC_Article_429.pdf

---

[8] FCA to banks: 'RegTech risks are your responsibility'. (Quote from https://www.fnlondon.com/articles/fca-tells-banks-RegTech-risks-are-your-responsibility-20170411)

continuous development. This RegTech enabling tool can be provided for a huge competitive advantage, as it may evolve to become a one-stop solution to weave open banking with RegTech, while addressing the ongoing changing regulatory challenges in its own parallel path.

RegTech tools as such ensure automation and faster compliance with regulatory obligations. They are intended to be flexible, are designed to simplify compliance tasks, and can work with the existing as well as upcoming technology stacks – RegTech tools proliferating around the proposed transaction model act in the same way regardless of what underlying technology is being implemented by the TPP/PSP, ranging from credit card schemes to blockchain-facilitated transactions. If a fully automated, end-to-end monitoring process is deemed necessary, it may thus be set up.

A Seat at the Table – Bringing the Voice of FinTech to the US Regulatory Process

By Lynn Bromley
Founder and Principal, FinTech Advocate

Another day, another sandbox – regulatory sandbox, that is. Countries around the world are deploying proactive regulatory strategies and establishing sandboxes to support growth and much-needed innovation in the financial services sector. They are popping up everywhere: the United Kingdom, Malaysia, Singapore, Canada, Bahrain, Australia, Hong Kong, Russia – everywhere but the United States, it seems.

Regulatory sandboxes present a clear and unambiguous signal to the market – to FinTech innovation. 'Bring it on', they say – everywhere but the United States, it seems.

To be clear, I am not a fan of FinTech for the sake of FinTech, or for the sheer brilliance of the many and various emerging technologies. It is rather the potential of FinTech to bring solutions to many of the world's most stubborn problems that inspires. Take but one example – the unmet need for small and medium-size enterprise (SME) loans.

The Case for Financial Services Innovation in SME Lending

There is broad agreement in the United States that small businesses are the primary creators of net new jobs in addition to spawning the lion's share of innovation, yet they struggle disproportionately for capital. In the past five years:

- 53% of SME's have applied for loans or lines of credit.
- 25% have applied more than once.

- 20% were turned down.
- 45% were turned down more than once.
- 23% do not know why they were turned down.
- and a critical economic factor – 26% had to forgo business expansion due to the difficulty of accessing capital.

This lack of traditional capital for SMEs has given rise to FinTech-enabled alternative/online lending.[1] SME enablement at this most basic level will invite thousands of new actors to be engaged participants in the economy. This will be profoundly transformative (including in the United States) if SMEs (including FinTech start-ups) can get a seat at the table – the regulatory table.

US Financial Regulation – Outdated, Complex

Though we look to FinTech innovation to bring much-needed solutions to financial services, FinTech has its own problems – it does not fit the complex and outdated US regulatory structure. Consider these facts:

There is a multiplicity of federal agencies with regulatory authority:

- Eleven of these regulatory bodies have no formulated approach to FinTech.
- Different bodies often have conflicting rules, making compliance difficult.
- Two major regulatory authorities – the Office of the Comptroller of the Currency (OCC) and the Securities and Exchange Commission (SEC) – are making efforts to develop FinTech-specific policy, but mainly independently.

---

[1] National Middle Market Summit, 2011.

Each of the 50 states has its own financial regulatory authority:

- Nearly every state has a money services businesses statute that requires companies to obtain a license before engaging in a money transmission business.

- FinTech innovator PayPal initially asserted that these money transmitter statutes did not apply to it. The company is now licensed in 53 jurisdictions in the United States.

- For companies operating in virtual currencies, the application of state-level money transmitter laws is particularly confusing.

Federal policy is in flux, thus creating uncertainty for innovators and investors:

- The Trump administration is in the process of rolling back a host of recently enacted regulations. Empowered by the seldom-used Congressional Review Authority (CRA), some 40 regulations dating back to May 2016 are in play.[2]

- Congress targets the Dodd-Frank Wall Street Reform and Consumer Protection Act for repeal or amendment. Anticipated changes in the operations, scope, authority, and structure of the Consumer Financial Protection Bureau (CFPB) will directly impact FinTech regulation.[3]

In the spirit of a picture painting a thousand words, note Figure 1, a chart of the US financial regulatory structure, for a hint at the scope of the problem.[4]

Figure 1 represents a perfect illustration of the regulatory maze and reporting obligations that every FinTech company in the United States will have to face.

In addition to this daunting complexity, unlike regulatory regimes such as that in the United Kingdom, the US system has no strategic objective to address the functioning of the relevant financial marketplaces by promoting competition as well as protecting consumers.

The US Financial Regulatory System Is Silent on Innovation in General and FinTech in Particular

Simply put, policy makers do not understand FinTech, and there is no formal process or expectation that regulators acknowledge innovation. Furthermore, FinTech innovators often don't understand or even contemplate how policy and regulation can aid, impede, or even prohibit the deployment of their innovation or business model. By way of example, attend a FinTech pitch contest demo day and ask of those pitching, 'What is the agency or entity that will have authority over your innovation or business model?' At some events, some will know. At most events, few will know, and I have attended events where none were able to answer the question. Even those most informed had relied on informal peer and mentor networks and the internet for this critical information.

Were it not for the sheer size of the US market, it would make little sense for FinTech companies to navigate this complex, confusing, and often contradicting maze of regulation.

Who's Speaking Up for the FinTech Sector?

Given that, as yet, there is no coordinated federal approach to FinTech, nor is there a regulatory sandbox in the United States.

---

[2] http://www.businessinsider.com/the-us-FinTech-regulation-report-2017-2?IR=T

[3] http://www.businessinsider.com/piecemeal-regulation-is-hindering-us-FinTechs-2016-10?IR=T

[4] US Government Accountability Office, 'Financial Regulation: Complex and Fragmented Structure Could Be Streamlined to Improve Effectiveness' (February 2016); http://www.gao.gov/products/GAO-16-175

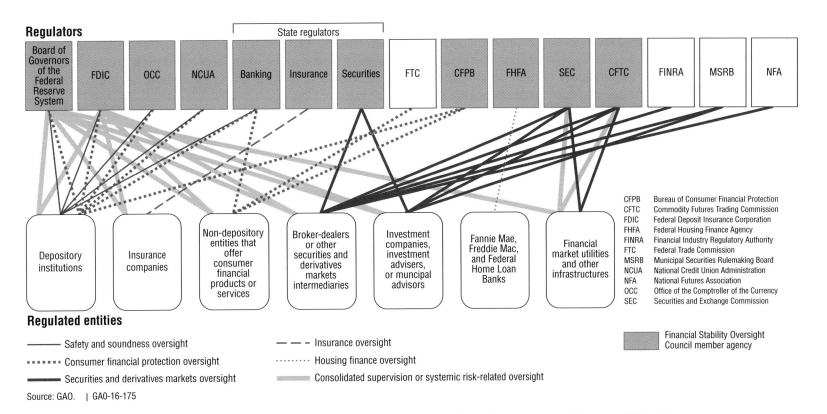

Regulators

Board of Governors of the Federal Reserve System | FDIC | OCC | NCUA | Banking | Insurance | Securities | FTC | CFPB | FHFA | SEC | CFTC | FINRA | MSRB | NFA

State regulators

Depository institutions | Insurance companies | Non-depository entities that offer consumer financial products or services | Broker-dealers or other securities and derivatives markets intermediaries | Investment companies, investment advisers, or muncipal advisors | Fannie Mae, Freddie Mac, and Federal Home Loan Banks | Financial market utilities and other infrastructures

Regulated entities

CFPB — Bureau of Consumer Financial Protection
CFTC — Commodity Futures Trading Commission
FDIC — Federal Deposit Insurance Corporation
FHFA — Federal Housing Finance Agency
FINRA — Financial Industry Regulatory Authority
FTC — Federal Trade Commission
MSRB — Municipal Securities Rulemaking Board
NCUA — National Credit Union Administration
NFA — National Futures Association
OCC — Office of the Comptroller of the Currency
SEC — Securities and Exchange Commission

——— Safety and soundness oversight
········· Consumer financial protection oversight
——— Securities and derivatives markets oversight
— — — Insurance oversight
·········· Housing finance oversight
▬▬▬ Consolidated supervision or systemic risk-related oversight

▢ Financial Stability Oversight Council member agency

Source: GAO. | GAO-16-175

Note: This figure depicts the primary regulators in the U.S. financial regulatory structure, as well as their primary oversight responsibilities. 'Regulators' generally refers to entities that have rulemaking, supervisory, and enforcement authorities over financial institutions or entities. There are additional agencies involved in regulating the financial markets and there may be other possible regulatory connections than those depicted in this figure.

Figure 1: US financial regulatory structure (2016)

There are individual lobbyists and lobbying groups who offer fee-based monitoring of upcoming regulation as well as fee-based direct advocacy for or against a specific bill, policy, or regulation. However, they cannot provide entirely comprehensive and timely information across all the issues from the many agencies to the entire FinTech industry – most particularly the smaller entities and start-ups.

Some established FinTechs are forming coalitions to educate, to advocate, and also to lobby. Notable among them is Financial

Innovation Now (FIN). FIN was formed in 2015 to 'encourage regulation in the technology-enabled financial services sector to enable a modern financial system that is more accessible, affordable, and secure'.[5] FIN's voice is not unimportant, but it is primarily that of the established companies, Amazon, Apple, Google, Intuit, PayPal, Square and Stripe. The issues of these larger players are not always the same as those of smaller FinTech entrepreneurs and innovators.

[5] https://financialinnovationnow.org/wp-content/uploads/2015/12/FIN-Policy-Priorities.pdf

REGULATORY INNOVATION AND SANDBOXES

It is important that FinTech establish and assert itself as a sector. This will, however, require new models of connection and collaboration, as the typical trade/professional association models in the United States are driven by dues-paying members who are not broadly representative of the sector. Again, most absent are the smaller, newer innovators and entrepreneurs.

No Sandbox? – RegTech to the Rescue

Countries and regulatory jurisdictions that include a sandbox approach are models we can look to for inspiration. The regulatory sandbox concept encourages innovators, protects consumers, and helps to educate regulators as they develop the relevant regulatory approach alongside the development of the technology. We can be inspired for sure, but the market will not wait for the US regulatory system to catch up with the rest of the world. What then?

In the same way that we look to FinTech to bring solutions to complex, inefficient, outdated, and redundant financial services and processes, so we can look to RegTech to solve these similar dynamics in the regulatory system. The same process of innovation – looking for pain points, weaknesses, and opportunities – is relevant here.

The window to transform regulation is open, but not for long. We need to show up with a FinTech sector-led approach to regulatory reform that supports innovation. Our collaboration must be robust, the participants and perspectives diverse (from zealots to naysayers), and our commitment clear. Innovation can no longer be considered a blip or an outlier. The US regulatory system must establish a process to expect and engage in the emerging realities of the entities that it regulates.

I offer two concrete steps and invite all to join the conversation and add to the list.

First, engage in a deliberate sector-wide dialogue and promotion of the FinTech subset – RegTech. As noted earlier, promoting

FinTech for the sake of FinTech is a bad strategy. Promoting FinTech for what it can do builds belief, trust, and support. All of us interested in the future of FinTech ought to be conversant with the concrete benefits of the sector as a whole, not just our own or favourite technology.

In a 2014 Harvard Business School working paper, the former head of the Small Business Administration outlined a road map and rationale for traditional banks to use digitization and RegTech innovation as a strategy to increase SME lending by adding efficiencies and reducing the cost of lending at 'every stage of the process'.

Since the global financial crisis, transaction costs have increased significantly with additional consumer protection regulations and the resulting compliance. The number of regulatory publications, changes, and announcements increased an astonishing 492% between 2008 and 2015. Existing compliance processes are not designed to handle the added volume and complexity. Individual systems do not easily interact with each other; data is often kept in different formats so that collating data about a particular client or transaction is often a heavily manual task.[6] The paper makes the point that transaction costs for a $100,000 loan are the same as for a $1 million loan, causing the banks to prioritize SMEs seeking higher loan amounts, leaving the majority of SMEs underserved. As RegTech products are deployed to streamline and automate compliance, costs decrease, banks make more profit on low-dollar loans, and more small businesses get funded.[7]

FinTech/RegTech innovators should not be shy about claiming victory for these sorts of win-win-wins. Banks, traditional lenders, and small business are key constituencies. It is a powerful

---

[6] Business Insider RegTech Report (January 2016).

[7] Karen G. Mills and Brayden McCarthy, 'The State of Small Business Lending: Credit Access During the Recovery and How Technology May Change the Game', Harvard Business School Working Paper 15-004, July 2014.

message that the very innovation that creates our current FinTech regulatory quandary in the United States can at the same time offer regulatory compliance solutions to traditional financial institutions.

Second, we must turn the capabilities of our own technology on ourselves by understanding the regulatory process; identifying the pain points, weaknesses, and opportunities; and developing RegTech solutions for the regulatory morass.

It will not be the regulators that bring solutions to the problem. Regulators do not set policy. It is important to remember that regulators in the United States only have the authority delegated to them by the Congress. Congress establishes broad policy mandates, and only then do the federal agencies create the detailed specifics of regulation and implementation.

The rulemaking process is governed by the Administrative Procedures Act (APA) of 1946, which designates the lengthy multistep process from notice of a proposed rule to final adoption and implementation.[8] There are two primary pain points in this process crying out for a RegTech remedy – one at the point of public notice and then again during the public comment period.

Public Notice

The public is notified of a proposed rule via an outdated and inefficient system. Proposed rules are announced in the *Federal Register*, which is published daily by the National Archives and Records Administration. It is distributed on paper, on microfiche, and on the World Wide Web.

Proposed and pending rules, statements of policy and guidance, and updates of any actions or proposed actions are published every day for every agency, from the Department of Agriculture to the Weights and Measures Division, in addition to the 11 financial services agencies with regulatory authority.

Sifting and sorting through this daily publication of every rule from every agency for sector relevance is mostly a manual process and not an activity that small entrepreneurs and innovators have the time or resources to undertake on a consistent basis.

A RegTech innovation is needed here!

Public Comment

After notice has been given and the rule is published, there is an open period where the public is invited to comment in order to provide data to the agency on the rule's likely impact as well as suggestions for amendment. These comments become part of the record that the agency is required to build. The open comment period is typically 60–90 days, and comments may be electronically submitted, mailed, or delivered in person.

Currently, 'public' comment is primarily made by lawyers, lobbyists, and special interests on behalf of their clients. Small innovators and entrepreneurs, again, are otherwise engaged and thus mostly absent in this process.

The balance between regulation and innovation for FinTech is critical, and should not be left to the uninformed or the self-interested, but rather to a broad community of voices. In the absence of a federal strategy and a regulatory sandbox approach, innovators must engage in the rulemaking process in order to smooth out the rough terrain and provide experiential data on regulatory barriers, best practices, and emerging technologies and business models. Yet, innovators and entrepreneurs are barely at the proverbial table, a table that is crowded almost exclusively with what could be described as 'the usual suspects'. We must be interacting with regulators in real time as the rules are being written.

A RegTech innovation is needed here!

---

[8] https://www.epa.gov/laws-regulations/summary-administrative-procedure-act

A Virtual Seat at the Table – Bringing the Voice of FinTech Innovators to the Process

One RegTech innovation currently in development is the dynamic feedback loop tool intended to access, engage, and aggregate the missing voices in the regulatory process. Using artificial intelligence (AI) and natural language processing (NLP), the feedback tool will bring curated information and alerts about regulations to the FinTech innovators and entrepreneurs, and send the crowdsourced feedback to the relevant regulators. Acting as both distributor and consolidator of information, the feedback tool will allow quick and effective responses from a widespread collection of FinTech innovators.[9]

Easy, accessible, and widespread access to proactive RegTech tools such as this one will enable FinTech innovators to take their virtual seat at the table.

Looking Forward

FinTech innovation will undoubtedly flourish in the years ahead, but it remains to be seen if the US regulatory system can move beyond the protection of consumers and turf to supporting innovation and emerging technologies important to the economy. One thing is certain: including the consistent voice of innovators will be a simple and powerful change that will be as disruptive to the regulatory process as FinTech is to financial services.

---

[9] Lynn Bromley, Mark Happe, and Divakar Goswami, 'The Dynamic Feedback Loop Tool', Massachusetts Institute of Technology FinTech Future Commerce Capstone Project, March 2017.

Sandbox Games for RegTech

By Dominik Witz

Head of Banking Compliance and RegTech, Swisscom

On 2 August 2017, the rules for the license-exempt innovation space, the so-called sandbox, came in to force in Switzerland. Their purpose is to promote financial innovation and to improve the competitiveness of Switzerland as a financial centre. This chapter discusses this new proposition and examines its potential for the testing of RegTech solutions.

Regulatory Sandbox in the Stricter Sense

Through changes to the Swiss Banking Act and the Swiss Banking Ordinance, the shortcomings of the previous regime shall be addressed. So far, a Swiss financial service provider required a banking license approval as soon as it accepted more than 20 public deposits. Unless it could rely on one of the limited exemptions, it needed to seek authorization and subsequently ensure continuous compliance with the regulatory requirements. To abolish this obstacle to innovation, the new regulation establishes an approval-free room for innovation, the so-called 'regulatory sandbox'. The regulatory sandbox allows financial service providers to offer new business models, products, and services and test their effectiveness, without having to seek approval and continuously ensure compliance with the regulations as well as without being supervised and monitored by the Swiss Financial Market Supervisory Authority (FINMA) in doing so.

Under the new rules, the parties eligible for the regulatory sandbox shall meet all of the following requirements:

- They continuously accept more than 20 public deposits or offer to do so, unless the public deposits exceed a total of CHF 1 million.

- They neither invest nor pay interest for the public deposits if they are mainly active in the finance business.

- They inform the depositors that they are not supervised by the FINMA and that the deposits are not covered by the deposit insurance.

For instance, if the financial service provider fails to observe its duty to furnish information, this will lead to its activity qualifying as a commercial activity that is subject to approval.

The room for innovation as provided for by the present draft bill is, of course, not only open to FinTech start-ups. The wording of the Swiss banking regulation also allows any established financial service provider that is already approved and supervised by FINMA to make use of the regulatory sandbox. For instance, it is possible that established institutions set up a subsidiary and use this subsidiary to test new business models, products, or services in the newly defined framework without requiring approval. In particular, the regulatory sandbox could be an opportunity to test the effectiveness of fully-automated risk management and compliance processes that are, for instance, based on artificial intelligence and self-learning software. For existing institutions, this would have the advantage that any liability would primarily be limited to the new company.

Today, financial market legislation requires banks to implement high standards of risk management and compliance measures as a precondition to the initial and ongoing authorization by FINMA. These requirements refer to both the process and the structural organization; i.e. each financial services provider must implement workflows, controls, and corporate governance in order to be allowed to pursue its regulated business activities. Specific requirements for risk management and compliance apply as a risk-based approach in line with the chosen business model, and ongoing adherence to these requirements is controlled by regulatory audits.

Testing RegTech Applications in the Sandbox

Companies that meet the criteria of the regulatory sandbox do not need authorization by FINMA. Without the need for an authorization, the financial services provider does not have to comply with any requirements for risk management and compliance. However, they can still follow regulatory requirements on a voluntary basis and act as if they applied. But why should a financial services company that is enjoying the exemption from financial market regulations wish to voluntarily follow them?

Banks, as well as supervisory authorities, rely on their experience with the old-fashioned analogous risk and compliance processes and instruments. Frequently, they prefer to trust well-known procedures rather than new ones, even if the former are not beyond all doubt. Displaying a certain risk aversion, banks are often reluctant to consider new methods and instruments, fearing the unknown and the possible consequences and scrutiny concerning their supervisory authority.

The protected environment of the regulatory sandbox is a suitable arrangement to try new solutions for risk management and compliance without jeopardizing the entire banking book and the good reputation. Obviously, experimenting with new approaches to risk management and compliance is not the primary scope of start-ups that primarily use the sandbox to test a new business model or product.

However, testing RegTech applications is likely to be of particular interest to banks, as in any case they have to meet stringent regulatory requirements and consequently bear high costs.

The sandbox's threshold of CHF 1 million customer deposits permits banks to work with a manageable number of customers. The newly established subsidiary does not try out a new, innovative business model, but should rather follow a well-known business activity, e.g. payment services or asset management.

However, due to the restrictions of the regulatory sandbox, they are not permitted to operate a lending business.

This setup – no regulatory requirements for risk management and compliance, a well-known business model, and a manageable number of real customers – allows the bank to simulate the existence of regulatory requirements and to implement them for all disciplines of risk management and compliance in order to test the full range of RegTech solutions. The parallel run of traditional methods and instruments of risk management and compliance will set the benchmark in order to classify the appropriateness of RegTech applications. Due to the small number of customers and customer deposits, traditional methods and instruments can be operated with a large number of control samples, which allows an accurate comparison with the new RegTech instruments to be tested.

To the extent that the rules for the approval-free room for innovation relate to the practical test of innovative new business models in the field of financial services or the testing of new RegTech solutions, this room for innovation is conceptually reasonable. However, contrary to other countries, there is no supervision or formal involvement by FINMA in the phase in which a company is still in the sandbox. This raises doubts as to whether FINMA can be convinced of the appropriateness and effectiveness of the tested RegTech applications, even if they prove highly reliable. However, this would be a prerequisite to their acceptance and future deployment as the essential, primary risk management and compliance measures.

'Light Approval' as Regulatory Sandbox in the Broader Sense

A thorough glance at the non-Swiss sandboxes shows, however, that the term *sandbox* has a broader meaning in these countries than in Switzerland so far. Outside of Switzerland, a company making use of the sandbox has to meet certain regulatory requirements, in particular with regard to minimum capital, equity ratio, and liquidity. Therefore, this can rather be compared with the promotion of innovation within the meaning of 'light approval', which was also introduced within the scope of the new regulation and came into force on 1 January 2019. The new 'light approval' will be necessary once public deposits from more than 20 persons exceed a volume of CHF 1 million. However, significant alleviations shall be granted with regard to minimum capital, equity ratio, and liquidity under special circumstances.

As soon as a company operating in the regulatory sandbox has exceeded a certain market-relevant size, it will be in close contact with FINMA in order to be granted the necessary regulatory license. In the course of the approval process, FINMA will thoroughly scrutinize the organizational measures on risk management and compliance and at the same time examine the appropriateness and effectiveness of RegTech applications deployed so far.

Conclusion

Since the requirements for 'light approval' are set out in an executive regulation on a more detailed level, high transparency and legal certainty are established in a form that cannot be found in many other countries. This should be a clear locational advantage of Switzerland over the other nations.

One possible point of critique remains, however: FINMA possibly misses a chance, as it does not observe companies from the very beginning within the new, narrowly defined sandbox. This is unfortunate because both the company and FINMA would benefit from such observation: the company could get feedback from FINMA at an early stage with regard to aspects that are problematic from a regulatory perspective, in particular with regard to the application of new technologies for risk management and compliance. FINMA could benefit to the same extent by familiarizing itself very early with the benefits of modern RegTech solutions, in particular to their own supervisory objectives. However, the threshold amount of CHF 1 million specified for public deposits is low enough to be exceeded quickly. Therefore, RegTech testers in the sandbox would be forced to contact FINMA at an early stage to discuss and organize the transition to 'light approval'. In this respect, FINMA can resort to its longtime pro-business practice regarding rulings on questions of law and – with regard to the scope of this chapter – deal with RegTech solutions.

In summary, the new regulations on the sandbox must be seen in close connection with the provisions on the promotion of innovation. The package of provisions has the potential of becoming a sustainable driver of innovation for Switzerland as a financial centre. It would be desirable for FINMA to seize the chance and deal with the different business models already within the scope of the sandbox and give companies the opportunity to consult with FINMA on matters requiring approval at an early stage.

Legal Guidance for Entering the Sandbox and Taking Advantage of Cross-Border Cooperation Agreements

By James Burnie
Senior Associate – Financial Services, Eversheds-Sutherland (International) LLP

and Andrew Henderson
Partner – Financial Services, Eversheds-Sutherland (International) LLP

Background: The Genesis of the Sandbox

With financial market participants embracing the benefits of FinTech, for example in creating new types of revenue and saving costs, many financial regulators and lawmakers are recognizing FinTech's inherent value. Perhaps uniquely, they are looking not only at how they should regulate FinTech, but also at how they can promote it. Of course, lawmakers, regulators, and market participants alike accept that FinTech is not without risk and may in reality introduce new risks. They need, therefore, to understand FinTech developments to ensure that FinTech does not become a means of subverting regulations and regulatory protection. Lawmakers and regulators like clear terms, but 'FinTech' is a vague concept, taking in a wide range of technologies. These range from simple automation of repetitive tasks to decentralized autonomous organizations (DAOs), which leverage smart contract and blockchain technology to organize complex networks. All of these carry risk, and regulators face a real challenge in understanding FinTech, particularly since the innovators who understand it best are more likely to be interested in creating new rather than monitoring existing technology. This challenge has prompted an innovative regulatory solution, the 'sandbox' – a safe(r) space with a tailored set of regulatory rules for FinTech firms to test and develop their businesses. In response to technological innovation, lawmakers and regulators have moulded an innovative regulatory solution.

Why Enter the Sandbox?

There is a misconception that the sandbox is the only way for firms to develop FinTech. Although sandboxes are important, one should see their potential value for a business in light of their purpose. Sandboxes are not all the same, but they tend to share three core characteristics:

1. *They allow product testing within a controlled environment.* New technology is inherently unpredictable. Testing new technology within a sandbox enables firms to work and experiment in light of this unpredictability.

2. *They provide a contact point between the industry and the regulator.* This gives innovators the chance to work with regulators to help them correctly understand new technical developments and monitor innovation in a secure regulatory environment that encourages a culture of regulatory compliance.

3. *They allow regulators to 'adapt the rules'.* Some technologies do not fit easily within existing legal frameworks. Sandboxes therefore let regulators suspend or alter a rule that is ill-suited to the relevant technology.

As such, whilst sandboxes are important for testing innovation, they are not always appropriate for launching a FinTech initiative. Generally, sandboxes are best deployed when:

- *There is a clear point an innovator wishes to test through using the sandbox, usually referred to as the proof of concept (PoC).* The sandbox is not a permanent state of affairs, but rather an opportunity to accomplish a specific aim with the regulator. Having clear, achievable goals when applying for sandbox entry increases both the chances of acceptance and the chances of achieving real value from the sandbox test.

- *There is a potential conflict between a new development and the regulatory system.* Sandboxes are, at their core, a regulatory device. Their value is therefore limited for firms operating outside the regulated sphere – in these cases, there is less regulators can help with through the sandbox, as there is no regulation to assist with. They are, however, useful as a means of ensuring that regulators understand a new product or showing that certain regulatory requirements are too prescriptive and should be adapted to take account of new technology.

- *A product is uncertain.* Even if there is no regulatory conflict as such, for example because new technology is designed to facilitate regulatory compliance, sandboxes may be useful as a way of acknowledging that things may go wrong when technology is being tested. An example of this might be a technology to facilitate mandatory regulatory reporting requirements – if such technology is tested outside a sandbox and fails to make the required reports, then this may incur penalties for the relevant firm. However, regulators may be prepared to waive such fines as part of being within a sandbox.

As such, when considering sandbox entry, it is worth considering whether this is the best route. The sandbox process can be inconvenient and expensive. As a testing area, regulators may restrict and limit the activities in a sandbox. Regulators may, for example, restrict the number and type of clients that a firm can deal with while in the sandbox. Wrongly used, a sandbox can hinder a business. It must be remembered that sandboxes are not the same as incubation hubs. Their purpose is not business growth and/or as places for receiving commercial business advice. If FinTech firms are looking for this, an incubation hub is likely to be a better option.

Which Sandbox?

Once the decision has been made to enter into a sandbox, the next question is: which sandbox? This is often overlooked; however, selecting the most appropriate regulatory environment may have a considerable impact on the business. A clear example is the Hong Kong Monetary Authority (HKMA), which is unusual in that its sandbox is available only to entities that are already authorized. It is slanted towards encouraging innovation in the banking sector

rather than other industries. In determining where to set up, firms need to take a holistic approach, including the following:

- *The appetite of the regulator for encouraging a particular business/product innovation.* For example, the Financial Conduct Authority (FCA) has typically been particularly open towards encouraging products based on blockchain and cryptocurrencies, whereas other countries have attempted to ban bitcoin altogether.

- *The regulator's level of understanding of a product.* For example, an Islamic finance product may benefit from input from a regulator with knowledge of Sharia law.

- *The flexibility of the local regulatory regime to meet an innovator's needs.* For example, many laws in the European Union are set by a central regulatory authority, which has the advantage of consistency, but the disadvantage that EU member states have less individual discretion to adapt laws to fit particular facts. An additional consideration here is whether there is a need in a particular regime for flexibility at all, as certain activities[1] are regulated in some countries but not others.

- *The wider local entrepreneurial culture in the relevant country.* For example, if a range of market players developing similar technologies coexist, this facilitates the trading of good ideas to mutual benefit.

- *The wider business plan*, e.g. considering where competitors are located.

One issue to note: although gaining entry to a sandbox may be a great achievement, it is a means to an end and not an end in itself. Sandboxes are only part of the journey for new products, designed to help get products up and running in a safe environment. As such, it is worth bearing in mind the anticipated end point

---

[1] A good example here is the act of lending to a business, as this is an activity where there is a lack of agreement among regulators regarding whether there should be regulation at all.

for a new technology from the point of conception; to give a simple example, there is no point obtaining regulatory approval in Europe if the whole of your intended market is in the United States. What this end point is will vary; however, a good illustration of the importance of a holistic approach is the current global development of cross-border cooperation agreements.

An Example of the Bigger Picture: The Impact of Cross-border Cooperation Agreements

The global regulatory landscape is changing, and this is particularly important for firms seeking a global footprint. This is demonstrated by the recent proliferation of cooperation agreements as a mechanism for encouraging information flows between regulators as well as assisting entities in one jurisdiction to set up in others. Many of these agreements cross continents; for example, there are agreements in place between Australia and the United Kingdom, as well as Singapore and France. This adds two further stages to any consideration of which sandbox to set up in:

1. Does the local regulator have cooperation agreements in each jurisdiction in which you wish to set up?

2. If your chosen regulator has agreements with a range of jurisdictions, which of these do you prioritize for expansion?

The result is an additional dimension to any consideration of which sandbox to use and, combined with the considerations just mentioned, can mean some difficulty in determining where is best to set up, and so it is worth taking this issue seriously. Once the decisions to both use a sandbox and which sandbox is made, the next step is to enter the sandbox.

What Are the Requirements When Entering the Sandbox?

Sandbox access is a privilege, not a right. Regulators have the discretion to determine who may enter into a sandbox, which they exercise through requiring firms to apply for entry. For example, in the United Kingdom, the FCA accepted only around 35% of applicants to its first sandbox cohort (although unsuccessful applicants may still get a regulatory steer to help their business moving forward). Before entering a sandbox, thought needs to be given on how to maximize the chances of successful entry. This involves being able to explain why entry should be allowed (on which, see previous discussion), as well as addressing the concerns regulators have when assessing an application, and in this respect care is needed to satisfy the relevant regulator's exact requirements. However, there are core themes, and most regulators will consider whether:

- *The product is innovative.* Although a vague term, innovation may be through using new or emerging technology, or using existing technology in an innovative way.

- *There is a nexus between the product and the regulator's jurisdiction.* Usually, this equates to a requirement that the product, once developed, will be deployed in the regulator's jurisdiction or assist the development of services in that jurisdiction.

- *The innovation offers a good prospect of consumer benefit*, such as through providing better risk management, efficiency, choice, accessibility, security, or quality of financial services. Conversely, regulators may also consider how the business can be exited, should testing in the sandbox fail.

- *There is a genuine need to test in the sandbox.* This may be shown by completing preliminary testing outside the sandbox and developing a realistic business plan.

- *The business is ready to test its innovation.* This can include demonstrating an understanding of relevant regulations, having a legal opinion to show how the business fits within the regulatory framework, ensuring partnership arrangements are formalized through contract, and securing any needed bank accounts.

The core themes here concern understanding the new technology, understanding its benefits and risks, and determining whether it is appropriate for a firm to enter the sandbox at the point of application. These are propositions of general application, and so are inherently worth bearing in mind when making an application.

Concluding Thoughts: The Wider Impact of Sandboxes

Sandboxes encourage positive regulatory interaction and help understanding. In this respect, this chapter has tried to give some practical guidance for those considering sandboxes, as well as briefly looking at the wider picture, using cooperation agreements by way of example. As a concluding thought, however, it is worth considering that the impact of sandboxes on the actual regulators may be greater than originally intended, in that they have created a new emphasis on interregulator competition. This means that different regulators are in direct competition to show that their regulatory 'product' is superior. Although competition between regulators may seem odd, regulators are providers of a regulatory solution. Regulatory innovation is certainly a good thing because it encourages safe practices, but also recognizes that FinTech is different and a different approach is required. This is very positive.

RegTech and the Sandbox – Play, Innovate, and Protect!

By Désirée Klingler

Attorney-at-Law and PhD Candidate, University of St. Gallen

The Rise of RegTech

RegTech vs FinTech

Regulatory innovation or the innovative use of regulatory technology – in other words RegTech – is a relatively new phenomenon that has emerged in the wake of 2016. Some authors understand RegTech as a logical continuation of FinTech. I see it as a phenomenon with a broader scope.

It is my claim that RegTech is not merely "a new domain within the financial industry"[1] but goes beyond. Rather than being limited to the application to the financial market, RegTech can be used in other regulation-intense industries like the health care sector or in public procurement. Due to its vast field of application and the large number of regulations, RegTech even holds the potential to outpace the velocity and scope of FinTech. Nevertheless, today's most prominent use cases of RegTech have emerged in the financial sector – this is why this article will focus on this matter.

Furthermore, I argue that RegTech is more than simply applying new information technologies like natural language processing (NLP), deep learning or data mining to make regulatory processes more efficient. It does more than just offer an innovative approach for the regulator to more efficiently and effectively oversee regulated institutions. RegTech has the potential to create new business models and eventually also a new area of law – as discussed below.

---

[1] Patrick Schueffel, *The Concise FinTech Compendium* (School of Management Fribourg, Switzland, 2017).

The Flood of Regulation

The pre-crisis *laissez-faire* regulatory approach towards financial institutions in many jurisdictions in Europe and the US was a major factor that led to the Global Financial Crisis (GFC) in 2008. To avoid its repetition and to fight against systemic risk, national regulators around the world have tightened and multiplied the laws and regulations for financial institutes.

Nowadays, financial institutions have to comply with a set of regulations that can be organized into three categories:

1. *Regulatory*: Reporting standards as introduced by Basel III and the Dodd-Frank Act, and regulatory requirements like stress tests performed by the European Central Bank (ECB) or the US Federal Reserve.

2. *KYC*: Know-Your-Customer (KYC), Customer-Due-Diligence (CDD) and Anti-Money Laundering (AML) requirements.

3. *Compliance*: Trading and market conduct rules as enshrined in the Markets in Financial Instruments Directive (MiFID II).

To handle the mass of regulations, especially the real-time reporting and very complex stress tests, the application of new technological means becomes more and more important, and opens up a gateway for RegTech firms.

Prominent RegTech Examples

The trend towards technological facilitation of regulatory processes has led to a new service industry: the RegTech companies. Start-ups have sensed the upcoming potential and entered the market with new products and software to tackle the data flood bashing against the walls of Wall Street and regulators.

A 2016 study of 100 RegTech firms shows that the majority of RegTech companies originates either from the United Kingdom or the United States (around 30% each). At the same time, firms from other financial hubs like Switzerland, Luxembourg or Singapore merely got a small slice of the pie (less than 5% each in 2016).[2]

To have a notion of what RegTech companies do, some successful and exciting RegTech start-ups that applied innovative technologies to comply with new regulatory requirements are introduced briefly:

- *Fintellix* is a RegTech company with more than a decade of regulatory experience, headquartered in New York with offices in the UK, India, Australia, Brazil, UAE and Singapore. The company developed a platform to convert internal data into regulatory reporting formats – which aspires to make regular reporting less time-consuming and more efficient.

- *Suade* was founded in 2014 in London and offers Regulation-as-a-Service (RaaS) in the form of a software platform, which interprets regulatory data, calculates risks and creates reports to put in place the necessary controls and governance.

- *Sybenetix* was founded in 2009 in London, acquired by NASDAQ in July 2017 and won the 2018 US Technology Award. The firm offers a surveillance platform that helps buy-side firms like asset managers to comply with regulatory requirements such as MiFID II. They use behavioral profiling algorithms to detect and flag manipulative behavior such as insider trading, front-running and market manipulation, which saves time and improves workflow efficiencies.

Other exciting, but less prominent RegTech examples outside the UK and US also deserve attention:

- *QumRam* is a Swiss start-up founded in 2011 that tracks all of a company's digital interactions to comply with record-keeping

requirements, fraud detection and customer experience analysis. The Swiss universal bank UBS is one of its recent customers. QumRam has won several awards, including the WealthBriefing Swiss Awards 2017, and was acquired by Dynatrace, a US-based private software intelligence company later that year.

- *Fundsquare* is a Luxembourg company, constituted in 2013 and a subsidiary of the Luxembourg Stock Exchange. It offers secure communication channels between funds and supervisors. The standardized communication line aims to decrease costs and risks for both funds and regulators.

- *Trulioo*, a Canadian start-up was founded in 2011 and is active in the field of KYC/AML. It provides electronic identity verification for businesses using government and private databases. It allows verifying more than 5 billion people using one single application programming interface (API), which helps large multinationals to verify customers across the world.

The above-mentioned success stories are – as all the first-wave RegTech companies – focused on cost and risk reduction. An interesting question is whether RegTech also has the potential to introduce *revenue-increasing solutions* such as new products or business models. Not to compare RegTech with the Industrial Revolution, but as for every technological progress I clearly see the potential of RegTech to create new jobs, business models and eventually also a new set of laws. This change does not necessarily need to happen within the financial services sector but may also – and I argue even more so – emerge in other regulated sectors, such as government procurement where new technologies are not only minimizing costs and time, but are introducing new mechanisms such as real-time and open tendering.

Attractive RegTech Hubs

To better understand which conditions attract RegTech firms, let's have a look at the top global hubs. Most of the RegTech firms are based in London, one of the largest financial centers in the world – and now also being the first jurisdiction that relaxed the regulatory

---

[2] Jan-Maarten Mulder, 100 RegTech Start-ups to Follow, June 2016, https://www.linkedin.com/pulse/100-regtech-startups-follow-jan-maarten-mulder/; Jan-Maarten Mulder, RegTech is Real and 120+ to Prove It, November 2016, https://medium.com/@janmaartenmulder/regtech-is-real-and-120-startups-to-prove-it-6b396d94dd8c.

requirements for innovative firms in the financial services industry. Other large hubs attracting RegTech firms are New York and the Silicon Valley, which is known for its tech companies and active financial investors. Last but not least, Singapore one of the large financial centers in Asia has started to attract RegTech firms and begun to relax their regulations for them.

Having a closer look at these locations, I see three major factors that play an important role attracting innovative firms like RegTech companies:

1. *Available capital* or funding as provided by venture capital firms or banks, i.e. large financial centers.

2. *High-quality education* due to near-by universities or military.

3. *Flexible laws and regulation*, including intellectual property rights, employment laws, tax laws and regulatory safe harbors like sandboxes.

Figure 1 shows an overview of the factors influencing the attractiveness of the top 10 RegTech hubs, based on a preliminary cross-country analysis (not final or exhaustive):

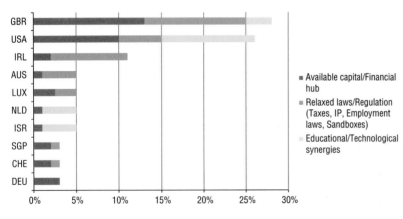

Figure 1: Top 10 RegTech Hubs

The existing host countries for RegTech firms show different combinations of the above-mentioned factors. While some of them are clearly profiting from their accumulation of capital like London, New York, Singapore, Switzerland and Frankfurt, others profit from technological synergies from near-by universities and tech companies as located in the Silicon Valley or Israel, which mainly relies on inventions from its military force. A new and here-discussed category of RegTech hubs has started to relax laws and regulatory requirements for financial institutions. As will be elaborated later, the UK was one of the first countries relaxing regulations for FinTech and other innovative companies. Other countries like the US or Ireland profit from the adoption of more lenient laws, like flexible employment or tax laws.

Concluding from this preliminary analysis, it appears that most jurisdictions have chosen a combination of the three factors, potentially with the goal to diversify risk. The coming years will show, which strategy will make the race and be the most successful.

RegTech for Regulators

The private financial institutions dealing with the increased regulatory burden is only one side of the coin. On the other side are the regulators and financial supervisory authorities that are under pressure to create regulations and monitor the compliance of financial institutions with the newly introduced regulatory requirements. It is no secret that many regulators around the world have reached, or are soon reaching, their limits in terms of capacity and infrastructure to deal with the mass of financial actors they need to oversee.

This means that in the current RegTech development, regulators are invested themselves and cannot merely take a backseat but need to take an active role. The regulators of the twenty-first century are mostly affected by and can potentially make most use of RegTech innovations in the following areas:

- *Data exchange* between regulators and financial institutions through cloud or online platforms.
- *Automated data processing*, especially APIs that create interfaces between different systems.
- *Digital compliance processes* to match KYC data from financial institutions and the regulator.
- Data analytics to understand and steer *macro-prudential financial policy*.

Regulatory Sandboxes for More Innovation

To foster innovation through FinTech and RegTech companies, a handful of jurisdictions have started to introduce regulatory relaxations, so-called regulatory sandboxes. Under these regimes innovative financial service providers can test their services and products in the market without being subject to the otherwise applicable regulatory requirements to financial institutions for a certain amount of time.

As a first-mover UK's Financial Conduct Authority (FCA) has launched the first regulatory sandbox in May 2016. The sandbox allows innovative companies in the financial services industry to test their products in the market during a period of 18 months. So far, the FCA has allowed four cohorts of companies to benefit from the exemption and accepted in total 89 out of 276 applications, which breaks down to an average acceptance rate of 30%.[3] Also, to broaden the reach of the UK sandbox, the FCA has established so-called *FinTech bridges* that allow FinTech firms from Singapore and Australia to participate

in the UK exemption. To apply for the UK sandbox, the FinTech firms need to meet the following eligibility criteria:

- The firm must be a *regulated business* in the UK financial services market.
- The *innovation must be new* or significantly different from what is offered in the marketplace.
- The innovation must *create benefit to customers*, e.g. through higher quality or lower prices.
- There must be a *need to test the offering* in the market, e.g. because a full authorization would be too costly to run a viability test.
- The innovation must be *ready to be tested* in the real market with real customers.
- The firm has measures in place to *mitigate consumer risk*.

Singapore has followed the UK in due course and established its sandbox in November 2016. It follows a very similar approach to the UK but with more rigid eligibility criteria. Most importantly, the sandbox rules ask for clearly defined exit and transition strategies and allow products to be tested only for 6 months on a customer base of maximum 50 people.[4]

Another country at the forefront of regulatory sandboxes is Australia. Since December 2016, the Australian Securities and Investment Commission (ASIC) allows financial start-ups to profit from relaxed regulatory requirements. The conditions for a licensing exemption are:

- For the firm: not more than 100 retail clients, customer exposure not more than $5 million, test no longer than 12 months, and have indemnity insurance and dispute resolution in place.

---

[3] Mekebeb Tesfaye, The FCA's FinTech Sandbox is Already Delivering Value, October 2018, available at https://www.businessinsider. com/fca-fintech-sandbox-delivers-value-2018-10

---

[4] MAS, FinTech Regulatory Sandbox Guidelines, November 2016, available at http://www.mas.gov.sg/~/media/Smart% 20Financial%20Centre/Sandbox/FinTech%20Regulatory%20Sandbox%20Guidelines%2019Feb2018.pdf

- For the products: payment, deposit and investment products not exceeding $10,000, consumer credits and loans not exceeding $25,000, and property and home insurance not exceeding $50,000 insurance value.[5]

While all of the aforementioned examples stem from common-law jurisdictions, similar initiatives have been launched in Continental Europe. One example is the regulatory sandbox created by the Swiss Financial Market Supervisory Authority (FINMA). In spring 2016, FINMA announced its support for the establishment of a sandbox and a 'banking license light' for innovative firms in the financial sector. In contrast to the common-law examples, Switzerland follows a one-size-fits-all model, which is open to all financial players, not only newcomers, gives them an exemption from FINMA's oversight and is not limited in time. The conditions to benefit from the Swiss sandbox are:

- The firm accepts deposits from no more than 20 persons.

- Funds do not exceed CHF 1 million, are settled in 60 days, and 3% are backed by capital.

- The firm informs its customers that it is not subject to FINMA's supervision and deposits are not covered by the deposit protection scheme.[6]

Sandbox Goals and Benefits

The primary and universal goal of a sandbox with relaxed regulatory requirements is to foster *innovation* in the financial services sector and thereby (implicitly) strengthen the attractiveness of the domestic

financial market. This goal also benefits consumers and the industry, most importantly in the form of increased *efficiency*, lower prices, eventually leading to better access to finance, as pointed out by UK's FCA and the MAS Guidelines 2016. The third goal is explicitly endorsed only by the UK and Singapore and encourages FinTech firms to create products and services that mitigate financial risk and identify new *consumer protection safeguards*. Other regulators like the Swiss and Australian supervisory authorities do not explicitly mention this goal.

So far, no large-scale or quantitative studies on the impact of regulatory sandboxes and their potential to create new and safe products have been conducted. What we have is a qualitative report from Deloitte about the UK sandbox from 2018, which is based on firm interviews and has identified the following added value:

- Increased credibility vis-à-vis investors and consumers.

- Possibility to identify and address potential consumer risks early on.

- Increased awareness and knowledge of regulatory requirements among start-ups.[7]

While all of these goals and benefits appear beneficial at first sight, they can often have a negative flip side, which is discussed in the following.

Trade-off: Innovation vs Consumer Protection

A major reason why only a handful of countries have created regulatory sandboxes lies in the antagonism of financial innovation

---

[5] ASIC, Licensing Exemption for FinTech Testing, available at http://download.asic.gov.au/media/4112096/licensing-exemption-for-fintech-testing-infographic.pdf.

[6] FINMA, Sandbox and Settlement Accounts: FINMA Amends Circular, September 2017, available at https:// www.finma.ch/en/news/2017/09/20170901-mm-rs-publikumseinlagen-bei-nichtbanken/; FINMA, FinTech Licence and Sandbox: Adjustments to FINMA Circulars, March 2019, available at https://www.finma.ch/en/news/2019/03/20190315-mm-fintech/.

[7] Deloitte and Innovative Finance, A Journey Through the FCA Regulatory Sandbox: The Benefits, Challenges, and Next Steps, October 2018, available at https://www2.deloitte.com/content/dam/Deloitte/uk/Documents/financial-services/deloitte-uk-fca-regulatory-sandbox-project-innovate-finance-journey.pdf

vs consumer protection. Since the financial crisis, national regulators have introduced new rules and regulations to restrict financial institutions in their activities, mostly for the benefit of consumer protection. Licensing systems, capital requirements, and reporting standards – all of these measures aim to protect clients from risky business.

For instance, in Switzerland the adoption of relaxed regulatory requirements for FinTech companies has taken almost two years for the sandbox exemption (beginning of 2016 until fall 2017), and three years for the relaxed FinTech license, which has entered into force in January 2019. One major reason for this lengthy procedure was the challenge to balance-off the two goals.

There is no use case (yet) teaching us about the most effective safeguards to protect consumers from the negative consequence of failed FinTech companies. I identify three types of safeguards that were put into place for sandboxes and that are more or less effective in protecting consumers:

- Arguably the most effective measure to protect consumers from harmful risky business of FinTech and RegTech firms is to *limit the negative effects* of a failure from the outset. Limiting the money amount of products, the customer base and the testing phase is an effective measure to constrain potential negative impacts of a failure and to avoid the accrual of systemic risk. The Swiss and Australian supervisory authorities have chosen this approach.

- The second most effective measures appear to be the *preventive safeguards*. One example is the disclosure obligation in Switzerland where FinTech firms have to disclosure to their customers that the Swiss regulator does not supervise them. This helps to create awareness among the customers about the potential risks involved. Also, the risk mitigation measures required under the UK and Singapore's regime are intended to have a preventive character. However, up to today it is not clear which measures this might entail. Hence, while preventive measures have the potential to stop crises from happening, often the measures are not concrete enough and are therefore often less effective than strict limitations.

- Finally, there are *ex-post safeguards* with a restorative effect that help compensate consumers for the harm they suffered from a risky business. For example, Switzerland requires FinTech firms to back up 3% of the accepted funds by capital. The higher capital reserves then increase the chances of customers to be paid back in a case of insolvency. A similar effect has the indemnity insurance required for FinTech firms by the Australian regulator. I acknowledge that these measures help restore justice, but they do not prevent the harm from happening, which is a clear disadvantage.

All of the aforementioned jurisdictions have chosen a combination of safeguards. While the ex-ante limitations often go hand in hand with the ex-post safeguards (Switzerland and Australia), the UK and Singapore put stronger emphasis on the outline of risk mitigation measures. Future will show, which approach – ex-ante limitations vs risk mitigation measures – will proof to be more successful in protecting customers.

One last concern relates to the signaling effect of the admitted sandbox firms. Often customers and investors take the acceptance into a sandbox as a quality seal. In my view, this inference is not correct and utterly dangerous. It is highly questionable whether the regulator is the savviest entity to select future innovators. Also, the regulatory exemption of a company is no guarantee for future success. To create awareness about this misperception, the disclosure obligations for Swiss sandbox firms might have a valuable countervailing power against the deceptive signaling effect.

Global Sandboxes: The Way Forward

Up to today, the development of RegTech firms and regulatory sandboxes is still in its infancy and under constant change (see Swiss revisions). As we have seen, each jurisdiction has chosen its own individual approach to deal with fostering innovation through regulation. However, I see some value in coordinating regulations and goals on a global level. Coordination and harmonization not only levels the playing field and eases the competition between hubs, which may eventually prevent a race to the bottom. They may also foster the development of stronger protection safeguards for consumers.

Hence, I see at least three good reasons to tackle regulatory relaxations through sandboxes on a global level. First, financial markets are highly interdependent – as the global financial crisis has taught us – and therefore deserve cross-border regulation. Second, new technologies like cloud applications, distributed ledger technologies (DLT), and other internet-based solutions do not stop at national borders but are cross-border by nature. Third,

this also means that in most cases, customers of FinTech and RegTech firms are scattered across the globe, which in turn asks for more universal rules of consumer protection.

A first step towards a "Global Sandbox" can be the incremental approximation of national rules. While the national regulators shall be given enough freedom to select FinTech firms that fit best into the existing legal and financial setting, the development and harmonization of mitigating measures to protect consumers seems universally beneficial. To achieve such harmonized schemes, cooperation between regulators is a crucial prerequisite.

In this sense: Let's go play in the global sandbox, but make sure we use the right toys!

A Call for Innovation or Disruption?

- Complexity and complication differ in that the former is about inter-connection and the latter about clarity
- Deployment of GRC solutions need to be rapid in order to ensure that their implementation is not made obsolete by a new change

- US$360Bn spent on IT in finance, with the majority going towards maintenance of systems
- Start-up approach of failing fast, is being challenged for RegTech as it is neither a suitable culture for banks nor acceptance to regulators
- RegTech solutions are more open to consortium collaboration as opposed to FinTech solutions which are treated as products

- Banks as data custodians represent both an opportunity in a tech world but a liability in a post-GDPR era
- Customers marketing in financial services can move industry towards universal to individual banking model
- Digital identity not just a consumer expectation but a business opportunity for banks
- PSD2 offers example of regulation driving innovation by opening up competition

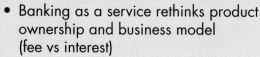

- Banking as a service rethinks product ownership and business model (fee vs interest)
- API strategy should be considered as part of a business transformation not just a technological upgrade

- Post-crisis regulatory interpretation cannot be strategies anymore
- Legal profession to participate in RegTech adoption by increasing their understanding of tech impact on their industry
- Progress still to be made to avoid automatic systems making errors whilst performing regulatory interpretation or enforcements

- KYC not just an onboarding requisite but an ongoing relationship management need
- Client sustainability can be better performed by looking at alternative customer data for a complete picture
- Need to move from a static to dynamic customer profiling

- FinTech and RegTech share founders with previous industry experience but varies in client base with former having B2C possibilities
- Blockchain naturally support consortium but its design needs to be aware of privacy standards as data is stored

Part 4 discusses the extent to which RegTech represents an efficiency gain or instead allows us to re-imagine the approach towards regulation. To do so, we will begin by providing readers with a distinction that needs to be drawn between RegTech solutions and regulatory reforms.

The bulk of current market activity is focused on efficiency gains. While not revolutionary, this state of the market is a reflection of the immediate low hanging fruits that have been created by the inflation of direct compliance costs incurred by financial services institutions. A metric to see this is the fact that out of the US$360 billion spent on the IT industry the clear majority goes into system maintenance, not replacement. Not only this but following the 2008 crisis, banks understand regulatory interpretation and innovation cannot be a strategy any more.

As a result, awareness is growing amongst corporate leaders that compliance obligations are no longer to be solved by throwing people at the problem but instead by leveraging technology that can automate newly implemented processes. Also, market perception is important, especially vis-à-vis regulators. RegTech again is prone to the development of a consortium approach to managing inter-bank risk or developed KYC utilities. RegTech startups will not in the short term be able to instil that 'fail-fast approach' as neither banks' or regulators' culture would allow it.

A noticeable evolution is occurring, especially within the KYC space. Indeed, an otherwise mundane onboarding process is now being re-imagined as a result of customer expectations. The development of technology companies has changed the way people identify themselves to access services. And while consuming a financial product differs from a social media facility, consumers want instant satisfaction of their needs. As a result, the digitization of the KYC process can represent a revolution in the industry.

KYC should no longer be considered only as a pre-requisite for service access but instead a differentiator for client onboarding and ongoing management. With this trend follows the redesign of what constitutes one's identity. If successful, this would move financial institutions from static legal identities (i.e. passport) towards dynamic digital identities (i.e. social media).

Finally, a series of European reforms such as PSD2 but also international initiatives, with banking licenses being issued to tech companies in Asia, is redefining financial services business models. The development of third-party product providers for banking platforms will radically transform the revenue model from one based on interest income to one based on fees. With it, however, comes a new chain of liability in case of misselling or data breaches. This highlights some potential 'known unknowns' of the disruption brought about by the change of regulatory standards.

Governance, Risk, and Compliance: Complex or Complicated?

By Bert Boerman
CEO, Governance.com

Is governance, risk, and compliance (GRC) complex or complicated? The answer is both; however, it should not be. We will get to complex versus complicated later, but it is worth clarifying what we mean by GRC first.

GRC has become a main topic of interest, or perhaps concern, and certainly a massively growing area of spending. The term is often made synonymous with technology, but in reality GRC relates first and foremost to operational matters. Given that the very definition is not uniform, we will start by establishing what each of the letters in this acronym represents:[1]

Governance. The establishment of policies and continuous monitoring of their proper implementation by the members of the governing body of an organization.

Risk management. The identification, analysis, assessment, and control of risks, and the avoidance, minimization, or elimination of unacceptable risks.

Compliance. Certification or confirmation that the doer of an action, or the manufacturer/supplier of a product, meets the requirements of accepted practices, legislation, prescribed rules and regulations, specified standards, or the terms of a contract.

While the common thread is to minimize threats to an organization and its stakeholders, our view is that governance is the umbrella process. It ensures that risk management, compliance, and other relevant checks are under control.

---

[1] www.businessdictionary.com

So, when this chapter refers to GRC, it means governance, risk management, and compliance as business challenges.

Asset Management: A Case Study

GRC is a generic topic, but asset management is one of the sectors most desperately struggling with it. Managing investment funds is not easy; making the right investment decisions is important, but managing and minimizing risks for investors is just as crucial. Unfortunately, the global financial crisis made it abundantly clear that many risks were not under control. As a result, legislators and regulators implemented an enormous number of additional directives, laws, and regulations, aiming to protect investors.

So, do you feel more in control than 10 years ago? Are the risks lower and do the procedures allow you to work more efficiently for clients?

Feedback from the industry tells us that the opposite is true. Financial professionals are less in control now than ever before, and risks continue to grow, not to mention the increased workload due to regulatory oversight duties. This has led to a corporate governance paradox:

- More regulation is introduced.
- More controls are implemented.
- Massive amounts of data and documents are collected.
- Data overload conceals previously undefined risks.
- Unexpected incidents and big losses occur.
- More regulation is introduced.

And this vicious cycle continues. In order to break it, we need to understand what specifically is complex and what is complicated.

Complex: 'Involving Many Different and *Connected* Parts'

Investment funds fit into this definition perfectly. Just think of the many parts of an investment fund: legal entities, accounts, assets, transactions, valuations, investors, share classes, net asset values, and so on. And then the service providers and stakeholders: directors, administrators, lawyers, auditors, valuation agents, regulators, distributors, and investment managers. And not forgetting that each of those areas can be linked to laws, regulations, procedures, checklists, due diligence, controls, committees, and risks.

In short, it is a complex puzzle involving many parts. However, complexity itself is not a problem, as people can usually deal with complexity through automation. To get there, however, we need to understand the problem first and to abstract it into smaller, connected pieces.

If we fail to take this structured approach, the problem becomes complicated.

Complicated: 'Involving Many Different and *Confusing* Parts'

The subtle nuance in definition between complex and complicated is important. The main difference is that a confusing problem cannot be solved. If the problem, and the reasons for it, are not clear, attempting to find a solution will be counterproductive. Unfortunately, that is exactly what is happening in the industry. 'A new regulation? Write a new procedure!' 'But we have one already!' 'Well, just link it to the new one'.

Doing so allows us to demonstrate that we are aware of the regulation and that we have taken action by implementing it into a procedure. However, it is almost certain that the procedure will not be followed. Procedures are no longer written as a clear manual of actions to be executed but as a protection mechanism against claims. A typical procedure may start like this:

> This client onboarding policy is implemented in accordance with the terms set out in procedures 2016-58, 2013-13, and 2011-35, and should be read in conjunction with EU Directive 2015/849, the laws of 17 July 2008 and 27 October 2010 on AML/CTF and local regulations X, Y, and Z.

Hardly something that we can expect our employees to read, let alone understand. Moreover, when the related directives and laws change, how do we ensure that the procedure is updated? Can we be certain that the actions of our staff are always in line with the procedure?

Time for a reset! Since we cannot solve a complicated problem but we can solve a complex one, the logical first step would be to turn the complicated problem into a complex one. Let us explain how.

From Complicated to Complex

Based on our experience in implementing a business and GRC framework in the financial sector, we have defined seven steps:

1. People first, supported by technology.

Data is ultimately produced and consumed by humans. Even if we have the best tools available, most of the qualitative assessments are still made by people. This means that we need to hire the best people available. But what qualifies someone as 'the best'? We often hear that it is all about level of industry knowledge. This is especially true for senior levels like directors, where fund boards are typically composed of executives with many years of experience. However, in these days of data overload, knowledge is only one part. An increasingly important skill is the ability to mine and analyse large volumes of data quickly. This requires the skills of digital natives: a younger generation of employees who do not have the experience but can process data with their eyes closed. The data, of course, needs to be presented most efficiently, which is where technology comes in.

2. Think big: map your territory.

What challenges and regulations are you trying to address? What kind of data are you dealing with? Before thinking of solutions and outputs (reporting), think of the different sources of data. Make a long list of every object you can think of. Think of things like entities, assets, committees, and documents mentioned earlier in this chapter. When the objects are known, what data points do we want to know about each object? For a transaction, we may want to know things like transaction amount, currency, transaction date, settlement date, buyer, seller, and so forth.

The final step here is to define where the data currently resides. Is it created and/or stored in other systems? Core banking system? Administration system? Spreadsheets? When we have finished this step, we have a full map of our universe of data. Don't worry – it will not make any sense yet; that comes later.

3. Connect the dots.

Now comes the time to connect the data. Laws are connected to procedures. Procedures are connected to committees. Committees are connected to clients, and so on. These links give us a full context of information around a task, but also enable us to analyse the impact of a change of one object on the next. If the law changes, we can immediately see which procedures and committees are impacted.

Objects can have hierarchical connections and ad hoc connections. A hierarchy is necessary to have predictable navigation around data. An asset is always connected to an entity or person. A transaction is always connected to an asset. And so on. However, objects may also have ad hoc links. A notary deed gives us information about a transaction (the hierarchical parent object), but it also gives us information about the buyer, the seller, the asset, and service providers involved. With ad hoc links we can create these links on the fly, meaning we can navigate to the data and documents reliably and predictably (hierarchy), but also in a more powerful and flexible way (search and drill down).

4. Start small: build a prototype.

Most big GRC system implementations fail. Some of the reasons for failure are:

- *User adoption.* If a system is too complicated to use or takes users too much time, it will not be adopted, and the project will fail.

- *Implementation time.* If a GRC implementation takes 12–18 months, you should not even start. By the time it has been implemented, the regulation itself will have changed again.

- *Endless customization.* User experience is critical for the adoption of a system. While customization of the data views should be left to each user, customization of the interface itself should be avoided. Focus on simplicity!

- *Dependency on legacy systems and external data sources.* A GRC solution that completely depends on legacy systems will fail. That does not mean that it cannot interface with external sources, but the solution must be able to operate on its own to start.

To avoid these traps, ensure that the project starts small. Identify the top 5–10 items from the list in step 3, and start only with that. Appoint a small pilot group of users. Get it right with these users before moving on to the next items.

5. Move the connections out of sight, and create work flows.

While the connections of step 3 are critical, they should be visible only when you need them. GRC systems like Governance.com can create these links out of sight so that the user can focus on the information required for the task at hand. When we want to see the link, we can, but only then.

The second part of this step is to create work flows. These work flows are automatically activated when the system recognizes a trigger for its activation. Rather than presenting the user with a complicated procedure, a workflow automates all the tasks that a machine can do better than a human, and provides the user with the key information needed to take more complex decisions.

6. Share data and collaborate.

One of the powerful aspects of connecting data is that we can now also connect it to people. This avoids duplication, increases efficiency, and typically gives a much better outcome. Why remind people that a task is overdue when the system can do that for us? If you have a board meeting or an internal committee meeting, make the agenda and all required information available to the participants through the GRC system, and collaborate on the minutes during the meeting itself.

7. Fail early, and then scale fast.

Remember that failure is an opportunity to learn, as long as the failure is small and identified early. Accept that not everybody will be happy immediately and that the output of the system will not instantly deliver on all its promises. By starting small and

soon, and getting feedback from users, we can quickly modify the output before confusion takes over.

When the first positive results are achieved, quickly roll out to a larger audience, and restart the cycle with the pilot group for a new set of data.

Technology

In his best-selling book *Don't Make Me Think*, Steve Krug described how a good software program should let users accomplish their tasks as easily and directly as possible, without confusing them. The challenge, however, is that the process of making the user experience simple is very difficult. Think of things like flexible data structure, easy application updates, on-premise and cloud deployments, and secure record-level access.

The good news is that you do not need to deal with any of that, as long as you don't complicate your life trying to build the technology yourself. Instead, focus on what makes you the best in your business, and let RegTech turn complication into complexity, complexity into simplicity, and simplicity into valuable business intelligence.

Innovation or Disruption: Not Always Black and White

By Sean Hunter
CIO, OakNorth Analytical Intelligence

As a result of their global power and influence, systemically important banks are subject to swathes of regulations, from data privacy to cybersecurity to anti–money laundering (AML) requirements. While regulators are working to protect the financial system and consumers, their regulations can also unintentionally impede the ability of banks and start-ups to spur innovation.

This chapter looks at the differences between innovation and disruption and why disruption can be difficult for highly regulated firms, forcing them to pursue innovation incrementally. Specifically, it discusses challenges with introducing new technologies at institutions with legacy systems and strict information technology (IT) requirements and ways around the clash of cultures between Silicon Valley's ethos of 'move fast and break things' and Wall Street's need for IT compliance.

Successfully merging these two cultures could transform the future of RegTech.

RegTech has the potential to go beyond merely helping firms to automate monotonous compliance functions and reporting. It can empower small, dynamic compliance teams to understand risks in real time, conduct advanced analysis that allows them to further direct technology towards addressing their greatest risks, and make data-driven decisions about both compliance and overall firm management. Much of RegTech's future depends on whether start-ups and incumbents can get it right.

Disruption or Innovation: A Tale of Two Cultures

Global enterprise IT spending was predicted to increase by 2% in 2016 to $2.77 trillion, with banking and securities, insurance, and healthcare, all highly regulated industries, leading the way. Banks alone were predicted to spend more than $360 billion on IT in 2016.[1] For much of Wall Street, annual IT spend is not targeted at introducing new technologies but instead is directed toward keeping old systems functioning.

Recent changes in technology, from cloud computing and large-scale data analysis to machine learning, mean that Wall Street has incredible new opportunities to profit, better serve customers, and provide transparency to regulators. However, many big banks have essential internal data and IT systems dating back to the 1970s. These systems hold important historical data and are often intertwined with other systems, forming a web of core legacy IT that can hinder meaningful technological progress.

Complying with expanding and evolving regulations makes the time and risks required for an IT overhaul for large institutions hard to justify. Increasing capital requirements also mean that outsized IT costs are heavily weighted against tightening profit margins. In this environment, it is easy to see how innovative solutions that might be labelled RegTech or FinTech could be overlooked by major institutions struggling to produce the results that were possible in the past. Paradoxically, these types of IT investments could be key to making sure major banks survive and innovate in a digital world.

RegTech start-ups specifically face the monumental challenge of trying to make compliance more efficient and transparent while

---

[1] Moutusi Sau, Derry Finkeldey, et al., 'Forecast: Enterprise IT Spending by Vertical Industry Market Worldwide, 2013–2019, 3Q15 Update', Gartner, 14 October 2015.

often functioning as vendors to large institutions, making them subject to the same regulations as their big bank customers. This can be a difficult burden for start-ups that lack the expertise or workforce needed to navigate these rules. The result is that RegTech companies can sometimes be inhibited by the very regulations they are working to address, uphold, or enhance.

Meanwhile, over in Silicon Valley, the absence of regulation in fields including new automotive technologies, 'sharing economy' apps, online content, digital advertising, wearable devices, and more means that start-ups have the opportunity to introduce new products, iterate quickly, and deal with emerging regulations later, even helping to shape those regulations to meet their needs.

Those who have spent enough time in Silicon Valley have likely heard the engineering crowd talk about 'disruption', the prize-winning cow of the innovation farm. The author of *The Innovator's Dilemma*, Professor Clayton Christensen,[2] categorises disruption as either serving an entirely new market or producing a simpler or more convenient alternative to an existing product so that it leads to the fall of the incumbent product.[3] Disruptive innovation can destroy old industries. In a non-syllogistic fashion, all disruption is innovation, but not all innovation is disruption. Non-disruptive innovation is incremental, taking an existing product and iterating and improving upon it over time.

Given the immense challenges that large financial institutions face, they are often capable of incremental innovation in the worlds of FinTech and RegTech, but not well positioned for disruption. They may come up with disruptive ideas, but in many cases pursuing

---

[2] Biographical details are available here: http://www.forbes.com/forbes/2011/0314/features-clayton-christensen-health-care-cancer-survivor.html

[3] Clayton Christensen, *The Innovator's Dilemma: When New Technologies Cause Great Firms to Fail* (Boston: Harvard Business Review Press, 1997).

such ideas initially appears uneconomic due to the competing pressures from regulators and shareholders. The trouble with that position is that it puts financial institutions at risk of eventual extinction by a more nimble actor, although, as previously stated, in RegTech even more nimble actors feel the weight of regulations when trying to bring disruptive ideas to market.

These related but ultimately separate concerns may be overcome by unlikely unions (coinvestments, incubation firms, joint ventures, or other partnerships). Such unions between financial institutions, with their compliance machines, and technology companies, with their engineering talent pools and agile development methods, can give Wall Street and Silicon Valley the missing ingredients for RegTech success.

Keys to Success for FinTech Partnerships

Wall Street and Silicon Valley can go a long way to bridge their cultural divides and work together in a cohesive and profitable way by keeping their differences in mind. Here are some important lessons from industry experiences that banks and start-ups alike can learn from.

Invest All the Way in Partnerships

Innovative partnerships require more than just money. No amount of money paid to a technology company will allow it to solve some of the regulatory challenges in today's financial system. To truly drive disruptive solutions, technology companies require access to subject matter experts, data, sufficient computing resources, and space to experiment.

For most large institutions this is a massive investment and requires some shift in company culture and practices. It may sometimes be difficult to balance their needs as a client with their role in fostering the partnership. This typically cannot be achieved without direct leadership and personal investment from the chief executive and the board.

One example of an innovative FinTech partnership is the collaboration between JPMorgan Chase & Company and alternative lender OnDeck Capital. CEO Jamie Dimon publicly announced and backed the initiative. He told shareholders 'Silicon Valley is coming', saying:

> There are hundreds of start-ups with a lot of brains and money working on various alternatives to traditional banking. The ones you read about most are in the lending business . . . they are very good at reducing the 'pain points' in that they can make loans in minutes, which might take banks weeks. We are going to work hard to make our services as seamless and competitive as theirs. And we also are completely comfortable with partnering where it makes sense.[4]

Incumbent banks have a great deal of leverage in pursuing partnerships with tech companies, from troves of data to regulatory know-how. Where they recognize clear threats and technological deficiencies, CEOs should be prepared to pursue partnerships rather than potentially waste resources trying to develop in-house solutions to compete.

Be Prepared to Take Risks

Investing all the way in a partnership also means accepting the possibility of failure. Some risk taking by bank leadership must be protected and encouraged at the board level. As Christensen writes, 'Successful companies want their resources to be focused on activities that address customers' needs, that promise higher profits, that are technologically feasible, and that help them play in

substantial markets'.[5] It is this very reasonable mentality that can keep major companies from taking the necessary risks to invest in potentially disruptive products. CEOs must be given some leeway to make risky technology investments.

For large institutions, this is perhaps the most difficult challenge and the crux of the problem that Christensen describes in *The Innovator's Dilemma*.

Not All Rules Are Made to Be Broken

Start-ups and IT engineering teams often have mentalities of fail, but fail fast; break things; or worry about rules later. Large financial institutions are adverse to some of these cultural principles and must maintain some adversity due to their systemic importance to the economy. This means that start-ups must be willing to compromise when delivering IT to large institutions. Tech companies looking to work with big institutions must rigorously test their technologies in sandboxes and push institutions towards new technologies while still playing by their rules.

Financial institutions face reputational and financial damage when their rules and regulations are not abided by. Start-ups should recognize that they have less room for trial and error when playing in highly regulated industries.

One of the most canonical examples of a start-up's failure to play by the rules is Zenefits. The disruptive company provided thousands of other companies with free human resources (HR) software, automating everything from health insurance to payroll. Zenefits made money from brokerage deals when companies bought insurance through the software. The company's incredible growth and valuation placed it well in the coveted Silicon Valley unicorn category, but its team of software engineers failed to keep

---

[4] Jamie Dimon, 'JPMorgan Chase & Co. Annual Report 2014' (JPMorgan Chase & Co., 8 April 2015).

---

[5] Christensen, *Innovator's Dilemma*.

up with the appropriate insurance sales training and licensing laws, ultimately resulting in high-profile resignations and layoffs.

Start-ups can realize tremendous benefits by learning from the compliance teams at big institutions. While rigorous compliance practices can slow growth, they keep companies from having to clean up major messes at a later date.

Openness Creates Lasting Value

Many start-ups must make a choice to develop open or closed systems. It can be tempting for start-ups that believe they have stumbled across a highly successful or disruptive solution to build closed systems to protect and grow their business. There is little room for this type of thinking in RegTech.

The potential network effects of regulatory technology are much more powerful than artificial monopolies built on proprietary technology: closed systems help no one and can ultimately threaten start-ups themselves. Start-ups should trust that their ability to execute is enough of an advantage, and work primarily to capture market share by creating value, rather than to entrench their position by locking customers into a closed system – the former will prove to be a much more sustainable competitive advantage.

Closed systems that don't play well with existing infrastructure are doomed to eventually fail. They will be difficult to adjust when regulatory requirements shift, which is inevitable, and they do not easily plug in and play with the legacy systems in place in most large institutions.

Partnerships as a Way Forward

The law firm Mayer Brown surveyed 120 senior industry leaders in the United Kingdom, 50 in FinTech firms and 70 in financial services. The survey concluded that partnerships between financial services and FinTech firms are on the rise; they are resulting in cost savings with incumbents saving time and money on new technologies, and a majority of these partnerships are resulting in increased revenue.[6] It is likely we will only continue to see increased partnerships among old firms and new players.

Partnerships between financial institutions and tech companies will not always be easy to navigate, but they may very well be one of the best recipes for innovation and one of the best chances for disruption. Furthermore, financial institutions and start-ups alike should not be making a choice between incremental innovation and disruption. In a rapidly changing world, they should be attempting to survive, but they also need to recognize the difference in these types of innovation and take different approaches based on what they are trying to achieve.

Setting up an in-house innovation lab at a bank is not going to be as powerful or as likely to develop effective or disruptive technology as choosing a specific problem to address and establishing a strong partnership. These partnerships will not all be successful, and that will partially depend on their ability to follow the lessons outlined here. Still, every company concerned with the RegTech space should be asking whether a potential partnership is right for it.

---

[6] Mayer Brown, 'The ABC of Fintech: Acquisitions, Brexit, and Collaboration' (November 2016).

How to Use Digital Marketing Data in Regulated Industries

By Dr Evelyn Thar
CEO, Amazee Metrics

Truly understanding your customer is vital in today's digital economy, particularly for a banking industry that lost trust during the financial crisis of 2008. This is not only in the effort to regain customers' trust but to be able to offer enhanced and targeted services, both of which can be achieved with a greater knowledge of the customers, their preferences, and their habits. Think about the success new digital companies like Amazon and Airbnb have had with their targeted customer approaches. Or the detailed information about potential voters that the Trump campaign used to win the US election.

The key to these new digital marketing approaches is the combination of personal and big data with targeted marketing interventions. For the financial industry, nominal personal data comes from companies' own data sources. Similarly, big data is usually available both from their own data sources or from industry-level research. This data needs to be enhanced with sustainable and appropriate behavioural data to gain valuable customer insights.

How do you start with collecting this behavioural data? Online user behaviour and social media networks fill this gap in collecting personal data about prospects and clients.

However, if we look at regulations in the finance industry we quickly see there are two regulatory stumbling blocks that would make collecting personal data out of the question. First, there are the regulations imposed specifically on financial institutions like the second Markets in Financial Instruments Directive (MiFID II) for the European Union, the US Department of Labor's new Fiduciary Rule, or the Federal Financial Services Act (FFSA/FIDLEG) in Switzerland. Second, there are more general privacy

protection issues that are currently a major point for governments across the world. The EU's strict new General Data Protection Regulation (GDPR) and coming amendments to Switzerland's Federal Act on Data Protection (FADP) will change the landscape for data usage globally.

This chapter proposes a combination of approaches to achieve this goal while remaining compliant with the regulations. The approach uses a mix of data collection methods, user consent, digital marketing campaigns, and digital services. To meaningfully understand the customer is possible for regulated industries by combining smart digital marketing strategies that adhere to compliance restrictions and clever marketing automation services.

To show how to handle digital marketing data, the chapter focuses on data in the finance industry using Swiss law.

First-, Second-, and Third-Party Data

First-party data is data collected by the company itself via different online marketing channels such as landing pages, mobile applications, or mobile websites. Second-party data is collected

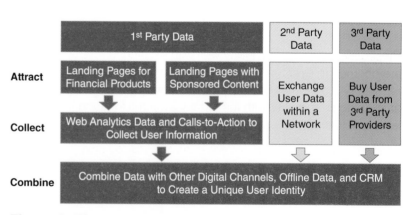

Figure 1: Three possible ways to collect online customer data to create user identities

through partners who are part of a network. An example of such a network would be a group of online retail companies that exchange customer data with each other.

The big advantage of this approach is that the online shop already knows the preferences of a new customer when this customer visits the online shop for the first time.

This means that the online shop can adapt its website and offering to the new user's preferences. The online shop already knows if this new user is a man or a woman as well as the user's purchase history on the other online shops in the network. If the user previously shopped mainly for women's shoes and especially for high heels, the new online shop can present its new collection of high heels directly on the start page. The user can benefit from a smooth shopping experienced adapted to her needs.

Now imagine what you can profit from if you buy user data from third parties. This can be user data from website services using third-party cookies to gain insights about user online behaviour. This could also be Facebook data, including personality profiles created based on the Facebook user's 'likes'.

The rest of the chapter focuses on first-party data, as second-party data and especially third-party data are complicated, and compliance with the FFSA/FIDLEG can be challenging. This is exactly why in regulated industries you have to be more creative with your online marketing strategies.

Attract: Search Engine Marketing

Search engine marketing is a great way to gain online visibility. Search engine marketing is made up of two main activities – search engine optimization and search engine advertising. Search engine optimization is the process of adjusting a website to ensure it appears as high in the nonpaid (organic) search results as possible. Search engine advertising is the

process of creating, optimizing, and running paid advertising alongside search engine results.

With search engine optimization, the website has to be well optimized both technically as well as from a content perspective. The landing page is key in this process to gain a high organic ranking.

It is best practice to focus on only one topic per landing page. This ensures that the message of the page has the best impact on search engine rankings. Make sure that the relevant page meta tags are filled in correctly and that the page itself contains enough written content about the topic. Preparing a list of keywords helps with this. These keywords should reflect the searches you want the page to rank for. All of this work assists in improving the landing page's ranking on the appropriate search terms.

A good quality landing page is also important for search engine advertising. The landing page content should be directly connected to the ad content and provide what is promised in the ad. This also applies to display and banner ads in display networks outside of search results.

As proposed in the chart, the landing pages do not need to be about financial products only. As we see a lot of sponsoring activity in the financial industry, this brings opportunities in digital marketing. Imagine a landing page where you can win tickets to the sponsored events or a sweepstakes competition entry directly on the landing page of the sponsored event. Adding questions about users' financial interests or know-how allows you to aggregate the user data with important information that can be used in the third step of our chart: combine user data.

Please be aware that search engine crawlers need to see content on your landing page – which will not be possible if a disclaimer is the first thing the user sees when entering the page. A common finance industry disclaimer asks the user to identify either as a professional or a private investor. This barrier prevents search engines crawlers from crawling the page, making such a landing page unusable for search engine optimization.

Collect: Calls to Action and Web Analytics Data

Once you have attracted users to your landing page, a prominently positioned call to action is crucial to the digital marketing data journey. For example, when presenting a landing page with general information about a product, the call-to-action button could lead to more detailed product information while first presenting the disclaimer regarding the distinction between private and professional investors. With this strategy, the landing page is usable for search engine optimization and compliant with current regulations.

As the call to action should follow a coherent conversion goal strategy, its appearance should not be underestimated. Regular and structured conversion optimization tasks help to find the best-performing position and design of the call to action, be it a button, form, or any other web page element.

Whether or not the user clicks on the call to action, there is still the possibility to gain valuable user insights by tracking the user's behaviour with a web analytics tool. If the user behaviour is recorded and stored with user IDs, the data can be used later to aggregate client data if the user decides to become a client.

General data privacy regulations apply here, from the new General Data Protection Regulation (GDPR) for Europe and in future from matching amendments to the Swiss law. They require explicit and fully informed opt-in consent to the collection and usage of user data. In addition and alongside other requirements, the data must be collected, stored, and processed in an EU country or a country with equivalent protections. As the GDPR applies to all companies doing business with citizens in the European Union, the GDPR also affects Swiss companies serving EU customers.

Combine: User Identity and Marketing Automation

In the last step of our data journey, the collected user data has to be combined with data collected in other channels. This creates a unique user identity.

Online data can be combined with offline data. If we think about the sponsored events mentioned earlier, you can use these events to collect client or potential client data that can be combined with a client's online user data to produce a more complete view of the client. This is the end goal: to really know your clients. This means to be able to combine all their data – online, offline, and the customer relationship management (CRM) data – in one user data repository. This provides the user with the possibility to choose the customer care touch points they prefer. With this 360° view of clients, their user experience can be enhanced with information available in all channels.

A highly effective use for this user identity is marketing automation. This process allows you to put the right message in front of the right person at the right time and on the right channel. It allows you to automatically send the client your marketing messages via email, text message, app notifications, or digital advertising, or even personalize your website content based on the client's data and actions.

As an example, if you collect data at a sponsored event about someone who is an existing client, you could send the person an email designed to cross-sell. However, if the data collected was for a potential client, then an email with a more appropriate message could be sent. These messages could be customized based on the person's location, language, or other variables. Additionally, if no action is taken on these emails, they could be automatically followed up with another email, a mobile message, or digital advertising depending on which channel makes the most sense for that client.

As the message you are putting in front of the client is specifically tailored to that person, marketing automation greatly increases the message's impact on potential new clients as well as the effectiveness of cross- and up-selling to existing clients.

The restrictions put in place by regulations are the same for marketing automation tools as those already mentioned for web analytics tools. This means that your users must give explicit consent for you to collect their data and to use it in a marketing automation program. The major difference here is that it is much more difficult to find a sophisticated marketing automation tool that stores the data within the European Union. The marketing automation industry is evolving out of web analytics tools on the one hand and email campaigning tools on the other, and there are not so many tools that combine the strengths of both these areas yet. In addition, the big players are mostly based in the United States. Nevertheless, there are tools that provide comprehensive functionalities and are compliant with GDPR and Swiss law. We can also expect more of the big players in the market to provide solutions to the data protection restrictions in the European Union and Switzerland in the future.

Conclusion

As shown in this chapter, it is possible to use data in regulated industries to create digital marketing strategies that are both effective and compliant.

Based on holistic marketing strategies that include the user journey from first contact to cross- and up-selling existing clients, it is possible not only to collect user data but also to use this data to improve client services, enhance the user experience, and increase sales.

The combination of digital marketing know-how with an understanding of the regulations is crucial to creating a successful digital marketing strategy.

Invention Versus Reinvention

By Natasha Kyprianides

Head of Omni-channel and Customer Experience, Hellenic Bank[1]

Innovation within financial services by FinTechs seems to have brought about only a user experience breakthrough as yet, rather than a true industry disruption. Banks need to address commoditization through business model innovation, rather than maintaining a focus on tweaking existing technology and products to perfection. Let's take Uber as a suitable example of a single company that has managed to disrupt an entire industry. The method rests on one principle: the application programming interface (API) economy.

APIs act as the messengers between systems to provide seamless, real-time communication amongst different applications. Furthermore, they allow companies to effortlessly and securely connect their services to build a better customer experience.

This is how Uber has managed to overlay its taxi booking software on Google maps. Making Uber's services possible requires a lot of highly complex components to be arranged and integrated into an app. It would necessitate a great investment of time and budget to develop each of them from scratch. Specialized players can provide the functions of every one of these components and make them available to other companies via APIs.

Now, how can this correlate to banking? By choosing to take full advantage of the possibilities that the second Payment Services Directive (PSD2) opens up, banks will be able to effortlessly deliver new products and services to customers while boosting revenues by adopting one or a combination of all three main open API strategies:

- Bank as a service
- Bank as a marketplace
- Bank as a facilitator

---

[1] Correct at time of submission, April 2017.

There are many great resources available that provide insights and explain the concept of the API economy from every angle. This chapter seeks to embody an applied experience at an incumbent bank and consolidates actionable specifics for implementing open banking as an early adopter.

What Is Open Banking?

Open banking is an emerging trend in financial services. It is based on using open APIs to allow third-party developers to build applications and services around financial institutions (FIs). It also facilitates increased financial transparency options for account holders while helping FIs to innovate and create new revenue.

The European Union appears to have identified open banking as one possible solution to an area of sluggish innovation and market development that seems to be holding back the competitiveness of its trading bloc. PSD2 aims to improve innovation, reinforce consumer protection, and advance the security of internet payments and account access within the European Union. Essentially, this type of regulatory intervention will compel banks to use an API layer to act as the entry point to their underlying technology, products, and services.

In short, open banking aspires to create more competition in the financial market, putting an end to customers paying high prices for substandard services. All the benefits of open banking rely on consumers and small and medium-size enterprises (SMEs) knowing how to make the best use of the services. The full capabilities and possibilities of open banking are not entirely known. However, the opportunities for innovation and, ultimately, improved services for consumers seem countless.

Building a Bank Through Partnerships

An API strategy and API-first approach can significantly accelerate digital transformations and will help banks become more agile to meet regulation requirements, achieve cost efficiencies, and overall harness innovation by not trying to reinvent things but to partner for everything.

The primary change is the acknowledgement that development does not all need to originate internally and that some of the best ideas can come from outside the FI. In fact, the API can be a key enabler to ensure frictionless partner integration and facilitate innovation by allowing third parties to build entirely new apps that can be combined with the bank's products, services, data, and processes. This means that the bank will be able to expand its customer-facing digital touch points and have them built faster and at no cost while also having the opportunity to monetize them!

Banks and FIs that will lead as disruptors are those that will recognize they cannot do it all, but instead identify the areas in technology reform where they do have an edge and partner with someone to do the rest. You do not go to the banking sector for technological excellence. Rethinking what a bank should look like means that you should also be reimagining how it should work.

Platform Banking Is How It Starts

This particular business model has been referred to using several terms such as banking as a service (BaaS) and banking as a platform (BaaP). The FI opens its APIs to anyone who is interested, including other FinTechs, potential competitors such as other banks, and third-party developers, so that they can utilize the data to build their own products to be accessed via a platform. The BaaS platform enables nonbanks to quickly deploy financial products without having to deal with banking regulation and setup requirements.

In essence, the FI reinvents its business model to change the competitive dynamics of the industry to its favour. Platform banking is similar to the Amazon model, whereby a new channel to the customer has become available through technology by eliminating

the traditional retail distribution channel and developing direct relationships with suppliers. This gives customers a greater opportunity to find a solution that best matches their specific needs.

Furthermore, corporate customers of the FI are able to do their banking directly through their enterprise resource planning (ERP) systems. Similarly, ERP vendors can plug in their products to the API platform, drive more customers into the FI, and potentially agree on a revenue-sharing model.

The main characteristics of the core model are:

- The FI has a banking license and manages the underlying technology signified by the core back-end systems.
- The bank's role ranges from just being a current account provider to being a supplier of a full suite of products and services.
- The bank creates a new channel through a platform and opens its API up to other FinTechs and third-party developers so that they can use their data to build their own products on top of this layer.
- Prototypes can be built in the sandbox by anyone after they register as developers on the platform.
- Appropriate governance is activated so that third-party providers can be evaluated for basic criteria and be approved to plug in their products to the live APIs of the platform.
- The bank does not curate these third-party services.

Marketplace Banking Is How It Develops

The platform-banking model can be further evolved so that customers of the 'plug-and-play' bank can benefit from a wider supply of bespoke products, services, and experiences.

The marketplace model primarily focuses on delivering better digital experiences by the FI through partnerships with third parties that will undergo a quality filter. The scope is to specify what is required to be built in order to accelerate meeting strategically prioritized customer needs and maintain a consistently superior product and branding. This method involves a high level of curation across what is offered, as the aim is to integrate the third-party services with the core system and execute the digital strategy.

There is, of course, a hybrid approach to this model. A bank can offer these third-party products or services attached to its core through an exclusive app store to give customers more choice (app store banking). This makes the FI more agile to bring new products to market more quickly and be accessible in other parts of Europe, expanding the organization's geographic footprint.

This principle is comparable to the concept of a smartphone device and its open mobile operating system that acts as an enabler for third parties to build apps and become part of this ecosystem for mutual benefit.

Co-ownership of Products and Customers

Regarding ownership of the product and the end customer, various strategic arrangements can be considered with third-party partners:

- The white-label agreement whereby the FI owns the product created and licenses the digital experience to other third parties (banks, FinTechs, product vendors, or any freelance developers) so that they can utilize them as accelerators in their deployment.

- The integration type where the third-party provider has built a product specifically for the FI's marketplace store, and therefore the exclusive customer of the bank will need to be onboarded to the partner service and agree to its terms.

- The most complex case is where a FinTech start-up or other bank with existing customers and the platform bank with its own customers will integrate services and digital experiences. In this type of scenario, customers will need to provide their consent to connect financial data to the third party and become customers of both institutions; and when a cross-border alliance is in place, they will need to be onboarded according to the corresponding regulator's know your customer (KYC) directives.

The Execution Model Is Fundamental to Succeed

To maximize the odds of success, it is essential that a PSD2-compliant API management platform vendor be selected, aiming to deliver at a fraction of the cost and time it would normally take for the FI to do it on its own.

A major challenge is to navigate through risk, compliance, and information security teams and get to the finish line faster. It is important to become an early adopter so as to start building digital experiences through partnerships before the competition. This is how you would turn open banking into a true commercial opportunity in the API economy.

API Monetization and Getting the Business Model Right

Giving away API access for free may drive brand loyalty and allow the API provider to uncover new revenue streams, but may also prove unsustainable over time. If executed properly, free API access (freemium) may act as a stepping-stone for other business models. Let's explore some of the billing prospects:

- *Freemium* is a model whereby developers are offered basic API capabilities for free and charged more for a more premium suite.

- *Revenue sharing* is where API consumers are paid for the incremental business they trigger for the API provider. This is an important model for a growth strategy to achieve cheaper customer acquisition and to increase revenue streams by cross-selling products through partners.

- *Data exchange* is a two-way model whereby the API provider receives data every time third parties use the API. This can encourage collaboration between banks that wish to offer account information aggregators.

- *Fee-based* model is the traditional case where the API provider charges service and transaction fees based on usage. Examples of this can be for service setup fees, service-level agreements (SLAs) for 24/7 support, and various fee tiers by transaction type and by volume of transactions. Subscription fees would also fall into this category and can be charged on a recurring basis at a preset frequency.

- *Charge by call* is a model where third parties pay each time a service offered through an API is called. An example is to initially offer free of charge up-to-the-minute balances and real-time payment activity to customers banking through their ERP systems so as to demonstrate the value. This can then transition into charging for API calls split into various price bands.

- *Balance sheet* is an important strategic resource, given that many FinTechs are seeking bank partners to provide core financial infrastructure for new products and services. A bank can benefit by increasing assets under management and providing deposits for capital requirements, as well as having the potential for additional interest margins if credit is involved.

Conclusion

An API strategy should be consolidated into the wider business strategy, with some initial business models identified as the first line of action. Open banking can help banks nimbly execute their digital strategy. A banking model that works more like an app store will create new revenue streams, will enable access to new customers, and can signal a whole new chapter for banking. A true partnership between banks and FinTechs through open APIs will bring novel products and services to the market and make an impact on the way we live. The future of banking is ecosystem-based.

Making Regulation Machine Readable

By Ralf Huber
Co-Founder, APIAX

For decades, lawyers such as myself have been mastering the art of interpreting regulation for financial services, but in a rapidly digitizing world, regulatory interpretation must also become binary. Moreover, a new wave of new RegTech solutions is just around the corner.

Dealing with regulations has sometimes felt like being caught in the treadmill: regulatory implementation project after regulatory implementation project, numerous unclarified case-by-case requests in between, more and more unhappy business stakeholders and clients – and no comprehensive solution in sight. For almost a decade, the industry has been trapped in a regulatory crisis.

While the problem statements around managing regulation remain complex, I am convinced that the following three courses of action would massively lower the pain of the financial industry:

1. Financial institutions should give up today's individual approach to regulations and start an *industry-wide collaboration*.

2. The mindsets of lawyers working for both regulators and the industry itself must shift towards a more *machine-readable and standardized interpretation of regulations*.

3. Instead of further building up legal and compliance teams to *manage regulations by hand*, the financial services industry should invest in more efficient processes – such as having a 'digital compliance officer'.

Invest in Industry Standards, Instead of Individual Approaches

When it comes to financial markets regulations, many countries, especially in Europe, have applied a principles-based approach whereby regulators govern more by principles compared to the very detailed rule books used in countries with a rule-based approach. While from a political angle this can be seen as a result of liberal and business-friendly societies, this approach was also strongly backed by financial institutions, providing them with the necessary freedom for their global growth strategies.

In this context, it made sense to believe that financial institutions could strategically play with their own interpretation of laws and regulations and whereby this interpretation was seen as a differentiator in an overall business strategy. At least for global players in the financial industry, however, this approach is outdated.

The sheer mass of regulations relevant when offering financial services in multiple countries combined with the complexity of global organizations makes managing regulatory change extremely difficult and resource intensive. Nowadays, regulation impacts a high number of very detailed processes within a financial institution. Managing these changes in a way that would allow senior management to evaluate their strategic impact is extremely complex and therefore often not happening. This leaves the interpretation of regulatory details to the vast groups of legal and compliance experts, who apply them on a case-by-case basis, which is not a strategic approach to implementing specific requirements. And while enforcement actions by regulators and justice departments have been intensified in recent years, the decreased risk appetite of financial institutions on both management and operations levels leads to a generally conservative interpretation of laws and regulations.

Therefore, the pretended freedom of a principles-based regulatory regime is, in fact, an inefficient concept where the responsibility for details is being pushed from the regulator to every single financial institution.

Regulatory implementation is not a strategic element or even a differentiation factor from competitors anymore and should therefore be seen as a *commodity* to conduct business. Moreover, as with every commodity, firms should start to become more efficient by standardization and cost saving.

Shift Lawyers' Mindsets Towards Digital

Since the early days of globalization, every international company expanding into new markets has faced the problem of unknown regulatory ground. However, in times of internet-based business models that are global by default, a physical, legal expert network in numerous countries is in opposition to the ambitious growth plans of the digital disruptors.

But why has there been so little effort for regulatory standardization in the past decades?

Richard Susskind, a specialist in legal technology since the early 1980s, has a very direct answer to this question: 'First, the professions do not themselves generally want to change, and so resist reform or revolution. Second, until now there has been no credible alternative to what they have on offer, no competing set-up to the status quo.'[1]

Today's lawyers have been trained in country-specific manual interpretational techniques still applied in legal and compliance offices around the world. Also, there is a clear lack of interdisciplinary focus, especially in training programs of today's law schools.

These might be reasons why lawyers have made too little effort in both science and politics to overcome today's country-specific regulatory regimes by providing more standardized regimes for highly regulated industries such as the financial, pharmaceutical, or food industries.

---

[1] Richard Susskind and Daniel Susskind, *The Future of the Professions* (Oxford, UK: Oxford University Press, 2015), 80.

RegTech and LegalTech solutions infuse the legal industry with the latest technologies and push them into a digital future that is inevitable. More and more, lawyers are tasked with becoming an integral part of information technology (IT)-supported processes, e.g. by using negotiation tools or contract analysis software.

Having the required IT end-user skills is one obvious requirement for future lawyers, similar to the emergence of Microsoft Office applications more than two decades ago. Today's law schools must go one step further in order to bring law and computer science closer together, e.g. by offering their students interdisciplinary lectures. I am convinced that only *lawyers with an understanding of IT concepts* and who are not scared of reading a line of code will be able to actively shape the future of their profession.

In addition, law schools should foster with the support of finance faculties the *establishment of global legal taxonomies* relevant to the financial services industry. Taxonomies, established with digital applications in mind, could support in-house lawyers in applying regulation to specific processes in a corporation. Today, most financial institutions individually deal with the interpretation and application of laws to their processes, services, and product landscape. By using global legal taxonomies, this interpretation could be massively simplified.

Managing Regulations Digitally, Instead of by Hand

Recently we have seen robo-advisers transforming traditionally human-centric investment advisory activities into a fully digital client experience. Much progress has been made to automate these processes, also by traditional financial institutions, but offering digital services internationally remains a challenge.

Not without reason, only four of the most popular robo-advisory solutions in Europe offer their services outside of their home country. Moreover, three of these four providers have an offering in only two or three countries.[2] This is a huge discrepancy if compared to today's largest private banks servicing clients in 50+ countries. One of the reasons why providers of digital solutions miss out on global markets and revenue potential is the variety and complexity of the different regulatory regimes in each country.

Especially in the areas of providing investment advisory services or distribution of financial instruments, regulatory authorities have raised the regulatory burden in past years. Detailed client suitability checks, cost transparency on financial services and products, or advisory documentation are just some examples of new regulatory requirements in this area.

At the same time, regulators often require more involvement of independent control functions, typically the compliance department. The typical reaction of financial institutions to such requests from regulators is the increase in human power in legal and compliance teams.

While increasing employees can make sense as a quick-fix solution, this approach can work only in a traditional, human-centric financial institution, where client advisers act as intermediaries and interpreters between law and client. In the case of robo-advisers or digital advisory processes, where clients request financial services with the click of a button, there is no room for individual regulatory interpretation.

The transformation of new regulatory requirements into digital rules that can be integrated into sustainable business processes is therefore not only a matter of increased efficiency but a key prerequisite for any financial institution wanting to enter the digital age.

In addition, by replacing generic prose-type policies and manuals with much more efficient digital solutions, financial institutions can enable employees to focus more on their core competencies such as advising clients or managing portfolios.

To be able to offer scalable solutions across multiple markets, regulatory advice as provided by legal and compliance experts today must also be digitized. Only an automated solution, a 'digital compliance officer', is the key to enabling a digital service offering in the financial industry.

How to Digitize Regulations?

The industry's silo-type approach to dealing with regulations, the mindset of lawyers, and the lack of focus on digital solutions in legal and compliance departments are three key elements of today's regulatory crisis in the industry. RegTech and LegalTech companies are emerging around the globe, applying tech-enabled solutions to these industry problems.

But How Can RegTech Platforms Digitize Regulation?

Even in a tech-focused environment, everything begins with having a deep understanding of the business problem: What services is the client actually requesting from the financial institution, and how are these services typically provided?

While being an obvious question, also, in this case, the devil is in the details: Is a financial institution servicing different client types in a country? Have country-specific client-type definitions been clarified, and are clients categorized accordingly? Are clients being serviced also outside of a financial institution's home country, and, if yes, are client advisers meeting clients abroad and in which context? Do the client advisers act in a non-licensed environment, or can they rely on a licensing exemption when offering services? Can the client adviser rely on a ready-to-sell product offering where all relevant financial-instrument-related parameters such

[2] http://robo-advisors.eu (accessed 16 April 2019).

as registration, inducements, structure, and so forth in a specific client context have been taken into account?

These questions and many more are relevant to ensure the offering of a financial institution complies with the financial markets regulation of a specific country. Therefore, the respective regulatory parameters related to the financial institution, the client or prospect, and the service or product must be taken into account to establish a rule set for a specific activity. As a matter of fact, a digital service offering of a financial institution requires a complete list of parameters for being able to provide yes/no answers for every specific client situation.

Clustering these regulatory parameters country by country and transforming them into digital rule sets is not an easy task. Building an efficient, tech-enabled approach allows sourcing of these rules as well as keeping them updated.

At the same time, taking advantage of already established taxonomies helps to describe these regulatory-relevant parameters. By doing that, one can get closer step by step to establishing an overarching and globally applicable legal taxonomy for the financial industry.

As with every new approach being applied to existing standards, also in case of digitizing regulations, new questions are coming up.

First, many regulators still today require policies or manuals as the governing basis for financial institutions on a specific subject, especially in the legal and compliance space. Therefore, when replacing manual guidance books or policies with digital platforms for managing regulatory requirements, being able to visualize and export digital rules relevant for a financial institution (e.g. for an audit review) is a must.

Second, knowing exactly which version of a regulatory rule is in force at what point of time is key. While respective requirements might be better understood when dealing with manuals or policies, requirements for maintaining an audit trail of a digital rule can become more complex. For example, strict data immutability must be ensured together with stringent access rights management for users.

However, while these two features require special care in the implementation of a RegTech or LegalTech solution, with today's technologies none of them will become a showstopper.

At this very moment, a number of RegTech companies worldwide are already working on the resurrection of the 'digital compliance officer' by making regulation machine-readable. In order to leverage its advantages, it is now the time to take action: on the one hand for the financial industry to increase collaboration on managing regulations, and on the other hand for lawyers and law schools to proactively approach technology and computer science.

Moreover, I am certain the financial industry is just the beginning, with further highly regulated industries still waiting for their very own RegTech revolution.

Can We Digitize Know Your Client?

By Shawn Brayman
CEO, PlanPlus Global Inc

Before we answer the question of whether we can digitize the know your customer (KYC) process, we need to look at how it is done today.

As part of an extensive research project on behalf of the Ontario Securities Commission in Canada, *Current Practices for Risk Profiling in Canada and Review of Global Best Practices*,[1] major regulators in the United States, Canada, the United Kingdom, Australia, and several other countries were interviewed. Every regulator in each marketplace was consistent:

- Robots must know your client to the same extent as a human adviser.

- No regulator prescribes what an adviser (or robot) must do to know the client.

- All regulators reference professional judgement as the foundation of knowing the client – educated, licensed professionals who are trained to know what to ask, when to ask it, and how to arrive at an assessment of a risk profile.

- A questionnaire is unlikely to be sufficient on its own, as they usually support only limited discovery and cannot adapt to unknown complexity in a consumer's situation. Advisers must dig deeper to determine whether other factors might be relevant.

Regulators worldwide are moving to higher standards of investor care, Trump and Department of Labor (DOL) issues notwithstanding. 'Investment suitability' is no longer sufficient – recommendations have to be in the client's best interests. With new fiduciary standards, advisers and firms are required to factor risk tolerance, time horizon, capacity for loss, experience, knowledge, financial need, objectives/goals, and more into their KYC process. Pressure also exists to have a defensible mapping of clients into portfolios and products, existing and yet to be launched. For 'best interests', the number of factors considered increases dramatically. However, here's the rub – both regulators and academics are silent about how to put the pieces together.

At this point in time, financial institutions see digitized advice as a panacea that will allow them to profitably serve the wealth management needs of a less affluent segment of clients without lowering advice standards. The rush to digitized advice delivery has created a dangerous nexus of conflicting requirements with no clear path forward.

Research to clarify the complexity of KYC by revealing both the number of contributing factors (see Figure 1) and the complexity of the actual decision making when combining factors is underway. It is in the trade-offs that the personalization of an individual's risk profile is at its highest. Some examples of the complexity include:

- Consider a client with a high *tolerance* for risk but who *prefers* less risk with more funds than are required to reach the goal. Should a more conservative portfolio be recommended?

- Two clients have the same *tolerance*; however, one's goal is largely funded by a pension (increased *capacity*). Should their portfolios be the same?

- A client with moderate risk *tolerance* and a high financial *need* increases the likelihood of running out of money prematurely. The consumer would *prefer* more risk rather than reduce the goal. Should this be allowed?

- If a client has *no experience* with equities but has a very high risk *tolerance*, should the client's first portfolio be aggressive equity?

---

[1] www.osc.gov.on.ca/en/Investors_iap_20151112_risk-profiling-report.pdf

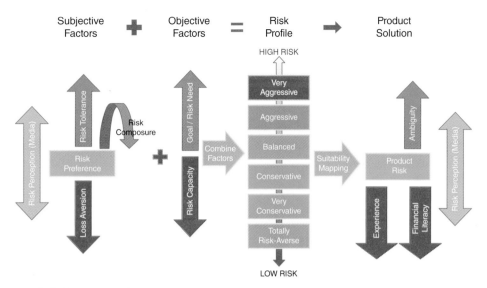

Figure 1: **Visual summary of risk concepts**

Online marketers want shorter KYC questionnaires because evidence shows that more consumers drop out as each additional question is asked until a tipping point is reached. So a tension exists between slick online processes keeping the user's interest and a proper KYC from a regulatory perspective that requires a level of data that will negatively impact the user experience. Because these risk profiling questionnaires (RPQs) are insufficient, the consequence is more costly offline human intervention. This limits the value of automation and reduces the number of consumers who can profitably be served. Some regulators are recognizing this tension and are exploring focused/simplified advice designed to facilitate online models. The regulations are not established enough nor the consequences clear enough to know whether this will be effective.

How Are We Doing Today?

Today, measuring or understanding the contributing factors, digging deeper and asking more questions, and then combining

all this information into an investor profile are largely the role of licensed investment advisers or firms. Based on this assessment, they recommend appropriate products. So how is the industry doing at this?

In Canada, the United Kingdom, and Australia, complaints to institutions, regulators, and ombudsman services over issues of 'suitability' (failure to match the client to the products recommended) outweigh all other types of complaints combined. In the United States, this also ranks at the top. Research has proven that advisers are more likely to insert their own interests into the process of making recommendations if they are biased by their compensation. Whether this is the cause or just a lack of training and understanding how to match clients to products is unclear.

Although regulators place the burden of professional judgement with the adviser or firm, advisers in mass market and mass affluent channels are often trained to use basic RPQs and rely on these completely. Compliance departments find it difficult to oversee a process that is bespoke rather than standardized. As a result, when an adviser gathers information about a client that includes factors not considered in the RPQ, they often coach the client on how to get the result they need. This, of course, compromises the validity of the RPQ entirely.

The research referred to at the beginning of this chapter found that most (83% in Canada) RPQs are flawed – with problems such as poorly structured questions, inaccurate scoring models, lack of ability to deal with extremes, and no form of consistency validation. Therefore, the short answer to our question of 'How are we doing?' is that we have significant challenges to get this right.

Aside from Biased Advisers, Why Is This So Hard to Get Right?

The science of risk profiling and financial planning has evolved along with our awareness of the complexities of behaviour. We have a better understanding of the component parts of risk and, more important, how to measure them:

- Psychometric risk tolerance tests have been in use since 1998, and dozens of academic papers show that they can measure a client's tolerance for risk and that the trait is stable over time.

- Recently, we have seen the use of 'gambling' questions, inspired by prospect theory and the work of Daniel Kahneman, to determine loss aversion of consumers. Portfolios with maximum likely losses are then matched to the client profile in an effort to recommend a portfolio that should not drop below the limits acceptable to the client.

- Financial planning tools that measure the consequences of failure to meet the client's goals or need and 'capacity for loss' – defined as whether the client has the resources to weather the downturns – are constantly being refined.

Most advisers believe a client's risk tolerance is not stable. Why? Let's use an example. Assume I complete a questionnaire that determines I am afraid of heights. If I am standing on the floor, I may feel no anxiety. However, if I am perched on the top of a ladder, my perception is not the same. My tolerance is unchanged; however, I see the environment differently. Although my risk tolerance can be measured and stable, my perception of the risk in the market can change, based on things such as media influences and more. Too many advisers confuse tolerance with perception.

Another crucial but poorly understood behavioural factor is 'composure'. While risk tolerance might be a stable trait under normal circumstances, what if the market crashes and CNN's economic pundit announces, 'We may never recover from this'. Do I stick to my plan because I know that in the past we have always recovered from major downturns? Or does my fight-or-flight instinct kick in, prompting me to sell my investments and crystalize a loss? Understanding composure or behaviour under stress cannot be answered by asking clients whether they might panic in the eventuality of a market crash.

So determining a client's profile in a manner that combines the various components of risk is complex. It involves gathering objective information that we can analyse (e.g. an individual's goals), subjective behaviour that we can measure (e.g. tolerance for risk), and behavioural information that is difficult, if not impossible, to extract from questionnaires. This is further complicated by the fact that few investors are willing to take the time to complete more comprehensive questionnaires and advisers are hesitant to use them. Even if we had all the components, there is no body of research or regulation that provides guidance on how to combine them into a concrete recommendation. Taking the time to implement a complex process for smaller investors that will not generate significant income is not deemed financially viable.

Cognitive Computing

One of the technology disruptors that might help in this regard is cognitive computing, which was demonstrated by IBM's Watson famously beating the human champions of *Jeopardy!*. IBM (as an example) has released a series of general application programming interfaces (APIs) to the programming world that open new doors to explore many aspects of data, including personality insights. By reading as few as 1,200 words of text from an individual, the system can map that person into what is referred to as the 'Big 5 Personality Traits'.

Research on these traits[2] indicates that people who score high on 'openness to experience' tend to make risky investments. Another study[3] found that 'agreeableness' and 'conscientiousness' lower people's willingness to take risks and that those high in 'extroversion' are more likely to make risky decisions. The inference is that this technology will allow us to understand a client's risk tolerance without the need to ask unnecessary questions.

Applying statistical averages to individual behaviour is like a form of racial profiling – an individual is not the average. Asking a question is always better than guessing. Asking multiple questions where we can confirm answers based on the internal consistency of the responses or validation from outside sources is best. Nonetheless, in the same way that a professional adviser might ask a senior citizen additional questions to ensure cognitive competency, we can use generalized indicators like the 'Big 5' to trigger further questions or inquiry.

In addition, insights from personality assessments might provide guidance on preferred ways to ask the questions. Some people are more visual in their thinking, while others might be more numerate. This could help us to determine whether we ask questions using graphics, charts, or simple text. So far, cognitive computing will

---

[2] M. Lauriola and I.P. Levin, 'Relating Individual Differences in Attitude Toward Ambiguity to Risky Choices', *Journal of Behavioral Decision Making* 14, no. 2 (April 2001): v–vi, 87–168.

[3] N. Nicholson, E. Soane, M. Fenton-O'Creevy, and P. William, 'Personality and Domain-Specific Risk Taking', *Journal of Risk Research* 8, no. 2 (2005): 157–176.

not solve the determination of a consumer's risk profile; however, it may start to allow more intelligent questioning to occur.

Finally, although we cannot ask people what their composure is, we may be able to explore their past behaviour to determine how they have reacted during previous periods of stress. It is unlikely this data will be nicely structured; however, intelligent systems may be able to distil information from the body of data now available on the internet.

Conclusion

So can we digitize KYCs? The simple answer is yes, but not well, given regulators' expectations. Regardless, automation will allow consumers to more easily self-serve, which, in turn, may reduce high-priced human intervention. We will still need mechanisms to recognize clients whom we cannot effectively categorize with a fixed RPQ.

For risk profiling to move beyond the simplicity of today to become a truly disruptive technology, we require a few key advances, including knowledge of:

• How to combine the factors based on evidence and not guesswork.

• When to ask additional questions and about what.

• How to explore past behaviours.

When we can combine these elements with the objective data from a client's financial plan and a selection of scientifically validated tests, we can produce a much richer and more useful result.

The whole exercise of understanding the client's risk tolerance will eventually be more standardized across the industry. It should become independent of the adviser or firm recommending products and a known attribute of the consumer. Until then – there is lots of work to do!

RegTech Investment and Compliance Spending

5

- Transformation will only be possible if we look at both legacy IT and culture in an organization
- RegTech's full potential will only be achieved once new architecture and teams are in place

---

- Human error and end user computing can be identified by RegTech solutions

- RegTech start-ups act not just as solution providers but also transformation consultants
- Onerous KYC process doesn't guarantee accuracy but can impact customer satisfaction
- KYC solutions to differentiation not just of data, but as to end-user usability

---

- The development of universal banks has generated a fragmentation of regulatory obligations
- Customer experience is not a compliance officer's mandate
- Need to bridge divide as both business and regulators have a goal of being pro-consumer

The fifth part looks at RegTech investment and where the majority of the market activity is currently occurring.

As discussed throughout this book, RegTech start-ups are approaching a market that now represents billions in spending following the increase in the last decade. To give a sense of scale, the six largest banks in the US spent over US$70 billion dollars in compliance in 2013. These are ongoing costs and exclude the over US$300 billion paid as one-off fines as a result of the 2008 crisis.

Looking at this from a human capital perspective, it is not unusual for financial institutions to have 20 to 30% of their staff within legal and compliance functions. In other words, Tier 1 banks have more compliance personnel than a tech company has engineers. The consequence of this large and ever-increasing employee base post-crisis is a recurring increase in overheads driven by the higher numbers of staff and pressure on talent availability.

Therefore the 300 RegTech start-ups globally are looking to take a piece of a billion-dollar opportunity. While financial institutions are investing heavily in digital transformation efforts, their multi-million-dollar strategies are starting to realize that compliance functions need to be part of that discussion and upgraded if not at least empowered. Seen in this way, broadly speaking RegTech start-ups have a higher success rate in working with financial institutions that their FinTech counterparts.

From the investor side, US$1 billion has been invested in the sector. Once again the comparison with the FinTech eco-system can be made, the latter having received over US$23 billion in funding. Although it is lower, the amount raised by RegTech start-ups is in proportion with the smaller numbers of start-ups in this space (300 vs 7000). As such, not only does the funding appear healthy, but investors have been able to find first-mover investment opportunities in this sector in the last few years, especially as the FinTech market has started to mature.

While public understanding of the RegTech market focuses on the KYC side, as it is one of the few compliance functions of a bank that has a client facing process, investment has not necessarily flowed in that direction. A fair amount of activity is happening instead on the AML and auditing side, especially as these combine both market demand as well as leveraging on technologies, often AI, which can then have other applicability within data analytics.

The following chapters will provide more detail on the market opportunity.

Why a Substantial Investment in Financial Services RegTech Now Will Strategically Reduce Your Future Regulatory Compliance Costs

By Nirvana Farhadi

Global Head Financial Services, RegTech Risk and Regulatory Compliance Affairs, Hitachi Vantara

A man who both spends and saves money is the happiest man because he has both enjoyments.

—Samuel Johnson

Since the 2008 banking crisis, the global financial services industry has been hit with a tsunami of regulation whose impact does not need explanation anymore. Being held ransom to large, shambolic, and messy systems that have grown far too large or risky to replace is costing firms billions in risk, operations, compliance, and audit (ROCA) costs alone.

Many of the large financial services institutions have been in business for a very long time,[1] and their technological software was highly likely to have been built or bought well over 40 years ago. This dated technology, which was once shiny and new, is now a gnarly, mechanical beast, creaking and fragile, yet still – bafflingly – running critical business operations such as general

ledgers, inventory management, and other back-office systems within organizations today.

The serviceability and functionality of these systems have not kept up with the times, and they are incapable of keeping pace with emerging regulatory requirements, let alone innovation. Many banking institutions run on infrastructure so old that they have had to encapsulate these systems with a patchwork of expensive data management tools in order to simply be able to give online access to their clients. These limitations not only prevent these organizations from progressing, but they also narrow their geographical reach as well as their customer service capabilities and inhibit the introduction of new products.

Through the years, these systems – which run at the core of these organizations – have been incrementally modified and enhanced to the point where they have become a nebulous mass of complexity with no room for duplication or replacement. In effect, they are enslaving the organization within the confines of its limitations and stifling progress and innovation. This is a risky and costly strategy. The colossal resources required to keep existing systems running while still patched and secure, coupled with managing the high levels of compliance requirements, will drain budgets over time. Beyond that, the high risk associated with manually sourcing data or using piecemeal solutions presents the very real risk of non-compliance.

However, it is essential to point out that it is not just legacy systems that are a problem in the financial services industry, but 'legacy thinking' from leadership. This old mindset of many of today's top industry leaders is in itself becoming a huge cost to organizations. The shortsighted tactical approach taken by leaders will, in the long run, end up costing organizations millions in unnecessary regulatory costs. These leaders are only concerned with the here and now and their revenue and profit-and-loss (P&L) balance sheets for the year – rather than thinking strategically and proactively and planning for the future while moving with the times.

---

[1] Banca Mote dei paschi Siena, established in 1472, is one of the oldest banks in continuous operation; other banks, such as Barclays Bank, established in 1690; Lloyds Bank, established in 1765; JPMorgan Chase, established in 1795; State Street, established in 1792; and Bank of New York Mellon, established in 1784, have been around for many years.

In the wise words of Warren Buffett:

> Someone is sitting in the shade today because someone planted a tree a long time ago.

So why are our leaders not thinking of intelligent strategic investments now, to avoid running their businesses into the ground eventually? We know that regulation will not cease to exist, despite the impressive rhetoric of every political party that wishes to create noise and say the right things in order to get into power. In fact, as FinTech continues to innovate, more and more regulation will come into effect to ensure that objectives of financial services regulations and regulators are met – by maintaining market confidence, promoting financial stability in the financial services ecosystem, reducing financial crime, and ensuring that the rights of the consumers are protected accordingly and that market abuse is prevented.

We know that the estimated cost of regulatory compliance in financial services in the United Kingdom will reach £17 billion over the next 10 years. The combination of Brexit and the Trump administration's bullish efforts to change or roll back elements of the Dodd-Frank Act are only making the problems worse, because changing regulations will add to the already burdensome workload of compliance and regulatory departments of financial institutions (FIs). The Markets in Financial Instruments Directive (MiFID/MiFID II) is an example of a regulation that will cost firms dearly to implement. Though it is a beast in itself, just being compliant with the regulatory reporting burden of MiFID/MiFID II will cost firms across Europe an estimated £2.2 billion.

Deloitte[2] estimates that in 2014 banks in Europe spent €55 billion on information technology (IT); however, only €9 billion was spent on new systems. The majority was used to bolt on more systems

to the antiquated existing technologies to simply keep the old technology going.

Many companies have invested heavily in their legacy systems to keep them going, but find themselves trapped and prohibited from being able to implement strategic growth. If these companies take a step back now and begin to implement a continuous investment cycle, instead of just spending on enhancements on a reactive basis, they will be able to keep up to date with evolving technology and be able to replace ageing components as required.

The C-suite leaders are sick of writing multibillion-pound cheques to consultants, lawyers, and contractors to help navigate them through the barrage of regulatory compliance changes that are coming down the pipe. Let's face it: regulation and compliance are a cost burden and do not generate revenue, but, ironically, being non-compliant will cost firms even more dearly.

So, faced with such heavy costs burdens, what's your average run-of-the-mill C-suite leader to do? Stop complaining about how hard life is chained to the tentacles of the brittle mechanical monsters they have helped create and make a wise strategic investment in RegTech now. If they do this, they will save themselves costs, reduce resource burdens, and create more efficient and streamlined processes and procedures! Leadership must, when looking at future technology investments, make sure that the decision made today will not be something that will imprison the firm in the future, and should consider agile systems that are adaptable to change; and this is how smart RegTech solutions can help. RegTech is a valuable partner for FinTech. As FinTech continues to evolve at lightning speed, regulators and compliance professionals alike will need to keep pace with the use of technology specifically geared towards solving regulatory problems. By making risk operations, compliance, and audit obligations less onerous and more efficient, and by reducing resource burdens, RegTech solutions will enable organizations to save on costs and focus on their core business.

---

[2] https://www2.deloitte.com/content/dam/Deloitte/ie/Documents/FinancialServices/ie-regtech-pdf.pdf

RegTech will also see new organizations entering the market, making regulation more pragmatic and workable. The monetary spend on regulatory compliance and control costs by the big banking institutions alone has been estimated time and time again in various industry reports and exceeds well over US$1 billion a year. As big players from other industries move in to seize new opportunities in the financial services sector, we will see current organizations rushing to become much more data-driven companies. Within the next three to five years, the traditional financial services institution will be known as a financial services technology institution.

From a regulatory viewpoint, we can see that many national competent authorities (NCAs) are leading the charge on RegTech and, like the UK's Financial Conduct Authority (FCA) – which issued a call for input on RegTech in 2017 – they are keen to encourage and promote RegTech. As a result of the feedback, the FCA has started to increase collaboration with RegTech companies, 'using our convening authority to help bring together market participants to work on shared challenges; and to act as a catalyst for change'.

In a paper published by the Institute of International Finance (IIF), it is stated that:

> FIs have a primary responsibility for supporting RegTech develop-ment, most importantly by creating IT and risk infrastructures that are capable of integrating these new solutions.[3]

According to this paper, areas such as risk data aggregation, data modelling, scenario analysis and forecasting, compliance monitoring, client identification, margin calculation, and identification of regulatory compliance obligations to the relevant

line of business are currently labour-intensive and complex processes, which could be enhanced through automated interpretation of regulations.

The accelerated pace at which FinTech has been adopted and is constantly innovating means regulators have struggled to keep up. However, far-reaching and broader regulations are now being established regularly – hence the requirement for RegTech to help manage this plethora of rules and procedures. RegTech is particularly relevant within the ROCA arena, where having oversight of the regulations is deep within their remit.

The financial services industry is heavily regulated through myriad interlinking global regulations. These regulations are implemented through reports – whether through trade, transaction, position, or periodic reporting or some sort of disclosure. Reports are the lifeblood of regulation and are based on data – therefore data is a crucial part of compliance. At the core of most regulations is the need for financial services organizations to locate, protect, and report on the data and information held within their systems. The regulations require not just audit trails; each report must demonstrate exactly how data is handled both internally and externally.

Reporting and regulation are unavoidable for all financial services organizations. FinTech, which is just developing and not regulated yet, will catch up very quickly as the regulators quicken their pace in keeping up to date with innovation and possible disruptions.

Financial services firms are now standing at a crossroads: do they continue responding piecemeal with multiple uncoordinated point solutions, compressed lead times, and inefficiencies, or, alternatively, do they adopt a proactive strategic approach allowing them to rationalize their processes and maximize available synergies?

Whatever happens, regulation and technology will play a very important role in the implementation of new regulations. Still in

---

[3] 'RegTech in Financial Services: Technology Solutions for Compliance and Reporting', Institute of International Finance, March 2016; https://www.iif.com/system/files/regtech_in_financial_services_-_solutions_for_compliance_and_reporting.pdf.

its infancy, the RegTech industry provides a set of technological solutions that address regulatory challenges across industries, including financial services, through innovative technology. Firms will need to prepare very carefully for changes, as the introduction of new rules and regulations will often change the way they collect, analyse, and report on their data. Applying RegTech could make an important contribution to increasing the profitability and efficiency of financial services firms while improving their effective compliance with financial regulations.

RegTech is not a silver bullet, and it is not going to solve all the compliance headaches businesses are suffering from. However, it will play a central role, especially when used to maximum effect. Take, as an example, reporting. We know through our research that this is an industry-wide challenge; on average, a firm has 160 reporting requirements under different regulations globally, all with different drivers and usually with different teams producing those reports.

By using RegTech, not only could those team resources be reduced, but the agility and speed with which reports can be produced will ensure compliance deadlines are adhered to. Additionally, resources can then be focused elsewhere, such as on driving innovation and helping to move the company forward.

Rather than focusing on what a burden the regulations are, by using RegTech, organizations will see them as an opportunity to get systems, processes, and data in order, and to use the intelligence and resources to drive the company to greater successes. To take it one step further, I believe regulation does not hinder or stifle innovation, but in fact, it breeds creativity and innovation.

Old Tech + New Tech = RegTech: Excel Spreadsheets and End User Computing in a Regulated World

By Brendan Bradley
Chairman, ipushpull

and David Jones
CTO, ipushpull

In the 2012 'London Whale' trading debacle, JPMorgan suffered a loss of at least $6 billion on a portfolio of credit default swaps. The bank's internal report[1] into the event described how misuse of Microsoft Excel spreadsheets had contributed to the loss. A set of Excel spreadsheets was being used to manage the risk on the portfolio. The risk management process was manual and involved copying and pasting data from one spreadsheet to another. More importantly, a calculation error in the spreadsheet had the effect of underestimating risk by half.

This scenario is all too familiar within financial institutions (FIs), where tools like Excel, Access, and MatLab are widely used by non-developers to implement end user computing (EUC) solutions. Regulators have recognized the risks that EUC solutions pose and have issued regulations aiming to oblige banks to monitor and control their use. In this chapter, we examine the regulations that aim to mitigate the risks of EUC solutions. We look at how FIs use EUC solutions and why this is likely to continue, and we summarize the RegTech solutions that can help banks implement these regulations.

---

[1] JPMorgan Chase, 'Report Regarding 2012 CIO Losses'; http://files .shareholder.com/downloads/ONE/2272984969x0x628656/4cb574a0- 0bf5-4728-9582-625e4519b5ab/Task_Force_Report.pdf, p. 128.

Which Regulations Apply to EUC Solutions in Financial Organizations?

A number of recent regulations apply to spreadsheet usage within FIs. It is important to note that they do not require EUC solutions to be eliminated; rather, they require that processes be put in place to manage their use. Some key regulations can be found in Table 1.

Table 1: Sample of applicable regulation for spreadsheet usage for financial institutions

Regulation	Selected clauses relating to management of EUC risk
Dodd-Frank Act, stress tests[a]	This Act requires banks to run stress tests twice a year to determine the impact of stressful economic and financial market conditions on the bank's capital. The stress test guidelines include this requirement: 'Banks must provide a comprehensive inventory of models … including any significant EUC apps that support projection of losses, revenues, expenses, balances and Risk Weighted Assets.'
Basel Committee on Banking Supervision, 239[b]	This regulation defines a set of principles to strengthen banks' risk data aggregation capabilities and internal risk reporting practices. Principle 3 includes this statement: 'Where a bank relies on manual processes and desktop applications (e.g. spreadsheets, databases) and has specific risk units that use these applications for software development, it should have effective mitigants in place.'

Regulation	Selected clauses relating to management of EUC risk
Sarbanes-Oxley Act[c]	The aim of this Act is to protect investors from the possibility of fraudulent accounting activities by corporations. While EUCs are not explicitly mentioned, section 404 asserts that corporate management bears 'the responsibility … for establishing and maintaining an adequate internal control structure.'
Solvency II[d]	The Solvency II Directive aims to codify and harmonize EU insurance regulation and improve insurance firms' resilience to financial shocks. It does not explicitly mention EUCs, but it states: 'Insurance and reinsurance undertakings shall have in place an effective risk-management system … necessary to identify, measure, monitor, manage and report, on a continuous basis.'

[a]Office of the Comptroller of the Currency, 'Dodd-Frank Act Stress Testing (DFAST) Reporting Instructions', https://www.occ.treas.gov/tools-forms/forms/bank-operations/DFAST-14A-Template-Instructions.pdf, p. 5.

[b] Bank for International Settlements, 'Principles for Effective Risk Data Aggregation and Risk Reporting', http://www.bis.org/publ/bcbs239.pdf, p. 15.

[c] Securities and Exchange Commission, 'Sarbanes-Oxley Act of 2002', https://www.sec.gov/about/laws/soa2002.pdf, p. 45.

[d] European Union, 'Solvency II', http://eur-lex.europa.eu/legal-content/EN/TXT/PDF/?uri=CELEX:02009L0138-20140523, p. 66.

These regulations address a variety of business processes in several sectors of the financial market, but the solutions that banks need to implement in order to comply with them are broadly similar. FIs need to be able to:

- Discover all relevant EUC solutions in use in the organization and rank them according to risk.

- Maintain an inventory of managed EUC solutions, control access, and track changes.

- Identify links between different EUC solutions used in the bank's risk and financial reporting processes and automate the data flows between them.

- Reduce the number of EUC solutions and minimize manual processes and complexity, both in the management of EUC solutions and in the generation of regulatory reports that depend on them.

It is therefore critical for FIs to implement policies and processes to manage EUC solutions and allocate the resources required to manage them. However, why are EUC solutions so pervasive in FIs? Wouldn't it be simpler to get rid of them altogether?

Spreadsheets in Financial Organizations

What Are They Used For?

Traders, risk managers, and quantitative analysts turn to tools like Excel when they need to respond to urgent customer requirements or to fill in the functionality gaps of enterprise applications. Common uses within the front office include:

- The rapid development of pricing models for new or exotic products.

- Flexible portfolio risk modelling, monitoring, and hedging.

- Cross-product and cross-trading system risk data generation and aggregation.

A front office developer at a Tier 2 bank reported that:

> The Front Office uses spreadsheets for both modelling and pricing of products for clients. Due to the dynamic nature of their business and the variety of client requests, IT cannot build systems flexible enough to price some of these products. They use Excel primarily as a UI [user interface] to build models and to set the parameters and structure of a deal.

While there is a desire to reduce spreadsheet usage, it is accepted that they will never be fully replaced, because it is impossible to be as agile as the market demands with a proprietary system. This reality is recognized even by cutting-edge technology solutions such as OpenFin, which include Excel integration as standard.

What Are the Problems with EUC Solutions?

EUC applications and the manual processes that surround them are exposed to a range of potential risks:

- *Coding errors*. Poorly written and untested formulas and code, leading to incorrect calculation results.

- *Process errors*. Mistakes arising from manual processes, e.g. 'fat finger' errors when entering data manually, copy-and-paste errors where incorrect or incomplete data is copied manually between sheets, or failure to update all necessary inputs leading to stale data being used in calculations.

- *Inconsistency*. Multiple instances of the same spreadsheet running on different desktops can easily become out of sync across the organization.

- *Access control risk*. Modification of sheet data or calculations done by unauthorized persons.

- *Key person risk*. Difficulty of supporting undocumented EUC applications when their original developer leaves the company.

- *Operational risks*. Poor version control, making it difficult to recover 'last known good' versions of EUC solutions or to rerun historical calculations during audits; EUC apps unmanaged by IT may not be available in disaster recovery situations.

- *Fraud*. Errors deliberately introduced to conceal fraudulent activity.

How Big Is the Problem?

Despite the widely acknowledged risks of EUC applications, their use is not decreasing. On the contrary, a report by Deloitte[2] noted that:

> The economic downturn curbed investment in IT resulting in a dramatic increase in the development and use of EUCs to address business needs not being addressed by IT.

Until they carry out a methodical audit of EUC usage within their organizations, it is highly likely that banks will underestimate the size of the problem they are dealing with. For example, a consultancy recently carried out a six-month audit of spreadsheet usage by the 300-strong front office team at a tier 2 bank. At the start of the audit, the expectation was that they would find around 3,000 unique spreadsheets. However, at the end of six months over 48,000 unique spreadsheets had been used, and 1,400 had been identified as being business critical. It is no surprise that, with such a lack of awareness and control, the somewhat menacing term 'shadow systems' is often used to describe these and the broader pool of EUC applications.

---

2 Deloitte, 'End User Computing: Solving the Problem'; https://www2. deloitte.com/content/dam/Deloitte/us/Documents/audit/us_aers_iat_end_ user_computing_solving_the_problem_mobile_020813.pdf, p. 2.

So how big is the problem across the entire market? A 2016 analysis by Chartis[3] attempted to quantify the risk of financial losses due to improper use of EUC systems, or *EUC risk*. They estimated that 'the current End User Computing (EUC) Value at Risk (VaR) for the largest 50 FIs is $12.1 billion'.

Increasing regulatory attention leaves little doubt that EUC is perceived as a big problem in need of an urgent remedy. Despite this, surprisingly, the analysis found that the uptake of RegTech solutions for EUC risk management was still 'low and uneven'. This will inevitably start to change as the regulators increase oversight.

How Can RegTech Help Financial Institutions Meet Their EUC Regulatory Requirements?

There follows a (non-exhaustive) list of products that aim to support FIs in reducing risk and meeting regulatory requirements by auditing, reducing, and controlling their EUCs:

- *Hub 85* provides an automated governance and insights solution, enabling organizations to manage their EUC inventory. End-user behaviour metrics allows firms to understand why and how spreadsheets are used. It uncovers risks, maps data-lineage, enhances internal controls and helps reduce the number of manual EUC processes.

- *Microsoft* provides its own solution for EUC management, to enable users to 'assess and categorize spreadsheets and databases based on relevance'.

- *Xenomorph* is an enterprise data management platform with integrated analytics capabilities. It aims to encourage users to port their spreadsheet calculations into a secure, audited environment, where both data inputs and outputs can be validated.

- *ipushpull* provides a means of auditing EUC usage and 'automating and controlling the data flows between spreadsheets used in the generation of pricing, risk or financial reporting'. It 'reduces the EUC footprint by offering an audited golden source for data and a means of distribution to the desktop and messaging platforms'.

Conclusions

Regulators globally are applying ever-increasing pressure on FIs to implement processes to manage their EUC estates. While it is impossible to guarantee that this will eliminate future spectacular failures like the London Whale, there is no doubt that the resulting reduction in operational risk, streamlining of business processes, and consequential reduction in IT costs associated with such processes can only be beneficial to FIs. RegTech solutions will play a critical role in this process.

---

[3] Chartis, 'Quantification of End User Computing Risk in Financial Services'; http://www.risktech-forum.com/research/chartis-quantification-of-end-user-computing-risk-in-financial-services, p. 6.

Will Financial Institutions Ever Achieve a 100% Compliance with Anti–Money Laundering and Combating the Financing of Terrorism Rules?

By Marcel Krist
CEO and Chairman, Photonfocus AG and Managing Director, KYC Exchange Net AG

The International Monetary Fund (IMF) explicitly states that money laundering and terrorist financing are financial crimes. Consequently, regulators in the different jurisdictions seek to outperform the anti–money laundering (AML) and combating the financing of terrorism (CFT) rules developed by the IMF's Financial Action Task Force (FATF) with more localized, specific, and stringent regulations.

Financial institutions (FIs) are cognizant of the rules, specifications, and, more important, consequences of non-compliance and non-mitigation. Compliance officers and risk managers acknowledge that they must comply with AML/CFT rules globally around the clock (24/7) in each legal entity and branch. However, taking a closer look, some FIs are 'managing' the AML/CFT regulations like fare dodgers. Regulations are deliberately ignored, and funds are set aside (as AML accruals) in anticipation of potential future fines.

So, how can regulators enforce the law and ensure an appropriate application of the AML/CFT rules, and what are the tools at their disposal? At the same time, do IT vendors offer appropriate know your customer (KYC) and client due diligence (CDD) tools and platforms to fight financial crime? Do they need to become more disruptive to the processes of money laundering and terrorist financing? And ultimately, will RegTech be the game changer to mitigate adverse effects of criminal economic activity?

This chapter explores the readiness and willingness of FIs to implement AML/CFT rules. Furthermore, it outlines potential pitfalls, challenges, and contravening incentives in the process.

Innovation and Disruption – The Magic Words for Investors?

Currently, many investors in FinTech and RegTech start-ups require them to provide innovative solutions that disrupt financial transactions and processes. These ensure a foothold in the market, generate revenues and profits, and enhance the appeal of the start-up to potential investors. Interviews with compliance officers in large American banks have shown that KYC checks in US institutions often rely on traditional verbal processes to collect the required information, so an offsite lunch is often the time and place where information is requested from an FI counterpart. Questions related to politically exposed persons (PEPs), ownership, business activities, products, dealings with sanctioned/high-risk countries, KYC policies, control procedures and enhanced KYC routines, shell banks, downstream clearing, and transaction monitoring are answered according to a paper checklist. As a result, the information-gathering process is removed from a digital process but remains largely accepted by local regulators.

Note that the switch from a manual process to a partially digitized solution can effectively disrupt an FI's illicit economic business flow. Initially, it can take months to modify and adapt current KYC processes to integrate an external partner's KYC solution or to be able to read and process data acquired from the provider. Many RegTech start-ups that are more agile and keen for acceptance of their innovative solution suddenly find themselves acting as business consultants. They must help clients to structure and streamline processes, assist with staffing and training employees, and thus earn unexpected but welcome revenues through an expansion of their business model.

Standardization, Digitization, and Automatic Validation

For some FIs, KYC began with 'know your customer' but ended up with 'kill your customer' as they ended relationships with customers from high-risk countries. The cost of the KYC information collection/validation process for those customers exceeded the earnings. During the initial onboarding process customers willingly provided the banks with necessary information. Over time the quality and amount of KYC information deteriorated dramatically. Companies in high-risk countries using multiple correspondent banks for payment clearing are often reluctant to hand over required KYC documents.

Unfortunately, the KYC forms used by the different banks are rarely standardized and/or digitized, despite containing similar questions. First of all, a standardized global, digital KYC questionnaire, covering the specific AML/CFT rules from all jurisdictions and a common set of documents, would greatly simplify and accelerate the allocation and preparation of KYC information and documents on the customer side. In addition, it would also allow the verification and validation of this information by compliance officers in different correspondent banks worldwide. A standardized digital data structure format would allow the requesting banks to compare and analyse discrepancies between the submitted forms and documents from the same customer and thus perform pattern recognition, identify malicious data, and generate customer blacklists. Naturally, such automatic and digital procedures make sense only if participating compliance officers are willing to process additional information and to initiate the necessary measures towards their customers.

There are cases where compliance officers deliberately request less information to avoid terminating a client relationship. The underlying reasons are obvious; regulatory bodies are constantly releasing new regulations, which lead to an increase of changes and updates. Because compliance departments in FIs are

typically not the areas where IT requirements are budgeted for, the compliance unit is lucky if it occasionally gets additional resources to deal with the overwhelming implications of the new regulations. In most cases, however, they do not receive an IT budget to invest in cutting-edge AML/CFT software or source data from RegTech providers.

Customer Identification and Verification

A long-standing client relationship often means FIs struggle to maintain up-to-date client information, as clients do not always respond to KYC-related enquiries. Nevertheless, the banks continue to clear payments regardless of potentially outdated KYC information. Frequently, FIs have long lists of non-responding clients, whose phone numbers or email addresses are no longer valid. Reasons range from customers' unwillingness to spend time on updating to forgetting to mention a change of work or living place. There are even cases where FIs consciously don't respond to a KYC request because they do not want to share the same amount of information with all of the requesting banks. Instead of submitting partial information, they simply don't provide anything at all.

Many auditors and regulators do not accept unanswered KYC requests, and banks know that they must terminate such relationships if the information is not obtained in due course. Outsourcing the data collection process to a third-party KYC provider is not a solution, as the external partner usually has even less access to the non-compliant counterpart and cannot rely on a legislative framework for the data request. Furthermore, many regulators do not accept the outsourcing of KYC data collection, and often external data validation is even prohibited.

Solid and constant customer identification and validation are crucial to sufficient KYC data quality. Compliance officers should focus on investigating legal entities and build up automatic real-time and ad hoc access to data centres around the world. Compliance data must be collected directly from primary sources and company and business registrations. FIs must have the ability to interrogate data fields from legal entities identifiers (LEIs) and bank identifier codes (SWIFT codes) and cross-reference this data with data from registrations and end users. The client needs to be identified in a single view across complex structures of large international corporate entities.

Especially in the case of speedy client acquisition (e.g. bankers anxious to achieve bonus-relevant objectives), FIs require accurate and certified client information to ensure correct and updated audit reporting. Automated identity, phone, and IP address verification and device and digital footprint analysis can be performed by RegTech companies and contribute to authorization or rejection of clearing payments from both trusted and fraudulent counterparts.

Finally, despite the need to fully digitize the information-gathering process, a personal meeting – even a Skype or videoconferencing session would be beneficial – between the individuals involved in the process is valuable. This would ensure the authenticity and authorization of the employee and organization they are dealing with. Business cards, passport copies, digital passports, organizational charts, and online identification tools are mere add-ons and cannot replace the recurring personal contact between those responsible for submitting KYC data and the FIs.

Repository, Data Ownership, and Self-Assessment

All KYC vendors proclaim their superiority, but in our experience, each solution has advantages and disadvantages. An omni-suitable KYC solution has yet to become available. The FI's customer base, its industry (banking, insurance, asset management, large international corporations or retail clients), and the specific phases of the KYC process (onboarding, data/document collection, data verification and validation, screening,

and reporting) are the determining factors when selecting a KYC requesting and collecting company. But do not worry – there is still ample room for new solutions and innovations from future RegTech start-ups.

In principle, KYC solutions have one thing in common: a (central) database and (secure) document storage. Solutions differ in storage options, secure backing up in databases or containers, and the respective involvement of the KYC requesting parties (KYC consumers) and KYC data-providing parties (clients) in data sourcing (or feeding), maintaining, validating, controlling, and data mining. Some KYC providers manually feed their repositories with publicly available data (annual reports, organizational charts, website information on management structures), while others use crawl agents – bots/spiders based on some specific algorithms directed towards the deepest of web pages (client websites, national/public websites, registration authorities, political organizations, and so on). Some extract information from local machines, databases, or the internet (e.g. bookmarked links) with data scraping methods. Others use automated data and document feeds from publicly available sources. Whatever outside-in approach is used, clients are rarely involved in data gathering and delivery, are often unaware of the data types originating from their organization being sold to the KYC requesting counterparts, and have no control over data consumption. Repository users have been known to complain that some KYC repositories store and use outdated data.

A further enhancement of KYC databases is achieved when clients are asked to submit their own KYC data in a structured and mandatory manner. This type of self-assessment produces more reliable, accountable, and binding data sets. Data ownership is an important incentive for clients to be transparent and diligent with their KYC data deliveries. If clients can decide, case by case, with whom they share their uploaded data or data subset, they become more inclined towards transparency and KYC compliance.

Such exclusive inside-out sourced KYC data platforms, with point-to-point connections and client-selected, secure data exchanges, combined with data from publicly accessible repositories, might be an approximation for a perfect database. To further enhance the content of such a master KYC database, data from multiple sources, at first glance not related, needs to be collected and analysed. The opportunities for big data, deep learning, and artificial intelligence need to be applied to manage the ongoing challenges to provide efficient and effective KYC solutions. They also have the potential to deal with already existing challenges around bitcoin transactions and also any criminal financial transactions in the dark web.

Conclusion

Although full compliance may currently be out of reach, certainly the steps outlined in this chapter will help edge closer to the 100% achievement mark.

RegTech and FinTech companies are crucial partners in this process, which should be based on mutual and transparent professionalism. Regulators, auditors, FIs, and KYC technology providers need to collaborate to harness the benefits of RegTech solutions and to check and control the readiness and implementation level of AML/CFT rules by using the same digital tools.

It is obvious that the current system of paying large fines for insufficient and noncompliant KYC solutions is not working. Instead, regulators should exert stronger and more consistent controls on FIs, and follow up on the documented findings and issues, similar to an audit process. The regulators would stipulate that FIs are required to address the issues and implement the necessary changes to their KYC solutions and processes within a specified timeline. Finally, regulators would need to check the FI, and only then would any unresolved issues be subject to a fine.

The fine would also need to include the costs to implement a compliant KYC solution and approach with an external, independent RegTech solution provider that is not biased with other goals of departments in the same institution. Presupposing the willingness of FIs to fight money laundering and the financing of terrorism, big data-based RegTech and digitization will be a game changer to mitigate the adverse effects of criminal economic activity.

Merits and Demerits of a Shared Risk Engine

By Rohit Ghosh
AI Scientist and Founder, Skyra Capital

and Harshwardhan Prasad
VP, Quant Analytics, Morgan Stanley

The idea of a shared risk engine (SRE) as a concept is to build a cloud-based, secure risk engine as a shared service that simulates all the major risk-related functionalities at significantly lower cost.

An SRE would be a common platform shared across multiple organizations albeit in a safe and secure way without compromising on any data privacy. SREs can replicate all major risk engine functionalities like value at risk (VaR) calculation, risk reporting, stress testing, and so forth on a cloud instance that is shared across financial organizations without any of them needing to expose their internal data and model publicly. The main advantage of such a model is extreme cost reduction for any organization, for two main reasons. Firstly, major cost operations and functions of model building, data storage and quality, model validation, and even risk report building would be shared across all participants. Secondly, the cloud-based architecture would mean pay per usage, customized to model complexity and data requirements of individual banks. In this chapter, we demonstrate how we can achieve this target, and offer a brief overview of the architecture involved.

Computationally, in the first step, the central module (I_0) in SRE produces organization-specific risk application programming interfaces (ORAPIs) – a set of APIs for all major risk functionalities for risk calculation. Consequently, the final risk calculation is done on yet another cloud instance (I_n) using the ORAPIs and the current exposure of the organization. This cloud instance (I_n), for obvious reasons, would be accessible only to the organization and opaque to the rest of the participants.

We will be describing the modules and architecture of the model along with discussions of possible advantages and disadvantages, followed by concluding thoughts on next steps forward in bringing such a system to production.

Cloud Infrastructure for Storage

Most organizations receive, trade, market, and associate reference data of several terabytes (TBs) every day for the risk engine computation. Currently, organizations use different means of data storage that vary from cloud to internal storage server racks.

SREs would reduce the storage costs along with the infrastructure maintenance costs drastically by storing the common data feed on the cloud. The data storage is therefore not replicated at multiple organizations, and storage cost is shared among participants. However, it is important to note here that organizations can still have their independent local storage, which can be fed into the storage for generating ORAPIs. The local storage would be interacting with the main storage instance (S_0 in Figure 1) through API calls and making the local storage inaccessible to other participants.

Data Handler

Currently, risk engines have multiple data sources contributing to an integrated feed. Most of the time, the majority of these sources present incoherent and missing data that requires extra monitoring and special preprocessing, incurring extra resource allocation on behalf of the organization.

Instead of compiling data feeds independently across organizations, SREs would compile multiple sources and use advanced analytics to maintain data quality and prune out noise. SREs would house an analytics powerhouse operating on central storage bucket S_0 to filter incoming data for preprocessing before using it for risk calculation.

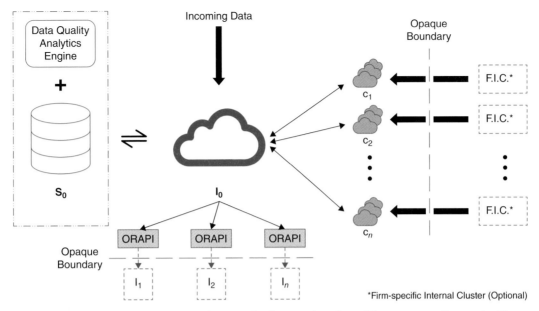

Figure 1: Architecture of SREs where I_0 communicates independently with storage S_0 and other computing clusters (C_1–C_n) to conglomerate a cloud-based shared risk engine

SREs would also contain modules for independent data entry as well, which would integrate seamlessly the collective feed from stand-alone sources in case an organization plans to integrate a private data source into its feed.

Model Silos

Most of the risk engines across the globe use advanced state-of-the-art modelling to calculate VaR or similar risk measures for their portfolios. The internal models could well be a differentiator for most risk engines across organizations. Hence SREs will have the option of supporting independent and opaque modelling clusters. The way privacy of such models would be ensured is explained with examples in the 'Architecture Details' section.

By default, SREs would have options to choose from a list of expert team–designed models, for most of the products that are widely used by almost all organizations. The expert team-designed models would be housed on the subclusters and interact with the main computing cluster to generate ORAPIs. These models would strictly adhere to the regulatory guidelines so that organizations using these models would not require any further validation.

Organizations can either choose from available models for their modellable pieces or choose to build internal models, which would interact with the subclusters via API calls. As explained earlier, in case they want to build their own models, they can get the models validated internally while the models would be completely opaque to other participants.

Stress Testing and Scenario Analysis

Banks are mandated to stress test their books to assess their readiness, resilience, and capital adequacy in case of a downturn. All scenarios for stress tests can be designed independently by the SRE, in line with regulatory guidelines.

By default, all the scenarios provided under Comprehensive Capital Analysis and Review (CCAR) by regulators would be generated uniformly for stress testing purposes. Scenario mapping to appropriate shocks can be defined with common rules. Further, scenario selection can leverage the availability of large common data to apply artificial intelligence (AI) and machine learning (ML) techniques and still give custom-built scenarios for each bank's position.

Integrated Risk Reporting

Reporting platforms to date are often outdated, rigid, and inefficiently built legacy systems. SREs can enable generating automated, customizable reports – both regulatory and business specific – in a click-and-drag environment. In smaller organizations, where different parts of data reside in silos, an integrated reporting dashboard offers a simple solution to generating reports at any point of time in the day.

Similar to the rest of the modules, the central module first generates a risk reporting–based ORAPI, which is in turn used by an organization-specific cluster to generate requisite reports. As the second part of the calculation is carried out on private clusters, the reports thus generated are again completely opaque to the rest of the participants in the SRE.

Architecture Details

Figure 1 depicts how the technical architecture would work. The main cloud computer instance (I_0) communicates with the data storage system (S_0) and the rest of the subclusters (C_1–C_n) to create ORAPIs.

ORAPIs are used by independent organization-specific submodules (I_1–I_n) to generate the final risk number or reports. A network of independent clusters (C_1–C_n) houses the different functionalities like risk modelling, stress testing, and reporting.

In cases where organizations decide to implement their own version of models for any particular risk class or customized report or for in-depth stress testing, they can design separate modules, which would only be interacting with respective submodules through API calls. For example, say an organization wants to build a very customized risk model for its Equity Vols risk class. It would be hosting the model on a separate cloud instance A_{EV}, which interacts with C_{EV} (where C_{EV} is the SRE subcluster that hosts the default expert-designed model for Equity Vols) and through API calls updates Equity Vols risk model outputs in C_{EV}, which would be used for reporting and modelling of organization A.

The clusters being modular, they thereby aren't affected when a firm wants to explicitly model only one of the risk classes or add a new report. The added benefit from such a modular structure is the extra safety of internal models and reports, as the key for these instances will be with organizations only and would be unavailable to the SRE. Also, for even more secure interactions, these custom clusters like A_{EV} can be hosted locally from the organization's premises.

After the generation of ORAPIs, I_n takes up the rest of the process for generating the risk values specific to the organization by passing current exposure as an argument to the ORAPIs. The current exposure would be available only to I_n and thus not visible to other participants in the SRE.

Rapid Scaling

Most of the legacy systems in almost all banking organizations suffer from the lack of scalability in their systems.

For SREs, scalability is a by-product of the entire process. Because of cloud-based storage and intra-instance data handling, SREs could easily be scaled up within minutes to tackle data storage at a larger scale (from new product categories or otherwise) along with the requisite processing horsepower.

Reduced Cost

The most evident and concrete advantage an SRE can offer is on cost-effectiveness. An SRE would be way cheaper than any other alternate solution by virtue of its shared architecture. Like any other shared service, an SRE can drive down the cost for an individual entity, and – like all such products – the higher the number of organizations adopting the SRE, the lower the cost.

Data acquisition, data storage, data maintenance, and integrated reporting are some of the areas where the costs are decreased dramatically with absolute certainty. Further, even the cost for customized implementations would still be far cheaper than conventional sources because of the pay-as-you-use model of cloud systems.

Improved Data Quality

The majority of preprocessing for data cleansing and monitoring could involve a lot of rigorous scrutiny along with the application of sophisticated technology for handling errors algorithmically. Let's consider a simple example: a spin-off, merger, or acquisition not only affects the incoming data but also requires adjusting historical data, which wouldn't be accounted for by the data vendor, as most of them are responsible for data feed but not historical data. Instead of replicating the adjustment for all data points across organizations, an SRE can streamline the entire process, and organizations can leverage the advanced algorithm and scrutiny efforts of the SRE.

The unified data feed and maintenance procedure also benefits regulators, as the monitoring for data quality can now be streamlined since most banks use a shared processing step.

Faster and Modular Modelling

In regulation technology (RegTech), modelling is the most important differentiator. Thus it is of utmost importance that risk models are designed in such a way that they represent the most advanced state-of-the-art methodology and models in respective domains. However, a good number of organizations would be constrained by the resources they could use to build up their systems and models to such a level. With SREs, the state-of-the-art implementation can be achieved easily at a marginally lower cost, as the cost of resources are shared across participants.

SREs would also be able to implement faster across-the-board implementations of any advanced model as soon as it is being talked about in one of the banks. This would reduce the cost of replicating efforts of building such a model at all organizations and be able to provide all participants with an edge in implementing such a model early on.

Improved Supervisory Comparability

Upcoming regulatory changes and new guidelines like Fundamental Review of the Trading Book (FRTB) advocate for more standardization and transparency across models. FRTB aims for better risk attribution for each risk model. Thus, it will obviously be easier for regulators to compare the results if banks are using commonly validated models and data. Also, any regulatory analysis can easily draw from common risk data, which would also be shared by other organizations for their modelling, thus ensuring maximum impact for their regulatory decisions.

Data Privacy

A crucial concern looming with SREs is data privacy. The architecture of SREs has been designed such that a firm can conceal all the internal modules it wishes to. The internal modules house all the internal models and private data, and only the results from these models are communicated to the respective subclusters in SREs through API calls. This makes the data and such models completely opaque. Also, as the final set of risk number calculation requires current exposure, they are also calculated in separate private organization-accessible-only instances (I_n) using ORAPIs generated by I_0.

Standardization of Internal Models

Another red flag for most businesses would be standardization of models, giving away their competitive edge. However, the platform allows building modules in addition to the choice to pick from prefabricated modules. Further, as with data privacy, model privacy would also be maintained in opaque silos with access limited only to specific members within the organization.

Systemic Model Risk

The systemic risk, one may argue, can be magnified by using a platform that brings greater commonality in model assumptions. As seen earlier in 2008, failure of common model assumptions can lead to widespread market failure. That said, diversification of model risk using the difference in model errors is far from optimal. A more rigorous and common model validation along with an incentive to contribute to sophistication will improve risk management globally.

Also, the severity of operational risk with an SRE can be considerable, given that the failure of any of the computing clusters could possibly spell doom for the SRE if the systems are not appropriately backed up. A business continuity plan to address such failures would give greater comfort to regulators and the market in moving towards such a common platform.

Conclusions

This chapter is written in order to lay out a blueprint for discussing and furthering the cause of SREs. A basic architecture explaining all the modules has been discussed at length, giving an insight as to how such a model would function, keeping the interests of all the stakeholders in mind. It has been demonstrated that SREs would be able to reduce cost and bring scalability to risk systems along with other benefits without compromising on data privacy at all.

Such a shared model not only benefits participating organizations but also greatly helps the cause of regulators. As explained earlier, the accumulation of data at one place and processing from a central unit makes it easy for regulators to be cognizant of the concerns associated with current risk management. Also, it would be much faster for regulators to discuss and implement changes, as all would be implemented centrally.

It is imperative to mention here that such efforts towards collaborative shared risk systems are already underway, with SunGuard building a hosted services platform or Markit and other firms providing FRTB suites with common modellability data and other modules of a standardized approach. Advancements like these indicate that with cooperation amongst financial organizations, regulators, data vendors, and product developers, SREs could soon see the light of day.

Spend on Compliance: A Necessary Evil or Business Enabler?

By Nicola Cowburn
Chief Marketing Officer, CUBE

and Patrick Barnert
Non-Executive Director, Evolute Group AG

Compliance, not banking, has been the real growth business since 2008. Unprecedented increases in the volume and complexity of financial services regulation are worrying senior executives, and are having a negative impact on profitability.

Compliance as a Cost Centre

The number of international regulatory alerts has topped 200 daily[1] (more than 51,000 annually) and is doubling every two years, indicating a gloomy outlook of spiralling costs. For most financial institutions, compliance is a cost centre that can represent as much as 10% of operating costs.

In a much-publicized 2015 Bloomberg interview,[2] Jamie Dimon, CEO at JPMorgan Chase, highlighted the problem: 'In the old days, you dealt with one regulator when you had an issue, maybe two. Now, it is five or six. It makes it very difficult and very complicated.'

Many regulated firms liken the cost of compliance to an insurance premium: expensive, yet mandatory. You hope you will never need to defend your firm from allegations of wrongdoing; nevertheless, you must pay whatever it costs to protect your firm, putting people, systems, and processes in place that would prove its innocence and demonstrate that you acted in a client's best interests, should the need arise.

Some people view spending on compliance as a necessary evil. It is 'necessary', certainly, considering that the cost of compliance can pale into insignificance, compared with the potentially devastating cost of non-compliance. Harsh penalties have been imposed for basic record-keeping misdemeanours. For example, a US regulator fined a global bank $3,750,000 for failing to keep proper electronic records, emails, and instant messages, and the Financial Conduct Authority collected a £3 million fine from one of the world's most prominent private banks for inadequate record keeping. Add to that the risk of reputational damage and the threat of personal liability (including possible senior executive imprisonment), and it is easy to see how compliance teams justify excessive budgets.

However, is spend on compliance really a necessary evil? Alternatively, have financial institutions simply failed to adapt constructively to the ever-changing regulatory landscape?

Compliance is a mainly manual process. Many firms have responded to escalating volume and complexity of financial regulation by throwing people at the process, which has inflated costs. Increases in compliance staff by 30–40% since 2008 have been commonplace; reports of ten-fold increases in compliance staff for some of the world's biggest banks have been reported. While this may help initially, it is not a scalable model, and the cash burn rate of the compliance function is rapidly escalating to the point of unsustainability.

The scale of the issue is about to rise further owing to the skyrocketing trajectory of digital transformation. By 2020, 75% of financial services client interaction will be digital, and this figure is likely to exceed 95% by 2025.[3]

---

[1] https://blogs.thomsonreuters.com/financial-risk/risk-management-compliance/cost-compliance-changing-world-regulation

[2] https://www.bloomberg.com/news/features/2015-06-25/compliance-is-now-calling-the-shots-and-bankers-are-bristling

[3] Qumram customer survey, 2017.

Today's people-heavy compliance efforts are no longer cutting it. They are backwards-looking, focused primarily on in-person meetings, phone calls, and emails. However, this is just the tip of the iceberg, compared with the explosive growth in e-communications. Most international regulations now include record-keeping requirements that encompass all e-communication channels, including websites and portals, instant messaging, social media, and mobile applications.

This migration to digital business is creating a huge blind spot for the majority of financial institutions. Many are failing to deliver on the digital manifesto that would satisfy customers, because they fear non-compliance. However, this digital blind spot is creating business risk for the future in the form of disengaged customers, which increases harmful churn and revenue loss.

Why Is Compliance Not Addressing the Blind Spot?

There are three main reasons compliance has not been addressing the digital blind spot:

1. *Inadequate systems and processes.* The majority of firms lack the ability to monitor and capture omnichannel records. As many as 92% of UK wealth managers have admitted that their data/record-keeping systems required – or still require – changes as a direct result of MiFID II.[4] US firms face similar challenges, as they tackle the regulatory demands of the Securities and Exchange Commission (SEC), Financial Industry Regulatory Authority (FINRA), and Department of Labor.

2. *Focus on business protection, not growth.* The compliance function has a duty of care to protect the firm, and its executives, from litigation. While some chief compliance officers

have one eye on the business as a whole, their teams have little or no focus on changing customer demands, new media trends, customer experience and preferences, and profitability. Compliance is often viewed as a 'business prevention team', inclined to block all business development proposals that increase risk. Until now, this has been bad news for digital transformation and social media initiatives, which, by their very nature, lead to more fluid and uncontrolled communication flows.

3. *Customer experience not a compliance consideration.* As you embark on your journey together, the abundance of form-filling entailed in the client onboarding and anti–money laundering (AML) process can lead to a poor customer experience, right from the start. Despite this, compliance officers are happy as long as the data captured conforms to regulatory requirements. Similarly, utilization of digital channels for customer communication is proven to increase satisfaction, yet compliance teams are concerned only with digital channels' propensity to increase risk.

Failure to address the digital blind spot is a lose-lose situation, which can lead to interdepartmental friction, as well as customer attrition. Keen to drive revenue growth and enrich customer engagement, business teams become frustrated when compliance thwarts their projects. The view of compliance as a function that simply haemorrhages cost, cannibalizes profit, and stifles innovation is perpetuated.

This battle between compliance and the business is unfortunate because at the macro level it is obvious that both parties share the common goal of client-centricity. Many regulations have the customer at their heart, having been formulated to protect their best interests. Equally, the majority of business initiatives aim to deliver to customers what they want: better products, more engaging service, higher returns, and more convenient and effective communications.

RegTech overcomes the technical limitations of legacy compliance automation tools and has paved the way for internal teams to begin pulling in the same direction, in pursuit of common goals.

---

4 'Compliance 2016 MiFID II: Will the Wealth Management Sector Be Ready in Time?' Compeer Ltd.

RegTech: A New Wave of Opportunity

The attempts to digitize the compliance and risk process have focused primarily on cost reduction and operational efficiency and are not new. However, RegTech in its present form is looking more broadly at the vast opportunity to mitigate risk across the board – operationally, reputationally, and financially.

Legacy technology systems deployed in the past to automate the compliance process have proven to be unwieldy, inflexible, and costly to maintain. Attempts to adapt these ageing systems to accommodate the complex, post-2008 regulatory landscape have been largely unsuccessful. They rely on outdated technology, and in most cases were not purpose-built for compliance.

This has spawned a new breed of agile and scalable RegTech solutions, which automate and streamline repeatable compliance processes and drive down costs. Crucially, these solutions also ensure transparency, accuracy, and accountability, thereby safeguarding the interests of both the customer and the firm, and providing a richer understanding of risk exposure.

The innovation of RegTech lies in leveraging the mass of data that is collected and retained by compliance for many years, to create actionable insights that generate business value, improve customer satisfaction, boost revenues, and drive growth. RegTech often includes advanced machine learning, artificial intelligence, and analytics tools that transform compliance into a business function that is capable of contributing to these goals.

A pivotal point to recognize is that banks and other financial institutions are now required by law to record customer identifiable data for regulatory compliance and legal e-discovery purposes – data that other departments, such as marketing or customer support, cannot capture without contravening data privacy laws. When used in anonymized form, compliance data converts into highly valuable business intelligence, which can be used to develop more saleable products and solutions, deliver more effective service, and drive customer satisfaction. Utilizing compliance data in this interconnected manner creates a holistic view of the customer journey and experience, which fuels enterprise-wide value across both compliance and business functions. Very quickly we see the perception of compliance alter from business

Figure 1: **Reuse data captured for compliance to drive business value**

preventer to business enabler. Figure 1 demonstrates how the collection of behavioural data allows companies to both be compliant and grow their business.

The so-called RegTech revolution has been welcomed by those professionals responsible for compliance technology, operations, and surveillance, whose challenge is to marry the growth and customer satisfaction needs of the business with the regulatory requirements of compliance.

Already, there are many working examples of financial institutions utilizing RegTech to secure their compliance status. These firms are saving millions of dollars in the process, and extending the value of their spend beyond compliance to enable more efficient and profitable operations.

Examples

Business Protection – Compliance and Fraud

- *Social media surveillance.* The compliant use of social media in financial services – for both internal and external communications – has become viable through RegTech. Many firms, including wealth managers, institutional asset managers, insurance companies, and global commodity providers, now communicate with each other, and with customers, via popular instant messaging and social media platforms (WhatsApp, WeChat, Skype, and LinkedIn, for example). Even unregulated providers of financial data, analytics, and research, supplying services to regulated investment managers, are leveraging RegTech to mitigate reputational risk.

- *Anti–money laundering (AML).* AML analysts can conduct online searches that are automatically recorded in their entirety from start to end, securely archived, and easily accessed for compliance e-discovery purposes. Previously, these analysts would have taken manual screen shots and archived them in jpg form. RegTech has saved an immense amount of time and

storage space; one global bank claims that every 30 seconds of time saved within the AML process results in a £1–2 million saving annually.

- *Fraud discovery.* Suspicious activity and patterns of behaviour, perhaps an out-of-hours lookup of customer account details by an employee or a download of the firm's customer list, automatically alerts the forensics team to be assessed and actioned if appropriate. The validity of whistle-blower alerts can also be investigated much faster and more efficiently.

Business Growth – Customer Experience and Engagement

- *Struggle detection.* Behavioural data captured for compliance purposes also includes rich online user experience insights. Many financial institutions use this compliance data to analyse user experience, detect user struggles, highlight hesitation, and detect a drop in customer conversion. Once this is understood, these firms can take remedial action.

- *Support and dispute resolution.* Sudden shifts in fund prices often result in an influx of customers contacting the call centre to question the timing, or price, of a recently executed transaction – especially when the transaction was self-executed online. Utilizing RegTech, first-contact resolution is completely viable. The customer service agent can immediately retrieve indisputable proof of the transaction without recourse to IT, saving considerable e-discovery time, loss of a client, or a potential fine.

- *Sales and marketing.* RegTech is revolutionizing the ability of financial firms and their relationship managers to predict their 'next best action' for every individual, throughout the entire customer life cycle. The use of predictive analytics for tracking and recording customer behaviour across all channels of communication generates revealing insights that can be utilized to ensure compliance, maximize satisfaction, and increase revenue.

How to Get Started

Returning to the title of this chapter, 'Spend on Compliance: A Necessary Evil or Business Enabler?', the answer is clear. While spend on compliance is necessary, it can become a constructive and profitable business enabler through the creative application of RegTech.

To get started, you should:

- *Understand the limitations and costs associated with your legacy platforms.* Be realistic about their ability to accommodate ongoing regulatory change, and to deliver sufficient value for money.

- *Utilize RegTech for compliance process automation*, to gain vast cost and time savings through operational efficiency.

- *Reuse data gathered for compliance purposes*, to fuel enterprise-wide value and achieve business growth.

- *Look beyond compliance, be open to innovation, and collaborate with colleagues*, to drive progress in pursuit of your client-centric goals.

- *Adapt your procurement criteria*, to quickly engage in flexible partnerships with small, yet innovative, RegTech firms. These firms offer fresh perspectives and creative approaches to compliance and risk management, but will not be on your approved suppliers' list today.

RegTech for Authorized Institutions

6

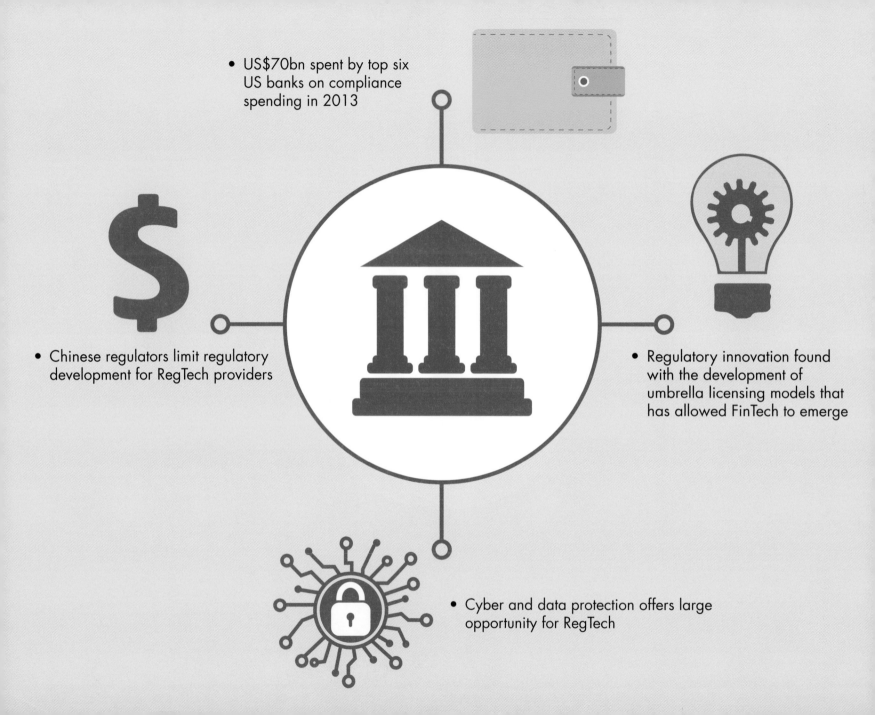

- US$70bn spent by top six US banks on compliance spending in 2013

- Chinese regulators limit regulatory development for RegTech providers

- Regulatory innovation found with the development of umbrella licensing models that has allowed FinTech to emerge

- Cyber and data protection offers large opportunity for RegTech

As Part 6 will show, the scope of business use cases of RegTech start-ups is diverse. Regulatory pressures have increased sharply in the wake of the financial crisis, giving RegTech a variety of applications in financial services.

New EU regulations aimed at preventing money laundering and terrorist financing provide considerable opportunities. The first chapter discusses how, as regulations increase the stringency of compliance obligations for both firms and regulators, RegTech can have an immediate impact in CDD, going further than existing manual processes to general holistic customer risk profiles. RegTech solutions such as in-depth reviews of data to identify customer's behavioral patterns will allow banks and financial services firms to go beyond a 'tick-box' approach to anti-money laundering, enhancing their ability to identify risks early and contributing to client relations.

The second chapter discusses current challenges related to 'passporting' in the EU and the opportunities this presents for RegTech. While investments firms in the EU authorized by their home states to provide investment services are able to offer their products to clients in other member states, European governments impose often ambiguous local regulations. Amidst the lack of uniformity and confusion, RegTech can facilitate supervisory cooperation between the financial services sector in home states and host member states through standardization and automation software.

China's financial services market also presents significant opportunities for RegTech: the financial services regulatory structure in China is complex, vertical and specialized, obstructing information sharing and cross-supervision in the process of applying for financial licenses. An integrated RegTech platform will assist in mitigating these regulatory constraints, opening the way for financial holding companies to obtain multiple financial licenses and generate economies of scope.

The increasing interaction of the regulatory sphere with the digital world entails both risk and opportunity. As regulated entities and regulators themselves adopt RegTech solutions, RegTech providers will need to address the cybersecurity implications of new technologies. Sandboxes present the opportunity for regulators to work with innovative and technology-focused companies from their inception, signaling a potential transformation in the role of regulators and the growth of industries whose regulatory culture is built on digital technologies. Sophisticated RegTech solutions that go beyond simple regulatory reporting and offer an integrated platform will benefit regulators, compliance officers and operational staff within companies as regulation becomes increasingly digitized.

The final chapter addresses the implications for banks and FinTech start-ups of the revised Payment Services Directive of 2015. The directive introduces two new types of entities to the financial industry – account information service providers and payment initiation service providers. As non-bank financial services enter the market, innovative opportunities as well as new compliance challenges will emerge.

Across these different use cases, successful implementation of RegTech solutions will require certain prerequisites from authorized institutions in terms of IT readiness and cultural alignment of compliance teams.

RegTech Opportunities in a Post-4MLD/5MLD World

By Jane Jee
CEO, Kompli-Global Limited

and Fleur Hutchinson
Enhanced Due Diligence Consultant, Seventeen Research Ltd

In June 2017 the then new UK government implemented the 4th EU Money Laundering Directive (4MLD) with regulations – the snappily titled 'The Money Laundering, Terrorist Financing and Transfer of Funds (Information on the Payer) Regulations 2017' or MLRs as we shall call them. The MLRs were set to make money laundering and terrorist financing more difficult and could have been much more effective had they been embraced and properly implemented by all member states and regulated firms.

However even 4MLD was soon seen as inadequate, due in part to the growing concerns over terrorist financing and the revelations of the Panama Papers. The Fifth Anti-Money Laundering Directive (5MLD) entered into force in July 2018 with an obligation for EU member states to implement it by January 2020.

5MLD builds upon 4MLD and extends it. For example, for the first time, 5MLD brings certain virtual currency service providers within the scope of EU anti-money laundering and terrorist financing regulations. The other main 5MLD provisions require EU member states to:

- increase transparency with respect to the beneficial ownership registers that they were required to establish under 4MLD;

- create and maintain a list of public functions that qualify as "politically exposed persons" or "PEPs" in their jurisdiction;

- establish centralized registers or data retrieval systems to enable financial intelligence units (FIUs) and national competent authorities to access information about the identities of holders of bank and payment accounts and safe-deposit boxes;

5MLD also:

- clarifies and harmonizes the enhanced due diligence measures that have to be applied to business relationships or transactions involving "high risk third countries";

- restricts the anonymous use of prepaid cards in order to mitigate the risk that such cards may be used for terrorist financing;

- grants new powers to FIUs who can request, obtain and use information from any obliged entity, based on their own analysis and intelligence, rather than just when triggered by a prior suspicious activity report.

Successful money laundering means that, essentially, crime pays. Criminals, whether they are drug traffickers, people smugglers, arms traffickers, terrorists, blackmailers, or any other form of organized criminals, disguise the origin of their criminal money so they can avoid detection and the risk of prosecution when spending it. Money laundering is critical to the effective operation of virtually every form of cross-border and organized crime. Anti–money laundering (AML) efforts, which are designed to prevent or limit the ability of criminals to use their ill-gotten gains, are both a critical and an effective component of anticrime activities.

Arguably, the 2017 MLRs were overdue, as many changes in the scale and sophistication of criminality had occurred in the 10 years since the Money Laundering Regulations 2007 were implemented. Some consider that the laws implementing 4MLD and 5MLD (yet to be implemented in the UK) represent an unnecessary burden and prevent legitimate business activities. However, those of us in the anti–money laundering compliance industry who are tech savvy have a far more optimistic outlook: we recognize that advancements in regulatory technology (RegTech) can significantly reduce both the burden and cost of compliance.

RegTech companies offer solutions that are flexible and agile – attributes that are often sadly lacking in the systems and processes of regulated firms. RegTech solutions enable data to be collated, sifted, manipulated, and stored securely; they are often cloud-based and can be adapted quickly when regulations change, as well as offering the speed and efficiency that legacy systems cannot provide.

Regulators have welcomed the entry of RegTech companies to the market and are encouraging regulated firms to engage with them and take advantage of their potential to deliver regulatory compliance in a shorter timeframe and at far lower cost. Both the Bank of England and the Financial Conduct Authority (FCA) have RegTech initiatives to promote innovation in this field, but more action and assessment of solutions are needed if the full benefits of RegTech are to be promulgated.

Many regulated firms have complained of the ever-increasing volume, complexity, and cost of addressing applicable laws in this field. However, the rapid growth of the RegTech industry should be seen as an unprecedented opportunity. Advancements in identity technology and automated screening can remove entirely the more manually intensive elements of customer due diligence, in favour of more meaningful data upon which to base better risk analysis, review, and management of high-risk customers.

A GLOBAL ISSUE

In January 2018 the UK government launched a new AML watchdog, the Office for Professional Body Anti–Money Laundering Supervision (OPBAS) that sits within the FCA. OPBAS is "a supervisor of supervisors" and has just issued its first annual assessment report (in March 2019).[1] The report makes somewhat depressing reading as it is very critical of the 22 supervisors OPBAS supervises – these supervisors cover mainly the accountancy and legal services sectors. OPBAS found that:

- the bodies were focused on representing their members rather than strongly supervising standards;

- too few of those bodies enforce the current standards;

- they fail to share intelligence on money laundering risks; and

- nearly a quarter of the professional bodies undertook no form of supervision.

OPBAS does not cover the three statutory supervisors, i.e., the FCA, Her Majesty's Revenue and Customs (HMRC), and the Gambling Commission. Many, including the recent Treasury Select Committee,[2] consider our AML regime in the UK is too fragmented and a single supervisor for all sectors would be more effective and efficient. Having said that, since money laundering is a global issue, it cannot be effectively addressed by any individual state in isolation. As we have seen from recent AML fines, the benefits of money laundering (higher bank profits) accrue nationally, while the costs of money laundering (more crime) are shared internationally. The failure of national AML and Counter Terrorist Financing (CTF) supervisors to co-operate and co-ordinate has led to inadequate enforcement of AML/CTF rules and, a reluctance to share information internationally with other bank supervisors, meaning significant intelligence is ignored.

A recent European report[3] made clear that better cooperation and information sharing among AML and prudential supervisors will be ineffective "as long as the underlying incentives to engage in international regulatory competition towards low enforcement of anti-money laundering standards are not addressed". Criminals will always seek out and exploit the weakest link wherever it exists in the world and are using increasingly sophisticated technology to achieve their ends.

---

[1] https://www.fca.org.uk/publication/opbas/themes-2018-opbas-anti-money-laundering-supervisory-assessments.pdf

[2] https://www.parliament.uk/business/committees/committees-a-z/commons-select/treasury-committee/news-parliament-2017/report-published-economic-crime-17-19/

[3] http://www.europarl.europa.eu/RegData/etudes/IDAN/2018/624424/IPOL_IDA(2018)624424_EN.pdf

The Financial Action Task Force (FATF) is now in its 30th year and is still a vital global standard setter. FATF has just been given an open-ended mandate[4] which reflects the fact that money laundering and terrorist financing are enduring concerns for the integrity of the financial system, and that a sustained political commitment to fight money laundering, terrorist financing, and proliferation financing is now more vital than ever.

A seamless global AML regime and enforcement may be some way off but there is a growing realization that RegTech is a vital weapon if the international community is serious about combating cross-border organized crime and creating better barriers against money laundering,

The Risk Based Approach (RBA)

The core principles underpinning 4MLD and 5MLD are not new: they largely build upon existing anti–money laundering legislation, but clarify ambiguous clauses and emphasize a move away from a tick-box approach in favour of the risk-based approach, which is now the cornerstone of compliance in this field. However, the MLRs involve subtle but significant alterations to compliance procedures for regulated firms (known as 'obliged entities'). The aim of the lawmakers is to force individual firms to assess the risks involved in the nature of the products and services they offer and to risk assess their customers more thoroughly. There is no room in the AML framework for complacency or abdicating responsibility; a board director has to be responsible for compliance and risk personal liability where practices and procedures do not meet the legislation. Regulators do ask to see documented risk assessments from obliged entities, and the regulators themselves are obliged to write up the risks faced by each of the sectors they regulate.

The MLRs place more emphasis on the treatment and management of politically exposed persons (PEPs), customers

with a presence in high-risk jurisdictions, and ultimate beneficial owners (UBOs), while removing the ability to take a simplified approach to lower-risk customers without explicit justification.

The Union of RegTech and Increased Regulation

In 2013, the six largest US banks reportedly spent US$70.2 billion on compliance, with some estimates claiming that some of the world's largest banks have each spent an additional US$4 billion a year on compliance since the financial crisis. The estimated costs of properly implementing 4 and 5MLD are anybody's guess, but without assistance from technology, the pressures could mean some firms will no longer be viable. MiFID II and GDPR have also been highlighted as a key challenge for both boards and compliance functions.

RegTech as an industry is developing rapidly and will help streamline many aspects of business by reducing the effort and time involved in compliance. Can RegTech solve all compliance issues? Of course not. Human judgement will always have a crucial role in determining where risks exist and their materiality; however, where RegTech is deployed in the right way at the right time, it will enable a firm to optimize the most expensive aspect of compliance: human resources. The area where RegTech can have the most immediate and obvious application is Customer Due Diligence (CDD) and its associated compliance requirements.

For many organizations, relying exclusively on existing manual processes to comply with the regulatory requirements of customer onboarding, approval, ongoing monitoring, and lifecycle management, will no longer be an option. Manual processes rarely go far enough in taking a holistic view of a customer's risk profile, often bringing up too many false positives or failing to identify information (especially if suppressed) outside of indexed web pages. Information gathering abroad can also prove to be particularly challenging and expensive, leaving obliged entities

---

[4] http://www.fatf-gafi.org/publications/fatfgeneral/documents/fatf-mandate.html

open to compliance gaps, increased risk, and the possibility of refusing lucrative new business. Finally, manual research processes are still susceptible to human error and are, above all, resource-inefficient.

New technological products are on hand to ensure that the usually labour-intensive processes of compliance are minimized, and in addition efficiently target the information gaps that the new regulations bring into scope. RegTech searches can be far more effective than commercial search engines – including offering searches of unindexed web pages – leaving less room for criminals and wrongdoers to hide their past.

Such advancements in RegTech should be seen as an opportunity to remove entirely the more manually intensive elements of CDD, such as the collation and review of identity documentation and verification and manual screening against international watch lists. New technologies offered by a raft of RegTech start-ups provide more sophisticated solutions, such as electronic identity verification for both corporate entities and individuals, automated screening and monitoring, and identifying adverse information in the depths of publicly available data.

While there is no question that the new regulations imply higher compliance costs, investment in today's regulatory technology will ultimately minimize the long-term cost burden of compliance, absorbing the expense of the changing regulations, minimizing human error in the onboarding process, and allowing for real-time monitoring of customers. Upgrading compliance technology should be viewed alongside replacing the legacy infrastructure of financial services firms with digital capabilities and recognized as an overall cost-benefit.

Beyond Regulatory Compliance

Money laundering regulation assists obliged entities in understanding the parameters of allowed activity in the financial services and related industries. Technology can assist with profiling customers within (and beyond) those parameters. If new technologies can complete identification verification more quickly and possibly better than a human, this frees up time to better *understand* customers.

Customer profiling means obliged entities do not have to merely rely on their customers' statements, but can track customers' behaviours, histories, corporate affiliations and integrity. Such reviews should identify and consider the risks associated with each customer relationship, including a comprehensive review of adverse media – an area that, in our opinion, obliged entities today do not address fully.

Such advancements allow obliged entities to move away from the tick-box approach that regulators frown upon to build a true, relevant, and contextual picture of customers from a range of publicly available information sources. This supports the ultimate aim of the regulations; increased consideration of risks and their materiality. The benefit to firms is threefold: it ultimately lowers their costs of compliance, frees up their employees' time, and vastly reduces their exposure to money laundering risk – and the costs and reputational risks associated with it.

Beyond the Regulatory Need for RegTech

Obliged entities look increasingly unlikely to meet the ever-expanding money laundering requirements without embracing new technology. We are fortunate today to be sitting at a crossroads where new RegTech products will enable simple, scalable, and affordable compliance – if embraced willingly and in spite of initial expense.

Beyond that, however, is a consequence that even the regulatory authorities perhaps had not considered: that embracing RegTech solutions will allow for enhanced and more sophisticated reviews of customers to identify material money laundering risks and catch the criminals early, preventing them from building up the fake identities and profiles needed to perpetuate, grow and maintain their criminal activities.

An Enhanced Approach

Obliged entities should look to minimize the processes employed to address CDD requirements, while changing their focus to more enhanced research techniques to mirror the ever more sophisticated methods used by criminals.

Such processes, which can also be addressed by new products in the RegTech space, can conduct in-depth reviews of structured and unstructured data for historical behavioural patterns, as well as employ sophisticated methods of reviewing vast quantities of data to identify relevant and material adverse information. Just as important as good data review are also good practices: not relying on a single information source to satisfy due diligence requirements, and ensuring that information is reviewed by a person with the relevant experience and one who understands the materiality of adverse information in the context of a client relationship.

A more enhanced understanding of a customer by a bank or financial services firm also has knock-on benefits of cross-selling, better customer financial management, and less pestering of customers for refreshed ID documents. Overall, embracing RegTech solutions has the potential to open up a new chapter in client relations – giving a whole new meaning and significance to the (often disparaging) term 'know your customer'.

Passporting in the EU – Is an Opportunity Also a Problem?

By Remonda Z. Kirketerp-Møller
Founder and CEO, muinmos ApS

The financial crisis had its impact on our daily lives. Blame was placed on the financial sector, on the governments for having little regulation, and on the regulators for lacking guidelines on existing regulation. *In the aftermath of the financial crisis, the regulatory pressure on the financial sector has increased, resulting in more complex regulation in an already heavily regulated sector.*

The Markets in Financial Services Directives 2004/39/EC and 2014/65/EC (MiFID) permit EU investment firms authorized by their home member state to provide any or all of the investment services for which they have received authorization in other EU member states. Many investment firms today offering their products to clients operate an online business model that is based on the cross-border provision of such products to mass markets (also known as 'passporting'). The passport system was built on the assumption that investment firms authorized anywhere in the EU will have met the same standards, and thus should in effect be treated as if they were locally authorized. However, European governments increasingly impose stricter rules or avoid creating clear guidance on very fundamental principles, thus creating a very uneven playing field. The local regulations may prevail and differ from one member state to the other, which reinforces the need for investment firms to review their compliance procedures and adapt their cross-border operating model to mitigate regulatory risk and protect their clients' interests.

There is heavy focus by the European Securities and Markets Authority (ESMA) in particular on the activities of third countries, representative offices, and branches of investment firms when operating a cross-border business, and whether these are operating in compliance with their regulatory status. However, little focus is placed on the following:

- What constitutes 'to provide any or all of the investment services' on a cross-border basis.

- The actual application form process an investment firm is required to complete when seeking an EU passport.

What Constitutes 'to Provide Any or All of the Investment Services'

Many investment firms in the European Union are confused by the phrase 'to provide any or all of the investment services', as there appear to be different definitions imposed by each EU financial services authority.

Does 'to provide' mean that an investment firm fulfils one or more of the following five points?

1. It actively distributes its products and services in another EU member state.

2. It markets its products and services in another EU member state.

3. It offers its products and services in another EU member state.

4. It sells its products and services in another EU member state.

5. It accepts clients who come unsolicited from another EU member state.

There are many examples of the discrepancy and lack of uniformity by the financial services authorities on what constitutes 'to provide any or all of the investment services'. This has led to mass confusion and resulted in many investment firms making passporting applications across the European Union without an actual business need, thereby creating a requirement for additional regulatory compliance oversight when in fact it may not be needed.

By way of example, the Financial Services and Markets Authority (FSMA) warned the public first in March 2017 against several investment firms operating unlawfully within the territory of Belgium, and reiterated that within the territory of Belgium no investment firm (authorized or not) is 'permitted actively to distribute' binary options via an electronic trading system. The same applied to derivative instruments, including foreign exchange derivatives and contracts for differences (CFDs) traded via an electronic trading system whose maturity is less than one hour, and those that directly or indirectly use leverage (collectively the 'products') specifically distributed to consumers, which is equivalent to the retail client category under MiFID. It moreover stated that any company wishing to offer the products must be an authorized investment firm. This appears to be a contradiction in itself. Is there a total ban in Belgium on the products, or is the ban on actively distributing and/or marketing and/or offering and/or selling the products and/or accepting consumers to buy the products?

The FSMA introduced the phrase 'permitted actively to distribute', and, to determine whether or not distribution is involved, the FSMA looked at indications such as the following to consider whether distribution is directed specifically to the Belgian public: the presence of specific information on the Belgian legal regime (particularly the tax regime), referral to contact persons in Belgium, the absence of a disclaimer indicating that the distribution is not addressed to the Belgian public, the language used, the possibility for Belgian consumers to register online, the fact that an investment firm has notified its intention to provide investment services in Belgium under MiFID, and whether advertisements for the products are disseminated via media within the territory of Belgium (collectively the 'criteria').

The criteria put forward by the FSMA appear to capture points 1–4, leaving out point 5, thus indicating that there is not a total ban on the products in Belgium, but that the FSMA allows an investment firm to in fact accept a consumer/retail client category from Belgium to buy the products as long as there is no active solicitation by the investment firm towards the Belgian consumer/retail client category.

Assuming an investment firm outside of Belgium but in the European Union accepts a consumer/retail client category from Belgium without any active solicitation, thus not caught by the ban, is the investment firm located in another EU member state not required to have a passport into Belgium in order to provide any and all of its investment services to a Belgian consumer/retail client category even if the consumer/retail client category came to the investment firm unsolicited? Based on the FSMA's application of the rules, it would appear that a passport is not required in this instance in Belgium to allow the investment firm to accept such a consumer/retail client category; otherwise, if the investment firm had a passport into Belgium it would in fact be caught by parts of the criteria, i.e. the fact that an investment firm has notified its intention to provide investment services in Belgium under MiFID, and therefore the investment firm in this instance may be caught by the ban imposed by the FSMA. This again raises the importance for both investment firms and financial services authorities across the European Union to understand the rules in each EU member state in order to avoid making passporting applications across the EU without an actual business need, thereby not only creating a need for additional regulatory compliance oversight when in fact it may not be required, but missing out on a potential business opportunity.

The Actual Application Form Process That an Investment Firm Is Required to Complete When Seeking an EU Passport

Financial services authorities across the European Union each have their own application form and process for when an investment firm wishes to passport into another EU member state. The EU passport application is often, if not always, completed by the investment firm wishing to provide its investment services to another EU member state. Rarely, the financial services authority sanitizes these applications, which has resulted in many investment firms being granted either more rights or fewer rights into the host member states than they originally had from their home financial services authority.

Under a standard financial services EU passport application, the following should form part of a standard application process:

1. What services or activities is the investment firm looking to passport?
2. What products is the investment firm looking to offer under the passport?
3. What client category is the investment firm looking to accept under the passport?

In the passport application process, most of the financial services authorities only ask about the services and activities that the investment firm wishes to passport into the host member state, thus allowing the investment firm to offer all available products under MiFID, whereas in many cases the investment firm in question may not even have an authorization from its home financial services authority to offer some of these products. The same applies to the client category; some investment firms may be limited to offer their services and products to professional clients and not retail clients. In some cases, they have been in fact granted a passport into another EU member state where they have been allowed to offer retail clients their products and services although they were never authorized by their home financial services authority to take on retail clients in the first place.

It is clear that many EU member states opted to apply their own terminology, which in some cases has left the investment firms confused during the passporting application process, thus creating errors in the application process. Taking the United Kingdom as an example, Table 1 highlights some of these differences where focus was placed on financial services and activities.

It is obvious that the terminology applied by the United Kingdom is quite different for a number of the services and activities when cross-referenced with MiFID. This will most likely result in confusion amongst the EU member states, especially when the financial services authorities of these member states are passporting the services into the United Kingdom. Many investment firms in the European Union have in fact received additional services and activities under their UK passport as a result of the differences in language used and interpretation applied by the United Kingdom and elsewhere in the European Union, and the same problem can be observed in other EU member states.

There is also no doubt, that at least for the foreseeable future, Brexit will add to the complexity for both financial investment firms and financial services authorities having to consider uncertainty, extension of deadlines and potentially a whole new legislation governing not just financial investment firms in the UK, but also UK citizens and residents wishing to become clients of EU financial investment firms and vice versa.

Conclusion

There is factual evidence that every EU financial services authority applies its own interpretation when it comes to defining 'to provide any or all of the investment services', which leaves many financial investment firms very confused as to the meaning, and in doubt whether they are required to have a passport into an EU host member state, resulting in unnecessary additional regulatory compliance oversight and potential missed business opportunities.

Furthermore, many investment firms have been granted additional services, products, and client categories from what they are authorized and permitted to have by their home financial services authority. Surely, these errors, which are detrimental, should have been captured during the application stage when the applicable home financial services authority reviewed the application.

It is clear that what is needed is not more regulation, but more active supervisory cooperation between financial services

Table 1: Comparison of terminology between European Union and United Kingdom for MiFID's implementation for services and activities

MiFID's terminology for services and activities	UK's terminology for the same services and activities under MiFID as implemented by the Financial Services and Markets Act 2000 (Regulated Activities) Order 2001 (SI 2001/544)
Reception and transmission of orders in relation to one or more financial instruments	Arranging (bringing about) deals in investment
Executing orders on behalf of clients	Dealing in investments as agent Dealing in investment as principal on behalf of clients (matched principal)
Dealing on own account	Dealing in investments as principal (own account – unmatched principal)
Portfolio management	Managing investments Dealing in investments as principal Dealing in investments as agent Arranging (bringing about) deals in investments Making arrangements with a view to transactions in investments
Investment advice	Advising on investments
Underwriting of financial instruments and/or placing of financial instruments on a firm committed basis	Dealing in investments as principal Dealing in investments as agent
Placing of financial instruments without a firm commitment basis	Dealing in investments as agent Arranging (bringing about) deals in investment
Operation of a multilateral trading facility	Operating a multilateral trading facility
Operation of organized trading facilities	Operating an organized trading facility

authorities of home and host member states supported by standardization and automation through software in order to ensure the safeness and soundness of the single market, and to protect the interests of clients across the European Union.

EU financial services authorities must work more together to try to harmonize areas that should be simple to harmonize. ESMA could lead this effort to secure consistency and investor protection across the EU. Otherwise, we are undermining the value of passporting in the financial sector across the European Union, due to a lack of consistency in the language used and the lack of oversight by the EU financial services authorities. Leaving it as is will simply become an opportunity for regulatory arbitrage, which will create a very uneven playing field in an already complex market.

What Do PSD2 and Similar Activities Mean for Banks and FinTech Start-ups?

By Vladislav Solodkiy
Managing Partner, Life.SREDA VC and CEO, Arival Bank

In 2016, the UK Competition and Markets Authority (CMA) implemented a widely ranging package of reforms[1] that required banks to (i) implement open banking by early 2018, so as to accelerate technological change in the UK retail banking sector; (ii) publish trustworthy and objective information on the quality of service on their websites and in branches, so that customers can see how their own bank shapes up; and (iii) send out suitable periodic and event-based prompts such as on the closure of a local branch or an increase in charges, to remind their customers to review whether they are getting the best value and switch banks if not. The CMA has also introduced specific measures to benefit unarranged overdraft users, who make up around 25% of all personal current account customers, and small businesses.[2]

However, the report was viewed with some disdain by the FinTech community and new entrants, who bemoaned the failure of the watchdog to impose tougher sanctions to break the stranglehold of the United Kingdom's top banks. In its final order, the CMA set out the timetable for introducing key advances such as open banking, the monthly maximum unarranged overdraft charge, standardized business current account opening procedures, and banks having to publish service quality statistics.[3]

---

[1] https://www.gov.uk/government/publications/retail-banking-market-investigation-overview

[2] https://www.gov.uk/government/news/cma-paves-the-way-for-open-banking-revolution

[3] https://www.finextra.com/newsarticle/30077/cma-issues-final-order-on-open-banking

At the end of 2015, the Directorate-General of the Financial Stability, Financial Services and Capital Markets Union (DG FISMA) of the European Commission revised its own Payment Services Directive, giving every member state of the European Union two years to incorporate PSD2 into respective national laws and regulations. The PSD2 revision was created to drive competition and foster innovation by lowering entry barriers for new payment initiation service providers (PISPs) and online account information service providers (AISPs).

PSD2 Introduces Two Types of Entities to the Financial Industry: PISP and AISP

- Account information service providers (AISPs) – service providers with access to the account information of bank customers. Examples of FinTech verticals: mobile-only banks, personal finance management robo-advisers, accounting.

- Payment initiation service providers (PISPs) – service providers initiating a payment on behalf of the user. Examples of FinTech verticals: peer-to-peer (P2P) transfer, direct debit, acquiring.

For banks, the new directive poses substantial economic challenges in many ways. For those acting as payment processors, PSD2 mandates even broader transparency and information requirements. Payment-processing banks might also face extensive competition from new PISPs, which will offer services at reduced costs.

Now every bank should allow access to third parties via application programming interfaces (APIs) to initiate payments directly from bank accounts. Moreover, access must be given on the same terms as if to the account owner. If the owner can initiate a payment at zero cost, then so must a third party. PSD2 has a number of impacts on banks providing payment services.

Transparency of Payment Services

Explicit information on the terms and conditions of the service should be provided up front when the payment is initiated, and the payer should agree to the terms before the payment is executed.

After the transaction, the payer's bank should provide the transaction amount, all charges payable by the payer with a breakdown of the charges, actual exchange rate, date of receipt of a payment order, and debit value date.

Payments Coverage

The scope of applicability of 'one leg out' (OLO) payments is widened and now includes transactions in any currency. They apply to payments from or to all of the 28 European Economic Area (EEA) countries plus Iceland, Liechtenstein, and Norway. Banks are still allowed to charge for the payment amount for OLO payments.

Payment Initiation Services

The market is now open for third party providers (TPPs) offering payment initiation services, which means a service to initiate a payment at the request of the user with respect to a payment account held at another payment service provider.

PISPs are now allowed to communicate securely with the customer's bank and seek information required for payment initiation. As an example, e-commerce and mobile commerce (m-commerce) companies can now access customer information to execute payment transactions without entering into two-sided agreements with the account servicing bank. These providers will be registered and supervised to enhance customer protection.

The European Commission believes customers will have easier access to products from competitors for financial services and might be provided with better quality services.

Another significant and interesting change made by the new directive for TPPs that can offer account information services and payment initiation services is that account-servicing banks are mandated to provide such information to these TPPs without any bilateral agreements. Two major themes should be highlighted: access to accounts and customer authentication and security.

Access to Accounts (XS2A)

AISP services that aggregate information on one or several accounts held with one or several account-servicing banks display information to the account owner in a consolidated way. Banks have to provide open access to account information to all authorized TPPs requesting account information via standard APIs.

Customer Authentication and Security

Now, banks are obliged to provide access to account and balance information freely to TPPs via APIs and transmit it securely to prevent fraud and illegal use of sensitive and personal data. PSD2 enforces requirements for strong (two-factor) customer authentication. Banks will face increased costs in implementing APIs for providing now-mandated access.

Altogether, PSD2 looks like banks have many obligations, but the trick is that every account servicing and payment service providing bank is at the same time a PISP and an AISP, which brings banks abilities they have never had before. Every bank is now able, with authorization from an existing customer, to get access to every other account of that customer in every bank across the EEA to offer new and competitive financial products. It is a challenge to increase banks' revenues they have never faced before.

Also, it presents marvellous opportunities for banks to extend their reach by providing new payment services to merchants to directly transfer funds from their customers' accounts, disintermediating card schemes and linked fees.

The rapid development of FinTech start-ups in 2016 has brought many leading players, such as Dwolla, Kantox, CurrencyCloud, Braintree, and OnDeck, among others, to integrate with each other via open APIs. This is very reasonable – why should one develop a product from scratch, while the competitive advantage is different and this can be done by offering a product from another company? On the other hand, plenty of connections with new services and obsolete custom back ends have forced banks to use automated external integrations via their APIs. In countries where such banks do not exist (the ones that are open to integration with FinTech start-ups), or there are start-ups that want quick scaling by connecting to many banks in different countries, bank as a service (BaaS) technologies start to emerge.

Big banks that realized the emergence of such platforms and FinTech start-ups with well-written open APIs felt a certain threat, so they started to promote an idea of bank as a platform (BaaP), where the bank is not limited to being a tech landing for start-ups, but is also the last mile seller of a start-up's product to its clients (examples: ABN Amro, Sberbank, and others). The core motivation of banks is to keep the last mile in-house – to deal with customers on the bank's behalf, rather than on the start-up's behalf. In China, the BaaP idea is followed by AliPay and WeChat.

The historical origin of BaaS[4] is in the United States. Such players as The Bancorp and CBW Bank have historically been active in hosting American FinTech start-ups. New players like Banco Bilbao Vizcaya Argentana (BBVA) are just entering such a niche to stand alongside the established peers. What's interesting is that in core markets for BBVA like in Spain, it acts as a BaaP, while in other markets where it is present, the strategy is linked to BaaS. Disadvantages of current Chinese and American BaaS platforms include the fact that they do not yet provide an international boost. In Europe there are 50 countries, Asia includes 58 countries, Africa includes 54 countries, and the Middle East includes 19 countries.

Europe is currently the region with a very balanced and mature BaaS market, with comprehensive government support provided to start-ups on the one side and financial institutions on the other, and market saturation with established players on the one hand and the rise of other professionals on the other.

The largest player in Europe is Wirecard. With a capitalization of €5 billion, it operates in most European counties and even opened an office in Singapore to actively expand in Asia and the Middle East. In every country where Wirecard is present, it aims to get a license, but some markets force it to partner with banks (so it becomes a BaaP solution for such a bank). It currently provides different types of infrastructure for N26, Curve, Monzo, TransferTo, Loot, Revolut, and others, but in quantitative metrics and volumes it lags behind its American peers. Wirecard's current main business is to partner with traditional players that are stepping up digitally: technology and media companies, telecoms, retailers, and banks. According to their own observations, the market is still very young, and the market can handle three or four more huge international players. And actually, there are more and more competitors emerging: solarisBank (Germany), IBanFirst (France), and UAccount (UK).

Asian, African, and Middle Eastern markets do not have examples of such platforms, except for Singapore with BAASIS. Moreover, if they do not emerge, the infrastructural unreadiness will kill FinTech undertakings and hopes of Singapore, Hong Kong, Seoul, and Tokyo to become FinTech hubs. This business model focuses on

---

[4] http://bank-as-a-service.com

building a platform in the Association of Southeast Asian Nations (ASEAN) region and is especially interesting because it does not aim to obtain all licenses from markets of operations, but chooses a single partnering bank in each territory. This gives traditional banks an option to lend their infrastructures, like Amazon does with its Amazon Web Services.

Traditional core banking providers for financial institutions like Swiss Crealogix and Malaysian SilverLake also see potential in working with nontraditional players and partnering with them, and are trying to find a niche to get closer with BaaS platforms. (So far they just provide services to upgrade banks' systems to be able to implement BaaP widgets.)

RegTech from a Regulatory Perspective

- AML and CFTE expands beyond financial regulation but enhances transparency and deters corruption
- Few regulations are universal, however AML and CFT is a fundamental prerequisite for any company handlings clients funds

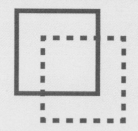

- Tech companies have distribution and scale that can challenge banks
- The establishment of FinTech contact points have aided regulators in their transformation journey

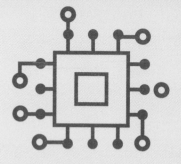

- Pull vs push compliance will change supervisory dynamics
- Regulators innovation will require inhouse tech capacity as well as internal upskilling
- RegTech value might not be in crisis prevention but faster identification of errors

- Emerging market and developing countries look to RegTech to provide resources to address constraints
- Explain regional use case in Kenya - pre-sandbox

- Large volumes of legislation and regulation have been implemented since 2008
- RegTech solutions need to create value either by simplifying fragmented regulatory obligations or finding a niche that is valid across jurisdictions (conduct risk management)

As mentioned at the start of the book, the RegTech industry has a diverse client base. While regulators are key actors in the promotion of this sector; they are increasingly direct consumers of these solutions as well. The following chapters will provide more detail on this trend.

This demand is the result of factors which each have their market and geographical specificities. While the UK has been at the forefront of RegTech development and Europe generally has been progressive regarding innovating regulatory reforms, growth in emerging markets has a different origin.

One such example is the R2A accelerator, a non-profit accelerator program co-sponsored by three central banks, each seeking to improve their supervisory capacity using technology. Regulators in emerging markets are facing a double challenge. Similarly to their Western counterparts, regulators often have resource constraints for market supervision, which in effect translates to limited if not limiting workforce capacity to properly oversee authorized financial institutions. Here RegTech solutions not only provide efficiency gains but become tools for more comprehensive supervisory capacity.

What is more, regulators in emerging markets are in the middle of a massive expansion in financial inclusion. While positive at a societal and economic level, the increasing number of individuals consuming financial products opens up many opportunities a path for misselling or fraud, which can occur if market penetration of financial services does not take place in parallel with end-user financial education. Thus already stretched regulatory resources will come under even more pressure as more individuals become banked.

Other markets, such as China, display regulators with different incentives to use RegTech solutions. It is clear that China's leading position in the deployment of financial services via tech companies is challenging the pre-existing regulatory model. Indeed, the effective supervision of large numbers of FinTechs and TechFins across a country of almost 10 million km^2 requires the use of big data analytics and AI, as was mandated by PBOC. Not only this but the emergence of tech companies entering finance means that they immediately have the scale and distribution impact of what would otherwise be considered a systemically important financial institution. Once again their adequate supervision requires new analytical tools.

While the incentive of regulators globally varies as to why they add RegTech solutions as part of their supervisory toolkit, the move towards RegTech is consistent. Market supervision will go from a push model, where firms fill in reports, to a pull model where regulators extract in real time the information they need to supervise a firm.

The Role of Anti–Money Laundering Law and Compliance in FinTech

By Christine Duhaime, BA, JD, CAMS
Founder, Digital Finance Institute

The disruption caused by the emergence of FinTech is transforming financial services, but the growth of the space is constrained by anti–money laundering (AML) and counterterrorist financing (CTF) laws that are in place to protect both the global financial system and consumers. However, AML and CTF laws do more than protect the global financial system – they protect the rule of law and democracy and are essential for international security because they operate to stop terrorism, to prevent the collapse of entire countries from the theft of national treasuries by corrupt officials, and to disrupt transnational criminal organizations.

Currently, some FinTechs are innovating in financial services in a vacuum, often providing financial services without understanding or complying with AML and CTF laws. Financial regulators all over the globe advocate for responsible innovation in FinTech, and that means providing services that incorporate AML/CTF. FinTechs that provide financial services without understanding and complying with AML/CTF laws as applicable will be inhibited in their ability to scale, particularly as financial crime controls are increasing.

Anti–Money Laundering Law

AML/CTF laws were initially drafted in response to mounting concern over drug trafficking, transnational organized crime, and global money laundering. In 1989, the Financial Action Task Force (FATF) was established by the G7 countries to develop policies to combat money laundering. It sets AML and CTF standards and works for the universal compliance of AML/CTF laws.

The FATF recommendations are what dictate the laws that set out obligations for client verification, onboarding, record keeping, and reporting obligations to financial intelligence units (FIUs) that arise when financial services entities provide services, and that establish procedures to provide law enforcement with data to pursue the prosecution of financial crimes. The FATF standards that are implemented nationally are a combination of regulatory and criminal law.

Offences of AML laws are often used to extradite corporate executives involved in financial crime, evidencing the seriousness given to adherence to AML/CTF law and its power to trump other laws.

Counterterrorist Financing Law

In the 1970s, Europe and the Middle East were affected by increased terrorist activities, and as a result the international community focused its attention on legal mechanisms to address these events. International conventions were adopted to address particular forms of terrorist activity (hijackings, kidnappings, bombings) occurring in different locations. The Convention for the Suppression of Unlawful Seizure of Aircraft and the International Convention Against the Taking of Hostages are two examples. Immediately before 9/11, there were 12 international antiterrorism conventions but no decrease in terrorist incidents.

As a result of the 9/11 terrorist attacks, the international legal community responded to address terrorism by adopting measures to stop terrorist financing. The United Nations adopted Security Council Resolution 1373 on 28 September 2001. It condemned the acts of 9/11 and called upon countries to work together to prevent and suppress terrorist acts, noting the link between money laundering, transnational organized crime, and international terrorism. The resolution directed countries to prevent and suppress terrorist financing, to criminalize funds used for terrorism, and to freeze terrorist assets. Countries agreed to impose punishments on persons supporting terrorist financing that reflected the harm to society of terrorist activities and to exchange information in respect of terrorist financing and money laundering.

Resolution 1373 specifically called for legislation listing terrorists and terrorist organizations and prohibiting dealing with their assets, facilitating financial transactions with them, or otherwise making property or other financial services available, directly or indirectly.

The FATF then incorporated more stringent counterterrorist financing obligations in the FATF recommendations, effectively creating a combined AML/CTF regime, and countries around the world then correspondingly adopted the AML/CTF recommendations into national laws.

Violations of terrorist financing laws are serious criminal offences and carry significant criminal penalties and jail terms ranging from 10 to 50 years.

Sanctions Law

I like to call sanctions law the third pillar of financial crime law – AML and CTF being the other pillars. Sanctions law is an important but often overlooked part of AML/CTF compliance. Sanctions laws are national. They prohibit financial transactions for certain sanctioned persons, entities, and countries. Sanctions avoidance is a predicate offence for money laundering, and therefore the proceeds of sanctions avoidance are the proceeds of crime.

The US Office of Foreign Assets Control (OFAC) remains the most important agency in the world in respect of sanctions that FinTechs, no matter where they operate, need to be familiar with. OFAC administers and enforces economic and trade sanctions based on US foreign policy, national security goals against targeted foreign countries, terrorists, drug traffickers, traffickers of weapons of mass destruction, and other threats to US national security, foreign policy, or the economy of the United States.

OFAC has jurisdiction over US denominated financial transactions that flow through the US financial system, and exercises that

jurisdiction to impose controls on financial and other transactions and freeze assets. Most financial transactions, wherever originated or destined, use the US financial system by virtue of the correspondent banking regime. OFAC's authority is derived from the exercise of the President's emergency powers, as well as by legislation, and because it derives from executive power, it can change on an hour's notice. FinTechs often think OFAC sanctions do not apply to them, but sanctions application is broad.

US sanctions apply to any person subject to the jurisdiction of the United States (a 'US Person') and those persons including US citizens and residents wherever situated; anyone physically in the United States; any corporation, partnership, association, or any other organization incorporated in the United States; and any corporation, partnership, association, or other organization, regardless of where incorporated or doing business, that is owned or controlled by a US Person. That means if a FinTech has material equity held or controlled by US Persons, even if it is a UK or French FinTech, US sanctions apply to it. It also applies if it has a US subsidiary to that subsidiary.

Therefore, when we refer to AML law, it means AML/CTF obligations and sanctions, each of which are crucial pillars of the financial crime landscape.

There are over 20 sanctions programs administered by OFAC and no two are the same, although they generally involve cutting off sanctions targets' access to the US financial system by prohibiting transactions in certain property or interests in property within the United States or involving US Persons and/or requiring US Persons to block the property of sanctions persons who are on OFAC's list of specially designated nations and its blocked persons list.

Each country has its own sanctions program that a FinTech needs to be cognizant of, and comply within its jurisdiction of operation. Determining what is required for each sanctions program is a formidable task. There are different regulations for each sanctions program, and each has different prohibitions.

Sanctions programs are directed against a number of countries and against thousands of listed persons, companies, charities, and entities considered to pose threats. Some sanctions programs are country-specific such as against Congo, Iran, Libya, North Korea, Somalia, Sudan, Syria, and Yemen. Then there are specific sanctions programs aimed at deterring certain types of activities, such as the counter-narcotics sanctions, diamond trading sanctions, Sergei Magnitsky sanctions, nonproliferation sanctions, and sanctions targeted at transnational organized criminal groups like the Mafia regardless of where they operate.

Generally speaking, all directors, officers, and shareholders of a FinTech, as well as the FinTech itself, are prohibited from engaging in any transactions with a sanctioned country, government, or prohibited person or entity, and they must review commercial and financial dealings and transactions and block or freeze assets in which the listed person, state, or organization has any financial interest, even if that asset or property is controlled or owned by someone else. This poses challenges for bitcoin and other digital currencies where the wallet holders can be anonymous.

Depending upon the country, violations of sanctions carry substantial civil and criminal penalties, including civil fines of up to $1 million and criminal penalties of up to $10 million, and in the United States, 30 years in jail. One of the areas in which OFAC compliance becomes complicated is in respect of beneficial ownership of companies. If a FinTech cuts corners, or does not have comprehensive AML/CTF procedures for sanctions or determination of beneficial ownership, they risk onboarding a sanctioned company or person and incurring liability risks.

AML Compliance 101

Depending upon the country, many FinTechs are deemed to be money services businesses or otherwise regulated by AML/CTF

laws, but not all. Where FinTechs are required to register with a national FIU, they are subject to that country's record keeping, client verification procedures, training, transaction reporting, and registration requirements.

AML/CTF laws in most countries are similar, and FinTechs that are registered with an FIU are required to undertake materially the same. KYC means 'know your client' and is but one small part of AML/CTF and of financial crime. The typical requirements of AML registration are as follows:

- *Report suspicious transactions.* FinTechs must report suspicious financial transactions and attempted suspicious financial transactions when it has grounds to suspect that the financial transaction is tied to the commission of a predicate offence. Predicate offences include things like murder, corruption, insider trading, drug trafficking, or tax evasion. It goes without saying that a FinTech must know the predicate offences to form the reasonable grounds to suspect proceeds of crime are involved.

- *Report terrorist financing transactions.* FinTechs must also report terrorist financing when they have money, bitcoin, or other property in their possession or control that they believe is owned or controlled by or on behalf of a terrorist or terrorist group. Terrorists and terrorist groups are listed, and their names are made available by governments and vary from country to country. There are no reliable private or public databases that include comprehensive lists of terrorists and terrorist organizations, except from the OFAC in the United States, which is limited to application in the United States and applies to correspondent banking relationships. CTF requires the constant review of such lists, and FinTechs usually have to report to a national law enforcement agency, in addition to an FIU, when a client or financial transaction triggers terrorist financing. A terrorist financing report is also a suspicious transaction and requires dual reporting to an FIU.

- *Large cash transactions*. FinTechs must report to their FIU when they receive an amount of money, usually $10,000 or more, in cash in the course of a single transaction or any series of transactions in 24 hours equal to $10,000 or more.

- *Electronic funds transfers*. FinTechs must report to their FIU when they send out of a country or receive from outside the country an electronic funds transfer of usually $10,000 or more in a single transaction.

- *Politically exposed persons*. FinTechs must also determine when they onboard a client if they are dealing with a politically exposed person (PEP) if amounts reach a certain threshold. A PEP is a person who holds a prominent public position (i.e. head of state, head of government, member of the legislature, judge, ambassador, military officer, or president or CEO of a government corporation). If it determines that the client is a PEP, it must verify the source of the client's funds above a triggering threshold. Determining PEPs is a difficult part of AML compliance because the obligation is a worldwide one. It is also difficult and time-consuming to verify a PEP's source of wealth and whether it is legitimate, especially from other countries where the translation of financial records may be involved. By way of illustration, at private banks, it takes an average of nine months to confirm the source of funds from a PEP from China for one person. When the PEP is a private company, confirming the legitimacy of the source of wealth with beneficial and legal ownership of shares is even more complex, requiring expertise in understanding corporate records, and debt financings that involve equity. PEPs represent a greater money laundering risk because of the higher probability that they will abuse their positions to carry out corrupt acts, such as accepting or extorting bribes or misappropriating state assets, and use the financial system to launder those proceeds.

- *Ascertaining ID*. FinTechs that have reporting obligations to an FIU must ascertain the identity of persons and companies using their services to complete financial transactions. The law in most countries requires that no client be onboarded by a financial services reporting entity unless the client's identity has been verified. This, of course, leads to financial inclusion problems – an issue we have commented upon often globally.

- *Records retention*. FinTechs are subject to fairly onerous record-keeping obligations if they report to an FIU. Among other things, they must keep records of the methods used to ascertain identity, records of transactions such as large cash transactions, and records regarding beneficial ownership and PEP compliance when certain transactions are conducted.

- *Risk assessments*. FinTechs that are registered with an FIU must undertake a risk assessment to evaluate and identify, in the course of its activities, the risk of the commission of money laundering and terrorist financing offences. The risk assessment involves an analysis of potential threats and vulnerabilities to money laundering and terrorist financing crimes to which the FinTech is exposed. This is a fairly involved process requiring significant review of clients, transactions, and geographical areas of service.

- *Compliance regime*. FinTechs must draft and implement a compliance program to meet the reporting, record-keeping, and client verification obligations under AML/CTF law and to address the risks identified in their risk assessment. A compliance program helps ensure that employees at all levels at a FinTech are aware of the unique obligations imposed on a FinTech as a financial services provider, and helps ensure those obligations are complied with as a matter of course at all levels of the organization. It also helps ensure that a FinTech has an ethical and compliant culture, minimizing risk to the company and its directors and officers of criminal, civil, and financial liability. The compliance program deters violations of the law, ensures fair and ethical business standards, and detects possible violations before they occur. If a violation has already occurred, the compliance program can help uncover the violation, forestall its continuation, facilitate and support an internal review to understand the facts and implications of the conduct, and promote appropriate remedial measures. The effectiveness of the compliance program ultimately depends on the extent to which a FinTech inculcates the program's standards into its corporate culture and places real importance on adherence. For the compliance program to be effective, the corporate culture must encourage consideration of compliance concerns.

AML/CTF compliance is a complex and expensive undertaking. The Arab Bank case, in which a financial institution was found liable by a New York jury for billions of dollars for unwittingly providing banking services to unlisted terrorists responsible for the deaths of American citizens in the Middle East is an example of the wide-reaching effects of getting AML/CTF law wrong.

The world of AML/CTF is evolving quickly with technology and in particular artificial intelligence (AI) and machine learning. AI is not new to AML/CTF. As early as 1993, FinCEN developed an AI system that links and evaluates financial transactions for indications of suspicious transactions characteristic of money laundering or terrorist financing, to identify individuals engaged in criminal activities.

We will see more interesting developments involving AI with AML/CTF in the years to come that one day will completely transform the way we conduct AML/CTF and will make our world a safer place.

Banking Supervision at a Crossroads – RegTech as the Regulators' Toolbox

By **Dr Tobias Bauerfeind**
Associate, Ashurst LLP

and Pascal Di Prima
CEO and Co-Founder, Lexemo LLC

Digital is tomorrow's battlefield for banks. While traditional credit institutions face enormous challenges and are suffering from a period of low interest rates along with simultaneously increasing costs and regulatory requirements, new FinTech companies hope to get a slice of the cake. Those FinTech companies plough through single segments and processes of traditional banking transactions more efficiently and with more agility than the old industry and are committed to achieving a leading role in financial markets.

In this context, agile technology does not have to be a threat to the financial industry but can help banks better understand and manage their risks. Therefore, RegTech companies can provide not only a more efficient way to report, monitor, and comply with prudential requirements but also a tool to strategically allocate, manage, and coordinate banking risks. With regard to banks, RegTech companies will help firms to automate compliance tasks and reduce risks associated with meeting reporting obligations by using analytic tools to intelligently mine existing big data sets and unlock their potential.

RegTech will be able to provide a new way of approaching regulation – for banks, as explained earlier, and also for banking supervision[1] itself. Within this framework, banking supervision can be reconceptualized. This also ties in with the quantitative prudential approach of Europe's supra-supervision, the European Central Bank (ECB) – unlike the qualitative approach of most national competent authorities (NCAs).

What will happen when the ECB as the competent authority is able to retrieve, process, and analyse necessary prudential (big) data flows in almost real time without any detours (via NCA or on-site assessments)? When prudential algorithms control and manage supervisory examinations? When the supervisor and respective bank management have access to the same risk management dashboard?

RegTech 'has the potential to enable a close to real-time and proportionate regulatory regime that identifies and addresses risk while also facilitating far more efficient regulatory compliance'.[2]

In the wake of the financial crisis, a wide range of new and revised rules, regulations, and practices have been imposed on the banking industry. While many of these steps are designed to strengthen the safety and soundness of the banking system, they also act as a tax on banks.[3] Banking regulation is an enormous cost factor for banks – especially with regard to compliance and reporting tasks – but is also a personnel and temporal burden for the supervisory authorities themselves.

A further workload for both the banks and the supervisors is the increasing complexity of regulation. The lack of clarity concerns all participants and complicates communication with one another, which, as a result, undermines the objectives of banking supervision.

---

[1] Within this chapter the terms 'supervision', 'supervisor', 'authority', and 'regulator' are used interchangeably, as well as 'supervision' and 'regulation'.

[2] Douglas W. Arner, Janos Nathan Barberis, and Ross P. Buckley, 'FinTech, RegTech and the Reconceptualization of Financial Regulation', *Northwestern Journal of International Law & Business* 37, no. 3 (2017).

[3] Goldman Sachs, Global Investment Research, Global Markets Institute, 'Who Pays for Bank Regulation?', June 2014.

Technology and Regulation

Using technology to help meet regulatory requirements is not new. However, the rise in digital products has increased incidences of data breaches, cyber hacks, money laundering, and other fraudulent activities. With the use of big data and machine learning technology, RegTech reduces risks. Therefore, RegTech companies tend to make regulation highly data acquisitive and to involve the use of real-time information and the incorporation of algorithms and analytics. A careful balance needs to be struck amongst regulation, innovation, and stability. RegTech is able to support regulators all over the world by analysing existing policies and regulatory standards to allocate space for innovation and automation. Due to highly manual regulatory and compliance processes that lack meaningful data for transparency, these processes are in dire need of digitization, automation, business intelligence, artificial intelligence, and predictive capabilities (e.g. anti–money laundering/know your customer [AML/KYC], risk management/mitigation, reporting, monitoring).

Regulators' key priority is to continue to promote innovation around regulatory compliance and to adopt an increasingly proactive role in driving efficiency and collaboration across the RegTech companies and the financial sector as the respective service recipients. They will also assist in the creation of common integrated standards and development of guidance on the rules of engagement. Finally, regulators bear the burden of responsibility for promoting initiatives focused on how to manage internal change resulting from RegTech, including a systematic prudential foresight from a global perspective.

Furthermore, continuously exploring the regulatory environment will improve the ability to assess regulatory overlaps, minimization of different interpretations of prudential rules, and enhanced timeline management.

All the more important is prudential rulemaking on a global scale – this is where the World Bank and in particular the Basel Committee on Banking Supervision (BCBS) as well as the Financial Stability Board (FSB) must meet their responsibilities in future.

In Europe, EU countries and institutions started in 2012 the initiative of the European Legislation Identifier (ELI), which is a system to make legislation available online in a standardized format so that it can be accessed, exchanged, and reused across borders.[4] Luxembourg's Central Legislation Service (SCL) has assigned ELIs to all legislation it has ever published. The persistent identification of legislation offers certain benefits. For example, identifiers can be used to show the relationships between laws by:

- Linking amendments to original acts.
- Linking acts and amendments to consolidated versions.
- Linking national laws to the EU directives they transpose.[5]

The visualization is a big step in the right direction, which is a great tool to cope with the increasing complexity of regulation.

This is in line with our approach at Lexemo LLC[6] to visualize and connect regulation by means of an online video commentary of the Capital Requirements Regulation (EU) No. 575/2013 (CRR), with the aim of bridging the gap between business and legal units or rather regulators.

Compliance and Reporting

RegTech, inter alia, focuses on the digitization of (manual) reporting and compliance processes, e.g. in the context of steadily rising AML and KYC requirements, which could offer tremendous cost savings to the financial services industry and regulators, particularly when – taking again the example of AML/KYC – banks

---

[4] http://eur-lex.europa.eu/eli-register/about.html

[5] http://eur-lex.europa.eu/eli-register/success_story2.html

[6] http://lexemo.com

develop internal rating methodologies[7] based upon AML/KYC data in order to reduce the systematic reliance on external rating agencies within banking supervision.[8]

This evolution would enable regulators not only to always have full insight into the banks' circle of customers (also with regard to tax honesty of the banks' clients) but to be able to directly retrieve data (close to real-time insights through deep learning and artificial intelligence filters) and to adapt requirements on a case-by-case basis (identify problems in advance rather than merely taking enforcement action after the fact).

RegTech could enable regulators to perform real-time regulation management (consistent with the ECB's quantitative prudential approach).

Firstly, real-time and system-embedded compliance and risk evaluation tools would allow a more preemptive and proactive risk management approach through automation of the latter to the collection, assessment, and presentation of (big) data, summarized in the risk management dashboard for both the management board and the supervisor. This would lead to a significant simplification of the communication between the supervised bank and the regulator as well as to more closely targeted measures.

Secondly, such an environment of regulators using RegTech solutions would drive down (personnel and know-how) costs and improve efficiency, including automation of compliance protocols and reporting to enable strategic business focus.

However in this context the question arises: how is the quality management with respect to the RegTech programs, sources, data handling (cybersecurity), and so forth used by the supervisory authorities as their supervision infrastructure appropriate in order to avoid errors, and how is this verified? Supervisory authorities would operate their (governmental) supervision via a (private) third party, which would result in new issues ranging from conflicts of interest to liability – similar to the Basel II regime of regulators relying on external ratings of third parties (rating agencies) for calculating banks' credit risk (standardized approach).

In Europe, taking the idea a step further, using RegTechs' algorithms and data processing for prudential purposes within a quantitative supervision approach, national central banks would no longer be necessary or rather would become the branches of the ECB – as the sole supervision authority – since the operating banking supervisors would consist mainly of a few information technology (IT) specialists rather than business graduates and lawyers. It is questionable, however, whether such a plan would be feasible politically and legally.

Either way, in the medium term RegTech will help institutions to automate their laborious compliance tasks and reduce operational risks associated with meeting compliance and reporting obligations.

As a further concrete example of data-driven financial regulation, one should mention here Suade Labs,[9] which – supported by the European Commission – established the Financial Regulatory (FIRE) data format that defines a common specification for granular regulatory data, which refers to the data that underlies regulatory submissions and is used for policy, monitoring, and supervision purposes while financial institutions face enormous challenges for consistency, quality, and transmission of data between systems.

REGTECH FROM A REGULATORY PERSPECTIVE

---

[7] Corresponding to the Internal Rating Based Approach (IRBA) introduced with Basel II that could be used not only by large banks (as is common at present) but by small and medium-size banks that are either regulated and controlled by supervisory authorities (in Europe e.g. by the European Securities and Markets Authority [ESMA]).

[8] Tobias Bauerfeind, 'The Modern Governance and Regulation of Credit Rating Agencies: A Legal Comparative Study to Reduce Dependency on and Relevance of External Ratings in US and European Banking Supervision', *ELSA Law Review* 2016 (1), 117–144.

---

[9] https://suade.org

Risk Mitigation

However, above all, RegTech offers the possibility of mitigating operational, reputational, and financial risk across the board.

Modern RegTech big data solutions could be able to reduce reporting and publishing periods from currently a quarterly basis (in Europe) to almost real-time analysis and classification.

The risk dashboard is part of the regular risk assessment conducted by the European supervisory authorities. This dashboard summarizes the principal risks and vulnerabilities in the banking sector within the European Union by looking at the evolution of specific risk indicators (RIs) among a sample of banks across the EU in order to provide an overview of financial stability.

The utilization, pooling, and assessment of big (risk) data would enable regulators to receive these RI and other data from all operating banks and firms (imaginable worldwide) in (almost) real time, being able to compare the data (benchmarking) within the relevant groups, to issue direct and immediate instructions (recommended action or rather supervisory measures) towards the management board of an institution to avoid financial distortions and, finally, to provide real-time banking supervision and regulation: early detection of prudential necessities, and gaps and deficiencies within the legislation. Institutions would be able to respond to regulatory change with minimal effort and cost in the future. Inter alia, regulatory arbitrage could be a thing of the past.

Obviously, such possibilities of using all the big (risk) data via risk dashboards would be offered to the management board itself, with the effect that a manager focused on company interests (customer-driven) would anticipate any supervisory measures without the intervention of the respective regulator (however, cf.

Goodhart's law[10]). Forward-thinking financial firms will now try to leverage spending on compliance and risk, and drive innovation by converting the vast amounts of big data, collected and retained for compliance and risk purposes, into smart data that offers actionable insights – using these insights to drive client retention and revenue generation initiatives, and support customer analysis.

However, it is questionable, in view of these trends, how far this system should be extended. If the regulator is able to make crucial adjustments within the institution itself, the regulator will be the bank's responsible chief risk officer. This would mean government bank control (i.e. expropriation). Such a result cannot be envisaged within a (social) market economy. Boundaries are therefore needed.

Conclusion

The challenges regarding compliance, reporting, and risk mitigation are influenced by a variety of factors like the complexity and interconnectedness of financial institutions, the increasing complexity of regulation, and the lack of comparability of the reported data. Technology can be a toolbox that can help the whole industry, including regulators, to better deal with these problems. RegTech itself will not prevent the next financial crisis, but using technology will make regulators better regulators.

---

[10] Goodhart's law: 'A risk model breaks down when used for regulatory purposes'. Jón Daníelsson, 'The Emperor Has No Clothes: Limits to Risk Modelling', *Journal of Banking & Finance* 26 (7) (July 2002): 1273–1296.

FinReg, FinTech, and RegTech – Quo Vadis, EU?

By Dr Ulf Klebeck

General Counsel, Montana Capital Partners and Partner/
Co-Founder, Excelerate

From a start-up perspective, the European Union holds the largest density of RegTech start-ups. However, in an industry that is defined by regulatory rules and dynamic dissociating, whether initiatives are fragmented or harmonized is key. As with any new trends, it is important to identify the position in the cycles to appreciate the factors impacting the development of RegTech in the EU, all of which is explored below.

Financial Market Regulations as a Game Changer

Is RegTech just a subset of FinTech? Is RegTech a key component of FinTech? Or is RegTech even the new FinTech? It does not really matter when one acknowledges the three common denominators.

Firstly, both FinTech and RegTech are the logical consequence of the ever-growing digitization of the way people are interacting – be it in business or be it in private life. Secondly, for both FinTech and RegTech, the future seems to be bright, following the various predictions of the business opportunities coming out of and relating to FinTech and RegTech. Thirdly, both FinTech and RegTech have had a key driving force behind their rise; the exponential increase in financial market regulations over the last nine years, mainly as a reaction to the global financial crisis (GFC) that started in 2007–2008.

This event has catalysed the growth of the new tech era in the financial industry.[1] Since the global financial meltdown, FinTechs have continued to crop up from all corners of the digitized globe – challenging and, to a certain extent, disrupting the business models of the traditional players. The GFC caused not only a lot of anger at the established banking system with its players, but also a widespread lack of trust with banks post-GFC.[2] The pressure on traditional banking and financial services providers is tangible. They are well aware of the threat of losing market shares, and they are now taking action, with some banks either developing their own tech offerings, establishing their own funds to invest in new technology, or appointing at least a new chief innovation officer (CIO). This follows the old principle: 'If you can't beat them, join them!'

But join what? This leads to the first and fundamental challenge of the current FinTech discussion within and amongst the industry, lawmakers and policy makers, as well as regulators, of attempting to define the business scope of FinTechs. There is no clear and precise definition or categorization. Whatever (sub)categories of FinTechs one defines – e.g. digital payment systems; alternative financing like crowdfunding and peer-to-peer (P2P) lending; digital asset management, trading, and robo-advice; distributed ledger technology (DLT) and blockchain – the lines will be increasingly blurred over time. Business models that evolved pre-digitization

---

[1] See Douglas W. Arner, Janos Nathan Barberis, and Ross P. Buckley, 'FinTech, RegTech and the Reconceptualization of Financial Regulation', *Northwestern Journal of International Law & Business* 37, no. 3 (2017) Available at SSRN: https://ssrn.com/abstract=2847806 (hereinafter Arner, Barberis, and Buckley, 'FinTech, RegTech and the Reconceptualization of Financial Regulation').

[2] See Douglas W. Arner, Janos Nathan Barberis, and Ross P. Buckley, 'The Evolution of Fintech: A New Post-Crisis Paradigm?' University of Hong Kong Faculty of Law Research Paper 2015/047; UNSW Law Research Paper 2016-62 (1 October 2015). Available at SSRN: https://ssrn.com/abstract=2676553

defined the historical financial services categories – i.e. retail, private, and investment banking or asset management – and with that (more or less) the applicable financial market regulation. FinTechs do not stop at historical and regulatory boundaries of categorization. These financial innovations currently operate within a regulatory system that originates in the analogue world, and it is struggling to keep pace with the new developments coming out of the digital world.

The European Securities and Markets Authority (ESMA), one of the three pan-European regulators (so-called European Supervisory Authorities), hit the spot when it confessed that the existing EU regulations were not necessarily designed with the digital industry in mind.[3] Following the outbreak of the GFC, the stabilization of the European Union's financial markets became a priority at EU level, and the regulatory reform of the EU financial sector became a crucial instrument through which to achieve it. Since then, the EU lawmaker has enacted and proposed various legislative measures to build new rules for the European financial markets in order to establish a safe, responsible, and growth-enhancing financial sector in Europe. To achieve this goal, more than 40 European legislative acts have been implemented, with others still on the way – including (but not limited to) well-known acronyms like AIFMD, EMIR, MiFID II/MiFIR, PSD2, CRD IV, MAR, PRIIPS, UCITS V, BRRD, SRM, Solvency II, SRM, IMD, and AMLD4.[4]

Speaking in the European Union's lawmaking terms, these examples are mainly major EU financial sector legislative reforms that are considered so-called Level 1 rules – providing an EU-wide regulatory framework to be implemented into the national law of each member state of the European Union. They are followed and specified by so-called Levels 2, 3, and 4 measures at EU level – in accordance with the so-called Lamfalussy approach.[5] Even after nine years, it is the common understanding that the EU's regulatory reform of the financial market has not reached the end of the road. There are more than 400 pieces of further Levels 2, 3, and 4 financial market rules to be adopted in the coming years – including regulatory technical standards (RTSs), implementing technical standards (ITSs), guidelines, advice, statements, and opinions issued by the European Supervisory Authorities in collaboration with the national regulators.[6]

At present, financial institutions are still occupied with implementing, and complying with, the various waves of new EU financial market regulations. The new rules have admittedly increased the compliance obligations and compliance costs for traditional financial services providers, and this compliance burden is considered to be one of the biggest barriers to investments in innovation.[7] The necessary prioritization of compliance means money is poured into the obligatory updates of their legacy systems to meet the new compliance standards. At this current stage, investments in new technology and adapting to the

---

[3] See manuscript of the speech by Verena Ross (Executive Director at European Securities and Markets Authority) at London Business School/ Bank of England Conference on 7 March 2016 (ESMA/2016/345): 'How Imminent Is the Real FinTech Revolution? Financial Innovation: Towards a Balanced Regulatory Response' (https://www.esma.europa.eu/sites/ default/files/library/2016-345_financial_innovation_towards_a_balanced_ regulatory_response_-_speech_by_v._ross_0.pdf), at 9.

[4] For an overview of the key EU financial market regulations and the prog- ress of financial market reforms in the EU, see e.g. European Commis- sion's website on financial reforms and their progress: https://ec.europa. eu/info/business-economy-euro/banking-and-finance/financial-reforms- and-their-progress_en

[5] For an overview of the Lamfalussy architecture, see e.g. European Commission's website on regulatory process in financial services: https://ec.europa.eu/info/business-economy-euro/banking-and-finance/ financial-reforms-and-their-progress/regulatory-process-financial-services/ regulatory-process-financial-services_en

[6] As an example of the workload at the level of the European Supervisory Authorities, see e.g. ESMA's work programme for 2017: https://www.esma. europa.eu/document/esma-2017-work-programme.

[7] See also JWG/RegTechFS, 'The RegTech Barriers: In Depth Analysis' (part 2 of 3): https://regtechfs.com/the-regtech-barriers-in-depth-analysis- part-2-of-3

changing financial landscape do not seem, understandably, to be a top priority for the traditional financial market players.

RegTech – The Helping Hand for Financial Institutions and Regulators

At this point, RegTech, simply defined as the application of new technologies for regulatory compliance,[8] comes into play, with new technology providers taking the new regulations as another business opportunity. As the incumbent institutions have to deal with greater reporting requirements and meet higher regulatory standards, new technology providers are offering innovative technologies that help financial service providers to better manage regulatory requirements and to reduce compliance costs. It is argued that RegTech can lead to considerable benefits for financial institutions and supervisors by using new technologies to address regulatory and compliance requirements more effectively, transparently, and efficiently, and in real time.[9]

Even if RegTech is still in its infancy, one can already outline many areas in which RegTech has begun to emerge. Examples can be found in the fields of shareholder disclosures, trading-behaviour analysis, trading compliance, organizational trust dynamics, and capital regulation (particularly in stress testing and risk management). Moreover, RegTech could be beneficial for regulators and supervisors too: among the most well-known examples of productivity-enhancing automation in the regulatory field is blockchain or DLT, the underlying technology of bitcoin,[10] which promises automated authentication and verification across a broad range of activities that regulators have traditionally had to monitor manually. There is even a sign of collaborative monitoring between regulators and financial institutions themselves, such that the data that are produced by the systems of the financial institutions are themselves also coded to provide real-time and ongoing regulatory information automatically.

Even if this collaboration has its statutory limits, given that regulatory supervision and operational risk management are separate activities serving different purposes,[11] the manual supervision of automated activities is entirely unrealistic. The automation of many of the regulatory tasks traditionally performed manually seems imperative for regulators. Against this background, it is fair to say that the seeds of a RegTech (r)evolution are sown.[12]

EU's Watchful Approach on FinTech and RegTech

The EU provides fertile soil for a RegTech (r)evolution. This is not only because of the ever-growing pile of EU financial market

---

[8] See European Parliament (Committee on Economic and Monetary Affairs), 'Draft Report on FinTech: The Influence of Technology on the Future of the Financial Sector', 27 January 2017 [2016/2243(INI)]; http://www.europarl.europa.eu/sides/getDoc.do?type=COMPARL&reference=PE-597.523&format=PDF&language=EN&secondRef=01), at 8.

[9] For the potential of RegTech, see e.g. the report of the Institute of International Finance (IIF), 'Regtech in Financial Services: Technology Solutions for Compliance and Reporting' (22 March 2016); https://www.iif.com/system/files/regtech_in_financial_services_-_solutions_for_compliance_and_reporting.pdf

[10] For an EU perspective on DLT and bitcoin, see ESMA's Discussion Paper on 'The Distributed Ledger Technology Applied to Securities Markets' (2 June 2016; ESMA/2016/773); https://www.esma.europa.eu/sites/default/files/library/2016-773_dp_dlt.pdf

[11] See Lawrence G. Baxter, 'Adaptive Financial Regulation and RegTech: A Concept Article on Realistic Protection for Victims of Bank Failure', Duke Law Journal 66 (2016): 600.

[12] See JWG/RegTechFS, 'RegTech: The Seeds of Revolution Are Sewn'; https://regtechfs.com/regtech-the-seeds-of-revolution-are-sewn

regulations, which in principle are a good thing for RegTech. The idea and concept of a single market[13] and a single rule book[14] are two of the biggest assets of the European Union. It has recently been acknowledged by the European Parliament, one of the EU lawmaking institutions, that FinTech, including RegTech and InsurTech, constitutes a building block of the modern digital society that the EU needs in order to face competition with the rest of the world.[15] Therefore, it has been recommended that the European Commission, another EU lawmaking institution, should present a comprehensive action plan that boosts FinTech in Europe – whether separately or as an integral part of two recent initiatives at EU level to deepen the European Union's single market idea. FinTech, as well as RegTech, shall be within the scope of the Capital Markets Union[16] and Digital Single Market[17] strategies. This commitment to FinTech and RegTech has been confirmed by the recently published consultation document of the European Commission, 'FinTech: A More Competitive and Innovative European Financial Sector',[18] as well as by its setting up of an internal task force on FinTech.[19]

Even if regulators and supervisors seem to have a natural tendency to search for risks and concerns within financial innovations, the pan-EU regulators aim to bring to the subject of FinTech and RegTech a balanced approach both 'protective and supportive'.[20] The challenge is to identify not only when the regulator should step in but also how to take regulatory action.[21] Regulators can take one of three approaches: (i) ban or restrict products, business models, or processes in light of the potential risks (restrictive approach); (ii) take a wait-and-see approach (watchful approach); or (iii) actively facilitate and regulate the products, business models or processes because of their potential economic and social benefits (facilitative or catalyst approach) and/or because of known threats to the regulator's objectives.[22]

---

[13] For an overview of the concept, strategies, and initiatives of an EU single market, see e.g. European Commission's website on the EU single market: https://ec.europa.eu/growth/single-market_en

[14] For an overview of the concept, strategies, and initiatives, see e.g. European Banking Authority's website on the single rulebook: http://www.eba.europa.eu/regulation-and-policy/single-rulebook

[15] See European Parliament (Committee on Economic and Monetary Affairs), 'Draft Report on FinTech: The Influence of Technology on the Future of the Financial Sector', 27 January 2017 [2016/2243(INI)]; http://www.europarl.europa.eu/sides/getDoc.do?type=COMPARL&reference=PE-597.523&format=PDF&language=EN&secondRef=01), at 3.

[16] For an overview, initiatives, and development of the EU Capital Markets Union strategy, see http://ec.europa.eu/finance/capital-markets-union/index_en.htm

[17] For an overview, initiatives, and development of the EU Digital Single Market strategy, see https://ec.europa.eu/commission/priorities/digital-single-market_en

[18] See European Commission's public consultation document, 'FinTech: A More Competitive and Innovative European Financial Sector': https://ec.europa.eu/info/finance-consultations-2017-fintech_en

[19] See European Commission's announcement on its website: https://ec.europa.eu/digital-single-market/en/blog/european-commission-sets-internal-task-force-financial-technology

[20] See manuscript of the speech by Verena Ross (Executive Director at European Securities and Markets Authority) at London Business School/Bank of England Conference on 7 March 2016 (ESMA/2016/345): 'How Imminent Is the Real FinTech Revolution? Financial Innovation: Towards a Balanced Regulatory Response'; https://www.esma.europa.eu/sites/default/files/library/2016-345_financial_innovation_towards_a_balanced_regulatory_response_-_speech_by_v._ross_0.pdf

[21] See also Arner, Barberis, and Buckley, 'FinTech, RegTech and the Reconceptualization of Financial Regulation', 38 et seq.

[22] See e.g. for ESMA's approach the manuscript of the speech of Patrick Armstrong, Senior Risk Analysis Officer, Innovation and Products Team at ESMA, at Oslo Børs ASA: Stock Exchange and Securities Conference: 'Financial Technology: Applications Within the Securities Sector' (23 January 2017; ESMA71-844457584-330); https://www.esma.europa.eu/sites/default/files/library/esma71-844457584-330_speech_fintech_and_asset_management_by_patrick_armstrong.pdf, at 3.

At EU level the European Supervisory Authorities have mainly taken, for now, the second approach towards FinTech and RegTech's innovation. There is a need to better understand the various innovations and their possible applications in the financial market. The pan-European regulators actively try to learn more about the innovation, but do so while it remains sufficiently immature to ensure that they are not placing their key objectives – stability, protection, and integrity – at risk by not taking action. At the same time, by waiting to see how the innovation develops, the EU regulators try not to risk stifling a potentially socially or economically useful product, business model, or process. It seems that at EU level the innovations coming from FinTech have not reached the tipping points where active regulatory participation is needed.

National governments and regulators of EU member states usually respond positively to the new players and their business models, recognizing the benefits of driving competition and increasing access to markets. Some of them have even taken a more proactive or supportive approach. In Europe, the United Kingdom is leading the way in many respects. Backed by the UK government, which aims and claims to be the leading hub for FinTechs and RegTechs in Europe and worldwide,[23] the Financial Conduct Authority (FCA) has established Project Innovate, which will support industry innovation to improve consumer outcomes.[24] It has launched the first 'regulatory sandbox' aiming to create a 'safe space' in which businesses can test innovative products, services, business models, and delivery mechanisms in a live environment, without immediately incurring all the normal regulatory consequences of engaging in the activity in question.[25]

The FCA has also recently issued a 'Call for Input: Supporting the Development and Adoption of RegTech', and it has provided a feedback statement on this call where various areas of potential support by the FCA were identified. All of these actions taken by UK regulators have been summarized by the recently released HM Treasury regulatory innovation plan with its vision for UK financial services to be the most competitive and innovative in the world.[26]

At first glance, these national efforts and the regulatory competition between EU member states for shares in the FinTech and RegTech market seem to be contradictory or even detrimental to the idea of a European internal, single market, and the goal of achieving the single rule book for financial services proposed by the de Larosière committee in 2009, which argued in favour of a European rule book for financial services based on maximum harmonization of financial market regulation.[27] Are we facing a new era of what Jacque de Larosière described as 'chacun pour soi' approach[28] in Europe – aimed at safeguarding the national interest?

Outlook: Call for Regulatory Interoperability

This question of countries safeguarding their national interests leads to one of the biggest challenges the emerging RegTech industry is currently facing. This challenge exists even within the European Union, and its goal of EU-wide harmonized financial market rules and passporting rights for financial service providers

---

[23] See HM Treasury Regulatory Innovation Plan (6 April 2017); https://www.gov.uk/government/uploads/system/uploads/attachment_data/file/606953/HM_Treasury_Regulatory_Innovation_Plan.pdf, at 5.

[24] For the various elements of FCA's Project Innovate, see the FCA's website on FinTech and innovative businesses: www.fca.org.uk/firms/fintech-and-innovative-businesses

[25] See generally FCA, 'Regulatory Sandbox' (2015): www.fca.org.uk/publication/research/regulatory-sandbox.pdf (providing an overview of the regulatory sandbox and its implementation).

[26] See HM Treasury Regulatory Innovation Plan (6 April 2017): https://www.gov.uk/government/uploads/system/uploads/attachment_data/file/606953/HM_Treasury_Regulatory_Innovation_Plan.pdf, at 5.

[27] See de Larosière report on financial supervision in the EU (25 February 2009): http://ec.europa.eu/internal_market/finances/docs/de_larosiere_report_en.pdf

[28] See de Larosière report on financial supervision in the EU (25 February 2009): http://ec.europa.eu/internal_market/finances/docs/de_larosiere_report_en.pdf, at 4.

throughout Europe. The European Union is still far away from a maximum harmonization of its financial market regulations. Without an established set of regulatory standards and legal certainty on the financial market rules, any RegTech solution appears to remain costly, complex, or even risky.[29] Due to the deluge of regulatory initiatives after the GFC, the complexity of the overlay and interaction of the new EU rules makes it difficult to see the bigger picture and adapt and implement EU-wide RegTech solutions.

The goal of harmonization within the EU has not yet been reached. This issue does not refer only to the timing of various EU regulations, which results in different deadlines for compliance in different EU member states. This also refers to the issues of 'gold-plating' EU financial market regulations by EU member states (i.e. supplementing EU rules with additional national requirements), divergent implementations by EU member states, and/or their opting out of certain provisions of EU rules.[30] This regulatory patchwork requires RegTech solution providers to deal with special

features for each EU member state and is an obstacle to providing a technological solution that is scalable throughout Europe. To make matters worse, when EU regulations are still changing, the majority of EU financial institutions are reluctant to invest in RegTech solutions that may become outdated due to future regulatory changes. This can be best summarized as the issue of failing to achieve 'regulatory interoperability' within the EU.

To conclude and to be fair, the EU has acknowledged this pressing issue, and the European Commission launched a call to facilitate regulatory interoperability. With the 'Call for Evidence: EU Regulatory Framework for Financial Services', the European Commission looked for empirical evidence and specific feedback on, inter alia, (i) unnecessary regulatory burdens; (ii) interactions, inconsistencies, and gaps in EU rules; and (iii) rules giving rise to unintended consequences.[31] Considerable feedback was provided by financial institutions, associations, and national regulators, but an indication as to whether and how EU financial market regulations may change is still pending.

The EU is, once again, taking a step-by-step approach that might offer further business opportunities for RegTech solutions in Europe. The European concept and toolkit to achieve a harmonized regulatory framework for EU's financial industry is vital for any commonly accepted and reliable RegTech solution. For this reason, I argue that it is worth waiting for an EU-wide harmonized regulatory framework beneficial for all stakeholders. A single digital rule book for understanding EU financial market regulations and their interplay and impact on financial service providers seems like a promising idea.

[29] For an overview of the current challenges for RegTech, see also Institute of International Finance (IIF), 'Regtech in Financial Services: Technology Solutions for Compliance and Reporting' (22 March 2016): https://www.iif.com/system/files/regtech_in_financial_services_-_solutions_for_compliance_and_reporting.pdf; JWG/RegTechFS, 'The RegTech Barriers: In Depth Analysis' (part 2 of 3): https://regtechfs.com/the-regtech-barriers-in-depth-analysis-part-2-of-3

[30] The EU regulatory system often grants to EU member states the right to implement the EU rules into national laws over different timescales and at their own pace, which requires one set of changes to be made, and then later followed by a further set of changes to the same systems, documentation, or processes; see e.g. FCA's response to the European Commission's 'Call for Evidence: EU Regulatory Framework for Financial Services': www.fca.org.uk/publication/corporate/eu-regulatory-framework-call-for-evidence-response.pdf, at 22.

[31] See http://ec.europa.eu/finance/consultations/2015/financial-regulatory-framework-review/index_en.htm

The RegTech Landscape from a Regulator's Perspective

By Benedicte N. Nolens

Chair of Advisory Council, Global Digital Finance and Board Member, Hong Kong FinTech Association

As noted by the World Economic Forum (WEF), the world is experiencing the fourth industrial revolution:

> We stand on the brink of a technological revolution that will fundamentally alter the way we live, work, and relate to one another. In its scale, scope, and complexity, the transformation will be unlike anything humankind has experienced before. We do not yet know just how it will unfold, but one thing is clear: the response to it must be integrated and comprehensive, involving all stakeholders of the global polity, from the public and private sectors to academia and civil society.[1]

This revolution is far-reaching, driven by the ever faster development of technology and automation, and the data it generates. It is transforming nearly all industries, with finance being only one of them. Experts have grouped the technologies that affect finance in several core clusters, including FinTech, RegTech, WealthTech, and InsurTech. These clusters, however, are not static and continue to evolve as new technologies see the light of day and affect industry dynamics.

As the WEF notes, the long-term impact on financial industry structure is not yet known, but we can draw some clues from the developments that have already materialized. This chapter sets out the landscape in which the term *RegTech* is emerging:

- The emergence of a new breed of technology-driven financial institutions.

- The need for traditional financial institutions to redesign their processes.

- The positioning of regulators in the midst of this evolution.

The Emergence of a New Breed of Technology-Driven Financial Institutions

In an interview in June 2015 at the prestigious Davos forum, attended by the world's finance ministers and most senior leaders, Jack Ma, a former teacher who is a self-made man and the CEO of Chinese e-commerce giant Alibaba, talked about the company's lofty goals. He noted he was visited by a Walmart executive in China, and that he made a bet with the man about Alibaba's future: 'In 10 years Alibaba will be bigger than Walmart on sales. If you want 10,000 new customers, you have to build a new warehouse. For me: *two servers*.'

The last sentence is salient and lies at the heart of the fourth industrial revolution: servers are much less costly to scale than warehouses and people.[2] The numbers are telling: Walmart's market capitalization is around US$300 billion, while Alibaba's market capitalization is around US$400 billion; Walmart's 2018 revenue was US$505.49 billion and its net income US$8.96 billion, while Alibaba's revenue was US$39.3 billion and its net income US$10.72 billion; for the period 2010–2017, Walmart's net sales rose by approximately 20%, while Alibaba's rose 15-fold;[3] the total number of Walmart's staff is 2.2 million worldwide, while Alibaba's is 101,958.

---

[1] See https://www.weforum.org/agenda/2016/01/the-fourth-industrial-revolution-what-it-means-and-how-to-respond

---

[2] For further context, Walmart was founded in 1962 by Sam Walton, whereas Alibaba was founded 37 years later, in 1999, by Jack Ma. Walmart's empire has been scaled over a period of 55 years, whereas Alibaba has grown to its current size in less than 18 years.

[3] Alibaba's revenue exceeds that of eBay and Amazon combined.

This thinking extends to finance: servers are much less costly to scale than branches and people. This is the very paradigm that underlies the FinTech (r)evolution in both East and West. Notwithstanding the similarities, it pays to look out for the differences.

While in the West, the payments space has seen the emergence of strong competitors to traditional banks such as PayPal with a market capitalization of around US$131 billion, challenger banks and robo-advisers have had a much tougher time gaining market share and often have seen themselves bought out by, or have seen their technology successfully adopted by, existing financial institutions, thereby not materially altering the competitive landscape.

The same is not true in China, where technology giants have very successfully expanded into all aspects of finance. Ant Financial, the financial subsidiary of Alibaba grown from Alibaba's e-commerce business much like PayPal grew from eBay, is valued at around US$150 billion, larger than Deutsche Bank, the market capitalization of which stands at around US$13.93 billion. Unlike eBay's PayPal, which mostly processes payments, Alibaba is operative across all the main verticals of finance, including payments, financing, wealth management, insurance, securities, banking, credit scoring, and crowdfunding.[4] The market capitalization of a close competitor Tencent has just surpassed US$302 billion, placing it in the top five companies by global market capitalization, comparable only in market capitalization to technology giants and JPMorgan, the market capitalization of which is around US$407 billion. Much like Alibaba, Tencent is operative across all main verticals of finance.

Therefore, unlike in the West where finance businesses remain to date dominated by traditional financial institutions, in China it is the technology giants that truly embody the meaning of FinTech and that have reaped the greatest benefits of the FinTech (r)evolution. China may therefore well be the world's leading FinTech market and at a minimum offers us a glimpse into what is still to come in other parts of the world, especially in white spaces such as emerging markets.

The Need for Traditional Financial Institutions to Redesign Their Processes

Brick-and-mortar institutions are being challenged by a new technology-centric breed of financial players. There are ample examples of traditional financial institutions that have already started to redesign their processes to face this new competition. For example, in commercial banking, ever since the global financial crisis (GFC), most global banks have been significantly reducing branch offices while improving their online offerings. Even though global bank share prices have partly recouped losses since the GFC, and though their revenues have improved, the trend to reduce brick-and-mortar branches has not stopped.

To a large extent, this is driven by customer preferences: most customer segments prefer the convenience of doing transactions at their own time, from their desktop or their smartphone, over a trip to the bank. According to a 2014 Viacom study, 33% of millennials, defined as a generation born between 1981 and 2000, believed they would not need a bank in the future, and 68% said that in five years the way we access our money will be entirely different.[5] According to a more recent Google study, 82% of smartphone users turn to their devices to help them make a product decision.[6]

---

[4] See IOSCO report on financial technologies at https://www.iosco.org/library/pubdocs/pdf/IOSCOPD554.pdf, Figure 4 on page 9 citing Ernst & Young.

[5] See Viacom study: http://www.millennialdisruptionindex.com

[6] See Google survey: https://think.storage.googleapis.com/docs/micromoments-guide-to-winning-shift-to-mobile-download.pdf

The competitive battle that is being played out at this stage within the financial industry, therefore, does not concern offline offerings, such as how good or well-decorated the brick-and-mortar branches are. Instead, it concerns the *online offerings*, such as how intuitive and frictionless the customer interface is, how quick identification and onboarding is, how instant online customer support is, etc. In tandem, the drive towards fee transparency and lower cost continues.

Against this new and improved RegTech solutions continue to see the light of day. Financial institutions can deploy RegTech to achieve a triple win: improved customer experience, increased institutional efficiency/cost-competitiveness, and better regulatory compliance. For FinTechs, virtual banks and even more novel players such as virtual asset service providers, RegTech is built into the technology stack and product proposition from inception.

While RegTech is a relatively new term that undoubtedly will continue to evolve in scope and meaning,[7] an attempt by *CB Insights* to map the RegTech landscape showed the following key areas that are relevant to finance: (i) compliance, monitoring, and reporting, including general compliance management, enterprise risk management, operations risk management, portfolio risk management, vendor risk management, tax management, and so on; (ii) anti–money laundering (AML), know your customer (KYC) and customer due diligence (CDD); and (iii) information security/cyber security.[8]

Of these three areas, the first – compliance and risk technology – is the more mature one. Compliance and risk departments of

financial institutions started automation of their functions more than 20 years ago and have improved such automation ever since. However, what is changing is that much more sophisticated compliance and risk management systems that blend big data analytics, natural language processing, machine learning, and artificial intelligence are available and can often be bought on a subscription basis. Data sets are much larger than they were ever before and now encompass millions of social media sources that can be analysed and concisely represented only through the use of such technologies. Trading has become more decentralized through the competition of exchanges, and much faster through investment by financial institutions and exchanges in technology, including algorithmic trading and high-frequency trading (HFT), therefore necessitating the use of much more sophisticated technologies to identify misconduct. In tandem, the regulatory expectations of compliance and risk departments to be able to supervise such fast and automated businesses have risen dramatically as compared to 20 years ago, further necessitating those departments to continuously improve their systems and to stay in step with the latest technologies.

The second area – AML, KYC and CDD – requires the direct interaction with the customer. Accordingly, for this area the customer experience is key. The traditional onboarding model consists of each financial institution individually and often manually collecting, record keeping, and updating KYC documents, often in hard copy format. This means that if a customer wants to open accounts with different financial institutions, the customer often cannot do it online, and has to physically provide the same KYC information to each of those different institutions individually. Such a process is cumbersome and inefficient, and it is not surprising therefore that a lot of innovation is happening in exactly this area of RegTech.[9] Firms are experimenting with replacing the current onboarding model with new approaches: many financial institutions and all FinTechs are adopting more advanced online authentication

---

[7] See Douglas Arner and Janos Barberis, University of Hong Kong – Faculty of Law, and Ross Buckley, University of New South Wales, Faculty of Law, 'FinTech, RegTech and the Reconceptualization of Financial Regulation', *Northwestern Journal of International Law & Business*, October 2016; https://papers.ssrn.com/sol3/papers.cfm?abstract_id=2847806

[8] See https://www.cbinsights.com/blog/regtech-regulation-compliance-market-map

---

[9] See 'The Identity Startup Landscape' at http://finiculture.com

methods, including through the use of biometrics; certain RegTech firms are creating central databases that financial services firms can subscribe to and on which KYC documents are stored; other RegTech firms and industry consortia are exploring the creation of 'permission-based distributed or shared ledgers' between groups of participating financial institutions; still others are experimenting with 'self-sovereign digital ID' run on distributed ledger technology (DLT). In this last model, individuals control their own digital identity, which becomes a combination of traditional identification methods such as passport copies, and novel methods such as biometric data and verification of identity details by public and private parties participating in the DLT network, including through zero-knowledge proofs.

As finance continues to move online driven by evolving customer needs and preferences, security is of the essence. It is therefore also not surprising that the third key area of RegTech focus shown on the *CB Insights* RegTech market map is cyber and information security. This area will continue to evolve and continue to grow in importance, in tandem with the vulnerabilities that more online activity and different technologies generate.

The Positioning of Regulators in the Midst of This Evolution

FinTech, RegTech, WealthTech, and InsurTech have not gone unnoticed by regulatory authorities. Many regulators have responded to the speed of evolution through the establishment of dedicated FinTech offices.[10] The dialogue between regulators and the industry through these dedicated FinTech offices has assisted in bridging potential knowledge gaps. Many regulators have issued research reports, guidance, and rule clarifications relating to and in response to FinTech evolution.[11]

Several regulators have also introduced regulatory sandbox frameworks, under which FinTech companies and traditional financial institutions may be granted certain regulatory flexibilities in order to experiment with FinTech, RegTech, WealthTech, and InsurTech solutions in a defined environment within specified timeframes.[12]

Some regulators have set up labs, accelerator programmes, and hackathons to explore whether certain new technologies can assist the regulator itself in better achieving its regulatory objectives and whether the regulator can adopt a more data- and

---

[10] Including Abu Dhabi, Australia, Botswana, Brazil, Canada, Chinese Taipei, Dubai, France, Hong Kong, India, Japan, Malaysia, Russia, Saudi Arabia, Singapore, The Netherlands, Thailand, United Arab Emirates, and the United Kingdom; https://www.sfc.hk/edistributionWeb/gateway/EN/news-and-announcements/news/doc?refNo=16PR117

[11] See for example the following research reports that in turn refer to rule clarifications:

- CPMI, 'Distributed Ledger Technology in Payment, Clearing and Settlements', February 2017.
- CPMI, 'Fast Payments – Enhancing the Speed and Availability of Retail Payments', November 2016.
- CPMI, 'Non-banks in Retail Payments', September 2014.
- CPMI, 'Digital Currencies', November 2015.
- CPMI, 'Payment Aspects of Financial Inclusion', April 2016.
- IAIS, 'FinTech Developments in the Insurance Industry', February 2017.
- IAIS, 'Issues Paper on Conduct of Business in Inclusive Insurance', November 2015.
- IOSCO, 'Crowd-funding: An Infant Industry Growing Fast', February 2014.
- IOSCO, 'Crowd-funding: 2015 Survey Responses Report', January 2016.
- IOSCO, 'IOSCO Research Report on Financial Technologies (Fintech)', February 2017.

[12] Including Australia, Canada, Hong Kong, Malaysia, Singapore, and the United Kingdom; https://letstalkpayments.com/international-fintech-regulatory-sandboxes-launched-by-forward-thinking-financial-authorities

technology-driven view.[13] Within this context, regulators are researching and testing DLT and its transformational capabilities as 'the golden record'. Many DLT proponents note that one of the benefits of DLT is that regulators can participate as one of the nodes in the distributed ledger, thereby having automated access to the data. This, in turn, would allow regulators to have more complete and better traceable, real-time records. If regulators want to become a node in a DLT this would, in turn, drive the need for the development of a much more advanced surveillance technology capable of handling much larger data sets, including through machine learning.

These topics will be delved into more deeply in the remaining chapters of this book. However, it is clear that the last word on RegTech has not yet been written, not even in this book, and that this exciting area of innovation will continue to evolve in the years ahead and may drive our financial services to be offered in a very different, more accessible, more inclusive, and more self-directed fashion than ever before. The age of virtual financial services to which RegTech is integral has only just begun.

---

[13] For example, Canada, www.osc.gov.on.ca/en/reghackto.htm; Hong Kong, http://www.sfc.hk/web/EN/files/Risk&Strategy/ITT%20-%20SFC%20 Data%20Strategy%20(June%202016).pdf; and the United Kingdom, www. bankofengland.co.uk/Pages/fintech/default.aspx.

RegTech is for Regulators Too, and its Future is in Emerging Markets

By Matthew Homer
Affiliate, Cambridge Center for Alternative Finance

and Mackenzie Wallace
Director, ZestFinance

RegTech companies continue to emerge at a strong pace, but most of these companies are focused on helping financial institutions comply with regulation, rather than retooling the regulators themselves. This is understandable. Financial institutions represent a more substantial initial market opportunity and have several benefits over regulators, including that there are many more of them, they are hungry to reduce compliance costs, and many have already set up platforms for engaging with innovators.

Regulators Are Starting to Innovate as Well

However, regulators are also starting to innovate. When we consider regulation as a life cycle, spanning from the licensing process to ongoing oversight and enforcement, we already see significant attention focused on reinventing the first part of the life cycle. This is where regulators engage with organizations that want to receive a license, as well as the licensing process itself. New product development by existing institutions could also fit here.

For example, we see a constant drumbeat of interest in regulatory sandboxes, with dozens of countries considering this and other test-and-learn approaches. These approaches have the potential to support innovation and new market entrants in well-defined settings that reduce risks, such as the risk of consumers being adversely impacted by a new product.

While sandboxes are garnering significant attention, they are just one of many innovative approaches regulators are exploring. In addition to RegTech we also see regulators experimenting with hackathons, advisory services to innovators, and more innovation-friendly licensing processes.

Once these new institutions are in the system, however, regulators must then find ways to effectively fulfil their mandate related to oversight and enforcement. This can be challenging when new entrants to the system are significantly different from existing firms, especially through more sophisticated use of technology. This is why regulators will need to become significant users of RegTech themselves if they want to keep up.

For Emerging Market Regulators, the Risk of Inaction Is Too High

Digital technology is transforming financial marketplaces in emerging economies in a more fundamental way than we see in more established ones. Companies new to financial services, such as mobile carriers, technology firms, and others are often leading the way in introducing new, digital-first solutions to consumers. This increasingly means mobile-first engagement with customers, the use of new types of data for the provision of credit and other products, and the possibility of more tailored consumer solutions.

While this can drive tremendous financial inclusion benefits, it also presents regulators with a distinct challenge: they must safeguard markets burgeoning with millions of first-time users by regulating new technology-driven entrants starkly different from the branch-based banks they have known. It is tempting for regulators to step on the brakes to hold back these forces, lest a new entrant or experiment crash upon their watch. The solution, of course, is not to stop the emergence of this new generation of financial services providers, but to ensure regulators have the tools they need to adequately understand and monitor these new institutions and take action, when necessary. Greater regulatory confidence reinforces healthier, inclusive financial markets.

Glimpses of a RegTech Approach to Regulation are Emerging

In the United States, we have seen the Consumer Financial Protection Bureau (CFPB) pioneer technology as a tool to oversee new types of institutions. When its oversight program was launched in 2011, the CFPB expected to supervise more than 3,000 companies, including a significant portion of nonbanks that had never previously been regulated. With limited staff and a broad mandate, the CFPB embraced technology to power its online consumer complaint platform. The platform provides a centralized place for consumers to lodge complaints and for financial institutions to respond. Perhaps most interestingly, the CFPB makes the data available publicly, so that regulators and the public alike can track and detect emerging bad practices and actors – creating incentives for markets to self-correct.

Now used by over 2 million Americans, the CFPB complaint platform demonstrates that technology can incorporate consumers and financial institutions in regulatory oversight in new, unprecedented ways to advance transparency and public confidence.

In Emerging Economies, We Are at the Beginning of a Wave of Regulatory Experimentation with RegTech

In light of all of these trends, emerging market regulators have begun to reimagine regulatory oversight and embrace a technology-driven approach. For example, an initiative launched in late 2016 called the RegTech for Regulators Accelerator (www.r2accelerator.org), which we conceptualized and helped design, has supported regulators to 'develop and test next-generation RegTech prototypes' such as chatbots, application programming interfaces (APIs), and machine learning. The initiative has already worked with regulators in the Philippines, and Mexico.

The day is soon coming when regulators may, for example, enlist consumers as their eyes and ears by crowdsourcing information on financial providers using surveys based on short message service (SMS) or interactive voice response (IVR), analysing publicly available social media comments, or using chatbots to source and collect data on consumer experiences. Regulators can also deploy technology to fully automate internal processes and leverage standardized, automated reporting tools to make real-time decisions. To combat illicit money flows, emerging market regulators can support machine learning to spot suspicious activity and encourage shared compliance utilities with industry.

Where RegTech for Regulators Is Headed

While the future of a RegTech approach to regulation is only just starting to come into sight, it will require new types of collaboration between regulators and technology innovators. Procedures that enable quick trials and experiments – before embarking down lengthy government procurement processes – will be critical. To be sure, RegTech is not a silver bullet but, combined with smart decision-making, it can much better position regulators for the challenges and opportunities that lie ahead.

Blockchain and AI in RegTech

- Expansion of entities subject to KYC has put pressure on talent availability
- Blockchain represent an opportunity of co-development of platforms
- AI represents a competitive advantage in analysis data

- Identities have evolved form from digital to digitized to analogue
- Identity remains sovereign and there are few cross-border successes
- Bilateral KYC standards to open up the way towards global KYC passports

- AI can solve confusing data
- Blockchain can solve complicated relations

- With reliance on AI for compliances purposes liability of algorithms becomes an issue

- Blockchain transparency enables chain of responsibility to be assigned

- Blockchain adds trust in supply chains
- Fair procurement practice limits exploitative behaviours of certain actors
- Blockchain can act as ownership registration infrastructure to guarantee provenance

The application of AI and blockchain across the financial services industry is without doubt one of the biggest technological trends in recent years. As a result, it is not unexpected to see RegTech start-ups focusing on these emerging technologies to provide better solutions for their clients.

In each case, the inclusion of these emerging technologies finds specific use cases. The chapters in this part provide in-depth details as to how broadly blockchain and AI are used. As a rule of thumb, the development of AI implementations tends to be less widely announced as often the methods underpinning data analytics can provide a competitive advantage. This is to be contrasted with blockchain-based solutions which often requires multi-party involvement and transparency to generate value whether in the context of KYC or provenance. To put it differently, where regulation is often characterized as complex and confusing, blockchain can solve complicated (inter)relations while AI brings clarity to confusing data and meaning.

As with any use of new technology legal questions arise as to the consequences of mistakes. This seems to be particularly true with the application of AI, especially when compliance mistakes are heavily sanctioned. A whole new field regarding AI regulation and liability is developing, including providing regulators with an understanding of algorithms used to avoid a Blackbox situation or the establishment of strict liability rules in case of an automated mistake.

When it comes to blockchain, the legal consequences of the use of this technology are presently unclear. Instead, it is more the potential of this record-keeping mechanism that is discussed. As an infrastructure, the use cases are numerous, with authors covering KYC management but also data access auditing capacities in the context of GDPR. As a segue into the next two chapters, the last chapter in this part looks at blockchain usage within the supply chain, as applied to diamonds. In short, the advantage of the technology creates three benefits, namely compliance with internal rules around diamond trading, transparency in the provenance of items, and the enhancement of fair procurement practices that avoid exploitative behaviours: reminders of how RegTech not only has a positive financial impact for its users but a positive social impact for society.

The ROI of RegTech

Brad Maclean
CEO, Regulation Asia

Technology continues to disrupt all manner of knowledge work, and regulation is no exception. Regulations and compliance continue to be a massive headache for financial institutions, regardless of size. They are not only costly but the costs and risk of non-compliance, even weak compliance, are astronomical. During 2015, in the US alone, financial institutions paid more than $160 billion in fines for non-compliance.

From this perspective, the potential of RegTech is massive – from improving compliance, efficiency and effectiveness, to a potential paradigm shift in their very natures. The change could be so substantial that it could transform the role of compliance from a necessary evil to a strategic opportunity. It can empower companies to improve behaviours for better compliance, lessen regulatory burdens, and build on relationships between different parts of their businesses and the compliance function. Ultimately, RegTech can give companies the knowledge and confidence to execute their business models while supporting a safe and sound global financial system.

Few would disagree that RegTech is still at a nascent stage, with only a handful of documented case studies to demonstrate its return on investment (ROI). In most situations, ROI will be difficult to calculate for a RegTech solution, and decision-makers will need to bear several principles in mind when evaluating a potential product:

- **Cost baselining:** Understanding the operational cost of regulatory compliance, including both the once-off and recurring costs. Companies need to understand these costs in the short-term as well as forecasted over three to five years for newer insurgent technologies, or an even longer time frame of eight to ten years for existing and traditional technology providers.

- **Technology needs continuous assessment:** There are gaps between technology and regulatory requirements today and there will be tomorrow. Companies need to continually map out the level of functionality, complexity and efficiency of their current technology, systems and data as new requirements kick in if they are to respond appropriately.

- **Vendor landscape:** Identify the RegTech providers which will add value to a financial institution's technology and capabilities, to close identified gaps or provide mitigating workarounds to current regulatory challenges.

- **Business case:** Evaluate options to deploy, buy, build or partner. A critical aspect to future ROI will be the decision to move forwards with an in-house, hosted or cloud-based single-vendor solution or through another form of partnership with firms that have access to the required technology.

Decision-makers also have to factor into the process that in recent years, there has been a significant and steady growth in fines for non-compliance. Most institutions also report a correlated increase in budgeted allocations for contingent liabilities. Innovation in RegTech by both established and new insurgent providers is poised to ease compliance burdens by automating many tasks and reducing costs, to the point that such burdensome contingency allocations may either not be needed, or can be reduced significantly.

Insight, not hindsight, will be a key driver of success for decision-makers. These forward-looking elements must also be factored into the investment process, with decision-makers asking the questions: "How will this solution help the company avoid any potential multimillion dollar fine?" or "How will this solution help us avoid dealing with regulatory issues that could involve multi-year remediation requiring millions of dollars in legal or consulting fees?"

Over the long run, banks that continue to adopt newer RegTech solutions will also reap other additional benefits such as smarter, cheaper and more efficient governance, risk and compliance (GRC) frameworks and a much-improved customer experience.

However, the effectiveness and benefits of any solution will be largely reliant on a company's ability to partner with RegTech firms and vice versa. This relationship too will be significantly shaped by regulators, as we have already seen in the rollout of GRC standards and the approvals and adoption of proposed technology solutions.

Decision-makers shouldn't expect their learning curve to slow anytime soon nor should RegTech providers. Surprisingly, the next big thing to drive ROI for decision-makers will not relate to their decisions on the "what, where, when and why", but external disruptive forces shaping their RegTech options.

For all their specialization and depth of market engagement, it is possible that existing RegTech vendors won't even see the next big thing disrupting their industry until it is too late. It is also possible that just as the new SaaS (software as a service) insurgents dethrone traditional licences vendors, so too will AI (artificial intelligence) disrupt seat-based SaaS providers.

As institutions continue to drive for smarter, cheaper and more efficient GRC frameworks, RegTech will inevitably shift focus from human to AI-based productivity. As a result, the buying process for banks will fundamentally change, and so too will the sales process for SaaS vendors. SaaS vendors that fail to start thinking about this inevitability, and pricing it into their models, will find their revenues cannibalized over time by AI.

With respect to financial institutions, ROI through AI will be achieved by transforming compliance functions such as Know-your-client (KYC), Anti-Money Laundering and Counter-Financing of Terrorism (AML/CFT), consumer protection, market conduct and surveillance, and finally regulatory and risk reporting and its management. AI will create value across these functions by actively reducing the need for human involvement over time.

So what does this mean in practice?

From a compliance perspective, for example, AI bots will work alongside humans so that humans can operate with greater productivity. Over time it's expected that SaaS companies will integrate AI into their services, but in doing so, if they continue on a "per-seat basis" pricing structure, then they will be actively disincentivizing improving user efficiency. The problem is that the more integrated, efficient and effective AI becomes, the lesser the need for individual users. Each user will be able to do more, and hence fewer people will be necessary to do the same job. Over time, as SaaS vendors increase their usage of AI, they will lose revenue, and this may push some SaaS vendors to drag their heels on these types of innovation – with a related domino effect being that we also see buyers of these kinds of technologies not maximizing their ROI from their investments.

One option for RegTech will be to charge based on usage. This could be through charging for actual AI work completed, measured through computing cycles. If considering the usage required for the process of onboarding a client –including KYC, AML/CFT, and the associated on-going data refreshes – the potential is massive. Straight-through-processing (STP) and increased process efficiencies will be the biggest drivers. Less risk and shorter processing times will further reduce messy manual touchpoints. Both vendors and institutions will be winners, because the more efficiency the customer demands, the more institutions will come to rely on AI processes. Institutions will end up paying vendors more for these services, and paying less for staff.

Usage-based pricing isn't a novel idea. Companies such as Amazon, Rackspace and many others have been pioneers behind the enterprise pay-as-you-go SaaS pricing. It is no surprise that these companies introduced pay-as-you-go options into their pricing models. Rather than relying on number of users or spending time on user account management, they instead rely on actual computing unit consumed, such as use of disk space in gigabytes or time spent on execution in seconds.

From a RegTech perspective, a usage-based pricing option opens the door to a more granular experience in which the institutions will only pay for what they use. But it also has the upside of other positive by-products. Customers will no longer be incentivized to "cheat" by sharing user licenses, nor will SaaS providers be incentivized to push customers to overbuy licenses to help them "plan for growth."

AI-enhanced RegTechs that move away from traditional or even hybrid pricing structures, charging instead based on usage, will help by potentially empowering customers with greater elasticity, creating better user experiences, and enhancing efficiency into their systems, possibly leading to lower churn rates and better long-term revenue stability.

In the coming years there are two trends we can predict with certainty: one, regulatory and compliance burdens will continue to get heavier; and two, the universe of RegTech firms will continue to expand, with each one scrambling to ease the burden of compliance in order to capture their slice of the bank-profit-pool pie.

We believe that over time, innovation from both established and insurgent RegTech firms is set to reduce the regulatory compliance burdens, but the longer-term potential and impact may well be more significant. We believe that in the long run, banks achieving the greatest ROI from their investment into RegTech will be those that looked beyond the immediate needs of today, and towards the potential of RegTech as a driver of change so significant that it transforms the role of compliance from a necessary evil to a strategic opportunity. In this respect, RegTech presents a significant opportunity to help companies to solidify compliance behaviours, lessen regulatory burdens and improve organization-wide relationships with the compliance function.

Even as technology cycles at most banks shorten, the fact is that decisions made by banks today will impact the landscape of RegTech tomorrow. The RegTech leaders of the future, be it established or insurgent firms, must be decisive in their pricing, and not fear potential revenue cannibalization. Only through shifting from a per-seat to a usage-based model will they truly have the ability to empower customers with greater elasticity, better user experiences, and improved efficiency, leading to lower churn rates and better long-term revenue stability, and creating lasting competitive advantage.

The Augmented Compliance Office

By David Craig
CEO, Refinitiv

The financial industry's first response to the global financial crisis and the initial wave of regulation was to commit large amounts of money – or, more accurately, large numbers of people – to the problem. Almost overnight the industry scaled up its compliance resources by employing more people to deal with the growing burden of regulation. Ten years on from the beginnings of the crisis that still casts its shadow over the sector, the approach is both more efficient and more effective, augmenting the compliance function with new tools and approaches that enable more accurate and targeted risk management.

Back in 2008, any of us in offices in London's Canary Wharf could see for ourselves that our world was changing irrevocably: the ranks of people in the Lehman Brothers building, their backs against the glass as they learned their company was collapsing. The legions of people carrying the contents of their desks in cardboard boxes, taking their commute home for the last time. We all knew the occasion was momentous, and we all knew things had to change.

As government and regulators responded to the crisis with thicker, denser rulebooks, the finance industry responded by building up its compliance departments.

As a consequence, we are now seeing the first wave of the industrialization of compliance.

Regulatory processes up to this point have been very manual. They are not a competitive differentiator for any company – nobody ever advertises a business on the effectiveness of its compliance team. Yet, they have the potential to ruin relations with customers – if indeed the firm succeeds in meeting all the regulatory requirements to onboard them.

Meanwhile, firms must also ensure the flow of information to the regulator is not impeded: regulators are seeking more and more detailed reporting from regulated firms. The more this can be automated and provided in readily accepted forms, the more efficient the compliance team can become.

So the good news is we are now seeing enhancements in how data can be created, stored, and managed; how machines can process, automate, and predict; and how utilities and standards can bring scale to the regulatory response.

The secret to successful compliance – to keeping regulators satisfied as effectively and efficiently as possible without compromising other business obligations – is to use technology to augment the skills of the team, deploying it so that humans can get on with the tasks where they can add real value.

There are three particularly good examples of this currently: compliance with know your customer (KYC) rules, enterprise risk management (not only analysing operational risks but also ensuring these can be reported to managers and regulators), and predictive regulatory modelling (using big data analytics to identify coming risks and the regulatory requirements that will stem from them).

Know Your Customer

The days of banks having to collect, validate, and maintain identity data and information on their customers are over. This activity is increasingly being outsourced. Moreover, banks are evolving towards a 'collective' rather than 'individual' effort: more and more financial institutions are seeing the benefit of combining their verified information about corporate customers on a shared platform so others can access it.

Complexity characterizes the regulatory backdrop against which all of this is happening. Disparate regulations around the globe, no recognized standard to which organizations can work, and increasing regulatory pressure are all converging to create an environment where KYC is becoming more and more costly and time-consuming for all participants.

Moreover, there are alarming inefficiencies in how financial institutions currently conduct their KYC. Research by Thomson Reuters has shown that financial firms are taking an average of 48 days to onboard a new customer. They are also spending more than $60 million per year on KYC and customer onboarding. An average of 68 employees work on KYC adherence and processing within each firm, and a lack of appropriately skilled people is one of the sector's biggest challenges in improving customer onboarding.

From the customers' perspective, all of this means their relationship with the bank gets off to a very bad start. It takes time, and it requires a great deal of information from the prospective customer and its senior staff.

Yet, progress is slow in standardizing the process for automation. The regulator is loath to be too prescriptive, but this invariably leads to inconsistencies in how firms interpret regulations. Firms will understandably err on the side of caution and hold on to outdated and laborious processes because of the perceived threat of regulatory action if they do not.

Therefore, standardization and consistency are desperately needed. And the good news is we are seeing progress.

The Financial Action Task Force (FATF) Recommendations of 2012 are globally recognized as the international standard for combating money laundering and terrorist financing. Additional to these are the FATF Mutual Evaluations, which:

> … assess global anti–money laundering (AML) and countering the financing of terrorism (CFT) compliance and identify jurisdictions that are not compliant or [are] deficient in attaining FATF standards.

Both are driving a degree of standardization globally.

There is also more precedent and experience to work from. Although some of the big banks that have been subjected to regulatory action are now more cautious and conservative in their approach to KYC, others that have escaped regulatory action to date are learning from them and applying those lessons to their own approaches.

The regulators themselves recognize the problem and are working together to simplify the rules. The first step is to improve the regulatory environment so that digital innovation can flourish; the second is to establish frameworks to provide guidance for compliance. Regulators in both Singapore and Australia, for instance, are working on frameworks to provide the necessary guidance without being overly prescriptive.

The next stage for regulators is to support digital innovation in regulated firms and to encourage widespread adoption of solutions. Ideally, this would mean regulators and the regulated working together, focused on ensuring customers can join the financial system and can use it with security and confidence. This is the approach pioneered in South Africa in 2016 with a utility model that not only benefits financial institutions and regulators but also boosts the economy by ensuring businesses have the access they need to financial services.

The regulators are turning their attention to these technological opportunities at an exciting time.

Blockchain's potential in managing digital identities is vast, so its application to KYC solutions is enormously exciting. The caveats still stand about its long-term resilience against coordinated cyber attacks, or its security from abuse by organized crime groups or terrorist organizations. However, its potential to help record global transactions in real time could prove to be invaluable for regulators as well as financial firms. The distributed ledger technology introduces transparency at every stage of the supply chain by revealing the provenance of each component to everyone involved. This could drastically reduce fraud and simplify documentation. It could enable an organization to have a single view of each client, avoiding the fragmentation and duplication of due diligence data by recording customer data centrally and then making this record available across the entire organization.

In short, 'one client, one view' is a goal for regulators and regulated firms alike – and technology to enable this is coming ever closer. What is needed is an open-minded approach from regulators to encourage innovation.

Enterprise Risk Management

Enterprise risk management (ERM) describes the collections of procedures and processes that organizations use to understand, measure, and monitor risk. It enables compliance teams more accurately to analyse and report on operational risks using advanced reporting engines with powerful search functions and a relentless focus on user experience. Not only is it more straightforward for compliance officers to identify risks; it is also easier to provide reports to management and regulators.

These types of risks can affect all parts of an organization and are not limited to particular business units or processes. The ERM process in place needs to be adaptable enough to accommodate a variety of risk types that cannot always easily be consolidated or aggregated.

Investment in ERM is typically driven by the level of regulation faced by an organization, the likelihood of high-impact events, and the importance the organization places on reputation.

The cost of compliance continues to rise for financial firms. Some estimates pin the cost of governance, risk, and compliance at 15–20% of the total cost of running the business at financial firms. That is nearly one-fifth of an entire firm's budget – just to stay in business and avoid fines from regulators.

For such firms, the opportunity of RegTech is the removal of one easily mitigated risk – the human element. Put simply, people are better employed in interpreting data than in collecting it and managing it.

ERM helps firms mine massive amounts of data in order to get the right information to regulators quickly. The sheer amount of data being dealt with means that humans performing these tasks will simply be overwhelmed, increasing an organization's exposure to risk.

Additionally, that information often overlaps: a piece of information on a trade or customer might potentially be used to satisfy multiple regulations. Condensing and making this data accessible may help bring real efficiency gains.

This approach particularly helps with the myriad new customer data laws. Many of these new regulations require similar information – just in different jurisdictions around the globe. Understanding the commonality of data across disparate geographies and how they apply can place a firm miles ahead of its competitors.

All of this can reside for easy access in the cloud. The sharing of mass data securely, combined with massive computing power, is enabling this new approach to the management of regulatory data.

Predictive Regulatory Monitoring

Data has more potential value when it can be shared or opened. It can be used by a number of different stakeholders and partners, within or outside an organization, for a variety of applications to gain new analytical insight and to build new products and services. Moreover, to effectively use data, it is important to understand how it connects to the real world. Big data analytics are powering systems that can identify coming risks from legislators and regulators.

The rise of RegTech and analytics on unstructured textual data means big data can be examined in new ways. We have already seen how firms are working to turn big data into actionable insights they can use. By pairing a large repository of unstructured financial content with the right automated technology solutions, firms can gain a real advantage. Predictive analytics and indicators can help firms to assess impacts and plan how to mitigate risks.

Artificial intelligence (AI) can support the mass processing of regulatory information when coupled with consistent taxonomy and tagging. AI is not a single technology: it is a collection of related technologies, including natural language processing and machine learning. Each of these technologies has specific uses. Natural language processing, in particular, is starting to come into widespread use in helping to analyse unstructured content such as laws and regulations. Together with machine learning, this enables the 'reading' of documents, extracting metadata, identifying entities that are referred to, and 'understanding' the intent or purpose of specific parts of the document.

Extracting metadata helps us to understand what the regulation is about, identifying financial products (such as loans or swaps), regulatory topics (such as AML or market abuse), and business processes (such as trade settlement or customer due diligence). With this information, we can determine whether the regulation is relevant, what parts of the organization are likely to be affected, and who needs to review it.

We can then identify all the entities in a regulatory document – whom it involves, whom it applies to, who else is involved (the regulator, any third parties).

And finally we 'understand' the content – we determine what we must do or must not do as a consequence of this information.

Such technologies that help manage regulatory developments and identify risks or events that could impact the business are helping firms move beyond manual spreadsheets and documents to a more automated and auditable approach.

The inevitable development of these technologies – the increasingly advanced data analytics – will enable firms to model future scenarios and to conduct trend and horizon scanning – to anticipate risks and therefore to prepare for them.

The potential applications are exciting.

Firms could be able to monitor transactions in real time, identifying patterns and trends in the data to help them to target their work to combat threats.

They could conduct behavioural profiling and analyse behaviourally driven risks within their organization to ensure their company culture supports not only compliance and best practices but also optimal and safe ways of working.

Moreover, they could learn from the past, analysing previous regulatory failures (theirs or others') to identify potential risk areas and their triggers so that they can be alert to early indicators, for instance in the financial markets.

In Conclusion

All of this exciting innovation is posited on one particularly and vitally important factor: verification of identity.

This extends beyond the need to know the people you are doing business with and is now inherent in every stage of a financial transaction.

The opportunity of blockchain and distributed ledger technology is that it effectively federates trust: it enables people who would not usually trust each other to trust each other. That is a very powerful concept.

However, these fantastic leaps forward in analytics ultimately are of little importance if you are not absolutely sure of what you are analysing. Digital identity is the foundation of all RegTech solutions: the identity of individuals, organizations, and assets is absolutely the first step. It is fundamental to how we do business, and to the opportunity that technology now offers us.

The downside? We have grown used to physical assets being the things we guard most closely: our wallets or our keys. The most precious thing we will be looking after in future is not our wallet or keys, but our digital identity.

Dissolving Barriers: A Global Digital Trust Protocol

By Ankit Ratan
Co-Founder, Signzy

In a globalized world, the need to be able to trust parties across borders cannot be understated. Any party when undertaking a transaction in a foreign jurisdiction takes an additional business and compliance risk. Thus in cross-border transactions, the due diligence takes months to complete, increasing not only the time but the cost, to the extent that it can determine the business decision itself when weighed against the size of the entire transaction.

To understand how tough it is to carry out a cross-border transaction, let's go through the process once for illustration:

> In a cross-border transaction taking place between two parties in the United States and India, the US party would hire a US law firm A and the Indian party will hire an Indian law firm A to ensure that the transaction complies with the local regulatory regime. Since the two parties do not trust each other, they will, in turn, hire lawyers in the other jurisdiction, i.e. the US law firm will hire an Indian law firm B, and the Indian law firm will hire a US law firm B.

That simple example shows how a single transaction now involves four law firms. This means time and cost escalations, which increasingly restrict such cross-border transactions.

A global digital trust system should allow multiple parties in different jurisdictions to transact through a single platform. It should also ensure that the transaction is meeting all compliances in each of the jurisdictions. Such a platform can enable cross-border transactions to be as simple as local ones, which can unleash the power of a truly globalized digital world.

Digital transactions, though, will require an element of digital trust like the human-based trust mechanism that forms the basis of offline transactions. There are three parts of building digital trust: authenticating unique identity, getting to know more about this ID, and having a digital record of the transaction. The first two parts are also covered in financial know your customer (KYC). So to create a global digital trust system, one would need a global way of verifying ID, doing a digital cross-border due diligence, and keeping digital transaction records that are globally verifiable.

Attempts at Unified Global Identity

There have been several attempts at a unified identity. These can be broken down into two categories: (i) creating generic digital identities and (ii) digital identities linked to unique physical identities.

Generic Digital Identities

There are multiple examples of generic digital identities. The most commonly used is email. It is often used as a login username, thus providing a simple-to-use digital identity system. Other examples are social media logins – Facebook, Twitter, Google, and so on, which are now using the digital profile itself as a login feature. In cases where you are not logged in to your profile, you end up first logging in to your profile and then signing in through it.

Email from a regulatory standpoint is an inadequate source of identity since it does not uniquely identify the individual, as one can create umpteen emails. Social profile, on the other hand, is not as easy to replicate. Further, using data from one's timeline and network, one can determine if it is a fraudulent profile. Facebook and Google also have recently started seeing this as an opportunity to become an identity standard. Facebook has been granted a patent to use social network data for lending, and several other start-ups, most famously Lenddo, have been using social profiles for giving creditworthiness scores. Google plans to use location and other behavioural data to help financial institutions assess risk and do basic KYC checks such as address.

Thus, it is evident that digital profile-based identity is getting more sophisticated and might be as good at identity fraud detection as, if not better than, offline systems. In spite of this, there is one flaw that might restrict its use in a regulatory scenario: the idea of a physical sovereign identity, i.e. a physical identity that uniquely identifies you to a country such as your passport.

Digital Identities Linked to Unique Physical Identities

This is a space that is seeing an increase in traction where companies are trying to link national identities to a global identity. Organizations are using multiple approaches, from verification using a large human team to storing data on the blockchain. The key steps are: (i) verify the national ID; (ii) if possible, verify the data on the national ID; (iii) prove that the person uploading the ID is the same as the one creating a digital identity.

The third proof is fundamentally a biometric proof that links the ID picture to the video/picture of the person uploading it digitally. Thus the method is more or less global in nature. In some cases even the biometrics are verifiable. In India, as an example, one can verify a person's fingerprint/iris/face using the centralized Aadhaar database. Further, this is available as an open application programming interface (API) for easy consumption.

However, (i) and (ii) are not global in nature. Each country would have different IDs and, based on regulation IDs, may even have different privileges. So all IDs may not be equal. As an example, while taking a vehicle loan in India the borrower's driving license becomes a mandatory ID. Further, ID frauds are prevalent, and there is no evidence to show that the frauds committed in the offline world will not transcend to the digital world.

Thus, even though this task of linking digital identities to a national ID might seem as easy as doing (i), (ii), and (iii), in reality, it is far more complex. Large regulatory departments in banks are a testimony to this fact. A single global ID hence might not be the answer.

Getting to Know More About This Identity (Due Diligence)

KYC does not merely imply establishing identity. KYC implies knowing your customer beyond the person's name, date of birth, and PIN code. This is where negative lists come into the picture.

Each country has a different regulator, and they have different negative lists based on differentiated criteria.

India, for example, has several industry regulators like the Reserve Bank of India, the Securities and Exchange Board of India, the Insurance Regulatory and Development Authority, the Registrar of Companies, and so on, which publish their own negative lists. There are several administrative and policing agencies like the National Investigation Agency, the Criminal Investigation Department, and the Central Vigilance Commission that keep publishing names of persons associated with anti–money laundering (AML) or countering the financing of terrorism (CFT) risk, whereas the United States has its own unique sanction list published by the US Treasury Department.

Moreover, different regulatory bodies are recording and furnishing KYC information in different countries. In India, there are multiple entity types such as a private limited company, limited liability partnership, partnership firm, sole proprietorship firm, HUF, trust, and so forth. Each entity type is governed by a different regulatory regime, which prescribes ownership and identity documents and other proof of business. In the United States each state has its own regulatory regime for incorporation of entities, and their identification and business proof documents. And each state allows multiple types of such entities, therefore leading to multiple types of documents for KYC.

Beyond One-time KYC: Keeping Records

The other dimension of trust is history. This is again a sovereign sensitive subject, for storing and sharing historical data may involve sensitive information. However, what is possible is putting all future global transactions on a record and using mere transaction party history itself, without revealing the nature of the transaction.

The creation of defaulter history has been one of the most critical regulatory processes within the banking domain. However, there are two broad issues: (i) input, as how one can trust organizations that are inputting negative data, and (ii) privacy, as collecting someone's past behaviour might not always be fully legal.

Thus today's practice is to have special access to industry centralized databases. Credit bureaus are one example. There is a practical challenge of real-time updating of these databases. However, even if that was to be solved, a critical sovereign aspect cannot be ignored: cross-border data sharing. It is a common instance that when people with current outstanding loans migrate from India to the United States, they have higher default rates. The reason is that their credit scores in the United States are unaffected by their credit history in India, as the US banks have no way to verify or link Indian credit history.

Underlying Core Global Regulatory Principles

There are two parts of KYC: identity and knowing more about the person. This discussion will limit knowing more to just AML/CFT.

While it may seem that identity documents are extremely disparate across the world, all regulatory processes establish just two things: proof of identity (PoI) and proof of address (PoA). Thus, at its core, identity verification globally can be described as a proof of sovereign identity and a physical local address.

While there are multiple negative lists, the conceptualization of AML/CFT has emanated from a global effort of the United Nations, and therefore the reasons and basic philosophies of AML/CFT are consistent across the world.

The UN General Assembly declaration in 1990 was the first constructive global step against money laundering focusing on prevention of financing to the illicit drug trade. Today the Financial Action Task Force (FATF), which is an intergovernmental body, recommends to countries a regulatory regime for prevention of money laundering and drives the global policy on AML/CFT. The global objective of the regime is to stop money earned through illegal means from coming into the traditional financial system and being converted into legitimate money. This is a combined effort to fight the funding of global terrorism and illicit trading and trafficking.

Core Function of Compliance Can Be Replaced by an AI Platform

In an increasingly digital world, real-time decision making is becoming an essential need of the business. As an example, multiple FinTechs are effectively creating online loan processes that take under five minutes. Thus all compliance checks also need to be concluded within this period and hence be done in real time.

While the compliance can also be done later in an offline mode, the speed of the digital world makes post-compliance a very risky affair. Hence real-time compliance has become a core value required of the regulatory environment of the digital world.

At the same time, the risks in the digital world are much higher, and severe damage can be done within hours. So what is essentially then needed is a real-time system that makes checks as strictly as today's human-based processes.

An AI-based KYC system then is itself a need in a future digital world. This KYC system will have three key components:

1. *Verification of identity.* Ability to link to a local identity system and authenticate a person digitally.

2. *Background check.* Ability to access local negative lists and databases, either public or industry-specific.

3. *Regulatory decision engine.* Makes decisions based on current prevailing guidelines and outputs from 1 and 2.

Verifying Identity

A human-based process requires the person to produce an ID document. An officer sees this, and then does the following three things: (i) establishes that this is a valid ID, (ii) establishes that the form details and ID details are same, and (iii) matches the customer's face with the picture in the ID.

This process is region agnostic. Plenty of companies (including ours) are now performing these processes using computer vision (a subset of the larger AI world) where the work flow is simple. The user does a video onboarding where he or she shows ID documents. The algorithms on the background have the ability to make all the three judgements and let the case pass or not.

Background Check

Background checks even today represent a fairly automated process. Moreover, a simple ability to connect and update the data should be good enough. Additionally, an ability to crawl and update negative lists would be desirable.

Regulatory Decision Engine

Outputs from both these engines would now have to be run through the particular case. This process will be an AI replica of a more manual process today, where risk teams using their understanding of compliance rules make a judgement in each case file. This engine can slowly evolve into a self-learning-based engine where digital frauds may throw up some interesting compliance best practices that have not been thought of today.

The Power of a Common Global KYC Platform

The power here lies in the common platform both parties rely on to do verifications. It may seem that the platform's advanced technological ability makes it acceptable. However, the real acceptance would be derived from two parties using the same platform to do local verifications.

Once Party A trusts this platform for its own local KYC, it is easier for Party A to trust the same for a global KYC check. Though this platform obviously has no single ID, it has a common intelligence layer. This layer decided, as an example, that it would use Aadhaar in India and SSN in the United States.

Keeping Records Beyond KYC

In a digital world, you need a negative database that gets updated in real time and still is able to ensure basic global principles are met: (i) privacy, (ii) quality of data, and (iii) global accessibility.

The author proposes that a decentralized digital ledger is the best way to carry this forward. The protocol will carry the following two types of data:

1. Unique identity

2. Transacting parties and their trust rating.

Trust rating would be a function of the number of past transactions. In this function, each transaction has weightage based on the trust rating. As an example, someone frequently transacting with low-trust parties might have a lower trust rating than someone with fewer transactions but with high-trust parties.

Today blockchain has become synonymous with a decentralized ledger. Furthermore, we already have globally decentralized ledgers with decent adoption. So one or multiple blockchains can be used to record transactions between parties and create trust scores that are verifiable by anyone across the world.

Conclusion

The offline trust mechanism performs two functions: (i) identify the person by look or feel and (ii) learn something about the person's behaviour. This AI-based platform would be able to do these two important things needed to replicate the offline human and paper-based trust mechanism:

1. Establish a digital KYC using AI that meets or even supersedes today's local human-based processes, thus satisfying local regulators.

2. Create a reward/punishment mechanism based on future digital transactions by assigning trust scores.

Thus, even though this system creates neither a global digital ID nor a common negative list, it can create a platform for enabling digital trust globally. The system will also ensure compliance with different jurisdictions and the differentiated regulatory regimes. This, in turn, will lead to seamless cross-border transactions to enable a truly digital global economy.

Can AI Really Disrupt Monitoring for Suspicious Activity?

By Malcolm Wright
Chief Compliance Officer, Diginex

At this moment, tens of thousands of anti–money laundering (AML) analysts are sitting glued to their screens poring through mountains of alerts generated by their transaction monitoring systems. Depressingly, most of these alerts will be false positives. Transaction monitoring in its current form is primitive, using a series of rules to detect suspicious activity. Such rules might include monitoring for a cash payment or series of structured payments that exceed US$10,000 and where an investigation then needs to be conducted or a report filed. The system is inefficient, and organized criminals are learning how to evade detection through ever more sophisticated laundering techniques. Similarly, terrorist financing behaviour, often viewed as money laundering in reverse, is even harder to detect, as transactions often appear to be normal.

Regulators view transaction monitoring as a fundamental pillar to detecting and preventing illicit money flows, and advocate that financial institutions not only invest in sufficient staff to review alerts generated but continually monitor and tune the effectiveness of their monitoring tools. However, even with appropriate resources and tuning, illicit money can and will flow through the financial network. The question is whether there is a new paradigm in which false positives can be reduced while anomaly detection improved and if so, how?

Grinding to a Halt

A study by Bain & Company in 2016 estimated that 15–20% of a bank's run cost comes from its compliance functions. That is a substantial overhead where any savings can go straight to the bottom line to improve operating margins. In parallel, we see an increase in regulatory enforcement actions; for example, the UK

Financial Conduct Authority's £3.2 million (US$4 million) fine of Sonali Bank (UK) Limited in 2016 was in part due to inadequate monitoring of transactions.

There is also a swath of new legislation driving greater compliance. In Europe, the fourth Money Laundering Directive (4MLD) came into force on 26 June 2017, and an amendment (5MLD) is already in the pipeline. At the start of the same year, the New York Department of Financial Services regulation came into force that required financial institutions to maintain programmes to monitor and filter transactions. These are not isolated, though, as similar pushes for greater compliance are taking place across Australia, Asia, and Africa as well.

Pressure is also coming from within the system, such as the move to real-time payments where existing batch-based transaction-monitoring systems cannot keep track fast enough, and where the illicit money may already have left the account by the time an alert is generated. New banks are also emerging that are not tied to incumbent technology, physical branches, or poorly connected data sets. This is allowing them to implement new systems far more quickly and create a competitive edge with customers. Further, new payment methods, including distributed ledgers, prepaid cards, and digital currencies, introduce ever more intricate transaction flows, which can mask illicit behaviour. Couple this with technologically adept criminals, and it is clear to see why the existing technologies are approaching their limits and why, before long, the cost of compliance will escalate to an unsustainable level.

A Definition

Before discussing artificial intelligence (AI) and big data analytics, it is useful to define a meaning or use case in the context of this chapter, given there is no common descriptor used by all. For clarity and simplicity, AI in this context refers to a technology that is able to accept multiple data sources, link and profile data, model unusual behaviour patterns, discount anomalies that are false positives, review alert decisions made by humans, and update identification models to allow for more accurate anomaly detection in future data sets. This definition also encompasses structured machine learning and big data analysis techniques such as data mining, classification, and graphing.

Linking with the Facts

Suspicious activity monitoring lacks foundation if we are unable to tell what 'suspicious' looks like for an individual customer. Very often, common rules are applied across a customer base such as looking for standard variances in volume, value, or velocity of an individual account over a defined time period. To truly be of benefit, activity monitoring needs to link back to

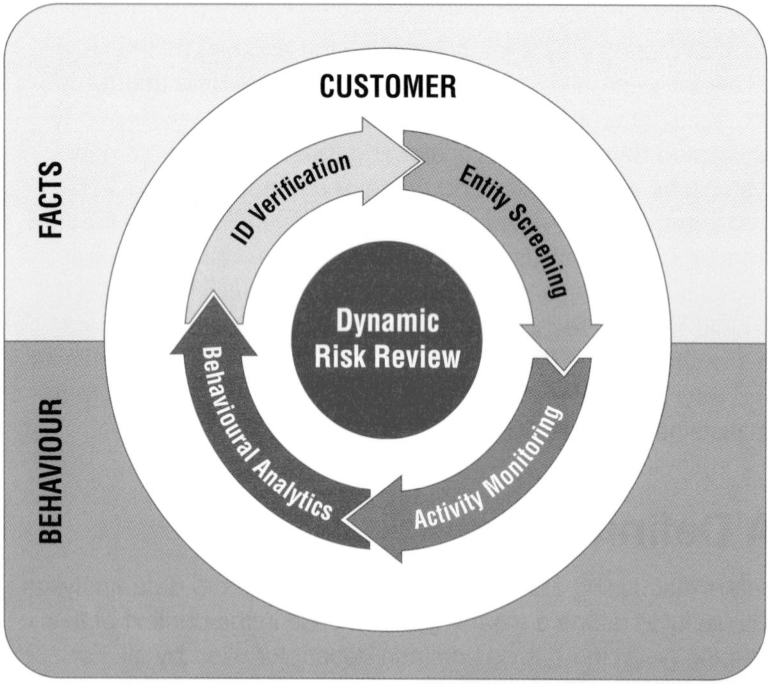

the facts known about a customer. For example, if a customer is known to be a cash-intensive business, it follows that the account will handle more cash than a card-based business, so monitoring thresholds may be set differently. Figure 1 demonstrates the AML life cycle.

Within the life cycle, identity is collected and verified, and the customer is then screened against sanctions, politically exposed persons (PEPs), and other watch lists. This then provides a factual profile about a customer, and activity monitoring can then commence. Through it all, a dynamically updating risk profile is maintained, allowing for a risk-based approach to be taken should fact-checking or behavioural monitoring risk thresholds be exceeded. In the course of monitoring, when an alert is raised, one of three things is true: the facts are incorrect, the rule is poorly configured and alerted incorrectly, or the behaviour is suspicious. However, there is something else going on too. How can the financial institution be sure that the identity data collected was genuine? It is not until behaviours are monitored that the truth of the facts surfaces. Suspicious activity monitoring is therefore ongoing identity verification. However, to operate well within this life cycle and at scale, tools far more refined than blunt rules-based engines are needed.

The Next Generation of Suspicious Activity Monitoring in Practice

With human capital costs, data complexities, and data volumes driving change, the opportunity for AI to make a significant difference to the paradigm is enticing. In a utopian world, a self-learning machine would be able to not only accurately identify suspicious transactions with a low false-positive rate, but also predict likely future trends on accounts through preemptive alerting. The goal is not to automate the entire process, but to surface accurate information for human review – in a sense, heading towards the film world of *Minority Report* starring Tom Cruise, which even then still had a human element at the end of the alert process.

CONCEPT BY MALCOLM WRIGHT.
(C) 2017 THOMSON REUTERS. REPRODUCED WITH PERMISSION.
Linked in. *https://uk.linkedin.com/in/malcolmwright*

Figure 1: AML life cycle

AI offers us six areas for consideration:

1. Compare transaction activity for customers who have similar characteristics – for example, type of business or occupation, geographic location, age, gender, and so on.

2. Provide hashed aggregated data to a shared data lake, allowing other financial institutions to build stronger detection models by accessing the lake. For example, if all financial institutions shared data on how typical pizza restaurants operate based on their customers' data, then using the wider pool of community data would make it easier to spot anomalies. Such data would also utilize secondary data such as business size, location, and so forth. This would additionally allow for a faster industry response to emerging threats.

3. Learn from previous false-positive discounting by human AML analysts, and adjust future detection models accordingly so fewer false positives are produced.

4. Learn which customer behaviours led to a suspicious activity report being filed, and use the learning to predictively identify other customers that behave similarly but that may not yet have been flagged as suspicious.

5. Provide deep-link analysis to uncover commonality in data sets. For example, multiple females living at the same address making small, regular cash deposits could be indicative of the property being used as a brothel. An option may also be to use broader data sets; for example, geolocation data could be used to trace a money launderer's road trip travelling from branch to branch making cash deposits into different, linked accounts.

6. Prioritize alerts based on the type of threat posed. Again, over time taking the ability to learn from human interaction as to what is critical and what is more routine. For example, a so-called freedom fighter preparing to depart for a war-torn country may be considered a higher risk than structured payments received into an account from the sale of street drugs.

Despite all of these options, hard rules will still be required, such as currency transaction thresholds or prepaid card limits, simply because in certain jurisdictions the legislation requires it. Thus, the end state for the industry will likely be a hybrid system that includes both AI and traditional rules to provide a sophisticated level of detection.

The Challenge with the Next-Generation Approach

We can see much of the next-generation approach already happening in fraud monitoring: real-time transaction analysis using big data, machine learning models, and rules to classify, identify, and block transactions. However, fraud and AML/countering the financing of terrorism (CFT) risk management differ in how the regulations handle them, and thus the ability to implement the utopian next generation has its challenges.

Three key challenges present themselves in adopting a new approach:

1. *Testing*. A rules-based system can be tested with thresholds. For example, testing that a US$10,000 deposit flags an alert, it is possible to test either side of the amount to determine whether the outcomes are as expected. However, how can a machine that learns be tested? At the outset, it can be trained with true data, or training data that is subsequently run against real data to determine if the system correctly understands what is, and what is not, suspicious. But, when that system has been running for some time and has learned new outcomes along the way, how can it then be retested? Sampling may go some way towards validation, but how big would the sample size need to be, and how can that sample data be validated itself?

2. *System knowledge*. An underlying governance principle that regulators draw on is that financial institutions can explain how

their systems work, and how a decision was reached. Regulators have highlighted this in response to automated screening systems. Within Europe, data protection legislation will take this further in that the data subject (in this case the customer) would have a right to understand why a decision was reached. To that end, how effectively can an AI system decision be explained by potentially non-technical bank compliance staff either to regulators or to their end customers?

3. *Data privacy regulation.* Some challenges are emerging in respect of data privacy. The European Union's General Data Protection Regulation (GDPR), which came into force in May 2018, presents the greatest threat to the emergence of a new approach. This legislation will apply to any organization that processes data on EU citizens, regardless of where the organization is located (even if outside the EU). Most significant are principles around customer profiling and automated decisions that would have a material impact on customers. Aside from a customer's right to understand a decision, as mentioned earlier, AI system design may need to account for a requirement to manually review machine-made decisions (such as changes to risk profiles) to ensure compliance to legislation.

It would appear that these will be the biggest challenges to the implementation of the utopian future. However, the fundamental question that needs to be answered is: can the regulator and the head of compliance or the money laundering reporting officer accept that a machine will make a decision (both positive alerting and discounting) on a transaction, and if so how demonstrable is that decision? The US appear to be considering this with the Algorithmic Accountability Act being proposed in April 2019.

Conclusion

Regulators have in the past tended not to take a proactive stance towards new technologies, or at least not until there is a groundswell of momentum that requires them to respond. Distributed ledger technology (DLT) is a good example of this with DLT having been gaining momentum in RegTech and FinTech circles for a couple of years; it was not until March 2017 that the United Kingdom's Financial Conduct Authority issued a consultation on DLT's potential use cases. Thus, now it would seem that the fledgling RegTech industry needs to draw on existing legislation and regulatory guidance that relate to more established technologies and to review reasons why some organizations have received fines. Although looking back retrospectively in this way may well appear to stifle innovation, failure to do so could prove equally costly.

Forging a Responsibility and Liability Framework in the AI Era for RegTech

By Brian Tang

Founder, ACMI and LITE Lab@HKU

Artificial intelligence (AI), and more precisely machine learning (ML), is now indeed no longer the exclusive domain of science fiction fans and cognitive science researchers at universities or in the military.

Four critical areas have undergone tremendous development, leading to both *Fortune* and *Forbes* naming 2017 'the year of AI':[1]

1. *Computational power*. Parallel computing for ML using graphical processing units (GPUs) originally developed for video games[2] has lowered the cost and wattage with increased computational power to dramatically broaden AI application.[3] As a corollary, cloud-based ML as a service (MLaaS) is now an important new business model.[4]

2. *Data*. The lower costs of data storage,[5] wireless communication for cloud-connected internet of things (IoT) devices

---

[1] '2017 Will Be the Year of AI', *Fortune*, 30 December 2016, http://fortune.com/2016/12/30/the-year-of-artificial-intelligence; 'Why 2017 Is the Year of Artificial Intelligence', *Forbes*, 27 February 2017; https://www.forbes.com/sites/forbestechcouncil/2017/02/27/why-2017-is-the-year-of-artificial-intelligence

[2] See, e.g. A. Coates, B. Huval, T. Wang, D. Wu, A. Ng, and B. Catanzaro, 'Deep Learning with COTS HPC Systems'; http://ai.stanford.edu/~acoates/papers/CoatesHuvalWangWuNgCatanzaro_icml2013.pdf

For context, according to Nvidia, a Google Data Center traditionally consisted of 1,000 computer processing unit (CPU) servers with 2,000 CPUs for 16,000 cores that used 600 kW and cost US$5 million; yet the Stanford AI Lab was built using three graphics processing unit (GPU)–accelerated servers with 12 GPUs for 18,432 cores that used 4 kW and cost $33,000: Nvidia presentation at seventh DBSx CAL Talk: 'AI or Human' in Hong Kong (3 March 2017).

[3] Concurrently, Google has developed proprietary tensor processing units (TPUs) with application-specific integrated circuits (ASICs) specifically developed for ML with higher volume and reduced precision and wattage that has been used to improve relevancy of search results in RankBrain, accuracy and quality of maps and navigation in Street View, as well as to 'think' much faster and look further ahead in AlphaGo: 'Building an AI Chip Saved Google from Building a Dozen New Data Centers', (*Wired*, 5 April 2017); https://www.wired.com/2017/04/building-ai-chip-saved-google-building-dozen-new-data-centers

[4] See, for example, Nvidia and Microsoft's HGX-1 hyperscale GPU accelerator; http://nvidianews.nvidia.com/news/nvidia-and-microsoft-boost-ai-cloud-computing-with-launch-of-industry-standard-hyperscale-gpu-accelerator; Amazon Web Services' (AWS's) Deep Learning AMI and three new AI services (Amazon Lex, Amazon Polly, and Amazon Rekognition): 'AWS Announces Three New AI Services', *Business Wire*, 30 November 2016; http://www.businesswire.com/news/home/20161130006126/en/AWS-Announces-Amazon-AI-Services; 'Cloud Wars: Google, Amazon and Microsoft Battle to Own the Future of Computing', *Telegraph*, 26 March 2016; www.telegraph.co.uk/technology/2016/03/25/cloud-wars-google-amazon-and-microsoft-battle-to-own-the-future. Cloud-based models also exacerbate concerns regarding magnification of coding error or failure across many at the end of the value chain as well as cyber security protocols being breached: 'Regulatory Hurdles for RegTech', SIA Partners, 27 March 2017; http://en.finance.sia-partners.com/20170327/regulatory-hurdles-regtech

[5] The rate of increase of hard disk density and corollary drop in price has been known as Kryder's Law, named after the founder of Carnegie Mellon University's Data Storage Systems Center and CTO of Seagate Technology: 'Kryder's Law', *Scientific American*, 1 August 2005; https://www.scientificamerican.com/article/kryders-law

(e.g. voice, text, images, video, biometric), and digitization of paper records[6] has resulted in an explosion of structured and unstructured big data that can be processed and analysed for better ML.

3. *Algorithms*. Silicon Valley and other US companies like Google, Facebook, Microsoft, Amazon, and IBM, as well as Chinese tech giants Alibaba, Baidu,[7] and Tencent, have been courting AI talent in a manner compared to top US National Football League quarterback prospects,[8] even resulting in lawsuits.[9]

4. *Infrastructure*. Leading software companies offer cognitive services through application programming interfaces (APIs), such as IBM Watson and Microsoft Azure. Increasingly, compa-nies such as Google, Facebook, Microsoft, and Baidu and many newer cloud computing services from Alibaba, Tencent and Huawei are experimenting with open sourcing deep learn-ing frameworks, tools, and platforms to 'democratize AI' and

encourage more developers, domain expert trainers, and use cases to embrace their frameworks.[10]

If AI can best be applied to areas of intense data, then its application to RegTech[11] for regulatory surveillance, monitoring, analysing, reporting, recommendations, and compliance seems ideal.

Compliance with regulations requires understanding and analysing many complex rules applicable to a multitude of factual permutations and possibilities.

Organizations such as financial institutions comprise a large constituency of employees and stakeholders whose behaviour and actions need to be monitored, analysed, and guided to influence behaviour and detect, report, and address breaches and perhaps predict rogue behaviour. Moreover, these firms are highly

---

[6] This has even been done on a nationwide basis, as can be seen by India's India Stack (https://indiastack.org) and e-Estonia (https://e-estonia.com).

[7] For example, 'Here's How Baidu's Founder Thinks AI Will Change the World', *Tech In Asia*, 26 August 2016; https://www.techinasia.com/baidu-founder-ai-future

[8] 'The Race to Buy the Human Brains Behind Deep Learning Machines', *Bloomberg*, 28 January 2014; https://www.bloomberg.com/news/articles/2014-01-27/the-race-to-buy-the-human-brains-behind-deep-learning-machines; see also Kai-Fu Lee, *AI Super-Powers: China, Silicon Valley and the New World Order* (2018)

[9] 'Uber v Google: And Now, the Self-driving Car War Gets Nasty', *Mashable*, 20 May 2017; http://mashable.com/2017/05/20/uber-vs-google-waymo-self-driving-car-wars-get-nasty/#2u5WgIWMC5qi

---

[10] See, e.g. 'Google Just Open Sourced TensorFlow, Its Artificial Intelligence Engine', *Wired*, 9 November 2015; https://www.wired.com/2015/11/google-open-sources-its-artificial-intelligence-engine; and then its DeepMind Lab training codebase 'Open-sourcing DeepMind Lab', 12 December 2016; https://deepmind.com/blog/open-sourcing-deepmind-lab; 'FAIR [Facebook AI Research] Open Sources Deep-learning Modules for Torch', 16 January 2015; https://research.fb.com/fair-open-sources-deep-learning-modules-for-torch; 'Deep Learning with Microsoft Cognitive Toolkit CNTK', Microsoft Research, 10 February 2017; https://blogs.msdn.microsoft.com/uk_faculty_connection/2017/02/10/microsoft-cognitive-toolkit-cntk; 'Baidu Follows US Tech Giants and Open Sources Its Deep Learning Tools [PaddlePaddle Toolkit]', *The Verge*, 1 September 2016; https://www.theverge.com/2016/9/1/12725804/baidu-machine-learning-open-source-paddle

[11] See definition in, e.g. Arner, Barberis, and Buckley, 'FinTech, RegTech and the Reconceptualization of Financial Regulation', *Northwestern Journal of International Law & Business* 37, no. 3 (2017); https://ssrn.com/abstract=2847806

incentivized to reduce costs and operational risks after the hefty fines of recent years.[12]

AI in RegTech is being used as part of FinTech[13] in areas such as:

- Risk management modelling and forecasting.
- Surveillance of employee behaviour.
- Know your client (KYC), anti–money laundering (AML), and fraud detection.
- Compliance chatbots.[14]

- Regulatory radar of new regulations, assessing applicability, and flagging for interpretation.[15]
- Surveillance by regulators.[16]

Tech giant IBM showed that it was a serious RegTech AI player when it acqui-hired Promontory and its 600 former senior government regulator employees[17] to accelerate Watson's development and ML of cognitive solutions for risk and compliance. In 2017, millions of Super Bowl fans learned of its tax preparation partnership with H&R Block.[18]

Applying Current Legal Frameworks in the AI Era

Common law courts developed the concept of tort, whereby all persons owe duties of care in relation to any breaches of such

---

[12] See, e.g. 'Banks Trimming Compliance Staff as $321 Billion in Fines Abate', *Bloomberg*, 23 March 2017; https://www.bloomberg.com/news/articles/2017-03-23/banks-trimming-compliance-staff-as-321-billion-in-fines-abate

[13] See, e.g. 'Application of AI in RegTech', *Let's Talk Payments*, 11 November 2016, https://letstalkpayments.com/application-of-ai-in-regtech; 'The RegTech Top 100 Power List: The Most Influential RegTech Firms', *Planet Compliance*, 21 March 2017, http://www.planetcompliance.com/2017/03/21/regtech-top-100-power-list-influential-regtech-firms; 'Rise of the Machines: RegTech and AI', RegTech Forum, March 2017, https://regtechforum.co/wp-content/uploads/2017/03/RegTech_Forum_Rise_Of-The_Machines.pdf; Institute of International Finance, 'Regtech in Financial Services: Solutions for Compliance and Reporting', 22 March 2016, https://www.iif.com/publication/research-note/regtech-financial-services-solutions-compliance-and-reporting

[14] 'In the Continuing Ascendency of Artificial Intelligence, Yet Another Investment Bank Hires Robots and Fires Humans', *Compliance X*, 2 May 2017; http://compliancex.com/continuing-ascendancy-artificial-intelligence-yet-another-investment-bank-hires-robots-fires-humans

---

[15] This would be helped by the development of a common and standard ontology of terminology: see Ireland's Governance Risk and Compliance Technology Centre's Financial Industry Regulatory Ontology: http://www.grctc.com/platform-research/firo; Chris Skinner, 'The Semantic Regulator (#RegTech Rules)', January 2017, https://thefinanser.com/2017/01/semantic-regulator-regtech-rules.html

[16] See e.g. 'Financial Regulators Embrace Artificial Intelligence' (*Institutional Investor*, 27 March 2017): https://www.institutionalinvestor.com/blogarticle/3667648/financial-regulators-embrace-artificial-intelligence/banking-and-capital-markets-trading-and-technology.html#.WR6ZklSGPIU

[17] 'IBM Buying Promontory Heralds AI Juggernaut for Bank Compliance', *Bloomberg*, 1 October 2016, https://www.ft.com/content/fd80ac50-7383-11e6-bf48-b372cdb1043a; 'IBM Is Set to Emerge as a Key RegTech Player', *Business Insider*, 16 June 2017, http://www.businessinsider.com/ibm-is-set-to-emerge-as-a-key-regtech-player-2017-6

[18] See the Super Bowl commercial: https://www.youtube.com/watch?v=UujLUcssIZU

duties that could reasonably result in losses to third parties (including customers and end users). Liability allocation is often sought to be contractually modified between the parties (vendor and corporate entity; corporate entity and end user), and addressed through insurance coverage.

Yet, regulators tend to focus on the accountability of regulated entities, and increasingly individuals,[19] and plaintiff litigators will seek novel causes of action. Product liability legislation also often exists to protect consumers, including potentially for defective software,[20] and the use of open-source software further complicates liability allocation.[21]

At the heart of legal policy is attributing responsibility for a decision (conscious or spur of the moment) made by a human actor or agent, where a judge and/or jury may determine culpability for civil monetary and/or criminal action for damage caused.

Civil liability of parents for minors[22] and of owners of domestic animals[23] provide some analogies to an AI agent acting independently from its human developers and trainers.[24] Yet, although there exists legislation against racial incitement for example,[25] teachers are generally not responsible for the acts of their students (a relevant analogy given the role of training in ML).

Key Issues for Forging a Responsibility and Liability Framework in the AI Era

Six key issues need to be addressed to forge a responsibility and liability framework in the AI era, and some are especially important to RegTech AI.

[19] See, e.g. 'Yates Memo', 9 September 2015, https://www.justice.gov/archives/dag/file/769036/download; 'Senior Managers and Certification Regime: One Year On' (see Financial Conduct Authority, 7 March 2017): www.fca.org.uk/news/news-stories/senior-managers-and-certification-regime-one-year; 'New SFC Measures to Heighten Senior Management Accountability', Securities and Futures Commission, 16 December 2016, https://www.sfc.hk/edistributionWeb/gateway/EN/news-and-announcements/news/doc?refNo=16PR143

[20] See, e.g. Levi and Bell, 'Software Product Liability: Understanding and Minimizing the Risks', Berkeley Technology Law Journal 5, no. 1 (January 1990); http://scholarship.law.berkeley.edu/cgi/viewcontent.cgi?article=1079&context=btlj

[21] See, e.g. Nimmer, 'Legal Issues in Open Source and Free Software Distribution' (adapted from The Law of Computer Technology, 1997, 2005 Supp.); http://www.ipinfoblog.com/archives/Open%20Source%20Legal%20Issues.pdf

[22] See, e.g. Matthiesen, Wickert, and Lehrer, 'Parental Responsibility Laws in All 50 States', 8 June 2016; https://www.mwl-law.com/wp-content/uploads/2013/03/parental-responsibility-in-all-50-states.pdf

[23] See, e.g. Law Reform Commission of Ireland, 'Report on Civil Liability for Animals', May 1982; http://www.lawreform.ie/_fileupload/Reports/rCivilLiabilityForAnimals.htm

[24] D.C. Vladeck, 'Machines Without Principals: Liability Rules and Artificial Intelligence', Washington Law Review 89, no. 1 (2014): 117–150; http://digital.law.washington.edu/dspace-law/bitstream/handle/1773.1/1322/89WLR0117.pdf?sequence=1

[25] Muntarbhorn 'Study on the Prohibition of Incitement to National, Racial or Religious Hatred: Lessons from the Asia Pacific Region', United Nations Human Rights Office of the High Commissioner, July 2011; http://www.ohchr.org/Documents/Issues/Expression/ICCPR/Bangkok/StudyBangkok_en.pdf

Data Reliability, Cleansing, and Consent

Data sets on which ML relies risk coming from bad data,[26] being tainted by malicious actors (internal or external), or even being subject to unconscious bias.[27]

How do we address 'garbage in, garbage out'?

Data wrangling,[28] or the capture, cleaning, and regularizing of data, is critical, including establishing appropriate data architecture and data lakes of centralized clean data for decision models. Appropriate consent for data use is also critical.[29]

Algorithm Model Bias and Law-breaking or Law-avoidance Activity

Algorithm models and not just data sets can be biased against communities and/or laws – intentionally or otherwise.[30] Volkswagen's 'defeat devices' were designed to fake nitrogen peroxide pollutant tests;[31] Uber's Greyball program detected law enforcement officials,[32] and its Hell program tracked its competitor Lyft's cars.[33]

---

[26] For example, defective IoT sensors, data feeds going down, or behavioural analysis based on accounts that are shared and/or purchases made for third-party gifts.

[27] See, e.g. Buolamwini, 'InCoding – In the Beginning', 17 May 2016; https://medium.com/mit-media-lab/incoding-in-the-beginning-4e2a5c51a45d . See also 'Twitter Taught Microsoft's AI Chatbot to Be a Racist Asshole in Less Than a Day', *The Verge*, 24 March 2016; https://www.theverge.com/2016/3/24/11297050/tay-microsoft-chatbot-racist; 'Big Data: A Tool for Inclusion or Exclusion?', Federal Trade Commission, January 2016; https://www.ftc.gov/system/files/documents/reports/big-data-tool-inclusion-or-exclusion-understanding-issues/160106big-data-rpt.pdf

[28] See, e.g. 'For Big-Data Scientists, "Janitor Work" Is Key Hurdle to Insights', *New York Times*, 17 August 2014; https://www.nytimes.com/2014/08/18/technology/for-big-data-scientists-hurdle-to-insights-is-janitor-work.html?_r=0

[29] See, e.g. 'NHS Gave Google's DeepMind "Legally Inappropriate" Access to Patient Records', *Financial Times*, 16 May 2017; https://www.ft.com/content/2cf5a8d7-932e-3d9d-809d-a92fd4db2112

[30] See, e.g. O'Neil, *Weapons of Math Destruction: How Big Data Increases Inequality and Threatens Democracy* (New York: Broadway Books, 2006); 'Algorithms Aren't Bad, But the People Who Write Them May Be', *Wall Street Journal*, 14 October 2016; https://www.wsj.com/articles/algorithms-arent-biased-but-the-people-who-write-them-may-be-1476466555; 'Hiring Algorithms Are Not Neutral', *Harvard Business Review*, 9 December 2016; https://hbr.org/2016/12/hiring-algorithms-are-not-neutral

[31] See, e.g. 'Volkswagen: The Scandal Explained', BBC News, 10 December 2015, http://www.bbc.com/news/business-34324772; 'How Volkswagen's "Defeat Devices" Worked', *New York Times*, 16 March 2017; https://www.nytimes.com/interactive/2015/business/international/vw-diesel-emissions-scandal-explained.html

[32] 'How Uber Deceives the Authorities Worldwide', *New York Times*, 3 March 2017; https://www.nytimes.com/2017/03/03/technology/uber-grey-ball-program-evade-authorities.html?_r=0

[33] 'Former Lyft Driver Sues Uber over "Hell" Tracking Program', *Fortune*, 25 April 2017; http://fortune.com/2017/04/24/lyft-uber-driver-lawsuit-tracking-program-hell

Yet, was there unconscious racial bias in the COMPAS algorithm for criminal sentencing risk assessments?[34] Do Facebook's algorithms have a confirmation bias because fake news has received more views than real news?[35]

Competition authorities are increasingly looking into the concentration of data with the emerging 'TechFin' companies.[36] They are also focused on the risk that autonomous repricing algorithms can collude to establish more effective cartels with no need for human intervention. In the words of EU Commissioner Vestager: 'I think we need to make it very clear that companies cannot escape responsibility for collusion by hiding behind a computer program.'[37]

Correlation-, Not Causation-, Based

For many years, enterprise systems have implemented expert systems, decision-tree work flows, and rule-based technology solutions to sift through documents for e-discovery during litigation, and for monitoring and reporting of regulatory compliance matters.

By comparison, AI based on ML and deep learning through layers of neural networks relies on large amounts of data, statistics, and pattern recognition, and has an evolutionary and even iterative dynamic:[38] it is based on correlation as opposed to causation, and on context more than content.

This raises two critical questions regarding responsibility and liability in the AI era.

[34] See 'Machine Bias', *ProPublica*, 23 May 2016; https://www.propublica.org/article/machine-bias-risk-assessments-in-criminal-sentencing; 'False Positives, False Negatives, and False Analyses: A Rejoinder to "Machine Bias: There's Software Used Across the Country to Predict Future Criminals. And It's Biased Against Blacks"', Community Resources for Justice, September 2016; http://www.crj.org/page/-/publications/rejoinder7.11.pdf; 'A Computer Program Used for Bail and Sentencing Decisions Was Labeled Biased Against Blacks. It's Actually Not That Clear', *Washington Post*, 17 October 2016; https://www.washingtonpost.com/news/monkey-cage/wp/2016/10/17/can-an-algorithm-be-racist-our-analysis-is-more-cautious-than-propublicas/?utm_term=.36b7b5bf3b9c; see also Pasquale, *The Black Box Society: The Secret Algorithms That Control Money and Information* (Cambridge, MA: Harvard University Press, 2015); 'The Code We Can't Control', *Slate*, 14 January 2015; http://www.slate.com/articles/technology/bitwise/2015/01/black_box_society_by_frank_pasquale_a_chilling_vision_of_how_big_data_has.html

[35] 'Facebook's Fake News Crackdown: It's Complicated', *Bloomberg*, 23 November 2016; https://www.bloomberg.com/news/articles/2016-11-23/facebook-s-quest-to-stop-fake-news-risks-becoming-slippery-slope; 'Of Course Facebook Is Biased. That's How Tech Works Today', *Wired*, 11 May 2016; https://www.wired.com/2016/05/course-facebook-biased-thats-tech-works-today

[36] 'The World's Most Valuable Resource Is No Longer Oil, but Data', *Economist*, 6 May 2017; http://www.economist.com/news/leaders/21721656-data-economy-demands-new-approach-antitrust-rules-worlds-most-valuable-resource. The phrase 'TechFin' is distinguished from 'FinTech' by Alibaba founder Jack Ma in seeking to 'rebuild the system with technology' rather than merely improving it: 'TechFin: Jack Ma Coins Term to Set Alipay's Goal to Give Emerging Markets Access to Capital', *SCMP*, 2 December 2016; http://www.scmp.com/tech/article/2051249/techfin-jack-ma-coins-term-set-alipays-goal-give-emerging-markets-access

[37] See 'EU Antitrust Enforcement 2.0 – European Commission Raises Concerns About Algorithms and Encourages Individual Whistleblowers', *Kluwer Competition Law Blog*, 21 March 2017; http://kluwercompetitionlawblog.com/2017/03/21/eu-antitrust-enforcement-2-0-european-commission-raises-concerns-about-algorithms-and-encourages-individual-whistleblowers. See also Ezrachi and Stucke, *Virtual Competition: The Promise and Perils of the Algorithm Economy* (Cambridge, MA: Harvard University Press, 2016), which warns of the 'frenemy' relationship between Frightful Five super platforms: 'Tech's "Frightful 5" Will Dominate Digital Life for Foreseeable Future', *New York Times*, 20 January 2016; https://www.nytimes.com/2016/01/21/technology/techs-frightful-5-will-dominate-digital-life-for-foreseeable-future.html

[38] Katz, 'Artificial Intelligence and Law – A Primer', 28 July 2016; https://www.slideshare.net/Danielkatz/artificial-intelligence-and-law-a-primer

First, what are the *accuracy and acceptable error rates* of such predictions? A fundamental analytical question is: if the same data without a machine were presented to a human, would a reasonable human make the same decision?

The law does not expect humans to be error-free: mainly that they did not have ill intent and/or they acted reasonably in the circumstances. Yet, even though machines can analyse more data and theoretically make better-informed decisions than humans, are we still viewing machines too mechanically and deterministically, and unreasonably holding machines up to an almost strict liability standard of care?

What would and should be the acceptable error rate for false predictions, especially in the context of RegTech AI?[39]

Second, if constant data capture through, e.g. internet of things (IoT) sensory, mobile communication, and transactional surveillance means that no one is effectively invisible and all behavioural data can lead to individual profiles for predictive analytics for future regulatory compliance, are we relying too much on *predispositions* rather than actions for determining culpability and liability (à la *Minority Report*)?[40]

This is important where ML is used for elective societal and financial access and pricing benefits such as credit ratings, search engines, bank loans, university applications, and health insurance, and is even more crucial when applied to RegTech (such as facial recognition for surveillance), which could lead to civil liability and loss of one's liberty.[41]

Diminishing Role of Human Agency in ML

Discerning the different levels of human agency in ML is essential.

Supervised learning is typically driven by carefully labelled data supervised by human labellers, which the machine repeats with more data (such as learning to identify cats on YouTube videos[42] or speech recognition).[43] Human agency remains in the data collection and training by the classifier with domain expertise.

Unsupervised learning draws inferences from data sets consisting of input data without human-labelled responses, through techniques such as cluster analysis and generative models.

---

[39] Could Six Sigma type approaches used for improving process output quality in manufacturing and business processes by identifying and removing defect causes and minimizing variability emerge for AI?

[40] Philip K. Dick, 'The Minority Report' (1956), a science fiction short story that became a 2002 movie of the same name directed by Steven Spielberg and starring Tom Cruise about a Precrime Division that arrests suspects prior to their infliction of public harm.

[41] See e.g, "MIT researchers: Amazon's Rekognition shows gender and ethnic bias (updated)" VentureBeat (January 2019): https://venture-beat.com/2019/01/24/amazon-rekognition-bias-mit/; "Florida is Using Facial Recognition to Convict People Without Giving Them a Chance to Challenge The Tech", ACLU (March 2019): https://www.aclu.org/blog/privacy-technology/surveillance-technologies/florida-using-facial-recogni-tion-convict-people

[42] 'Google's Artificial Brain Learns to Find Cats', *Wired*, 26 June 2012, https://www.wired.com/2012/06/google-x-neural-network; Le, Ranzato, Monga, Devin, Chen, Corrado, Dean, and Ng, 'Building High-level Features Using Large Scale Unsupervised Learning' (2012); http://ai.stanford.edu/~ang/papers/icml12-HighLevelFeaturesUsingUnsupervisedLearning.pdf

[43] Xiong, Droppo, Huang, Seide, Seltzer, Stolcke, Yu, and Zweig, 'The Microsoft 2016 Conversational Speech Recognition System', Microsoft Research, 2016; https://www.microsoft.com/en-us/research/wp-content/uploads/2017/01/ms_swbd16.pdf

New methods like *reinforcement learning*[44] involve AI agents that take actions in an environment so as to maximize some notion of cumulative reward,[45] such as DeepStack and Liberatus AI separately learning to beat human professional card players at Texas hold 'em poker[46] (an imperfect information game), and OpenAI being used to learn to play Atari 2600 Pong from raw game pixels.[47] Other methodologies such as *generative* *adversarial networks (GANs)*[48], *transfer learning*[49] and Google's *federated learning*[50] are emerging too.

'Augmented intelligence' seems the preferred industry phrase,[51] but the increasingly reduced role of human agency in AI decision-making, and current ongoing research directions.[52] complicated by the real possibility of human mischief,[53] add to the complexity of whom to hold culpable for damage caused by RegTech AI.

Philosopher's Trolley Problem Applied to ML

The moral philosopher's classic problem has become a touchstone AI question when literally applied to autonomous driving – is a trolley hitting a child instead of a couple a justifiable choice, or vice versa?

[44] See, e.g. 'OpenAI Gym Beta', 27 April 2016; https://blog.openai.com/openai-gym-beta; 'Deep Reinforcement Learning: Pong from Pixels', *Andrey Karpathy Blog*, 31 May 2016; http://karpathy.github.io/2016/05/31/rl; Jaderberg, Mnih, Czarnecki, Schaul, Leibo, Silver, and Kavukcuoglu, 'Reinforcement Learning with Unsupervised Auxiliary Tasks', 16 November 2016; https://deepmind.com/blog/reinforcement-learning-unsupervised-auxiliary-tasks; Minh, Kavulcuoglu, Silver, Graves, Antonoglou, Wierstra, and Riedmiller, 'Playing Atari with Deep Reinforcement Learning', 19 December 2013; https://arxiv.org/pdf/1312.5602.pdf

[45] These could involve, e.g. policy gradient methods that attempt to learn functions that directly map an observation to an action, and Q-learning, which attempts to learn the value of being in a given state and taking a specific action there.

[46] 'Artificial Intelligence Goes Deep to Beat Humans at Poker', *Science*, 3 March 2017; http://www.sciencemag.org/news/2017/03/artificial-intelligence-goes-deep-beat-humans-poker; Moravcik, Schmid, Burch, Lisy, Morrill, Bard, Davis, Waugh, Johanson, and Bowling, 'DeepStack: Expert-level Artificial Intelligence in Heads-up No-limit Poker', *Science*, 2 March 2017; http://science.sciencemag.org/content/early/2017/03/01/science.aam6960; 'Inside Libratus, the Poker AI That Out-bluffed the Best Humans', *Wired*, 1 February 2017, https://www.wired.com/2017/02/libratus; Brown and Sandholm, 'Safe and Nested Endgames Solving for Imperfect-information Games', Carnegie Mellon, 15 December 2016; http://www.cs.cmu.edu/~noamb/papers/17-AAAI-Refinement.pdf. This is unlike AlphaGo, which analysed 30 million Go moves from human players before refining skills by playing with itself.

[47] 'Human-level Control Through Deep Reinforcement Learning', *Nature*, 25 February 2015; http://www.nature.com/nature/journal/v518/n7540/abs/nature14236.html

[48] See, e.g. 'Google's Dueling Neural Networks Spar to Get Smarter, No Humans Required', *Wired*, 11 April 2017; https://www.wired.com/2017/04/googles-dueling-neural-networks-spar-get-smarter-no-humans-required

[49] See, e.g. '"Transfer Learning" Jumpstarts New AI Projects', *InfoWorld*, 9 January 2017; http://www.infoworld.com/article/3155262/analytics/transfer-learning-jump-starts-new-ai-projects.html

[50] See e.g., "Federated Learning: Collaborative Machine Learning without Centralized Training Data" (April 2017); https://ai.googleblog.com/2017/04/federated-learning-collaborative.html

[51] See, e.g. 'IBM: AI Should Stand for "Augmented Intelligence"', *Information Week*, 4 August 2016; http://www.informationweek.com/government/leadership/ibm-ai-should-stand-for-augmented-intelligence/d/d-id/1326496; see also Ito, 'Extended Intelligence', 10 April 2017, https://www.pubpub.org/pub/extended-intelligence

[52] Furthermore, research and ideas grow in complexity, including backpropogation (backprop), convolutional neural networks (ConvNets), and long short-term memory (LSTM) recurrent neural networks. See, e.g. Domingos, *The Master Algorithm: How the Quest for the Ultimate Learning Machine Will Remake Our World* (New York: Basic Books, 2015).

[53] See e.g. "Hackers are the Real Obstacle for Self Driving Vehicles" MIT Technology Review (August 2017): https://www.technologyreview.com/s/608618/hackers-are-the-real-obstacle-for-self-driving-vehicles/; "Voice Fraud Climbs 350%" Security Magazine, September 2018: https://www.securitymagazine.com/articles/89432-voice-fraud-climbs-350

When Mercedes's initial response was to protect its passengers first, it understandably faced tremendous criticism.[54] Should algorithm writers programme frameworks of comparable values or pricing as 'ethical guidelines', especially given cultural ethical variations as shown from 40 million decisions by users from 244 countries and territories who used MIT's Moral Machine?[55] Or should a randomizer ensure processes and responses are unscripted? Alternatively, should the law's need for a responsible human agent ultimately limit the full application of AI?

Assessing Model Risk in ML Black Boxes

When Google Search transitioned from rule-based to neural net-based algorithms, some former Google employees were concerned that 'it was more difficult to understand why neural nets behaved the way it did, and more difficult to tweak their behaviour'.[56]

Without explainable AI,[57] how would a regulator or court know what an AI has learned in the past that led to it making its decision that led to loss suffered, to help determine culpability?[58]

The Road Ahead: Addressing Opacity and Complexity for AI Responsibility

To address concerns such as those just described, amongst many solutions being proposed,[59] the European Union has already

---

[54] 'Mercedes-Benz's Self-Driving Cars Would Choose Passenger Lives Over Bystanders', *Fortune*, 15 October 2016; http://fortune.com/2016/10/15/mercedes-self-driving-car-ethics

[55] See Awad, Dsouza, Kim, Schultz, Henrich, Shariff, Bonnefon and Rahwan, The Moral Machine Experiment, *Nature* (24 October 2018): https://www.nature.com/articles/s41586-018-0637-6.pdf

[56] See 'AI Is Transforming Google Search. The Rest of the Web Is Next', *Wired*, 4 February 2016, https://www.wired.com/2016/02/ai-is-changing-the-technology-behind-google-searches; 'Google Translate AI Invents Its Own Language to Translate With', *New Scientist*, 30 November 2016; https://www.newscientist.com/article/2114748-google-translate-ai-invents-its-own-language-to-translate-with

[57] Explainable Artificial Intelligence (XAI) is actually the name of a US Defense Advanced Research Projects Agency (DARPA) program focused on this important issue: see 'Explainable AI: Cracking Open the Black Box of AI', *ComputerWorld*, 10 April 2017; www.computerworld.com.au/article/617359/explainable-artificial-intelligence-cracking-open-black-box-ai

[58] Ribeiro, Singh, and Guestrin, '"Why Should I Trust You?" Explaining the Predictions of Any Classifier' (2016); http://www.kdd.org/kdd2016/papers/files/rfp0573-ribeiroA.pdf. See also description of 'The Dark Secret at the Heart of AI', *MIT Technology Review*, 11 April 2017; https://www.technologyreview.com/s/604087/the-dark-secret-at-the-heart-of-ai

[59] Some ideas include: a US federal agency that certifies AI (see Scherer, 'Regulating Artificial Intelligence Systems: Risks, Challenges, Competencies, and Strategies', *Harvard Journal of Law & Technology* 29, no. 2 (Spring 2016); https://ssrn.com/abstract=2609777); and California introducing the world's first law on autonomous vehicles in 'California's Finally Ready for Truly Driverless Cars', *Wired*, 11 March 2017; https://www.wired.com/2017/03/californias-finally-ready-truly-driverless-cars. More radical suggestions include recognizing AI agents as legal persons (see Samir Chopra and Laurence F. White, *A Legal Theory for Autonomous Artificial Agents* (Ann Arbor: University of Michigan Press, 2011); Asaro, 'The Liability Problem for Autonomous Artificial Agents'; http://www.peterasaro.org/writing/Asaro,%20Ethics%20Auto%20Agents,%20AAAI.pdf; AI oversight systems as AI Guardians in 'Designing AI Systems That Obey Our Laws and Values', *Communications of the ACM*, September 2016; https://cacm.acm.org/magazines/2016/9/206255-designing-ai-systems-that-obey-our-laws-and-values/fulltext

passed the General Data Protection Regulation (GDPR)[60] that came into effect in May 2018.

Under Article 22, all natural persons have a 'right to an explanation' regarding automated evaluation and decision making,[61] including the right to 'meaningful information about the logic involved' and the right to safeguards, including 'the right to obtain human intervention...to express his or her point of view and to contest the decision'.

Data privacy laws worldwide are going in only one direction – tighter and requiring data to be held onshore – and blockchain distributed ledger technology (DLT)[62] and Merkle trees[63] have been suggested as depositaries of knowledge that change over time to help provide a searchable audit-like trail of AI data, training, and models.

Yet, this disclosure paradigm raises the issue of the technical literacy gap and a 'mismatch between the mathematical optimization in high-dimensionality characteristic of machine learning and the demands of human-scale reasoning and styles of interpretation'.[64] This, in turn, points potentially to the ultimate need to develop RegTech algorithms to examine RegTech and other ML algorithms, and direct real-time regulatory reporting.[65] The increased open sourcing of AI tools complicates the liability analysis.

Historical AI applications and successes arose primarily in rule-based games with zero-sum outcomes, such as chess, *Jeopardy!*, Go,[66] and poker, with machines that can 'experience' more than any human can in a single lifetime with a time horizon that can outlast the lives of its creators and those of its progeny.

As Viktor Mayer-Schonberger and Kenneth Cukier remind us, for every *Moneyball*[67] example about the effectiveness of data analysis, there exists the risk of catastrophic decisions made under a 'dictatorship of data' as seen in US Secretary of Defense Robert McNamara's focus on body counts during the Vietnam War.[68] Especially given that RegTech AI can apply to regulation of nearly all aspects of our human lives on this planet, including markets, elections, and even our food chain, and its network effects can

---

[60] 'EU Data Protection Law May End the Unknowable Algorithm', *Information Week*, 18 July 2016; http://www.informationweek.com/government/big-data-analytics/eu-data-protection-law-may-end-the-unknowable-algorithm/d/d-id/1326294

[61] Goodman and Flaxman, 'European Union Regulations on Algorithmic Decision-making and a "Right to Explanation"', 12 July 2016; https://arxiv.org/pdf/1606.08813v2.pdf

[62] 'Blockchains for Artificial Intelligence', *BigChainDB*, 3 January 2017; https://blog.bigchaindb.com/blockchains-for-artificial-intelligence-ec63b0284984. Blockchain can provide provenance in a cryptographically verifiable manner of input data to identify and catch supply chain leaks; training input/output (X/y) data; testing input (X) data and output (yhat) data; model building and model simulation; and models themselves.

[63] Google's DeepMind is experimenting with Verifiable Data Audit as Merkle trees rather than blockchains for UK health data: 'Google's AI Subsidiary Turns to Blockchain Technology to Track UK Health Data', *The Verge*, 10 March 2017; https://www.theverge.com/2017/3/10/14880094/deepmind-health-uk-data-blockchain-audit

---

[64] Burrell, 'How the Machine "Thinks": Understanding Opacity in Machine Learning Algorithms' (*Big Data and Society*, 6 January 2016); http://journals.sagepub.com/doi/abs/10.1177/2053951715622512

[65] See, e.g. Austria initiative in 'Reforming Regulatory Reporting: Are We Headed Toward Real-time?' (Bearing Point Institute, November 2015); http://www.bessgmbh.com/ecomaXL/files/BearingPoint-Institute_006-19-Regulatory-reporting-1-1.pdf

[66] See, e.g. 'The Rise of Artificial Intelligence and the End of Code', *Wired*, 19 May 2016; https://www.wired.com/2016/05/google-alpha-go-ai

[67] Michael Lewis, *Moneyball: The Art of Winning an Unfair Game* (New York: W.W. Norton, 2004).

[68] Viktor Mayer-Schonberger and Kenneth Cukier, *Big Data: A Revolution That Will Transform How We Live, Work and Think* (London: John Murray, 2013), 163. See also Emanuel Derman, *Models Behaving Badly: Why Confusing Illusion with Reality Can Lead to Disaster, on Wall Street and in Life* (New York: Free Press, 2011).

lead to algorithm collusion[69] equivalent to being 'too big to fail', it is critical that we get this right.

It is hoped that human ingenuity, foresight, and humility will lead to the emergence of a new framework[70] and ethos of ML developer and trainer professionalism[71] together with objective ML verification and balanced oversight. Increased and inclusive international, interdisciplinary, intergenerational and private-public discourse on global algorithmic development and deployment best practices will serve us all.[72]

[69] See, e.g. Organisation for Economic Co-operation and Development, 'Algorithms and Collusion – Background Note by the Secretariat', 16 May 2017; https://one.oecd.org/document/DAF/COMP(2017)4/en/pdf

[70] For example, Donella Meadows provides a framework for thinking about places to intervene in complex and dynamic systems – see Meadows, 'Leverage Points: Places to Intervene in a System', Sustainability Institute, December 1999; http://donellameadows.org/archives/leverage-points-places-to-intervene-in-a-system

[71] Mayer-Schonberger and Cukier call such professionals "algorithmists"; Cathy O'Neil suggested a Modeler's Hippocratic Oath; after the 2008 global financial crisis, Emanuel Derman and Paul Wilmott developed 'The Financial Modeler's Manifesto' (*Risk Management*, September 2009) (file:///C:/Users/user/Downloads/jrm-2009-iss17-derman.pdf), which could be a good starting point:

- I will remember that I didn't make the world, and it doesn't satisfy my equations.

- Though I will use models boldly to estimate value, I will not be overly impressed by mathematics.

- I will never sacrifice reality for elegance without explaining why I have done so.

- Nor will I give the people who use my model false comfort about its accuracy. Instead, I will make explicit its assumptions and oversights.

- I understand that my work may have enormous effects on society and the economy, many of them beyond my comprehension.

This is analogous to the promotion of capital markets professionalism for human financial services actors: see Tang, 'Promoting Capital Markets Professionalism: An Emerging Asian Model' in Buckley, Avgouleas, and Arner, *Reconceptualising Global Finance and Its Regulation* (Cambridge: Cambridge University Press, 2016).

[72] While private initiatives such as Partnership for AI initially arose, increasingly, the broader push has recently come from data commissioners worldwide, including the Declaration on Ethics and Data Protection in Artificial Intelligence by Data Protection and Privacy Commissioners from the EU and 17 different countries (October 2018), that reflect the approach of the IEEE Global Initiative for Ethical Considerations in Artificial Intelligence and Autonomous Systems, to which the author is a member of the Policy Committee.

Compliance with Data Protection Regulations by Applying the Blockchain Technology

By Bartłomiej Klinger

Former Co-Founder and CEO, Positiverse

Nowadays it becomes obvious that blockchain, and distributed ledger technology more generally, is going to become mainstream for many business domains. Since the blockchain was recognized as something more than only a base technology for the bitcoin network, it has infused business with fresh ideas and opened up a lot of new opportunities. Visionary authors like William Mougayar,[1] Chris Skinner,[2] and Alex and Don Tapscott[3] have inspired many to devise the best way this technology can be implemented.

One of the most promising approaches seems to be the application of blockchain to regulatory technology (RegTech). More and more demanding regulations and consequences of not being compliant generate serious operational risks for companies around the globe. At the same time, customers are more and more aware of their rights, and the regulations require a high level of compliance from service providers. Because of these considerations, some fresh ideas for how to ease the fulfilment of regulatory requirements using the blockchain technology could truly revolutionize the market and help to build a sustainable competitive advantage.

Even though compliance is vital for many regulated business activities, it is not usually homogeneous for different business domains. However, there is one area of regulations that covers almost all customer-facing activities: personal data protection. It is a hot topic nowadays, especially due to many significant personal data leaks and unauthorized usages being reported recently.[4] Corporations and governments around the globe are joining forces to address this challenge and all related issues. It has been and still is widely discussed, especially in the European Union as a result of a new EU law that came into force in May 2018. The new law is the General Data Protection Regulation (GDPR), and it is the same for all EU member states. The regulation seems to be the first serious attempt to implement a very strict, user-centric approach to personal data protection that is homogeneous across many European countries. Even if the GDPR is not the first regulation to introduce strong privacy protection rules (for instance Canada's Digital Privacy Act came into law earlier), the broad impact of the European regulation can also affect non-EU countries interested in doing business within the EU.

There are a lot of complaints from many parties that obligations established by the GDPR are extremely demanding and will negatively impact or even bring down many businesses. Can we do something about that? Can we find the solution to ease compliance with the GDPR, minimize this potentially negative impact, and use this new regulation as a growth factor? My answer is: yes, we can – and the means to achieve that is the blockchain technology!

---

[1] William Mougayar and Vitalik Buterin, *The Business Blockchain: Promise, Practice, and Application of the Next Internet Technology* (Hoboken, NJ: Wiley, 2016).

[2] Chris Skinner, *ValueWeb: How Fintech Firms Are Using Bitcoin Blockchain and Mobile Technologies to Create the Internet of Value* (Marshall Cavendish International (Asia) Pte Ltd, 2016).

[3] Don Tapscott and Alex Tapscott, *Blockchain Revolution: How the Technology Behind Bitcoin Is Changing Money, Business, and the World* (New York: Portfolio, 2016).

---

[4] https://en.wikipedia.org/wiki/List_of_data_breaches

Distributed and Transparent Source of Truth

Distributed processing and transparency are very important characteristics of the blockchain network. The distributed nature of the blockchain eliminates a single point of failure, so data remains unchanged even if a part of the network is damaged. What is more, the damaged entities (nodes of the network) can be easily recovered and can reload precise and actual data sets from other nodes. There is no need for either sophisticated and usually very costly database replication or real-time backup mechanisms – all is built into the blockchain. Transparency ensures that all network participants or entities have access to the same data and no one could present or treat any unsynchronized data as valid.

Thus, both companies that have to be compliant and regulators using the blockchain technology can maintain their own nodes of the same blockchain network without appointing anyone from this network as the most trusted data source. There is no risk that someone could undergo either significant data destruction or a loss after infrastructure damage or a cyber attack.

How could this help with GDPR compliance and what are the measurable benefits? Here are a few examples:

- Blockchain as a common platform for exchanging information amongst data controllers, data processors, and regulators could significantly reduce the costs of this data exchange.

- All required evidence of personal data processing and GDPR documentary obligations tracked via the blockchain could be conveniently reported, and these reports are easily verifiable by auditors.

- Thanks to using blockchain it is possible to avoid an implementation of the complicated database replication infrastructure and related significant, long-term costs of maintenance.

It is easy to understand that the distributed and transparent nature of the blockchain not only is an answer to specific GDPR challenges, but also helps with compliance with other regulations.

Immutable and Tamper-proof Ledger

Key features of the blockchain that determine the strength of this technology are immutability and being tamper-proof. Such a distributed ledger is resistant to any change of historical data. Once stored, the data remain unchanged to the end of the given blockchain network's life (or forever in case of any copy of this blockchain node). Any attempt to change the historical data can be easily recognized, so that no one can tamper with the ledger.

These features play a key role in compliance solutions. Every participant in the blockchain network can be sure that others cannot change the historical data and what is stored in the blockchain is trustworthy. Regarding the GDPR, all facts related to personal data processing – e.g. data processing purposes or consents given by the data subject – become immutable as soon as they are registered in the blockchain. Everyone can check if and when the fact was registered. Let's imagine a scenario in which a data processor, e.g. a well-established, global corporation, cooperates with a marketing agency or other partner that collects personal data on behalf of this company. If the corporation would not be exposed to the risk of significant GDPR fines, it should not trust only the verbal or written statements of the partner, which is usually smaller and most often has limited financial liability. This corporation can use an independent source of trusted information – the blockchain – to easily check if the subcontractor operates in a full compliance with the GDPR and does not provide any unlawful personal data. Also, an auditor who would like to check the lawfulness of data processing is able to check the ledger and will get reliable confirmation immediately. Finally, the immutability shows all its potential in case of any disagreement between the data subject (end user) and the data controller (e.g. online service provider). In the case of any claims, thanks to using an immutable ledger, it will be straightforward to prove whether or not the consent for the personal data processing has truly been given.

Some of the benefits seem to be obvious:

- None of the cooperating parties is able to tamper with the historical data in the blockchain, so there is no 'super admin' who would be able to change the data quietly in order to present his or her own version of 'truth'.

- Data processors could reduce their operational risk by validating independently whether data controllers provided the data to the processing with compliance to the GDPR rules.

- A compliance ecosystem based on the blockchain is capable of providing strong evidence of what was registered and when, and it could simplify the procedures of auditing and any regulatory checks.

- Data subjects could control all their given consents from one place.

- Data subjects could also be equipped with a very convenient and reliable tool to execute their rights to personal data protection.

The immutable and tamper-proof ledger suits the GDPR challenges well, especially because all parties to the GDPR process can cooperate without needing to trust one another. The trusted party will be the blockchain network – a neutral technology controlled by no one.

Secure Space to Process Transactions

Another important and built-in mechanism of the blockchain is the security based on strong cryptography. Current blockchain networks, both public and private, are based on the most advanced cryptographic algorithms. These algorithms ensure that, as long as private keys are kept in secret, the data is protected against cyber attacks. Using security mechanisms also ensures that in the predictable future messages stored in the blockchain will become almost impossible to decrypt without knowing private keys. The keys themselves will not be able to be hacked. The foundation of the data processing in the blockchain is strong asymmetric cryptography, which allows secure processing of peer-to-peer transactions and prevents double spending of any assets under processing.

The transactional nature of the distributed ledger based on the blockchain technology accompanied with strong security features could be useful in the context of GDPR compliance. If we look at several activities related to the GDPR such as managing consent's life cycle or exchanging information between the data controller and the data processor (without a doubt these are transactions, and even more: they are peer-to-peer transactions), it drives us to an obvious conclusion: blockchain could be an ideal technology to handle a majority of transactions related to the GDPR compliance process. If we assign the individual key pairs – an account in the blockchain – to data subjects, data controllers, data processors, and auditors, we immediately achieve a common, shared platform ready to securely exchange transactions between those parties.

So we could achieve the following, thanks to the transactional nature of the blockchain in the GDPR context:

- A transactional platform for secure and reliable exchanging of information between actors of the GDPR processes.

- The confidence of information stored in the blockchain and nonrepudiation by adding an extra layer of digital identification of participants.

- Regulators as counterparties to a specific reporting transaction, which could greatly simplify the whole required documentary work flow.

What is more, the blockchain seems to be a cure for issues raised by extensive and ongoing interactions between actors of the GDPR compliance processes. For sure, one such issue is the high cost of doing the same things many times (e.g. implementing the same GDPR reporting mechanism by different companies across the entire European Union), and it could be easily avoided.

Recently we have more often heard about attempts to regulate the bitcoin network and sometimes even about attempts to regulate blockchain, although it is hard to imagine what that could mean. A better approach is the opposite: a wide usage of the blockchain to simplify regulatory procedures and to ease compliance with more and more demanding regulations.

Customer-centric personal data protection regulations like the EU GDPR are not amongst the easiest regulatory burdens imposed on companies. The GDPR causes anxiety primarily due to extremely high fines of up to €20 million or 4% of the annual global turnover – whichever proves to be more. However, there are also other worrying aspects of the GDPR such as freely given, specific, informed, and unambiguous consents that can be withdrawn at any time, the right to be forgotten, or ensuring the possibility of transferring one's own data to another service provider. Companies under this regulatory pressure have to equip themselves with reliable technology that not only fulfils functional needs but also ensures that additional operational costs of maintaining GDPR compliance will not increase radically. The blockchain technology with its core features of transparency, immutability, and secure distributed transaction processing without a doubt can make GDPR implementation much easier.

Blockchains Are Diamonds' Best Friend: The Case for Supply Chain Transparency

By Julia Walker
Head of Market Development, Risk and Regulatory Technology, Asia Pacific, Refinitiv

and Leanne Kemp
Founder and CEO, Everledger

Globally it is generally accepted that supply chains are becoming too complex and lack transparency, raising risks and compliance concerns. Blockchain and regulatory technology (RegTech) have the ability to reconceptualize regulation and bake it into the fabric of the supply chain. The potential is immense, crossing boundaries and assisting in global concerns such as human rights and financial inclusion, as well as combating corruption, modern-day slavery, and financial crime.

Globally there has been a raft of regulations that have come into force due to society's drive to protect our most vulnerable members of society. Brand impacts and regulations, such as the US Foreign Corrupt Practices Act (FCPA), conflict minerals rule (US Dodd-Frank Act, section 1502), UK Bribery Act (UKBA), UK Modern-Day Slavery Act, French Corporate Duty of Vigilance Law, Australia's new compliance reporting legislation, and a host of other global regulatory initiatives, have significantly increased the importance of establishing transparent supply chains.

Hewlett Packard, Nestlé, and Coca-Cola have enforced new standards for their suppliers to address human rights issues like modern-day slavery. Indeed, Hewlett Packard also requires standards to be applied further down the supply chain, where, disconnected from scrutiny and accountability, slavery is more likely to occur.

By forcing disclosure, regulators empower third parties to confront global corporations about the business practices in their supply chains. In the past, technology has not been able to keep up with fragmented supply chains. Blockchain, however, has the potential to transform the supply chain and disrupt the way we unearth, transform, market, and purchase goods. Adding transparency, traceability, and security to the supply chain can go a long way towards making economies safer and much more reliable by promoting trust and honesty and preventing the implementation of questionable practices.

When investing in certain high-end items, particularly rare and desirable objects, there is often a risk as to authenticity and provenance. An example of this is in the diamond industry. Buyers want to be able to screen for stone mines in regions where forced labour is common or where proceeds from previous sales were used to fund violence.

A report from Amnesty International from 2014 found at one diamond mine in the Central African Republic (CAR) several children working in hazardous conditions, including an 11-year-old boy. In December 2012, a rebel alliance known as the Séléka – predominantly from the CAR's Muslim minority – began a military offensive, overthrowing the then government in March 2013. More than 5,000 people have died so far.

The Séléka and anti-balaka profit greatly from CAR's internal diamond trade. In some cases, they take over mine sites. More commonly, they demand 'taxes' or 'protection' money from miners and traders. Artisanal miners often work in dangerous conditions, and the state provides little in the way of protection. Miners are exposed to serious health and safety risks at unregulated mine sites. They are frequently trapped in exploitative relationships with the middlemen who trade diamonds and therefore carry out backbreaking work for very little money. Human rights violations have been identified in Zimbabwe, some South American nations, and throughout Asia.

Due to a previous lack of provenance technology, bad actors can continue to thrive by exploiting the most vulnerable members of society.

In situations where provenance is broken or not validated, risk emerges. Risk fuels opportunities for theft, counterfeiting, terrorist financing, and money laundering, four main drivers for black markets globally. Such risk also allows for the movement and trafficking of counterfeit goods and commodities such as blood diamonds that contribute to funding conflict.

The risks, particularly focused around trusting sellers and the information they are providing, make blockchain a valuable tool for authenticating and validating transactions. It also helps governments to ensure that there are no unreported value-added taxes (VATs) or goods and services taxes (GSTs) for goods moving across various borders.

Blockchain also has the potential to validate those industries in certain countries that may otherwise be shunned due to uncertainty around the production supply chain's authenticity. Ultimately, this could increase countries' gross domestic products (GDPs) and ability to be global contenders where they would otherwise be overlooked.

Provenance of a moveable item has become more important since the inception of the internet. If we look at artefacts or moveable items (chattels) of value, there has always been a need to ensure that a party has good title to the asset prior to any business dealing involving that asset. Today the buyer has little information on where the goods came from and their authenticity.

What Is Provenance?

One area where promising work in the blockchain space is being developed is in provenance tracking. Understanding the origin and identity of the commodities we create, sell, and trade in open marketplaces globally has never been more important to both the producers and the end consumers. Additionally, there are strong incentives for various stakeholders across global supply chains, from insurance companies to banks, to have clear visibility on an asset's authenticity and movement.

For example, authenticity and transparency are everything in the world of luxury items. Provenance is the chronology of the ownership, custody, or location of an object. In the case of fine wine, the provenance would include where the grapes were grown and picked, where the wine was bottled and stored, and then where it was sold and on what platform. The history of the wine creates its identity and verifies its authenticity by providing the producers, distributors, and consumers with authenticated and proven information on the provenance of the wine, thereby assuring current and future owners of its authenticity and history.

The blockchain allows for digital certification, verification, and smart contract enablement, in order to:

- Protect against the occurrence of fraud, theft, trafficking, and black markets.
- Address significant problems with double financing in the supply chain.
- Reestablish trust and widen financing channels in industries that are suffering from such deficits.
- Bring transparency and authenticity to the provenance of high-value assets, increasing saleability and liquidity, and reducing risk.
- In the diamond industry, identify and reduce conflict stones, and improve identifiability of synthetic stones throughout the supply chain.

What Technology Solutions Are Available?

The blockchain is a data structure that can be used to create digital ledgers of transactions shared among a distributed network of participating organizations.

When data is to be added to the ledger, the participating organizations that hold copies of the blockchain must agree that the transaction is valid before the new transaction is approved and the block of data associated with the transaction is added to the ledger.

While blockchain is still new and experimental, there is worldwide interest in the technology and how it might be used to facilitate transactions between participating organizations without a central authority.

Major tech companies see the benefits of this technology and are in the process of investing in the development of infrastructure that will allow businesses and governments to implement custom solutions that do not rely on open, public blockchains. To meet the demands of modern markets, IBM and other companies are collaborating to develop an open-source, industry-focused implementation of blockchain technology for business use, called Hyperledger Fabric, hosted by the Linux Foundation's Hyperledger project. Hyperledger Fabric is a platform for distributed ledger solutions on permissioned networks. Its modular architecture delivers high degrees of scalability, privacy, and confidentiality.

Blockchain has the capability of creating and validating provenance by holding an immutable digital record of an item and following the life cycle of this item through a chain of custody. Once items are registered, the records are permanent and cannot be changed, thus providing a clear audit trail to be used by multiple parties throughout the supply chain to verify authenticity. Empowering these records with smart contracts, new financial offerings and exchange models are able to form on the basis of these records.

This application of the blockchain replaces industry-wide paper-based processes that are fragmented, susceptible to tampering, and often unavailable as an item changes ownership or location throughout its lifetime journey. Blockchain can act as the infrastructure for registering and authenticating asset ownership between untrusting parties with common interests. It also has the ability to prove sourcing in a sustainable manner, as well as prove that no slavery or exploitation was involved.

One key application that removes paper-based processes is the implementation of provenance tracking. To give an example, let us look at diamonds. Diamonds rely on records of origin, identity, and custody to prove authenticity and provenance. In recent years, the industry has been impacted by the proliferation of blood diamonds, synthetic stones peppering the pipeline, and an increase in the number of fraudulent certificates accompanying diamonds. Most recently, fraudulently certified diamonds were discovered in a shipment from Sierra Leone to Hong Kong, and in 2017 a trader on Alibaba attempted to sell 10,000 carats' worth of synthetic diamonds, accompanied by certification declaring the stones authentic.

Most of the current systems in place are paper-based, which results in issues with banking regarding financing of the pipeline, where invoices have been double and triple financed. This has resulted in a dramatic reduction in the number of financial institutions willing to provide funding to the diamond industry.

Beyond document tampering, issues with fraudulent claims and double financing continue to plague the industry, most recently resulting in the retreat of major banks from financing the diamond supply chain. Following a review, banks view the diamond industry to be very high risk, with little reward – for example, Standard Chartered Bank, which was caught up in the Winsome Diamond default; Antwerp Diamond Bank, which was completely closed down; Bank Leumi; and Barclays.

Blockchain's decentralized and secure environment for joint record-keeping provides the ideal foundation for building a global, digital ledger for high-value assets by creating a permanent record that can be used by the industry as a clear audit trail for the asset that proves authenticity, and in turn leads to a reduction of fraud, theft, and trafficking.

Knowing Your Object (KYO)

In the fight against money laundering, traditional approaches have focused on clients and how well a bank knows them – i.e. knowing your customer (KYC). Provenance tracking creates the ability to know your object (KYO) – for example, what raw materials it is made of, where it came from, how it was manufactured or formed and by whom, and where it has it been. In the world of financial crime, being able to marry objects and people will be a powerful way to fight financial crime.

KYO leads to reshaping a new era of global trade based on the pillars of transparency, sustainability, and ethical sourcing. Increased visibility along the supply chain will help to reduce friction and inefficiencies for stakeholders taking on the highest risk when it comes to financing and insuring objects.

To create an object's unique digital identity, new data points and technologies are utilized to capture unique identifiers and other specifications of the object; these might include scanning, microlens, chemical analysis, and so on. This digital incarnation or thumbprint of an object adds a reputational layer of trust across an industry that allows insurance companies, banks, and open marketplaces to detect whether transactions, certificates or objects are fraudulent. The process provides the first barrier of defense when it comes to trading and ensures transparency at every stage of a diamond's object life journey from raw materials to the marketplace.

Blockchain technology can then capture a complete life cycle of a diamond by extending the technology to tackle the trade of rough diamonds as well, certified through the UN-mandated Kimberley Process Certification Scheme (KPCS), and thus enabling transparency at every stage of a diamond's journey from mine to jewellery, ensuring it is ethical and conflict-free.

The Kimberley Process imposes extensive requirements on its members to enable them to certify shipments of rough diamonds as 'conflict-free' and prevent conflict diamonds from entering the legitimate trade. Under the terms of the KPCS, participating states must meet 'minimum requirements' and must put in place national legislation and institutions, as well as export, import, and internal controls, and also commit to transparency and the exchange of statistical data. Participants can legally trade only with other participants who have also met the minimum requirements of the scheme, and international shipments of rough diamonds must be accompanied by a Kimberley Process certificate guaranteeing that they are conflict-free.

The blockchain not only replaces industry-wide paper-based processes that are fragmented and susceptible to tampering, but also ensures the ownership and authenticity of a diamond are securely recorded on a digitized, incorruptible ledger. This enables companies to track the provenance of diamonds, allowing buyers to screen for stones mined in regions where forced labour is common or where proceeds from previous sales were used to fund violence.

For industries like insurance, the implications become endless as to where a ledger can be used to secure assets and process claims. The potential of blockchain applicability goes beyond diamonds into most luxury markets where provenance matters, such as the world of fine wine.

This application ensures the ownership and authenticity of an item are securely recorded on a digitized ledger, which, unlike the paper records that can be enhanced, can't be altered or fraudulently copied. From blood diamonds mined out of Africa to the movement of counterfeit goods over borders internationally, blockchain can provide a global verification system that ensures transparency at every stage of the supply chain process and encourages ethical sourcing.

Blockchain's Potential

What are the areas of concern or industry deficits that blockchain can remedy? Consider the following applications:

Fraudulent claims. Fraudulent claims cost the insurance industry over £2 billion annually in Europe, with 65% of fraudulent jewellery claims going undetected in the United Kingdom alone. Blockchain's distributed and immutable nature provides a more secure way to record the transaction history, ownership records, and identification papers associated with an asset being insured. When a fraudster attempts to upload an incorrect set of information, the ledger will be able to identify suspicious activity and stop the attempt as the records cannot be changed without shared consensus among all the stakeholders invited. Blockchains can be fraud controls and potentially cyber security controls; they are utilized in digitized transactions that represent the performance of legal contracts, and can and do operate across multiple jurisdictions, and simulate or interact with banking and finance systems.

Smart contracts for processing claims. Smart contracts are agreed-upon terms written into computer protocol. Smart contracts hosted on the blockchain make it easier to execute an agreement, as the process is automated and distributed without reliance on a centralized authority or a person's verification, as this is already built into the code. The potential for the insurance industry is best exemplified through claims payouts, applied to anything from delayed travel times to an automobile accident. Smart contracts can ultimately automate the process previously required to distribute these claims that resulted in numerous back-and-forth movements between the customer, the insurer, and associated organizations.

Insuring assets. Blockchain allows both offline and online assets to be tracked in a distributed ledger where records on an asset's ownership, storage, and insurance are tied to the object itself, instead of being connected to the current owner. This allows for assets to be insured throughout their lifetimes, without disruption every time an item changes ownership. This becomes important when we start looking towards a future world enabled by the internet of things (IoT) – where all the devices we use and engage with in daily life are connected on the web and, more likely, on the blockchain. For the insurance industry, blockchain gives access to a single version of the truth – a linear, permanent record connected to an asset that replaces an object's paper identity with a digital one.

Future Challenges

We are at a critical moment with blockchain technology. The industry has woken up to all the possibilities, but careful planning is required to move forward with the proofs of concepts and pilot programmes that have been introduced.

As with any digital transformation, the paradigm is not focused on displacement and replacement but is instead aimed at connectivity and recombination. This responsibility rests not only with entrepreneurs building in the blockchain space but also with leading businesses and industries that are looking to adopt this technology.

With blockchain, we have the ability to bring imagining into existence with careful thought, collaboration, and consensus on setting the foundation and guidelines for how the technology can and should be applied, and, more important, under what protocols. The largest hurdle faced will be in industries where regulation is inflexible and where considerable cooperation will be required to determine the best way forward.

The biggest threat for blockchain is the application of the technology to all manner of problems across any industry. When looking at the fabric of the technology, one has to think about where it can best be applied – what information or objects require the immutability, security, and scalability that blockchain provides. We have seen projects pursued where blockchain is not required, where other methods work better. Entrepreneurs and industry leaders have a big role to play here in identifying where they should be investing in blockchain.

Working at the forefront of a technology like blockchain is exhilarating and comes with its share of responsibility. If we as an industry move on implementing projects where blockchain is not required, we fail collectively. However, if we build out commercial systems where blockchain has the potential to solve critical path and last mile problems, then there is no limit to what we will be able to achieve.

RegTech Applicability Outside the Financial Services Industry

- RegTech extends beyond finance, with data protection rules such as GDPR being central to this process, and will build consumer trust and confidence in any industry

- RegTech is key to information security and its use will make the public feel safer from digital threats

- Building blockchain systems to support the art market is one example of RegTech outside of financial services

- Environmental protection is another area where RegTech has great potential

- Because of growing compliance obligations outside of the financial sector including those around corruption, data protection, insider dealing and others, RegTech will grow dramatically in the coming years, including providing impetus to support further industry digitisation

- RegTech is particularly powerful in combating fraud and money laundering

Unlike some definitions of RegTech which reduce it to a sub-set of FinTech, the editors apply a broad characterization of what RegTech covers. In short, application of technology in the context of any regulatory or compliance process falls under the RegTech umbrella, meaning that other regulated industries ranging from Manufacturing, Medicine, Environment etc. have a series of use cases for RegTech solutions.

The justification for this book's focus on the financial services industry is a reflection of the fact that the term RegTech has been coined within this sector and that investment to date in RegTech has primarily been in financial services. Once founders have demonstrated the value of their technology within this sector, they will rapidly expand beyond finance, looking at other industries that are heavily regulated and in need of efficiency gain if not outright disruption.

Therefore, readers should look at the previous chapters as a framework of understanding for a transformative trend that will repeat itself in other industries. As for these specific chapters, a series of use cases are shown. GDPR illustrates this trend as it covers any industry, globally as long as EU citizens' data are processed. On the technology side, the opportunity of blockchain to trace the provenance of goods has applications in the art business where the value of a work of art is dictated by its origin. The application of AI to identify suspect transactions in rapidly growing e-commerce companies and before that online gambling is yet another illustration of how compliance obligations in other sectors can be automated. Finally, the market for carbon emission or micro-energy trading has already shown why tokenizing it delivers values for actors.

However, the arrival of new regulatory obligations is also creating new pressure on businesses that otherwise had no, or limited, compliance functions within their organization. The potential consequences of a GDPR breach should matter equally to a bank CEO as to a founder of a fashion start-up, since a breach will impact customer trust and financial operation of the business. For those industries that have not previously thought of compliance as a pre-requisite for operation, the hiring of full-time staff might be disproportionate, and they may instead prefer to rely on outsourcing these obligations to third-party tech solutions.

Protecting Consumers and Enabling Innovation

By Stuart Lacey
Founder and Director, Trunomi

What Is RegTech?

Regulatory technology (RegTech) was previously defined as a subset of financial technology (FinTech) and applied to technology that focused on solving regulatory challenges in the financial services sector. RegTech meant innovative, agile technology that helped financial service providers comply with regulations more efficiently by helping them better understand and manage their risks and automate their compliance processes. Now, RegTech is being applied beyond financial services and has the potential to revolutionize customer experiences across all industries.

The financial sector is one of the most regulated globally, and regulation is seen as a necessary evil to protect consumer rights and fight money laundering and fraud. However, few people associate regulation with innovation, and most firms see it as a straitjacket that can reduce operational agility. The rise of RegTech in financial services opens the door for innovation beyond compliance – a way to enhance the customer relationship while reducing compliance costs and operational inefficiency.

The term RegTech was first promoted in 2015 by the UK Financial Conduct Authority (FCA); It was heralded as a welcome solution to banks globally, as the snowballing rules and regulations and escalating costs of compliance were resulting in what has been called 'regulatory fatigue'. Compliance departments worldwide were overwhelmed by the scope and volume of regulatory change and were experiencing resource and staffing challenges, budget restrictions, and lack of awareness surrounding the complicated regulations, as well as fear over potentially record fines for non-compliance. The costs of compliance are staggering, with reports that UBS spent nearly $1 billion in 2014 alone in order to meet regulatory requirements, and in September 2016 Bain & Company estimated that governance, risk, and compliance costs accounted for 20% of banks' total spend.

So why is complying with regulation so hard for banks? In the simplest terms, this can be attributed to the fact that banks have massive amounts of sensitive, confidential, protected, personal, and financial data – typically unstructured and in different bank legacy systems. This means banks have struggled to devise a robust and efficient approach to data use and compliance, meaning they are unable to leverage their data to innovate. RegTech has solved this in multiple ways: from automating compliance standards to allowing straight-through processing and to implementing interface layers that allow banks to leverage third-party solutions and data providers.

Data Revolution

However, banking is no longer the only industry collecting, consuming, and producing massive amounts of data. The internet of things (IoT) (the interconnection via the internet of computing devices embedded in physical objects, enabling them to send and receive data) has transformed the way we live. Being IoT-enabled is also referred to as 'smart', and every aspect of our lives and almost every object we use can now be 'smarter': smartphones, smart watches, smart cars, smart homes. From travel to health, energy, retail, and real estate, this 'datafication' has affected every industry.

What do all these devices have in common? Autonomous cars, health wearables, smart home thermostats, fridges that know you are out of milk, toys your children can talk to: all are reliant on collecting your data. Gartner Technology Research estimated that 5.5 million connected devices came online every day in 2016. In 2020 the total number of IoT devices is expected to have risen to

20.4 billion. Taking these numbers into account, it is no wonder that 90% of data in the world has been generated over the last two years. This is our personal data, produced by devices that make our lives easier, better, more efficient – but why is it so valuable to businesses, and why must we implement RegTech to protect it?

In this digital age, consumers emit a binary vapour trail wherever they go – but this vapour trail does not disappear: it is devoured by businesses that can profit from it. These technological advancements and subsequent data provide an opportunity for business to achieve transformative improvements in customer experience by providing access to personalized customer data flows.

Data is the 'new oil' – fueling our digital, personal data economies.

The freemium model that has been so prevalent over past years has emboldened brands to capture significant amounts of customers' personal data 'in lieu of payment', often without their knowledge or informed opt-in consent. From that point, the data are no longer the property of the original data owners, meaning they lose their rights – eroding trust in the system, losing transparency and surrendering any value from the data's subsequent monetization.

At the same time, we are confronted with the rise of data privacy and security concerns: cyber attacks and data breaches and increasing stories of smart devices collecting data without consent. This privacy breach (or total collapse) was never more obvious than in February 2017 when it was discovered that a smart sex toy was illegally collecting customers' use patterns and time and data information, along with personally identifiable email addresses. Data capitalism is rising, and our privacy has been the collateral damage.

Consumers are now more concerned than ever over data use and are demanding privacy and control over their data. The lack of trust in IoT is already a market problem; with hacks increasing and non-transparent data usage stories breaking, consumers are

starting to reject smart devices. It has also become a top priority for governments and lawmakers. Companies face a monumental challenge: how to use these vast amounts of data to create value for themselves and their customers while simultaneously avoiding crossing the line into unethical, illegal, or unwelcome use. How do businesses effectively balance opportunity and risk? There must be regulation.

Enter Data Protection Regulation

New data privacy regulations such as the recently enacted EU General Data Protection Regulation (GDPR), the proposed ePrivacy Directive, and the US Federal Trade Commission Consent Order are driving a shift in the data landscape and giving consumers more transparency and control over who is using their data.

The GDPR specifically will revolutionize the data privacy landscape in Europe. It went into effect automatically across all member EU states in May 2018 and will strengthen and unify the data privacy landscape across all industries in Europe. Its extraterritorial effect means it will apply to all global firms processing or holding EU citizens' data. This means large multinational companies must adopt the rules throughout their operations if they want to continue to market to EU citizens and compete in the European market. The GDPR will force companies to be more transparent about the types of data they collect on customers, how that data is used, and when it is exposed in a breach.

What makes this regulation different is the size of the fines for non-compliance. Under EU GDPR businesses could face fines of 4% of global revenue or €20 million, whichever is greater. To put that into perspective: the 2016 security failings that allowed a customer data breach at UK telco TalkTalk cost the company a fine of £400,000, whereas under GDPR this could be as much as £59 million. This risk means businesses across all industries will no longer be able to treat personal data as a commodity owned by them and must move to protecting it as a fundamental right.

Consumer Empowerment

So what are the changes for individuals under GDPR? GDPR requires higher standards of consent: consent needs to be active, represent affirmative action, present genuine choice, and be time-limited. Consent will not be valid unless separate consents are obtained for different processing activities or purposes. Forced or pre-ticked consent mechanisms will not be valid. Data subjects have the right to revoke their consent at any time. GDPR introduces new rights to data rectification, to erasure, and 'to be forgotten'. Individuals have rights to view the data held by businesses and review the data's accuracy. A customer has the right to request access to both the personal data and information on processing, recipients, and data transfers. Should inaccurate personal data about a data subject be held by the data controller, the data subject has the right to supply the correct information and request rectification. The inaccurate information should be updated 'without undue delay'. A data subject can also request erasure of his or her personal data ('the right to be forgotten'), subject to certain conditions, such as compliance with a legal obligation, public interest for public health, and legal claims. The right to data portability allows data subjects to request that the personal data they have supplied to a controller be shared with another data controller in 'a structured, commonly used and machine-readable format'.

In contrast to previous data privacy laws, the GDPR introduces a responsibility on the controller to demonstrate compliance and show 'privacy by design'. This means businesses' organizational structure and technological solutions must be built with data privacy as a key tenet. Importantly, supervisory authorities are required to take into account the organizational and technological measures that have been implemented when determining the severity of non-compliance fines.

Consumer empowerment also lies behind the proposed ePrivacy Directive. If enacted, this regulation will align the rules for electronic communications with the new GDPR. The latter imposes new rules on businesses that store customer data, stipulating they have unambiguous customer consent before sharing or processing their data. The ePrivacy Directive builds on GDPR by extending consent to the processing of customers' electronic communications data and metadata.

The RegTech Solution

Luckily, there is a solution to these extensive and strict new regulations – the same technology that has eroded privacy can also restore and reinforce it. Enter RegTech. Companies that are able to prove compliance with GDPR will have the chance to create trust in the IoT and create market opportunities.

The need for personalized, effective, legal, and regulatory-compliant digital user experiences is clear: RegTech can improve efficiency of businesses and provide an auditable trail and clear proof of consent for regulators, and build loyalty and trust for customers. We are beginning to see the introduction of technology (RegTech), which allows customers control and transparency over how their data is being used, by whom, and for what purpose. RegTech will solve the data rights complexity and consent issues that have hampered the enhancement of customer experience and data monetization efforts.

Consumer trust in data privacy is essential to business success. We must therefore embrace the idea of informed consent and be willing to work with customers in true data partnerships. This customer consent and participation in data flow (and value exchange) will be necessary for all businesses to ensure their customers are protected.

This is a consent-based consumer-centric approach to regulation, governance, risk, and compliance management that is fit for the digital age. RegTech will no longer be a vertical of financial services, but a pan-industry horizontal, with customers in control.

RegTech Impact on the Private Security Industry

By Benjamin Weld
CEO and Co-Founder, Falcon DHQ

In a world of uncertainty, safety and security are in ever-increasing demand. Growing concerns of crime, terrorism, and insufficient public safety measures, coupled with an improved economic climate and a booming construction industry, have facilitated the rise in the requirement for real-time regulatory compliance, situation management, and evidenced best practice in the private security industry. This chapter discusses how the security industry has changed since 2001, and how advances in technology have seen an increased appetite from regulators and security providers alike. It will help determine whether RegTech – which has been incredibly successful in the financial services industry – has the potential to be as prosperous in the private security industry and create a stronger, more robust, and more pertinent industry that is capable of facing the demands of an ever-changing always-on interconnected world.

Security, in any world, is of paramount importance, as is evident from 2012 figures stating that the private security industry contributes £6.5 billion to the UK economy. Yet, pre-2001 the UK government had little interest in the industry, and regulation did not feature highly on any government manifesto despite the private security industry suffering from an endless amount of deep-rooted problems. Security was treated as a grudge spend, meaning companies had little money available for training and staff development. A temporary workforce, high staff turnover, and nothing to encourage loyalty from employees meant there was little incentive to provide training for the security staff outside of the bare minimum. This drove standards down, shrank already small margins, and created an environment for criminality to breed. This locked the industry in a downward spiral of diminishing returns and deteriorating public perception that it could not break itself away from.

This changed with the creation of the Security Industry Authority (SIA), formed as a result of the Private Security Act 2001, designed to 'reduce criminality and improve standards [so as to ensure that] … the public is, and feels safer'. The rationale was that having created a professional industry, there would be an immediate increase in demand for adequately trained and SIA-certified security officers. This would mean the security companies could charge more for the security officers, increasing their margins and willingness to invest in training, and would incentivize staff to become more loyal to 'reputable' companies. These combined outcomes would ensure a more professional and competent workforce and help remove the criminal element from the industry, thereby helping the public be – and feel – safer. The SIA assumes responsibility for the training framework, vetting, and licensing of people wishing to work in the industry. The accreditation of companies through the Approved Contractor Scheme is also covered. The combination of the 2001 Act and the involvement of the SIA has meant that local authorities now require licensed venues that operate with security staff to maintain detailed logbooks of those working as well as any other incidents that may occur.

The use of logbooks is an archaic process, yet despite this, from 2001 logbooks were the sole method used to accurately collect data from dynamic workforces and customers to ensure regulatory compliance. A process that once signaled change is in reality riddled with problems. Firstly, the accurate pocket-books kept by individual security officers are being loosely transcribed into logbooks – collected monthly for audit and storage. Discrepancies are commonplace, with incorrect information and missing evidence the norm. Secondly, when moderated, it is unlikely that these errors are corrected, emphasizing the pitfalls of this method, with regulatory breaches and public safety issues exposed only when auditing logbooks.

It is clear that this overreliance on logbooks is damaging trust and costing the industry hundreds of millions in administrative expense and lost contracts. This inefficient process is jeopardizing public, staff, and infrastructure safety and is significantly preventing the industry from accurately fulfilling its sole objective of protecting people, property, and assets effectively. At the same time, it is obvious that this type of practice is not benefiting anyone. The lack of accurate records leads to no improvement in standards or conditions, and no scope to empower organizations to enhance security capabilities through meaningful data-driven insights.

There have been attempts from the major players within the industry to modernize and improve the obvious problems. However, all have been ineffective, and, in reality, the current tools have increased workloads and generated more unanswered questions. None have combined real-time regulatory compliance with the day-to-day operations of security officers and companies.

When exploring the uses of RegTech outside of the financial services industry, it would be inaccurate to simply consider replacing manual reporting and compliance processes. Real-time situation management is the logical and correct methodology for the security industry to progress to, ensuring its survival and allowing it to constantly adapt to an ever-changing world. The word *situation* can be defined as 'a set of circumstances in which one finds oneself'. So, if we apply that to the private security industry, then 'situation' can combine both circumstances of regulatory breaches, such as unlicensed staff, overcrowding, duty-of-care issues, understaffed contracts (and staff not showing up for work), and overworked staff, with incidents like the everyday occurrences faced in the industry such as theft, violence, suspicious activity, intoxication, substance possession, missing people, antisocial behaviour, and trespass.

The real benefit of real-time situation management is that it can create a framework for how RegTech can be used in the industry to benefit all stakeholders involved, from the security officers to security companies and their customers, as well as the regulators and the public. The use of a web- and app-based real-time end-to-end platform allows the framework to be relevant for all

involved within the industry – it is multifaceted and acts as a security officer's companion, a security company's workforce management tool, an insights dashboard for the client, and a compliance management tool for the regulator. The ability to generate a real-time data capture of an entire industry allows the data to be repurposed for local authorities and insurance companies.

Technology is constantly evolving and is generating new opportunities regardless of industry such as the explosion of handheld internet-ready devices, which shows no sign of stopping. Crucially, that is exactly where RegTech for the private security industry begins – in the hands of the security officer. Creating a process that is simpler to use will ensure that the correct data is captured, thus allowing greater opportunities to develop new data-driven insights for security companies. Risk-data warehouses that require models for staffing and hardware requirements (such as closed-circuit television [CCTV], entry/exit points, and building/public space design) are now able to focus on new projects, based on pinpoint-accurate data sets. The dynamic management information tools generated by the risk-data warehouses allow real-time data and monitoring on current workforce activity and performance, from anywhere in the world. This will prove invaluable for an industry that operates almost entirely remotely, with contract sites operating as satellite offices – which report situations back to a control room or central headquarters.

Data-driven training guidelines become a consequence of real-time situation management. Each situation has guided outcomes based on the security company guidelines coupled with regulatory requirements. Although each situation is unique, it ensures that each incident can be automatically analysed against the existing entries in the risk-data warehouses. Importantly, this will provide learning outcomes on how future similar situations should be managed and potentially averted.

The correct management and execution of each situation will allow for greater regulation and training for the industry. This improved understanding together with compliance universe tools can ensure the foundations for future legislation and regulation gap analysis – cementing the view that potentially the UK security industry could move towards a self-governance model. Regulations are only ever created and implemented to help improve and structure industries. It is evident that ineffective technology has hampered regulation to date, and there has been no viable way of effectively implementing it. However, the world is constantly evolving, and technology is now so sophisticated that a user can be pinpointed to within metres – something that was unimaginable 20 years ago. With stronger cellular data reception and the capabilities of creating peer-to-peer networks amongst security teams, there has never been a better opportunity not only to improve but to enhance the private security industry.

The most practical way to deliver real-time situation management is deploying an end-to-end app to security officers that is connected in real time to a centralized platform. Using an app-based real-time end-to-end platform that connects security officers, security companies, their customers, and also the regulator will create the most secure and operationally effective regulation going forward. Being able to ensure end-to-end compliance through an app on the security officer's device opens the door to an unlimited potential for improving training standards, customer service, public perception, and job satisfaction.

The implementation of an end-to-end real-time situation management platform is soon to become a reality. The ability to have interconnected stakeholders and connected information will help strengthen an industry that was previously abandoned by significant technological advances. An ageing system will be revitalized, allowing a greater, less intrusive regulation of the industry while increasing security effectiveness. It is evident that the implementation of RegTech should not be underestimated, and the opportunities generated are limitless. Ultimately, RegTech creates a much more cohesive system, which will improve best practices and increase public, asset, and infrastructure safety. Private security is an industry that still needs huge human input; RegTech is the first step in intertwining technological advances in hardware with people and software to create a powerful hybrid. Perhaps the most important aspect of RegTech, which should not be underestimated, is that it will allow the public to be – and feel – safer, which is difficult when fear is becoming the norm in this ever-changing world of uncertainty.

ArtTech: How Blockchain Can Improve Provenance

By Javier Tamashiro

Head of Technology Risk and Compliance, Maecenas and Founder, Ospree Pte. Ltd.

Art provenance provides a critical foundation for assessing the authenticity and ownership of an artwork. A good provenance increases legitimate ownership and should leave no doubts that it is a genuine object. The capacity to successfully perform a good provenance is highly dependent on the existence of solid, documented evidence that proves its ownership and the owner's identity and helps to establish that the artwork has not been altered and is not a forgery or a stolen object. This complex and expensive authentication process significantly increases the transaction cost and is considered one of the biggest threats to trust in the art industry, as not being able to prove the provenance impacts the value of an art piece that could be suspected of having been previously stolen or faked. With the art market moving from a small niche market towards a global industry, the need for improved art provenance solutions has become imperative. This chapter evaluates the benefits of blockchain technology in the registration and authentication processes of artworks and analyses the advantages of a collaborative framework that includes multiple participants. The art market is still considered an immature industry, while blockchain is starting to disrupt many of the existing ways of doing business. To unlock their mutual benefits, it is essential to understand some of the key challenges that must be overcome, in particular in the area of provenance standards, governance, and regulations.

Introduction

Regulatory compliance and high transaction costs are increasingly pushing the art industry to look at more transparent and streamlined solutions operating under the radar of regulatory bodies. An illustration of this trend is given by the European Union's fourth Money Laundering Directive[1] (4MLD) of 2015, which addresses the threat of money laundering in high-value goods requesting protective measures, such as the identification of payee or fund origins, for cash payments equal to or more than €10,000. Pointing in the same direction, the Financial Action Task Force (FATF) Mutual Evaluation Report of Belgium[2] of 2015 mentions 'antique and art dealers' as 'particularly vulnerable' to money laundering risks, along with precious metals dealers. The 40 FATF Recommendations[3] do not explicitly refer to art dealers. However, precious metals and stones dealers have already been classified as 'designated non-financial businesses and professions'.

These regulatory constraints are taking effect at the same time as the online art market is proving to be a viable alternative to the traditional offline market. The growth in sales among online businesses such as Artsy, 1stDibs, and Saatchi Art suggests that people are getting increasingly comfortable buying and selling art online. A recent report[4] has shown that online art market sales reached an estimated $3.75 billion in 2016, up 15% from 2015, amounting to an 8.4% share of the overall art market. The

---

[1] 'Directive (EU) 2015/849 of the European Parliament and of the Council', *Official Journal of the European Union* (2015), 84. Retrieved 10 April 2017 from http://eur-lex.europa.eu/legal-content/EN/TXT/PDF/?uri=CELEX:32015L0849&from=EN

[2] 'Anti–Money Laundering and Counter-terrorist Financing Measures', *Belgium, Mutual Evaluation Report* (2015), 27. Retrieved 10 April 2017 from http://www.fatf-gafi.org/media/fatf/documents/reports/mer4/Mutual-Evaluation-Report-Belgium-2015.pdf

[3] 'The FATF Recommendations' (2012), 19. Retrieved 10 April 2017 from http://www.fatf-gafi.org/publications/fatfrecommendations/documents/fatf-recommendations.html

[4] 'The Hiscox Online Art Trade Report 2017: A Market Yet to Awaken?' (Rep.) (London: Hiscox, 2017); www.hiscox.co.uk/sites/uk/files/documents/2017-05/hiscox-online-art-trade-report-2017.pdf

larger the volume of online transactions, the more important it is to demonstrate capacities to operate across digital channels assuring high-quality provenance. In a world where nearly every individual has a powerful digital device at his or her fingertips, technology is adding to the burden of compliance while breaking the barriers to entry to more and more markets. It is not surprising that the art industry is increasingly looking to more robust and sophisticated solutions to facilitate provenance.

This chapter discusses the benefits and key requirements of a blockchain-based provenance solution. It will not focus on technology; rather it will attempt to provide direction on which configuration would be the best to solve key problems faced by the art industry nowadays.

Provenance and Blockchain Background

Provenance as a research practice has been used to document and testify to the history of artworks as they changed ownership through time. Except in exceptional cases, provenance is tightly attached to a specific artwork, and it supplies information that helps to reconstruct the memory of an object by collecting data attributes such as ownership, style, physical state, and origin. Interest in provenance has traditionally been rooted in the incentive to provide evidence that supports the authenticity of an artwork and demonstrates that it was part of a distinguished collection. This confers value on the object and can be used as proof of superior qualities.[5]

From an economic perspective, provenance is understood as a market mechanism to ameliorate the problem of asymmetric information.[6] This problem refers to the market conditions in which one party has more or better information than the other. In the art market, when selling an artwork, the owner is likely to have full knowledge about its provenance history and authenticity. The potential buyer, by contrast, will be in the dark and may not be able to trust the seller. Therefore, provenance is a big word when it comes to the art industry, as it has effects on essential problems, including financial crime prevention; it requires documentary records to support ownership and authenticity, and it is also a market response to the problem of asymmetric information where a trusted party is needed to validate the attributes of an artwork and bring trust to the market.

In recent years, blockchain has attracted the attention of governments and companies across the world. It has built its reputation as a disruptive technology that could truly transform several sectors of the economy. Key features of blockchain enable the accurate, secure, and decentralized sharing of databases with multiple writers with a certain degree of mistrust. For organizations operating in the art industry, blockchain may hold considerable promise to address problems related to provenances such as authorization, authentication, and asset identity. However, blockchain implementations will need to address three major areas before a wider adoption becomes possible: multiple trusted participants, governance challenges, and digital provenance standards.

Multiple Trusted Participants

A number of ongoing provenance projects involving the use of blockchain are focused on registration and authenticity of artworks. Many of these projects operate virtually like stand-alone solutions. However, a blockchain provenance solution does not need to be

[5] G. Feigenbaum and I.J. Reist, *Provenance: An Alternate History of Art* (Los Angeles: Getty Research Institute, 2013), 22.

[6] D. Autor, 'Lecture Note 17: Private Information, Adverse Selection and Market Failure' (lecture presented at 14.03/14.003, Microeconomic Theory and Public Policy, Massachusetts Institute of Technology, 2011).

provided by a single entity; it can be designed as a collaborative network that integrates multiple trusted parties. In fact, the ability to perform a good provenance relies on documents supplied by a wide range of participants. For instance, an artwork may require[7] provenance history, certificate of insurance, certificate of authenticity, exhibition catalogues, restoration history, and documented evidence that screening against the Interpol Art Database and Art Loss Register has been done.

Blockchain offers a broad spectrum of models to suit different business needs. Permissionless blockchain and permissioned blockchain are two of the distinctive models. In a permissionless blockchain, participants do not need to register and can also become miners to create new blocks and contribute to the network. The permissioned blockchain, by contrast, is a form of blockchain where participants must first be acknowledged by the network before they can contribute to validating blocks and updating the ledger. In other words, in a permissioned blockchain only specified parties such as artists, galleries, or restorers would be allowed to participate in the ledger. For an industry looking for higher transparency and regulatory compliance, permissioned ledgers are likely to be a more appealing model.

Governance Challenges

Technology alone cannot bring benefits to the art industry; blockchain needs to be coupled with industry collaboration and legal frameworks. In this regard, establishing a governance body would be critical to the successful implementation of a permissioned blockchain. A blockchain provenance solution may involve a wide range of participants providing different services. Offering voting rights and a governance structure that safeguards participants' private interests can result in increased stability

and growth of the network, with better capabilities to solve a wide variety of circumstances. A governance body can continuously adapt requirements and standards while encouraging transparency and accountability.

Digital Provenance Standards

Any blockchain provenance solution will require the implementation and adoption of data standards to transform traditional written provenance records into standardized, digitized, and structured data. Much of the work for creating such standards for digital provenance has already been done by initiatives such as the Art Tracks project with the support of the Carnegie Museum of Art[8] and the Getty Research Institute.[9] Perhaps these standards can be adopted to build blockchain solutions going forward.

Conclusion

Recent regulatory changes suggest that the art industry is facing more stringent compliance requirements focused on transparency, fraud, and money laundering risks. These regulatory constraints are taking effect at the same time as the online art market is proving to be a viable alternative to the traditional offline market. This shows a shift in how buyers and sellers interact, adding more pressure to develop more efficient provenance solutions to operate in digital environments. In response, a permissioned blockchain solution can be designed as a collaborative network comprising members of the art industry. In addition, a blockchain provenance

[7] T. Christ and C. Von Selle, *Basel Art Trade Guidelines*. Working Paper 12. (Basel, Switzerland: Basel Institute on Governance, 2012).

[8] 2016 Digital Provenance Symposium (n.d.). Retrieved 10 April 2017 from http://www.museumprovenance.org/pages/scholars_day_2016

[9] The Getty Provenance Index Databases (n.d.). Retrieved 10 April 2017 from http://www.getty.edu/research/tools/provenance/search.html

solution should be designed upon a governance structure with explicit decision-making processes to safeguard participants' private interests.

Provenance is the backbone of the art industry. It provides a critical foundation for assessing authenticity, valuation, and ownership of artworks. Although there is great room for growth in the art market, without more advanced and sophisticated provenance solutions the art industry as a whole will be constrained. Blockchain may represent the best hope to solve this problem while opening up new opportunities and challenges.

The Potential of RegTech in Improving the Effectiveness of Environmental Regulation

By Dr Inna Amesheva
Associate, ESG Research and Advisory, Arabesque S-Ray

Regulatory technology (RegTech) is not confined to just revolutionizing the financial services, or FinTech, industry. Instead, it has the potential to spur numerous breakthroughs in diverse areas such as consumer protection and environmental sustainability, among others. This chapter explores the impact of RegTech on ensuring the effectiveness of environmental regulatory measures such as greenhouse gas reduction schemes aimed at tackling climate change. RegTech developments are particularly apt to tackle information and reporting asymmetries inherent in environmental compliance. Indeed, recent technological advancements have the potential to streamline and even revolutionize a number of areas such as the monitoring of energy consumption and the facilitation of renewable energy projects financing, as well as designing more effective emissions trading schemes. This can be done through the adoption of 'smart meters' in the premises of polluting enterprises, which measure and report real-time data of a company's emissions. Compliance can also be facilitated by blockchain-enabled 'smart contracts', which can be self-executing and make sure that the parties to a contract automatically comply with their reporting and monitoring obligations. As this chapter demonstrates, correctly tracing, reviewing, and taking account of the data generated by carbon-intensive enterprises and industries, with the help of RegTech, has the potential to restore the credibility of environmental regulatory measures and to ensure that they result in substantive ecological improvements.

The Clean Energy Revolution

The global market for clean technologies is expected to reach US$1.3 trillion by 2020.[1] Just in developing countries, this figure is estimated to amount to US$640 billion per year within the next 10 years.[2] Clean energy investment and capacity have grown to unprecedented levels in recent years, spearheading what is nothing short of a modern-day energy revolution. Having accessible, affordable, and reliable energy access is an essential prerequisite to achieving an adequate standard of living and meeting the United Nations' Sustainable Development Goals, promulgated in September 2015, as a successor to the Millennium Development Goals.[3]

Still, 20% of the world's population (particularly those living in developing nations), do not currently enjoy reliable energy access. Moreover, energy production is the single greatest contributor to climate change, being responsible for 60% of global greenhouse gas emissions.[4] This poses not only an enormous challenge but also an immense opportunity for rethinking the present-day unsustainable fossil-fuel-dominated energy system. Indeed, substantial renewable energy investments have been made in recent years that aim to ensure a robust and sustained clean energy transition. According to figures from Bloomberg New Energy Finance, global clean energy investment reached

---

[1] http://www.carbonbrief.org/the-rise-fall-and-future-of-the-cleantech-industry

[2] World Bank. See also National Bank of Abu Dhabi, 'NBAD Report: Growing Opportunities for Renewable Energy in Middle East'; https://www.nbad.com/en-ae/about-nbad/overview/newsroom/2016/06-03-2016.html

[3] United Nations Sustainable Development Goals; http://www.un.org/sustainabledevelopment/sustainable-development-goals. Particularly, Goal 7 on ensuring affordable and clean energy for all.

[4] United Nations, 'SDGs, Energy'; http://www.un.org/sustainabledevelopment/energy

US$332.1 billion in 2018, the fifth in a row in which investment exceeded the US$300 billion mark.[5] Despite a drop in investment, and spurred by falling equipment and operation costs, installed renewables capacity, in fact, *increased* year on year, global PV installations increased from 99GW in 2017 to approximately 109GW in 2018.[6]

The clean energy transformation currently underway has, at least partially, been spawned by a robust international regulatory framework, underscoring growing global consensus on the need to collectively tackle environmental challenges such as climate change. In this regard, the international community adopted the landmark Paris Agreement on climate change in December 2015.[7] The accord provides unprecedented impetus for world governments, municipalities, and corporations alike to effectively address the threat presented by climate change. The Paris Agreement, however, purposefully left a great deal of detail regarding the concrete implementation of its pledges vague, making them subject to ambiguous interpretation.[8] This is particularly the case in the area of market mechanisms aimed at reducing greenhouse emissions. The Paris Agreement does promote reliance on market-based measures such as carbon trading while emphasizing the importance of ensuring that no double counting of emissions reductions take place. The emphasis on eliminating double counting is an essential aspect for the

successful operation of the international climate change regime, ensuring its integrity and reliability. Nevertheless, the Agreement furnishes little or no detail regarding the precise operation of emissions trading schemes and their adequate implementation.

Regulatory Uncertainty in Monitoring Environmental Data

At their root, cap-and-trade emissions trading mechanisms represent market-based measures that allow businesses to trade a certain number of pre-allocated carbon credits. Thus, polluting enterprises can purchase the right to discharge greenhouse gas emissions either from entities that are not involved in carbon-intensive activities or from those that have already installed the necessary technological improvements that curb emissions and hence have a surplus of carbon credits at their disposal. At the same time, the overall level of emissions is held constant, so that emissions credits are being redistributed to those willing to pay the market price for pollution. However, a major problem with global cap-and-trade schemes is the double counting that occurs when emissions reductions are being counted twice, both on the books of the seller and on the books of the buyer of the relevant carbon emissions credits.[9]

Indeed, the monitoring and recording of environmental data have so far proven to be a difficult and elusive exercise. This can be illustrated by a number of examples, such as China's severe

---

[5] https://about.bnef.com/clean-energy-investment/

[6] https://about.bnef.com/blog/clean-energy-investment-exceeded-300-billion-2018/

[7] The Paris Agreement is a successor of the 1997 Kyoto Protocol to the United Nations Framework Convention on Climate Change (UNFCCC).

[8] This was arguably done so as to ensure a maximum level of participation from countries.

---

[9] An additional problem with carbon trading schemes is the inadequate price of carbon, which severely limits the effectiveness of such projects by making it cheaper to just purchase carbon credits (for about five euros per tonne in the case of the European Emissions Trading Scheme), as opposed to undertaking substantive improvements. This issue, however, does not fall under the scope of this chapter.

underreporting of its coal consumption by as much as 17%.[10] Double counting of emissions reductions is also prone to occur in the area of forest conservation when the country undertaking a reforestation exercise and the country purchasing the accrued emissions credits both count this towards their national emissions reduction pledges.[11] This is where the potential of RegTech to address issues relating to environmental regulation and its implementation can be realized.

The Use of Technology in Achieving More Effective Environmental Regulation

Newly emerging, cutting-edge technologies such as blockchain, artificial intelligence, machine learning, and big data analytics can help fill in the gaps between environmental monitoring and compliance.

Cryptocurrencies and blockchain technology, for example, have far-reaching implications for the recording, accounting, and executing of multiparty transactions and exchanges. In the field of energy generation, 'blockchain allows for peer-to-peer energy microtransactions and accounting. They are an open, distributed system that can record transactions between two parties across borders in a verifiable and permanent way.'[12] There are multiple

advantages to the operation of a blockchain-enabled energy or carbon 'ledger', which would practically eliminate the likelihood of double counting and would also provide a much-needed boost to the transparency of different parties' environmental compliance records.

In addition, smart contracts can revolutionize the way environmental transactions are executed. Once a party has fulfilled its obligations (i.e. by issuing a set number of carbon credits), the contract becomes self-executable, ensuring speed and accuracy of the outcome: 'Transactions can be programmed to automatically trigger under certain conditions through so-called smart contracts, thus doing away with the need for a trusted intermediary in a transaction.'[13] The definition of 'smart contract' dates back to 1994, having been coined by Nick Szabo:

> A smart contract is a computerized transaction protocol that executes the terms of a contract. The general objectives are to satisfy common contractual conditions (such as payment terms, liens, confidentiality, and even enforcement), minimize exceptions both malicious and accidental, and minimize the need for trusted intermediaries. Related economic goals include lowering fraud loss, arbitrations and enforcement costs, and other transaction costs.[14]

In addition to the regulatory enabling implications of new technologies, the role of continuing innovation and entrepreneurship in fostering the impending clean energy transition should not be understated. In this connection, data-driven 'greentech' companies already fulfil that function along a broad spectrum, focusing on a variety of angles and environmental metrics. The specialization of such start-ups ranges from solar energy remote monitoring to water treatment analytics

---

[10] See 'China Burns Much More Coal Than Reported, Complicating Climate Talks', *New York Times*, 3 November 2015; https://www.nytimes.com/2015/11/04/world/asia/china-burns-much-more-coal-than-reported-complicating-climate-talks.html

[11] 'Who Takes the Credit? The Risks of Double-counting in a REDD Carbon Trading Mechanism', 11 June 2015; http://www.redd-monitor.org/2015/06/11/who-takes-the-credit-the-risks-of-double-counting-in-a-redd-carbon-trading-mechanism

[12] 'Renewable Energy Trends to Keep an Eye on in 2017', 24 April 2017; http://www.eco-business.com/opinion/renewable-energy-trends-to-keep-an-eye-on-in-2017/?utm_medium=email&utm_campaign=April%2026%20newsletter&utm_content=April%2026%20newsletter+Version+A+CID_07058b90d698e30e944293b6b82b2678&utm_source=Campaign%20Monitor&utm_term=Renewable%20energy%20trends%20to%20keep%20an%20eye%20on%20in%202017

---

[13] Ibid.

[14] Don Tapscott and Alex Tapscott, *The Blockchain Revolution: How the Technology Behind Bitcoin Is Changing Money, Business, and the World* (New York: Portfolio/Penguin, 2016), 72, 83, 101, 127. Szabo is speculated to be the creator of bitcoin.

enabled by machine learning and big data[15] to real-time energy saving via smart devices and internet of things applications,[16] as well as using machine learning to provide energy use optimization,[17] to name but a few examples. Some greentech companies operate devices that monitor household electricity consumption and urge users to reduce their electricity demand (especially during peak hours so that the use of unsustainable electricity sources can be minimized). The data is then sent to local utilities and governments, which in turn monitor usage and adjust power plant operations accordingly. Exciting developments have also occurred in the area of renewable energy financing, which has been transformed with the help of crowdfunding-based financing models[18] and one-stop-shop clean energy marketplaces.[19]

These practical illustrations of RegTech-enabled greentech entrepreneurship provide a great level of momentum towards the sustainability transition already underway. Therefore, it is all the more important that policy makers ensure a level playing field as

well as regulatory certainty for upcoming energy disruptors and established incumbents alike.

Conclusion

This chapter's main objective is to illustrate the relationship between newly emerging regulatory technologies and their impact on ensuring more effective environmental governance, monitoring, and compliance. The secret of success underpinning a more sustainable, long-term energy strategy involves an unprecedented collaborative effort by national governments, the private sector, academia, and individual consumers alike. The scope and complexity of this challenge are extraordinary, but it also presents an unrivalled opportunity to create a truly viable system of universal energy access and independence, underpinned by sustainability at its heart. As this chapter demonstrates, RegTech is poised to play a crucial role in realizing a more positive environmental vision of the future.

[15] Pluto AI (http://www.plutoai.com/).

[16] Ohm Connect (https://www.ohmconnect.com/).

[17] Tempus Energy (https://tempusenergy.com).

[18] The Sun Exchange (https://thesunexchange.com).

[19] Solageo (http://www.solageo.com/).

RegTech Applicability Outside the Financial Services Industry

By Robin Lee
Market Development, Risk and RegTech, Refinitiv

and Sharifah Nursyafiqah Binte Syed Isha
Senior Consultant, Datarama

Since its inception in 2016, RegTech has traditionally been associated with the financial industry due to compliance inefficiencies and challenges faced by this sector, which can be viewed as RegTech's low-hanging fruit.

For example, the US Banking Secrecy Act stipulates that any transaction greater than US$10,000 needs to be flagged and reported to the Internal Revenue Service (IRS). The 10,000 number holds little ambiguity, so applying this to a RegTech application is very straightforward.

The types of regulations and ultimately compliance in the non-financial industry contain much more ambiguity. Therefore, we currently see very few RegTech companies focusing on this area. As technology progresses, we should see some interesting solutions emerge. We look forward to exploring this area further.

Non-financial Compliance

In today's non-financial world, the role and background of a compliance officer is very different from that of a financial industry compliance officer. Non-financial compliance officers are typically lawyers (or ex-lawyers) and work very closely with the legal team, whereas in the financial industry compliance has moved away from legal risk and is more aligned with operational risk. As a result, there is less of a focus on areas like anti–money laundering (AML) and risk management and more of a concentration on topics such as anti-bribery, anti-corruption, and combating internal fraud.

Non-financial compliance officers usually have a tougher job because many of the regulations they are required to comply with revolve around *human behaviour*. Trying to figure out if your sales representative has bribed an official is much more difficult than determining if a transaction over US$10,000 should be flagged. With scenarios of this nature, designing RegTech solutions for non-financials is not easy.

Eliminating compliance officers altogether is not going to be possible for a while until artificial intelligence is developed further. Therefore, in the interim, RegTech for non-financials can be viewed more as a *Robocop* offering (human + technology) as opposed to a *Terminator* scenario (technology alone).

Tone from the Top/Ethics

Today, many non-financials try to set the tone from the top and develop a culture of integrity with the belief that ethics is the precursor to compliance. In other words, if you run an ethical shop, the chances of corruption, fraud, or any other form of misconduct befalling your organization should (in principle) be slimmer.

So how do we address this, and do we even need RegTech? The short answer is 'It depends'. With respect to the tone from the top, we need leaders who not only have that distinct level of integrity but possess the knowledge of how to leverage technology to ensure that culture prevails. An example of this is Larry Page from Google. One of our good friends is a former executive at Google and was telling us the story about how he personally put together a deal with one of Google's then-prospective partners. He presented the deal to senior management, and Page's first response was 'Is this fair?' After sifting through the details, they decided to rework the terms of the deal so that they were more favourable for the Google partner and furthermore utilized Google's internal communications tool to re-emphasize Google's motto and corporate code of conduct of 'Don't be evil'.

It can also be addressed with training. There are several RegTech solutions available for non-financials, and the more effective ones focus on user experience and account for the following:

- *Convenience* (training should not have to be done in one place).
- *Engagement level and interaction* (not boring).
- *Leveraging emotions* (best way to learn).

We have first-hand experience in this with a previous start-up, the Governance Risk AML Compliance and Ethics Foundation (GRACE), which was subsequently acquired by RHT Taylor Wessing, a Singaporean law firm. One of the products we developed at GRACE utilized digitally blended learning, which consisted of multiple short, bite-size videos (vs. one long video) with the lectures loaded on an app combined with virtual face-to-face (for discussions). We deliberately hired ex-TV producers to make the videos (no one does a better job at keeping your eyes on a screen) and made sure that each video (which explained a different topic) was of a different genre (with styles ranging from animation to documentary to kung fu fighting to Korean drama!) – that way the knowledge and messages more effectively stay in your head. Australian RegTech Create Training continues this trend with founder Nicole Rose being a former lawyer and compliance officer as well as an animator and psychologist.

Due Diligence/Enhanced Due Diligence

Due diligence is required for multiple reasons, including mergers and acquisitions (M&A), third-party risk assessments, and supply chain management. For example, if you are a cellphone manufacturer and you have outsourced screen production to a third party, you need to ensure that it adheres to your own policies and regulations. This may involve assessment of the third party's financials (is it financially positioned to take on your order?), assessment of its previous activity (has it had issues fulfilling orders for you or any other cellphone manufacturers in the past?), and even assessment of its culture and practices (for example, you do not want to be working with a firm that employs child labour).

Traditionally, solutions are available aplenty on the financial assessment side for public companies (spreadsheets, Bloomberg, and so forth) and even for private companies, as most governments in developed countries have an application programming interface (API) that is essentially a feed that provides company financials. However, in certain jurisdictions, manual retrieval is required, and in some cases there is no central repository, and the financials must be manually retrieved from each province! For the assessments of previous activities, cultures, and practices, a risk consulting firm is typically hired to make that assessment, but that can get expensive. One report on one company can cost as much as US$35,000.

The one RegTech firm that addresses all these issues is Datarama. Datarama can be viewed as the 'Netflix of risk consulting reports' whereby an annual subscription is purchased, and access to reports for *all* the companies (including the financials, which have been manually retrieved in bulk) is granted.

Anti-bribery and Corruption

The two main regulations that (practically) all companies must adhere to are the US Foreign Corrupt Practices Act (FCPA) and the UK Bribery Act.

Merriam-Webster defines a bribe as 'money or favor given or promised in order to influence the judgment or conduct of a person in a position of trust'.

From a RegTech perspective, we can look at this from two angles:

1. *Preventive* (making sure the bribe does not take place).

2. *Reactive* (if a bribe did occur, identifying it and bringing it to the attention of the compliance officer and senior management to act on it).

For *preventive*, other than setting limits on company credit cards, the only form of useful RegTech available today is a policy sign-off system that will ensure employees sign off that they have understood the magnitude of both company and personal liability when it comes to bribery cases. Dynamic governance, risk, and compliance (GRC) is an effective example of such a solution. In addition to this, the RegTech training methodology described in the 'Tone from the Top/Ethics' section can also be applied.

For *reactive*, it becomes an actionable intelligence exercise. Actionable intelligence can be defined as *leveraging big data to have the right information, at the right time, in the right person's hands, to improve business outcomes*. RegTech systems should be able to sift through expense reports, communications, and travel logs to pull up potential bribery activities and bring them to the compliance officer's attention.

Trust and Safety

This is an interesting area and one that we believe will become a focus for the compliance space and currently involves the social media industry.

Tasks include analysing posts, pictures, and videos and screening them for hate speech, illegal actions, and possible terrorist activity. Recent examples of this are murders that have been committed and streamed live via Facebook; online harassment of celebrities; unsuitable postings of a sexual, violent, or discriminatory nature; and online terrorist recruitment videos posted on YouTube.

There are audio, image, and video content analysis solutions that are used to detect facial or object recognition, shape recognition,

and even flame/smoke detection. Commercial RegTech solutions are not yet available, but it is only a matter of time before we see applications of this nature emerge for use outside the social media space. In fact, much of this technology is already being utilized in closed-circuit television (CCTV).

Communications Archival/ Monitoring

This intersects with the financial industry but also applies to corporate entities. The Sarbanes-Oxley Act requires companies to archive three years' worth of official communications and ongoing monitoring. As technology has evolved, so have these official communications channels. What was previously applicable only to email must now encompass short message services (SMSs), WhatsApp, Telegram, Slack, Skype, and so forth. RegTech solutions that address this include Qumrum, KyoLAB, and Finchat.

Insider Trading

With respect to insider trading, the financial industry usually addresses the recipient of the insider information, but corporations need to handle the source. This means not only the monitoring of employee communications (as described in the prior section) but also linking employee relationships to determine if there is a relationship with the source. They also need to be aware that governments may be doing this already. An example of this is that shortly after the insider trading scandals of 2008, the US Department of Justice hired a team of data scientists (before they were even called data scientists!) to match hedge fund managers and analysts with corporate employees via common schools they may have attended at the same time, places where they may have worked together in the past, or even if they were college roommates! The US government was using RegTech before the private sector!

Conclusion

Due to the human nature of non-financial compliance, RegTech solutions are few and far between. This will be an interesting space to watch and seems to be where regulators are shifting focus anyway (much of what has been previously described has already started to hit the financial industry, with JPMorgan and Deutsche Bank both managing anti-bribery cases).

Therefore, it will be only a matter of time before RegTech solutions emerge that can measure human behaviour, and leveraging predictive analytics will take a more preventive approach to addressing much of what we have discussed.

Using RegTech as a Cross-Industry Digitization Tool

By Peter Lancos
Co-Founder and CEO, Exate Technology

and Sonal Rattan
Co-Founder and CTO, Exate Technology

RegTech has traditionally been defined as a subset of FinTech. This is primarily as a result of the abundance of regulation that has been applied to the finance, and specifically the banking, sector. Given the advent of new privacy-based regulations such as the EU General Data Protection Regulation (GDPR), the EU e-Privacy Directive (to become a regulation), and the Privacy Shield in the United States (which is being reviewed by the Trump administration), the scope of RegTech has been expanded to include all industries that process personally identifiable information (PII). Examples of industries that process large quantities of PII include the recruitment Industry, third-party service providers (such as software as a service [SaaS] providers), and the automotive industry. Whereas the financial Industry has extensive experience in dealing with regulatory change (Markets in Financial Instruments Directive [MiFID], Dodd-Frank Act, Volcker Rule, Market Abuse Regulation [MAR], second Markets in Financial Instruments Directive [MiFID II], and so on), other industries have not previously been subject to these requirements. The requirement to digitize in the finance industry in order to deal with regulatory change, customer expectations, and an evolving technology landscape may need to be applied to other industries as they begin their transformational process. This chapter discusses the lessons learned in the finance industry with respect to RegTech, as well as specific use cases whereby this type of technology can be used to provide accelerated cross-industry solutions.

Lessons Learned in the Financial Services Industry

The primary lesson learned in the financial services industry is that the many different regulations have required multiple new data attributes to be created or modified, sometimes in a contradictory manner. As banks digitize, it very quickly becomes apparent that digitization relies on strong management of data, especially personal data. Given that data is the new currency of digitization, it needs to be protected at all times. In many large organizations, the protection of data, including PII, is managed at an application, or system, level. The manner in which data flows internally within an organization, and externally to and from an organization, means that firms are at risk from every system and employee that touches or processes PII. This is often a significant number, and the risks are increased, as the security built into each system is rarely consistent. The only way to protect and manage data is to have it held centrally and securely. Managing access at the data source has the effect of eliminating the dependency on each individual system, person, and end user computing application (such as a spreadsheet or share point that holds the data). RegTech firms have provided solutions to allow this form of data management to occur.

Data Protection Is a Now a Cross-industry Problem

Whereas regulation in the past has primarily impacted only financial institutions (MiFID, Dodd-Frank, Volcker, MAR, MiFID II, and so on), this is now changing with the implementation of the EU GDPR. The GDPR applies to all companies globally, in all sectors, that process the PII of an EU citizen. Much like financial institutions have to identify US Persons under Dodd-Frank, firms will now need to identify and track which clients and employees are EU citizens. PII is defined as anything that can identify an individual, including genetic, mental, cultural, economic, social, or photographic information. The penalty for non-compliance is severe, with fines up to the greater of €20 million or 4% of global turnover, as well as class action lawsuits by people whose data was compromised.

Consequences of Not Protecting Data (and the Benefits of Doing So)

Once again looking at the lessons learned from financial institutions, history has shown that a large number of people will change their bank or insurance company in the event that their personal details are lost or stolen. This is further corroborated by the UK Information Commissioners Office, which produced research indicating that 75% of the adults in the United Kingdom do not trust firms with their PII.[1] These statistics illustrate that the key issue concerning protecting PII is trust. Client trust is essential, and the GDPR is a proactive regulation, driven by this loss of trust in companies by consumers. In a recent speech, Elizabeth Denham – the UK Information Commission Officer – noted that it was her job to re-establish trust, and the GDPR can help with this by giving people a chance to reconsider their data protection approach. A loss of trust can produce irreparable damage to a firm, its brand, and its reputation. Fortunately, the RegTech solutions that were created to help financial services companies deal with their regulation can be leveraged to assist in protecting against this. Utilizing RegTech in order to protect data should be a competitive advantage for companies that make optimal use of it. RegTech should help to retain existing clients and offer opportunities to attract clients of competitors that neglect to invest in these solutions.

___
[1] https://www.sogeti.com/globalassets/global/clickable-images/ our-services/cybersecurity/privacy-and-cybersecurity-in-fs__ dti-research-report.pdf (Figure 9).

Issues Related to Industries Outside of the Financial Services Sector

RegTech data protection solutions developed for the financial services industry typically focus on two key sets of attributes: client data and employee data. It is essential that both be protected. These sets of attributes are not unique to just the financial services industry, as every company has both clients and employees. The following are examples of data privacy issues in other industries and how RegTech solutions can be applied to address them.

The recruitment industry is heavily dependent on client PII, as it is marketing people to firms. If you look at a curriculum vitae (CV), you will have a name, address, phone number, email address, employment history, and salary history. The CV will typically be sent to companies looking to hire the individual, thereby exposing all of that PII to a third party. Additionally, you will have a copy of identification, such as a passport or a driving license. As recruitment firms digitize, all of this data will be stored electronically and will need to be protected from both internal and external actors in order to comply with the GDPR requirements. Similar to the wealth management industry, there is a large amount of internal data theft in the recruitment industry. This is due to the fact that it is a relationship business. When recruiters leave for a new firm or to set up their own firm, they will typically look to take with them their portfolio of candidates and hiring firms.

The SaaS industry has new challenges in a GDPR environment, as the rules have changed. Previously, the owner of the data (called the 'controller') was solely liable for data loss, even if the loss was by a third party to whom they gave the data (called the 'processor'). Under GDPR, both the controller and the processor will be liable in this instance. This will require an enhanced level of security when sharing information outside of an organization, especially when the processor is located in a different country than the controller.

The automotive industry is also unique from a data privacy perspective. Given that 81.4% of buyers finance the purchase of a new car through borrowing, the industry has massive financing subsidiaries. This makes companies within the automotive industry appear to have similar characteristics to financial services providers. One other more intriguing area is a result of cars becoming more digital with the advent of onboard computers. These computers track everything about your journey, including not only engine diagnostics, but also where you went and how fast you drove. When your car is brought in for servicing, the onboard computer data is uploaded to a server within the automotive company. It would be unfortunate if, for example, data indicating that a driver was regularly driving above the speed limit could be accessed by insurance companies as a way of avoiding a payout on a claim.

How RegTech Can Be Applied to Industries Outside of the Financial Services Sector

The same RegTech solutions that were developed for the financial services industry can be used to address the data privacy concerns in the recruitment, SaaS, and automotive industries. It all comes back to protecting your data currency. One solution for this is to apply a three-lines-of-defense model, in line with how the regulators view risk. The first line of defense is to protect data at rest, in line with the GDPR requirements. Acceptable methods of data protection referenced in the GDPR legislation include encryption, tokenization, and pseudo-anonymization. The first line of defense is in essence just good business practice. The second line of defense involves managing who is permitted to view data within a firm. This is the solution for managing data centrally. Each data attribute is

controlled at the source and is wrapped with rules regarding who is permitted to view it. These rules can be at a country level, a firm level, an employee level, or any other level that a firm requires. Managing access to attributes at a central level helps a firm in any industry to implement a proper data strategy. The third line of defense is an immutable audit trail that tracks who was granted access to a data attribute and who was blocked from accessing a sensitive attribute. As part of the third line of defense, your chief information security officer (CISO) or data protection officer (DPO) can generate real-time reports to determine where attempted unauthorized access has occurred.

Looking back at our three examples, it is easy to see how a RegTech solution can protect a firm's data currency across any industry. In the recruitment example, sensitive PII about job applicants can be secured and available to recruiters only, while restricting access to colleagues in the finance or information technology (IT) department. Additionally, a cap (after which there is management sign-off) can be placed on the number of attributes viewed by a recruiter in a day, thereby preventing the recruiter from downloading all job hunters in order to steal the list. CVs can be sent in a secured format with the ability to decrypt them provided only to the relevant people in a hiring firm. In the automotive example, the information related to engine performance can be viewed by the car mechanic, but the sensitive information regarding driving speed and locations visited can be blocked. In the SaaS example, decryption keys for sensitive data can be held within a controller's firewall, and access to sensitive countries, such as Germany, can be blocked. In all of the examples, to the extent that there is an unauthorized attempt to access PII, immediate alerts can be sent to the relevant DPO, thereby greatly reducing risk.

Conclusion

The RegTech industry has been developed to address the multitude of regulatory requirements that have been applied to financial institutions over the past several years. Most, if not all, of these requirements require data to be either protected or reported. As new cross-industry regulations, such as GDPR, are launched, the same technology that financial institutions have been using can be applied to other industries in order to solve similar problems. Using RegTech to solve data protection problems can accomplish two outcomes: (i) client trust can be ensured, and (ii) market share can be increased by attracting the impacted clients of those competitors that neglect their responsibility to properly protect data.

RegTech Unleashed: Discovering the Pathways Beyond Finance

By Sebastian Ko
Co-Founder and Chief Operating Officer, DHB Global

RegTech is defined and analysed extensively in this book as a category of FinTech or in the context of financial services (FS), but this limits our imagination and the potential for innovation. Legal and regulatory issues do not exist in silos. The same facts, for example, surrounding a conflict of interest situation could lead to claims in tort, contract, and equity. Similarly, industry divisions and jurisdictional boundaries cannot confine online data flow. Moreover, contrasting regulatory and compliance approaches adopted in FS and non-FS sectors can provide fertile grounds to cross-pollinate innovation. This requires seeing RegTech broadly.

While considering the lessons provided by FS RegTech solutions, this chapter examines the factors impacting RegTech in (i) its development as a business and product, (ii) its ability to attract investment, and (iii) its potential social impact to attract buy-in from the public and the public sector – and thereby the conditions for unleashing the potential of RegTech.

More than FinTech and Finance

While some RegTech solutions address compliance issues unique to banking, corporate finance, and securities regulations, most commercially available solutions, especially those in the enterprise solutions market, target issues that are also relevant and easily adaptable to non-FS regulations. Numerous RegTech products (e.g. Abide Financial and FundApps) focus on transactional and regulatory reporting because information disclosure is the linchpin of company and tax laws and financial regulations. These laws and regulations have elaborate requirements of record retention, financial reporting, and self-reporting of potential breaches, and authorize regulators to request filings, document productions, inspections, and interviews.

Many regulatory regimes have similar procedures and requirements, including reporting, monitoring, and customer and vendor due diligence.[1] Solutions that digitize and automate compliance with these requirements are low-hanging fruit for translation from one regulatory context into another. MetricStream helps retailers manage product quality and safety as well as health, safety, and environmental compliance by monitoring internal activities and communications with third-party partners. In this vein, educational and advisory support tools in the governance, risk, and compliance (GRC) market are also low-hanging fruit; such tools might cover staff training (e.g. Unicorn Training Group and GRC Solutions) and legal and regulatory analysis (e.g. Ascent and Suade Labs). Highly marketable RegTechs are readily customizable and have many use cases because their implementation requires integration with existing work flows of adopting organizations. So, it makes sense that RegTech is increasingly customizable across regulatory regimes.

Financial crime is another domain demonstrating regulatory and technological convergence. RegTech has been adopted prevalently in sectors such as construction, export/import trade, gaming, logistics, and oil and gas, and to combat financial crimes across multiple channels (e.g. ComplyAdvantage, SAS, Squirro, and Truven Health Analytics). These solutions help monitor sales, payments, and other financial activities in order to flag suspicious activities (e.g. potential bribery, corruption, fraud, theft, money laundering, and tax evasion). Financial crimes, cyber security, and data protection are tightly interrelated in commerce today.[2] Many

---

[1] See S. Ghislandi and M. Kuhn, 'Asymmetric Information in the Regulation of the Access to Markets' (2016) at https://epub.wu.ac.at/4886/1/wp219.pdf

[2] FINRA in the United States, FCA in the United Kingdom, and the SFC in Hong Kong all require licensed persons to take substantial steps to protect customer data.

cyber security and data protection solutions (e.g. CloudCover and Privitar), and even data warehousing, are considered RegTech. The Actiance Platform, for example, helps users in the FS and healthcare sectors to manage data protection and information security compliance. Indeed, cyber security and data privacy laws are highly relevant to RegTech development, as applications often collect and process personally identifiable information and other sensitive information protected by law.

The definitional scope of RegTech seems overbroad and very fuzzy around the edges. Could, for example, computer forensic tools and e-discovery software, which are often applied in regulatory investigations, also be part of RegTech? Perhaps not by current industry views if they are applied to regulatory activities primarily on a project basis. In covering a wide array of subjects, the RegTech market has enormous potential outside the FS sector to reshape regulatory practices with the promise of real-time insights, predictive analytics, and other unprecedented compliance capabilities.[3]

Regulatory Costs Driving Cross-sector Demand

To make RegTech truly flourish, the RegTech community should consider strategically where investments in innovation could yield optimal returns. In 2014, the US National Association of Manufacturers found that, on average, manufacturers spend more than US$19,500 per employee per annum on regulatory costs, while companies in other sectors spend over US$9,900 per employee per annum.[4] In 2017, the US National Small Business

Association found that American small businesses spend more than US$12,000 annually to deal with federal regulations.[5] Many businesses in highly regulated industries struggle to reduce costs while meeting regulatory schedules and other mandatory conditions and reducing risks of errors and liabilities.

We should break down the costs of regulation, including inefficiencies arising therefrom, to determine regulatory areas and practices that would likely create high demands for RegTech. There are two types of costs: (i) compliance costs imposed by the regulatory structure and environment and (ii) remedial costs in cases of enforcement and disputes. Higher spreads are associated with the latter type of contingency risks. Businesses must commit operating expenses and time to meet their licensing conditions, and those subject to fast-developing and complex regulations must budget more for updating know-how and staff training.

Regulatory breaches could lead to administrative and criminal penalties. In some jurisdictions, the quantum of fines is a percentage of profit or revenue or might attract punitive multipliers.[6] Under certain regulations, collateral civil litigation could be brought in parallel to the administrative or enforcement action. Major infractions could result in loss or suspension of license – disrupting business, devastating revenue, and damaging reputation. There are also secondary compliance costs. Businesses would retain accountants, lawyers, and other advisers and sponsors to ensure compliance ex ante and mitigate loss and damage ex post.

---

[3] C. Gust and J. Marquez, 'International Comparisons of Productivity Growth: The Role of Information Technology and Regulatory Practices', *Labour Economics* 11, no. 1 (2004): 33–58.

[4] W.M. Crain and N.V. Crain, 'The Cost of Federal Regulation to the U.S. Economy, Manufacturing and Small Business' (2014) at http://www.nam.org/Data-and-Reports/Cost-of-Federal-Regulations/Federal-Regulation-Full-Study.pdf

---

[5] National Small Business Association, '2017 NSBA Small Business Regulations Survey' (2017) at http://www.nsba.biz/wp-content/uploads/2017/01/Regulatory-Survey-2017.pdf

[6] K. Yeung, 'Quantifying Regulatory Penalties: Australian Competition Law Penalties in Perspective', *Melbourne University Law Review* 23 (1999): 440.

Depending on the business nature, significant multipliers may apply to the costs of regulation. A restaurant, whether large or small, would be subject to multiple licensing regimes, including business and employment registrations, food service establishment permit, liquor license, and other local permits – all with their own specific requirements. An additional layer of complexity exists for multinational corporations (MNCs) that engage in day-to-day cross-border transactions and manage jurisdictional differences in their international compliance programs. A global healthcare provider or insurer might need to track dual compliance with the US Health Insurance Portability and Accountability Act and the EU General Data Protection Regulation in maintaining the same patient records. The calculus of regulatory costs mentioned earlier adds to transactional friction and obviously hits bottom lines.

Big Data Also Drives Demand in Business

Big data trends magnify the costs of business and regulation as a result of the exponential data growth in 'volume, variety, velocity, veracity, and value'.[7] Data from chat, social media, and internet of things (IoT) devices are becoming prevalent in the workplace, and they may be stored across mobile and desktop devices and in the cloud. Any business tomorrow should be a big data business. Digitization and automation of compliance processes enable corporate entities to benefit from an ensemble of advanced technologies (e.g. natural language processing, blockchain encryption, and biometrics authentication). With big data and analytics, keeping one's information technology (IT) house in

order (e.g. enterprise-wide data cleaning) can unlock business intelligence and machine learning capabilities.[8]

RegTech solutions are cost-efficient and scalable because they can be quickly set up and accessible globally. Typically, solutions are delivered as software as a service and take the form of cloud-based databases with low up-front costs and on-demand resourcing. The universe of business data is stored on a platform with a stack of database and work flow management services. Analytics could further serve the platform by facilitating data aggregation and scenario analysis. RegTech can provide abundant data insights and accelerate processes to velocities where near-instant feedback, tightly modelled risk-based approaches, and data-driven forecasting become practicable.

Developments in big data and regulation drive the narratives for RegTech growth. MNCs face challenges of cross-border data transfers and the costs of operating in multiple regulatory frameworks. However, these challenges are also opportunities for arbitrage and scaling efficiencies. MNCs, like Microsoft and Samsung, are examining their information governance and upgrading their systems to address data complexities in their businesses, compliance programs, and legal operations. They realize that, done right, they could leverage technologies not only to save costs and manage risks, but also to develop competitive market strategies.

Co-opting Public Sector for Vibrant Ecosystem

The predominant providers of RegTech are in the private sector; this aspect of RegTech must be disrupted to foster a climate for innovation. Regulators and enforcement agencies are key stakeholders in RegTech. They administer the regulations and

---

[7] A. De Mauro, M. Greco, and M. Grimaldi, 'What Is Big Data? A Consensual Definition and a Review of Key Research Topics', *AIP Conference Proceedings* 1644, no. 97, edited by Georgios Giannakopoulos, Damianos P. Sakas, and Daphne Kyriaki-Manessi (Melville, NY: AIP Publishing, 2015).

---

[8] E.g., Ayasdi offers a predictive analytics software platform driven by machine-learning in the FS and healthcare sectors.

set the intensity and expectations of enforcement. FS regulators in the post-global financial crisis era were often requesting all-encompassing information disclosures from licensed persons. Recently, the intensity of requests has somewhat subsided due to the vast data volumes received and the lack of computing power and human resources to cope with them. One of the key challenges for effective private and public collaboration in technology use has been connectivity and interoperability of the solutions. This challenge could be met if the government could set a common application programming interface (API) exchange and open data standards for public adoption of RegTech.

Regulators should keep up technologically with the private sector. There is an essential case for the administration of justice in adopting RegTech, which could help regulators optimize the time allotted to each case and reduce public spending. MeWe CoInspect provides a mobile app-based platform for restaurants, food trucks, and other licensed operators to conduct self-inspections and share the hygiene and safety data to relevant municipal authorities in the United States. The authorities' app client to the platform helps them aggregate inspection data for each licensed operator and conduct spot checks, which demonstrably saves government resources. Government authorities applying technologies to their regulatory agenda could enable innovative supervisory and enforcement measures.

RegTech: The Next Generation

Strong demand for RegTech is expected amongst highly regulated industries and by stakeholders in these industries with significant data needs. Existing FS RegTech provides useful lessons for predicting the developmental pathways of RegTech in non-FS sectors.[9] A comparative law understanding of FS and non-FS

regulations and their market impact would provide valuable insights to stakeholders. RegTech will thrive in a particular sector after it is properly aligned in function, purpose, and value with the underlying regulations. Beyond FS, major adopters of RegTech in the near term should be healthcare, pharmaceutical, and technology MNCs.

In the future, RegTech should transform regulation and compliance in substantial ways. RegTech solutions are more than efficiency and risk management. They will be enablers of emerging forms of regulation. Market-based regulation, such as carbon cap-and-trade, often fails because the pricing mechanism is inefficient. Pricing efficiency could be achieved with better solutions integrating IoT-enabled sensors and advanced data analytics for real-time feedback. These will develop upon existing products that track carbon emissions and footprints (e.g. Carbon Trust Footprint Expert and IHS Energy and Carbon Solution).

RegTech will be critical when society entrusts more autonomous machines (physical and virtual) to make decisions vital to human beings (e.g. self-driving cars). The governing systems of these autonomous machines are RegTech, which might themselves be part of state-sanctioned but privately controlled regulatory networks. At that stage, we can expect deep embedding of regulation into computer codes (broadening the application of the 'code is law' concept of smart contracts). RegTech would directly affect performance and minimize the need for human intervention.[10]

Conclusion

RegTech has enormous potential to reduce regulatory burdens for businesses and government agencies. FS RegTech is already thriving and has shown fast growth in innovation and adoption.

---

[9] D.M. Katz, 'Quantitative Legal Prediction – or – How I Learned to Stop Worrying and Start Preparing for the Data-Driven Future of the Legal Services Industry', *Emory Law Journal* 62 (2012): 909.

---

[10] A related issue here is developing RegTech with robust ethical frameworks, albeit this is beyond the scope of this chapter.

Non-FS and cross-sector/industry solutions exist commercially and have similar functionalities to FS RegTech. This is not surprising, as FS and non-FS regulations share comparable procedural requirements, and the same data trends have an impact across virtually all industries. While conceptually separate in law, these requirements can be addressed holistically as part of the same software design problem – to integrate data (created in various operational contexts during the course of business) and work flow to meet a wide range of legal and compliance objectives.

There is a clear and simple economic case to increase adoption of non-FS RegTech. However, without active promotion, innovation will languish. The success of FS RegTech should be leveraged to enhance RegTech broadly in terms of development, investment, impact, and public adoption. RegTech should therefore be rebranded, reconceptualized, and reimagined ambitiously to break out new paths of development.

RegTech Outside Finance: Four Options, One Clear Choice

By Chionh Chye Kit
CEO and Co-Founder, Cynopsis Solutions Pte. Ltd.

Wait a minute. Isn't RegTech only meant to help banks comply with ever-increasing regulations?

After all, banks are the ones with the most regulatory problems. They have the financial muscles to pick and choose from a variety of solutions – FinTech, RegTech, InsurTech, LegalTech, and so on. Who else needs RegTech?

This chapter discusses RegTech applicability outside of the financial services industry in respect of a specific regulation that has gained global attention of late.

In an abysmal web of anti–money laundering (AML) and counter-terrorism financing (CTF) requirements prescribed by the Financial Action Task Force (FATF), more commonly known as the FATF 40 Recommendations,[1] there are at least three recommendations that affect non-financial sector participants too. This sector is known as Designated Non-Financial Businesses and Professions (DNFBPs).

Who are DNFBPs?

Succinctly, these include casinos, real estate agents, lawyers, accountants, corporate service providers, precious metal and stone dealers, and trusts. It is a fairly large and diverse group.

I am sure your minds will wander to the glitzy casino scenes in Las Vegas and Macau where high rollers wager their bets at the tables, and then move quickly to well-suited real estate agents trying to sell high-end properties, and to lawyers and corporate service or trust providers structuring and incorporating legal vehicles on behalf of their ultra-high-net-worth clients – or even shady back-alley transactions in diamonds and other jewellery.

That is exactly what we are talking about. It is not just in the movies. Money laundering typically involves a large and complex web of providers in the middle as intermediaries before actual money gets moved.

In other words, money laundering does not occur just in the banks. Crooks have become more sophisticated and have now gained access to a variety of services that will help disguise, conceal, and transfer their ill-gotten gains into numerous forms.

FATF Recommendations

The point here is that standard AML requirements of performing customer due diligence, taking a risk-based approach, screening, and so on with which the financial services industry is very familiar have now dawned upon DNFBPs in all 36 FATF member jurisdictions and 2 regional organizations. In fact, more than 190 jurisdictions globally have committed to adopt and implement FATF Recommendations.

FATF carries out periodic mutual evaluation reports (MERs) on its members' compliance and effective implementation of the 40 Recommendations. A quick review of the various MERs published on the FATF website[2] suggests that a large proportion of its members are achieving rather poor outcomes in respect of the recommendations applicable to DNFBPs.

---

[1] http://www.fatf-gafi.org/publications/fatfrecommendations/?hf=10&b=0&s=desc(fatf_releasedate)

[2] http://www.fatf-gafi.org/publications/mutualevaluations/?hf=10&b=0&s=desc(fatf_releasedate)

This could be a result of regulators and government agencies in the member countries not legislating or enforcing the requirements as much as they should have or that DNFBPs are clueless how to comply, or a combination of both.

Four Available Options

In the 1900s, Professor Walter Bradford Cannon expounded the fight-or-flight response in human and animal reaction when faced with a perceived harmful event, danger, or even threat of survival. Some may call it natural reflexes or survival instinct.

I would like to take the concept of fight-or-flight response and extend that to the situation currently experienced by DNFBPs coming face-to-face with new regulatory requirements on AML/CTF.

Whatever the case may be, like their counterparts in the financial services industry, DNFBPs have four options, as shown in Figure 1, when faced with this new and Herculean task to ensure AML compliance. There is only one sensible choice.

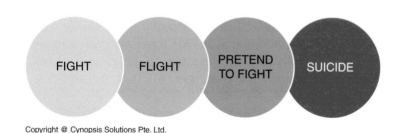

Copyright @ Cynopsis Solutions Pte. Ltd.

Figure 1: Four options

Fight

This is what most people would like to do. However, the choice of tools and weapons will make a huge difference whether the fight is futile or worthwhile. This is where RegTech applicability comes in. Unlike the banks with much deeper financial pockets, DNFBPs

may not be able to purchase expensive systems or afford to throw bodies at the problem.

That is why DNFBPs have to think outside the box in order to solve the compliance issue without going through the unnecessary and painful processes that banks have been going through all this while. There is an opportunity to leapfrog and stay ahead of the regulatory curve without always trailing behind passively.

Flight

With increased compliance costs, some may choose to get out of certain business given it is no longer lucrative if they need to put in place costly compliance solutions that may not even work in the first place. In the financial services sector, this is more commonly known as 'de-risking'[3] where large global banks are cutting off certain markets, sectors, and customers in order to manage their ever-increasing regulatory risk of non-compliance.

In the DNFBPs space, if de-risking were to occur too, it will likely have an unintended consequence of driving activities underground, which will make it even more difficult for regulators and law enforcers to detect potential wrongdoings. That will have undesirable knock-on effects on the global fight against money laundering and terrorism financing.

Pretend to Fight

There is always an option to try to cover the minimum and surface level only and to pray for the best. This is akin to putting up a good front without substance underneath. Where internal control is concerned, you just cannot pull a fast one, because

---

[3] http://www.worldbank.org/en/topic/financialmarketintegrity/brief/de-risking-in-the-financial-sector

cracks and gaps will show very easily when the system is put to the test. Although it may somewhat get you over the line to some extent now (if the regulators are not paying attention), in the long run the ineffectiveness will certainly come back to haunt you. I call this penny wise, pound foolish.

Suicide

A risky approach is to simply not do anything, take the chance, and await sanction, if any; hence this can be suicidal. Whether anyone in the DNFBPs sector will adopt this approach depends a lot on the extent of enforcement efforts that the local regulators take. If you know that your regulators are not going to check, and your peers are not doing anything, then perhaps this is not an entirely bad option to consider in the short term.

However, you run the risk that one fine day the regulatory approach changes and you fail to react in time or you are the first one to be hauled up for non-compliance. That is when you wish you had not taken this option right at the beginning.

The Option to Fight

As with all battles, you need to equip yourself with the right mentality, strategy, resources, and tools in order to win.

Acknowledging that compliance is not optional is the first step towards ensuring compliance with regulatory requirements, be it in AML/CTF or other areas. It is smarter to deal with the issue correctly right at the start, which will save you much time and effort to remediate in the future.

Figure 2 summarizes vital AML/CTF regulatory requirements for both financial and non-financial sectors globally. I call it the four pillars of AML/CTF. The holy grail of RegTech applicability lies in the ability to automate and digitize the first three pillars – risk-based approach, record keeping, and screening.

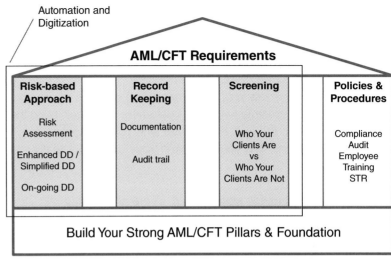

Figure 2: Four pillars of AML/CTF

There Are So Many Solutions Out There

True enough, there are indeed quite a few RegTech solutions in the market at the moment, with more to come given the amount of money banks are dumping into AML/CTF efforts since the financial crisis in 2008.

Apart from casinos, which are often flush with cash, there is a very long tail in each segment of DNFBPs where the small to medium-size enterprises are constrained by the lack of (i) resources, (ii) access to regulatory expertise, and (iii) knowledge of technology.

Think about the sole proprietor accountant, lawyer, and real estate agent. They do not have the financial strength and technological know-how to automate and digitize AML/CTF processes. Given a limited budget, DNFBPs need something that can tick more boxes for them.

For example, under the screening pillar, it is typical for banks and even DNFBPs to merely subscribe to commercial screening databases that cover politically exposed persons, sanctions, and negative news. However, that only gets one part of the pillar covered – telling you who your customers are not. There is the other aspect of the know your customer (KYC) process where you need to find out and verify who your customers really are. Note the difference between the two. If you know who your customers are not, it does not mean that you know who your customers really are, and vice versa.

RegTech comes in at this point to help. There are identity verification and authentication tools available in the market to make non-face-to-face onboarding of customers a breeze subject to regulatory approvals.

Taking another example, this time in the risk-based approach pillar. The ability to automate and digitize risk assessment and risk bucketing of customers is something that exists in large banks that are willing to spend millions of dollars to build the system on their own or to outsource to a large IT vendor. However, with RegTech, where deployment is often done in the cloud, the cost is tremendously reduced without taking away effectiveness. This is undoubtedly what DNFBPs need.

The record-keeping pillar is an interesting one. I believe a significant proportion of DNFBPs globally are still operating in a manual and analogue manner in terms of keeping documentation, an audit trail, and evidence of work done. This is something that was done in the previous century but still continues to be done in the same manner. I view record keeping as a constant evolution process that can be summarized in Figure 3.

Analogue > Digital > Token

Copyright @ Cynopsis Solutions Pte. Ltd.

Figure 3: Constant evolution process

As said, many DNFBPs are operating in an analogue environment. This means there are a lot of hard-copy papers and files. Most forms are handwritten and physically signed and dated.

Besides automating processes, RegTech should digitize records. In its simplest form, the ability to centrally store records in various formats in the cloud where they are easily retrievable puts DNFBPs in a much better position in respect of AML/CTF compliance.

The next stage of evolution on record keeping could be tokenization involving hashing, encrypting, and decrypting records to be shared securely and widely with people who need to know. This could even be in a blockchain or a distributed ledger technology that is being discussed in other chapters.

Control of information need not always be centralized. Where decentralization leads to better management of records, improves efficiency, and enables flexibility, DNFBPs should seriously consider the option.

The last pillar of policies and procedures is unfortunately not able to benefit from RegTech at the moment, although it can be argued that training is one potential opportunity. The need to write your policy, implement compliance and audit arrangements, and have procedures to report suspicious transactions still relies on human judgement and discretion.

Conclusion

What does this mean for DNFBPs struggling with new AML/CTF requirements?

Do not fret, because there are solutions out there that are cost-effective, flexible, and scalable. RegTech enables DNFBPs to leapfrog their positive compliance outcomes without the need to go through the pain that incumbents in the financial services sector have gone through over the past 20 years. Unlike the banks where they are stuck with numerous legacy systems that cannot be easily replaced, small to medium-size DNFBPs are light on technology and can genuinely reap the benefits of cloud computing offered by RegTech solutions.

In the current environment, after more than 20 years of efforts by FATF in addressing money laundering and terrorism financing issues around the world, we continue to see new criminal trends evolving every day.

The fight against money laundering and terrorist financing is not just about catching the next prominent politician stashing millions or billions away in personal bank accounts or evading taxes. It is more about the underlying victims suffering from many other heinous crimes and the ability for such criminals to abuse the financial and non-financial systems to achieve their goals.

Everyone has a part to play, however small it may be, as you never know if the next KYC question you ask a prospective customer may well indirectly save an abandoned child from a global human trafficking syndicate.

RegTech: A Safe Bet for Tackling AML and Fraud in the Gambling Sector

By Jay Patani
Business Insights Lead, CompareAsiaGroup and former Technical Evangelist, ITRS Group

Compliance rarely evokes passion or enthusiasm in companies. It is seen more often as a necessary burden than an opportunity, an extra cost rather than a future revenue generator. However, a new breed of companies is changing this image. Welcome to the world of RegTech.

RegTech is a moniker that has been doing the rounds in recent years. Although there has long been technology that tackles regulatory challenges, the RegTech phenomenon signals a leap in applying bleeding-edge technologies to the issues of regulation. While the status quo so far among banks has been to begrudgingly cope with (and occasionally breach) regulatory requirements, RegTech brings financial institutions one step closer to automation. It is proactive instead of reactive; predictive (or prescriptive) instead of descriptive.

Since the 2008 financial crisis, regulators have worked tirelessly to write new legislation that curbs risky activity among market participants. The precrisis laissez-faire attitude has given way to greater scrutiny and an ever-growing complex web of rules that vary across different jurisdictions. Meanwhile, in the big data world, academics and practitioners have made significant strides towards developing and applying the latest big data techniques in industry.

The confluence of these two phenomena has led to the emergence of RegTech. In the face of the regulatory changes of recent years, technology companies have been quick to respond and have designed flexible and scalable systems to help banks manage data across an organization to meet new compliance standards.

However, RegTech tools go beyond this. It is no longer a case of blithely managing and reporting data to regulators. Both banks and regulators want to extract meaningful insight from data and have a deeper understanding of what is happening in real time, where the risks lie, and how to fix them.

However, although today RegTech is inextricably linked with the financial world (and is commonly classed as a subset of FinTech), its underlying principles have much to offer in other industries. While RegTech's bigger brother FinTech concerns itself with new technologies applied to the financial sector, RegTech should adopt a more horizontal approach. Regulation exists in most industries, and therefore existing RegTech principles and technologies can be coupled with domain knowledge to create innovative regulatory solutions in different contexts.

The RegTech Technology Toolbox

It is first worth identifying the six critical big data technologies underpinning RegTech:

1. *Data integration*. Regulatory data comes in different shapes and sizes. RegTech solutions need to offer a way to ingest data from multiple data sources and data types. This data could include granular user or customer behaviour, content from emails, transactional data, and customer relationship management (CRM) information.

2. *Big data storage*. Traditional relational databases no longer suffice to store the vast amounts of regulatory data coming in at breakneck speeds. More flexible NoSQL-type databases provide more scalable storage, which can scale in and out based on demand.

3. *Artificial intelligence*. Artificial intelligence (AI) is powered by machine learning algorithms, which 'learn' from relationships within data to provide powerful predictive or pattern-finding capabilities. This allows organizations to proactively identify risk before it escalates.

4. *Streaming analytics*. Managing risk is a time-sensitive business. Streaming analytics technologies are capable of processing millions of events per second, thereby allowing companies to extract insights as complex multidimensional events unfold and not before it is too late.

5. *Cloud*. RegTech solutions are increasingly offering cloud solutions so that data is remotely stored and maintained. This often provides cost savings, greater scalability, and less maintenance.

6. *Domain knowledge*. RegTech software providers need to offer a firm understanding of the specific regulations in the sector in order to develop relevant product features to meet compliance obligations.

RegTech in a Gambling Context

A fruitful application of RegTech outside of financial services is in the gambling sector. Both industries share many of the same compliance challenges such as combating fraud and establishing robust anti–money laundering (AML) or know your customer (KYC) procedures, and are subject to expanding regulation. For example, in Europe, the introduction of the fourth Money Laundering Directive (4MLD) in 2015 places a greater onus on gambling operators to enforce AML procedures. It will now cover the entire gambling sector while previously it applied only to casinos. Among other requirements, the 4MLD states that gambling providers must carry out due diligence on transactions valued at more than €2,000.

In order to carry out more nuanced due diligence on customers and transactions, RegTech helps gambling companies evolve from a strictly rules-based approach to a machine-learning-aided approach to compliance. The rules-based approach involves hard-coding rules that describe what money laundering looks like. For example, the system would flag cash bets over a specific currency amount and block transactions from certain individuals, amongst many other predetermined rules.

The use of these types of systems is widespread, but they are manually intensive and require employees to thoroughly review the transactions that are flagged to filter out the false positives. In addition, a rules-based approach to AML will be unable to adapt to changes in criminal behaviour without recognizing and manually updating the rules. This is problematic because not only is it difficult to even recognize what fraud looks like in a static context, but illegal tactics also continuously change over time.

Machine learning algorithms can partially automate this process by inferring relationships and patterns from a vast body of historical records. As data grows, the possible unique combinations of variables expand, and machines can more subtly understand relationships and dynamically spot abnormal behaviour.

Supervised Learning Techniques

In a fraud detection use case, a classification model can be designed by training algorithms to learn from past incidents of fraudulent transactions. These are categorized as 'supervised learning' algorithms, as the historical cases are clearly labelled as fraudulent transactions or nonfraudulent transactions. The algorithms learn the mapping or relationship between the input features (e.g. customer demographics and transaction behaviour) and the output labels (whether the transaction was fraudulent). Since there are significant repositories of available fraud data, it is possible to train these supervised technologies to have a relatively high level of accuracy in predicting which combinations of input features lead to fraud.

However, money laundering poses a more difficult challenge as there is little labelled data from which to learn. While there is a diverse set of data regarding players and their behaviour, there are just too few recorded cases of money laundering in the gambling sector. Therefore, supervised learning techniques applied to AML are often ineffective.

Unsupervised Learning Techniques

In the next five years, more gambling companies will start to use 'unsupervised learning' techniques, which are able to learn patterns and relationships from unlabelled data (i.e. where no data on past instances of money laundering exists). In the context of classification algorithms for identifying money laundering, the aim is to segment the unlabelled data on players into different clusters. These clusters exhibit distinct risk profiles. The bettors or betting actions that do not fit into any cluster should be deemed anomalous. These cases should be flagged as suspicious and require further research or action (see Figure 1 for a simple unsupervised clustering example with two features).

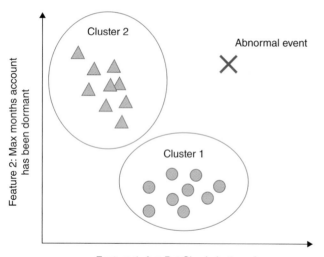

Figure 1: Clustering algorithms to identify abnormal behaviour (e.g. money laundering or fraud)

360° View of Bettors

The unsupervised learning algorithms for identifying anomalies are most successful when a big data platform ingests data from multiple different sources. Designing a system that can process different data types is essential in building a 360° profile of a player. Essential features to monitor include the inflow and outflow of funds in a bettor's account, speed and volume of betting activity, links between different accounts, use of multiple accounts and account types, reactivation of dormant betting accounts, and a player's demographic data along with his or her social media activity.

Improving Efficiency by Centralizing Data for Compliance Teams

In order to achieve a 360° view, RegTech companies should focus on enabling data harmonization in companies. The lack of foresight that banks suffered before the financial crisis was in part due to silos, where every division had separate data storage and processes that were mutually incompatible. RegTech companies must be able to ingest and securely store different data types coming from different parts of a financial institution.

Banks usually have access to massive data sets of public and proprietary information, including criminal records and property records, along with information from internal databases. The gambling industry similarly amasses lots of data from radio frequency identification (RFID) monitoring of chips, detailed records of historical bets, facial recognition, and CRM systems. By unifying all these data collection processes and making the results available to investigation teams, compliance will become a more efficient process.

Assembling Everything in a Real-time Architecture

So far, we have focused on addressing the volume and variety of data in a gambling enterprise. Building a big data platform to take account of these two factors is a challenge in itself for any big data architect. However, the ideal system should also consider the velocity of data. Gambling is a fast-paced industry. Moreover, identifying money laundering or fraud yields maximum value when compliance teams anticipate and prevent instead of recognizing what has occurred after the damage has already been done.

Adopting a real-time processing architecture ensures that anomalous patterns can be spotted and acted upon in real time. With streaming algorithms, bettors' risk profiles and clusters can also be updated in real time as new behavioural activity data comes in. Gambling companies can also set automated triggers to respond to suspicious activities.

In addition, bettors can be checked in near real time against a comprehensive set of global watch lists from all the relevant sanctioning and law enforcement agencies. It may also be useful to find mentions of a gambling company's customers in ancillary streams of data such as news or social media activity.

Machine Learning's Black Box Problem

As RegTech charges towards automation, we need to carefully look at the machine algorithms behind these offerings. Although learning algorithms sometimes appear to have almost magical predictive properties, they will need to be transparent in the future so their decisions can be challenged. RegTech companies need to provide audit trails or rationales to help gambling companies understand how the algorithms reach their conclusions on why a player is fraudulent, cheating, or involved in money laundering.

Spurred on by the rapid technological development in the use of data, the European Union has overhauled its data security policy. In December 2015, the European Commission announced that the new European General Data Protection Regulation (GDPR) would replace the current Data Protection Directive in May 2018.

Though nonbinding, a section in the GDPR gives a taste of things to watch out for in the future of data policy: 'The data subject should have the right not to be subject to a decision evaluating personal aspects relating to him or her which is based solely on automated processing and which produces adverse legal effects concerning, or significantly affects, him or her.' In a compliance context, this may mean that algorithms cannot be solely responsible for making important decisions such as automatically rejecting a user creating an account or placing a bet. Therefore, while AI-driven RegTech solutions hold much promise, gambling companies need to establish supervision and prevent algorithms from operating as opaque black boxes.

The Positive RegTech Externality

While RegTech is primarily targeted at compliance teams, its benefits can be wide-reaching. In economics, a positive externality is when one party's activity has an unintended beneficial effect on another party, who did not incur the cost of the action. Executives should see return on investment (ROI) in RegTech in a similar way, and the big data projects are likely to have positive spillovers to other areas of a company. Through collecting, analysing, and storing various data to 'know your customer', both gambling and financial institutions can not only meet compliance service-level agreements (SLAs) but also have the opportunity of translating the data into revenue for other sides of the business.

Gambling companies have many questions unanswered due to insufficient analytics capabilities. For example, what is a particular customer most likely to bet on? How can the customer be encouraged to place a bet? Which is the most profitable segment of the customer base?

Therefore, RegTech projects should be seized as an opportunity to re-envision a gambling company's data architecture: to not only address regulatory issues but to answer fundamental questions that will impact the company's bottom line.

Social Impact and Regulation

10

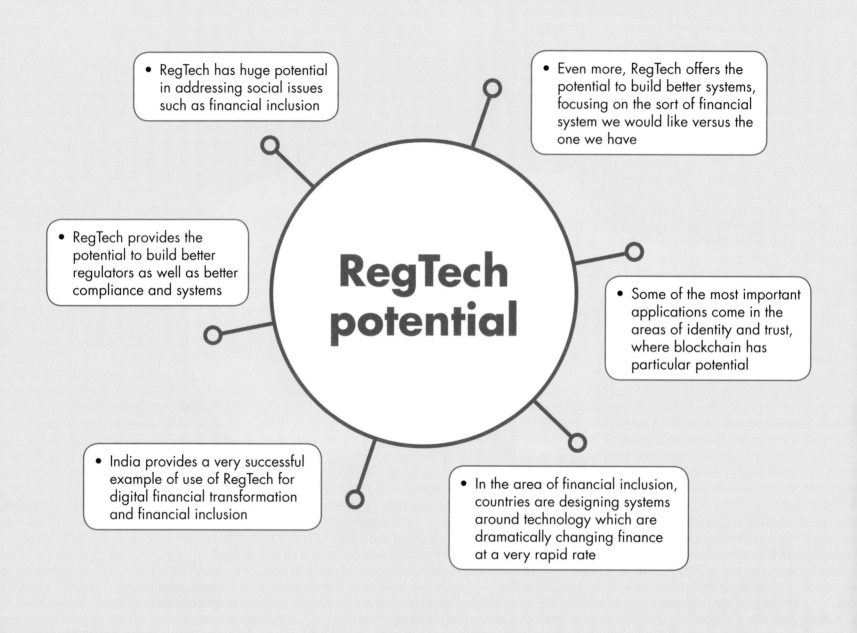

The human cost of the 2008 financial crisis has been dramatic, both in the immediate aftermath with a direct increase in unemployment as well as value destruction of middle-class savings. Even a decade later slower economic growth has led to the under-employment of millions among the younger generation, fueling political dissatisfaction and international disagreements. The authors that have contributed to this part have provided examples of how RegTech can be a force for good.

While the creation of FinTech solutions has primarily been a reaction to the crisis to avert certain symptoms (e.g. reduction in credit supply spurred the growth of P2P lending and mistrust in banks facilitated the arrival of challenger banks) the question remains: what role can RegTech play?

From the contents of this book, it appears that RegTech solutions form part of a broader reform that is occurring across finance. While the short-term impact of the RegTech industry will be about driving down operating costs of compliance, in the long run we can expect a brand new regulatory architecture stack allowing for real-time supervision and compliance.

The opportunities of cost decreases and new paradigm shifts hold significant potential for financial inclusion. Indeed, when we look at some of the reasons for financial exclusion, which impacts 1.7 billion people, we find that the origins can be traced back to regulatory obligations that do not fit market reality (e.g. requiring formal ID documents when a segment of the population does not have any); financial institutions which are afraid to operate in high risk markets (e.g. UK to Somalia remittance corridor); to questions of viability to maintain accounts of poor customers.

However, the last decade has provided a formidable illustration of the opportunities that can be created when regulators, banks, start-ups and governments work together. The development of M-Pesa in Africa has been made possible by a regulatory exemption that pre-dated the concept of the sandbox, the development of Adhaar as a new form of Identification is solving the KYC process in rural areas, and the decreasing operating cost of onboarding new customers goes one step closer towards affordability in maintaining small value accounts.

Understandably, financial inclusion discussions have been taking place for years and so the narrative can lose its strength. Yet we should be reminded of how India created a new digital identity for billions of people and China included hundreds of millions into a new financial eco-system provided by tech companies. As a result, the level of financial inclusion is gradually increasing and will continue to do so as RegTech solutions keep arriving to market: from 2010 to 2017, over 1.3 billion people gained access to an account for the first time.

But we should not be complacent: the refugee situation is not improving, with over 70 million displaced persons in the world. These represent a tremendous opportunity for RegTech start-ups and founders to do good because this market if addressed has significant opportunities and social impact potential.

The FinTech Ecosystem Between Legal Compliance and Social Dimension

By Francesca Gaudino
Local Partner, Baker & McKenzie

EU Commission President Jean-Claude Juncker recently stated that:

> Digital technologies are going into every aspect of life. ... We need to be connected, our economy needs it, people need it.[1]

This statement well depicts the fact that digital technologies are meant to play a key role in our lives. Technology and innovation are essential business factors; this is not a new concept. What is brought about by the digital revolution is that our world, our personal lives, and the global economy are 'going digital', meaning that the focus is on the fact that digital technology is the driver and at the same time it is the cornerstone in terms of our personal lives and the global economy.

In 2015 the European Commission launched the Digital Single Market strategy,[2] which is composed of the following three main pillars: (i) better access for consumers and businesses to digital goods and services across Europe, (ii) creating the right conditions and a level playing field for digital networks and innovative services to flourish, and (iii) maximizing the growth potential of the digital economy. Among others, implementation of the Digital Single Market will foster economic growth and boost the competitiveness of the European continent in the global dimension. A crucial part of this initiative is the setting up of a clear, firm, and modern legislative framework to take care of the protection of personal data. The new legislative framework has been shaped taking into account the digital ecosystem so that many issues posed by the use of new technologies such as analytics, big data, the internet of things (IoT), and so on are captured.

The massive impact of digital technologies has made its path also towards the banking industry, giving birth to the so-named FinTech phenomenon. In fact, even banks and financial institutions, which traditionally have been more reluctant to embrace technology-based solutions, are now finding themselves in a position to be somehow forced to enter the digital ecosystem. It should be highlighted that moving within this ecosystem fosters higher efficiency of internal business organizations, which is also usually associated with the delivery of higher-quality products and services to the market. In addition, digital technologies are also the primary enablers of the bilateral, continuous, often virtual conversation that is the pillar of any customer relationship management (CRM).

These considerations lead to the conclusion that digital technologies are no more a question of whether a financial institution will go digital; it remains only a question of how the institution can make the best of it while staying compliant when this happens.

There are different possible scenarios for FinTech companies to make use of substantial data sets in order to improve their product or service offerings and their internal organization management.[3]

---

[1] EU Commission President Jean-Claude Juncker in his State of the European Union speech addressed to the European Parliament, 14 September 2016.

[2] The Digital Single Market strategy was adopted on 6 May 2015 – refer to the European Commission's website for more details: https://ec.europa.eu/digital-single-market/en/digital-single-market

[3] For example, 'FinTech – The Digital Evolution in the Financial Sector', Deutsche Bank Research, 11 November 2014. Part 1 is available online at https://www.dbresearch.com/PROD/DBR_INTERNET_EN-PROD/PROD0000000000345837.pdf

An innovative and technically driven use of data fosters efficiency and cost saving, and it is a path that the banking and financial industry is somehow forced to take in order to remain competitive in the market.

This FinTech revolution, among others, is also about a different approach to personal information. We observe not only a material increase in the amount of data collected but also a different way of using and processing the data. This combination of a new approach to personal information and new possibilities made available by technological innovation, combined with the need of FinTech companies to embrace innovation somehow in order to maintain competitiveness in the market, raises a number of concerns regarding the right to privacy and data protection of individuals.

In this direction, in April 2016 the European Commission issued the General Data Protection Regulation (GDPR),[4] to take effect in May 2018, setting forth the boundaries within which companies may collect, process, use, and share personal information of individuals. Regarding compliance, the path for FinTech companies is a hard one. However, we observe that there are also other considerations that should be taken into account in digital initiatives. Indeed, digital initiatives are mostly about the collection, analysis, use, and sharing of personal information of individuals, which results in deep encroaching into individuals' lives and in depicting clear profiles of individuals. In addition, decisions that may have a material impact on individuals' lives are taken based on the individuals' profiles and their automated evaluations.[5]

However, being compliant with legislative and security standards may be regarded as the starting point, or better as the minimum compliance level for FinTech companies. The reality is that the digital ecosystem offers a number of possibilities to exploit personal information, so that it may happen that a certain processing activity may be carried out adopting the specific rules set forth by the law, but the result of the processing may have an impact from other perspectives, notably from a social, historical, or ethical perspective.[6]

In general, we observe the increasing attention of companies to the ethical dimension of their business operations. Indeed, many companies are involved in projects relating to the protection and fair treatment of workers, sustainability, environment, and so forth. These initiatives are usually taken on a voluntary basis and are driven by key individuals within the company. They also have a material impact on the reputation of the company, as they foster the creation of advocates among customers.

When it comes to the way in which FinTech companies may collect and use personal information of customers and prospects, it is clear that they will have to come to grips with something more than mere provisions deriving from the GDPR, as well as security- and sector-specific laws and regulations.

The core of the matter is that new technologies allow penetrating (in some cases) intrusively into individuals' lives and that the potential use of personal data (so-named 'secondary use') is

---

[4] Regulation (EU) 2016/679 of the European Parliament and of the Council of 27 April 2016 on the protection of natural persons with regard to the processing of personal data and on the free movement of such data, and repealing Directive 95/46/EC – http://ec.europa.eu/justice/data-protection/reform/index_en.htm

[5] As an example, we may mention credit scoring, credit liability, and hiring processes, among others.

[6] For reference, see 'Data Protection Law and the Use of Analytics' by Paul Schwartz, Professor of Law, Berkeley Law School, University of California; https://www.law.berkeley.edu/files/bclt_Schwartz_Data_Protection_Law_and_the_Ethical_Use_of_Analytics.pdf; and also see 'Big Data Ethics' by Neil M. Richards, Professor of Law, Washington University, and Jonathan H. King, LLM Graduate in Intellectual Property and Technology Law, Washington University, and Vice President of Cloud Strategy and Business Development for CenturyLink Technology Solutions; https://pdfs.semanticscholar.org/84f7/8d5dd2772aabf006576201bf0a7e09f6f31b.pdf

often unknown and not considered when data are first collected. For example, personal data collected to provide an individual with a certain financial service may then be associated with other information, gathered also from public or external sources, and may be used to build a very specific individual's profile, evaluated when the individual asks for other services or products. This profile may also be shared with third parties for different purposes – for example with prospective employers in the course of the hiring process, with other companies for marketing purposes, and so on.

In addition, this fluent environment makes it possible that a certain data processing, meant to make use of a defined set of data, leads to production of a new set of data that may cause data protection and/or ethics concerns, for example because it contains data of a sensitive nature (such as data relating to racial or ethnic origin; to religious, philosophical, or other beliefs; to the health status or sex life of individuals) or data relating to children.

It should also be taken into consideration that it may happen that a set of data that as such does not relate to an identifiable individual, and thus is not subject to data protection laws, by association with other information or through profiling and aggregation operations may lead to single out and thus to identify an individual, which would then trigger application of data protection laws.

The question why compliance with the law would not be enough for FinTech stakeholders is that the personal sphere of individuals raises concerns not only from a legal perspective (data protection laws) but also from an ethical, human, and social perspective. Considering that the reputation of a company represents much of its goodwill, especially regarding the trust of its customers, of its commercial partners, and of its market of reference, as well as of public authorities and governmental agencies, it is crucial for stakeholders to establish and maintain this trust. Operating in an ethical manner is an effective tool to achieve this goal.

This is true especially in light of the requirements of the GDPR, which obliges companies to notify (in certain cases) the privacy authorities and the individuals affected by the data breach. It is self-explanatory that if a company reveals the fact that its information technology (IT) systems have been breached, customers will be reluctant to continue using affected online services and may fear that further threats may occur to their financial and economic information.

We have said that attention to the ethical and social sphere is a sort of extra mile that FinTech companies are asked to go through. The issue is what FinTech companies may do in this direction.

If rules are not in the law, an alternative possible source of regulation may be found in self-regulation involving more specific mechanisms such as codes of conduct. They are based on voluntary adhesion, and usually they are set up and issued at the industry/business sector level. The great advantage of codes of conduct is that they are issued by the stakeholders themselves or associations representing them. Thus they are (i) well accepted in general; (ii) already transposed in the specific market or industry sector, so specificities and factual aspects of the same are already taken care of; and (iii) written in a language that can be easily understood by the addressees.

Codes of conduct, together with certification, are given an enhanced role under the GDPR.[7] Leaving aside their role as an element to prove compliance with the GDPR, to rule the relationship between the data controller and data processors, and also to transfer data to third parties, one of their main goals is to serve as facilitators to understand the GDPR rules and how to comply with them. Similarly, specific codes of conduct drafted to address ethical and social aspects may also play an important role in raising awareness among stakeholders. The use of codes of conduct to rule in specific areas is something known in the banking and financial sectors. Thus FinTech companies should already be well acquainted with them.

---

[7] See artt. 40 and 41 of the GDPR for codes of conduct; artt. 42 and 43 of the GDPR for certifications.

As to the content of these codes of conduct, first of all, there should be a procedure in place to consider ethical and social impacts before starting new processing activities and also in relation to already existing data processing operations. For this purpose the privacy by design approach envisaged under the GDPR in relation to compliance with data protection rules may be borrowed, modifying the concept into a sort of 'ethics by design' approach.[8]

In practice, FinTech companies should take into account, among other things, the quantity of data intended to be collected, the quality of data, the purposes of the processing, the security measures adopted to protect data, and the extent of data access and sharing. These items should be assessed from a legal perspective, yet at the same time they should also be compared with current ethical and social considerations in order to assess whether the data processing may be regarded as ethical.

All stages of the data processing should be scrutinized, including collection in order to evaluate how data are gathered and whether individuals are aware of what is being done with their personal information. This also applies to the means used to process data and to how the results of the processing will be evaluated, together with the actions that are intended to be taken on the basis of said results. The whole process should be under constant revision and updating, in light of new purposes for which data are intended, in light of changes in the environment where data are to be used, and in light of new social and ethical considerations.

Another important item to be factored in is that the ethical and social dimensions should be translated into procedures, policies, and guidelines in order to guarantee a holistic approach that takes care of all stages of the processing and all kinds of processing operations.

In order to be effective, codes of conduct should also provide for accountability and enforcement actions. Accountability means identifying the individuals who are in charge of the decisions within a company, while enforcement means that there should be in place transparent and coherent sanctioning mechanisms in case of breaches. Indeed, the GDPR when setting up the new legislative system for certifications and codes of conduct poses specific attention on the enforcement element since real enforcement is a crucial factor for the effectiveness and reliability of these mechanisms.

For FinTech companies operating worldwide, it may be an issue to find a common benchmark, and to find coherent standards regarding ethical and social matters, especially because these matters are usually the results of local and historical evolution. In these situations, finding a standard that is a level higher than the local one usually allows finding a right balance that may apply worldwide.

As a general consideration, proponents of codes of conduct and certifications under the GDPR may take into consideration the GDPR requirements and the social and ethical dimensions at the same time, and so have robust tools that not only would allow compliance from a purely regulatory perspective, but also would act in line with social and ethical principles.

It should be noted that the issue of the ethical dimension in the digital ecosystem is on the radar of European authorities. Indeed, the European Data Protection Supervisor (EDPS)[9] has set up an independent Ethics Advisory Board[10] with the specific task

[8] See art. 25 of the GDPR for the concepts of privacy by design and privacy by default.

[9] The EDPS is the European Union's independent data protection authority. Among others, its task is to advise EU institutions and bodies on data protection issues. More information is available at https://edps.europa.eu/about-edps_en

[10] Decision of the EDPS dated 3 December 2015; for more information, see https://edps.europa.eu/sites/edp/files/publication/15-12-03_ethicsgroup_decision_en.pdf

of examining and reporting on the ethical perspective in the digital dimension, and promotes workshops for the purposes of information and raising awareness.[11] Giovanni Buttarelli, the current secretary of the EDPS, referred in this regard to '[e]thics at the root of privacy and as the future of data protection'.[12]

It may be argued that FinTech companies, like all private companies in general, act to pursue an economic interest, not an ethical interest. This is true, yet, as underlined earlier, the trust of customers and potential customers, business partners, stakeholders, and the business industry at large is vital, and the potential negative feedback of a data processing initiative that is outside the ethical and social boundaries should have a material deterrent effect. Indeed, the trust and reputation of a company translate into its business success and opportunities.

It follows that acting not only within the boundaries set forth by the applicable legislative framework but also in line with the ethical and social dimension represent the next necessary compliance step for FinTech companies.

---

[11] On 18 May 2017 in Brussels a workshop was held on Data Driven Life (digital ethics), the second event of the EDPS.

[12] Giovanni Buttarelli on 19 April 2016, Berkman Center for Internet and Society – Harvard University and the MIT Internet Policy Initiative and the MIT Media Lab; https://edps.europa.eu/data-protection/our-work/publications/ethical-framework/ethics-root-privacy-and-future-data_en

The End Justifies the Means: Putting Social Purpose Back at the Heart of Banking and Financial Regulation

By Anne Leslie
Senior Managing Consultant, IBM

When the year 2008 is mentioned, it is associated with the untimely demise of Lehman Brothers and the ensuing financial chaos that engulfed the global economy and rocked it to its very core.

Lost output in the United States alone amounted to as much as $13 trillion – an entire year's gross domestic product (GDP) – with paper wealth lost by US homeowners totalling $9.1 billion.[1] On the other side of the Atlantic in the United Kingdom, conservative estimates of the lost growth in Britain amount to £1.8 trillion.[2] Moreover, that is without taking into consideration the economic losses caused by higher foreclosures on mortgages and increased unemployment since 2008.

Even if the 2007–2009 bust was synonymous (just like previous collapses) with a sharp decline in GDP, the direct costs of the crisis paled in comparison with the slump in growth that followed.

Today, we are still paying the price.

Lessons Learned or Business as Usual?

Benjamin Disraeli once said, 'There is no education like adversity'. Yet, despite all the suffering and hardship that the financial crisis wreaked in the real economy, we continue to see banking scandal upon banking scandal in financial centres across the globe, from the rigging of foreign exchange markets and the manipulation of the London Interbank Offered Rate (LIBOR) to the heinous conduct of shadow lenders in China.[3] The adversity caused by the crisis has not been sufficiently felt in the quarters of society where the need is greatest for meaningful lessons to be learned and behaviours consequently changed.[4]

In 2009, Lord Adair Turner (then chairman of the UK Financial Services Authority) famously pronounced a sensible heresy when he suggested that finance should concentrate on useful activities, discarding useless ones, and asserting that not all financial innovation is socially desirable even it if is highly profitable to individual institutions.[5]

Unsurprisingly, Lord Turner incurred the wrath of the mainstream financial community in making this distinction. The prevailing view within the financial elite since the 1970s was, and largely continues to be, that such a distinction is not only irrelevant but dangerous.[6] It is likely, given the current enchantment of the industry with FinTech innovation, that his comments would be received with just as much (if not more) hostility today as back in 2009.

However, in his book *Between Debt and the Devil: Money, Credit and Fixing Global Finance*,[7] Lord Turner refers to the 'strange amnesia of modern macroeconomics', which largely ignored the

---

[1] GAO-13-180, 'Financial Crisis Losses and Potential Impacts of the Dodd-Frank Act', 16 January 2013.

[2] Andrew Haldane, 'The 100 Billion Dollar Question', *BIS Review*, 30 March 2010.

[3] *The Economist* Special Report – Finance in China: Shadow Banks', 5 May 2016.

[4] Charles Goodhart, 'Why Regulators Should Focus on Bankers' Incentives', *Bank Underground* (blog), 5 April 2017.

[5] Adair Turner, 'How to Tame Global Finance', *Prospect Magazine*, 27 August 2009.

[6] Milton Friedman, 'The Social Responsibility of Business Is to Increase Its Profits', *New York Times Magazine*, 13 September 1970.

[7] Adair Turner, *Between Debt and the Devil: Money, Credit and Fixing Global Finance* (Princeton, NJ: Princeton University Press, 2015).

details of the financial system, preferring mathematical precision and elegance at the expense of realism.

We all know where that got us.

The Collapse of Trust and the Spread of Inequality

However, for all the economic damage that the financial crisis is credited with causing, the year 2008, in fact, marked the genesis of a societal phenomenon far more pervasive, divisive, and corrosive than was initially appreciated.

When Lehman Brothers collapsed, governments, central banks, and trusted financial intermediaries such as banks found themselves brutally exposed: at best, the public perceived them as hapless and impotent bystanders, caught in an economic maelstrom of a scale and complexity never seen before; at worst, they were unveiled as cynical and self-serving constructs that sacrificed the greater good on the altar of individual capitalistic gain.

The events of 2008 effectively opened the floodgates to a crisis that is not just financial in nature: what we are experiencing is a profound and unprecedented collapse of trust, confidence, and legitimacy regarding the public servants who govern us and the organizations that serve us. The people, the voting public, have lost faith in the very institutions that are meant to represent, protect, and further their interests.[8]

From a macro perspective, the world economy has never known so much wealth, and yet never before has the global prosperity gap been so enormous, both between geographical regions and within the frontiers of individual countries.

In today's global economy, there are more than two billion people worldwide who still do not have a bank account or access to basic financial services,[9] and those who do are too often victims of predatory lending and abusive credit-card practices. At the other end of the spectrum, the concentration of wealth has reached such staggering proportions that eight high-net-worth individuals currently possess riches equivalent to those held by 50% of the earth's population.[10]

With the insidious creep of patrimonial capitalism, the advanced economies of the world are increasingly showing the characteristic traits of rent-seeking oligarchies.[11] In a world that is more wealthy in the aggregate and more technologically advanced than ever before, it is indeed an egregious state of affairs that modern 'progress' should be constructing a bleakness that is all too Victorian in its guise – bleak, that is, unless you happen to be part of the privileged 1%.[12]

> The sole meaning of life is to serve humanity.
>
> – Leo Tolstoy

However, let there be no ambiguity: this is not the 'politics of envy'. It is a non-partisan fact that growing economic inequality is bad for us all – it undermines aggregate growth and social cohesion, even if the consequences for the world's poorest people are disproportionately severe. Apologists for the status quo often cite the overall reduction in the number of people living in extreme

---

[8] YouGov, 2013.

[9] Valerie Bockstette, Marc Pfitzer, Dane Smith, Neeraja Bhavaraju, Cara Priestley, and Anjali Bhatt, 'Banking on Shared Value – How Banks Profit by Rethinking Their Purpose', FSG Shared Value Initiative, 24 June 2014, p. 7.

[10] Deborah Hardoon, Sophia Ayele, and Richardo Fuentes-Nieva, 'An Economy for the 1%', Oxfam, 18 January 2016.

[11] Paul Krugman, 'Challenging the Oligarchy', *New York Review of Books*, 15 December 2015.

[12] Hardoon, Ayele, and Fuentes-Nieva, 'An Economy for the 1%'.

poverty as proof that inequality is not a major problem, but this is only cynical obfuscation of the real issue.

The balance has tipped so far in favour of the few that adopting approaches to creating shared value is nothing short of a strategic imperative for our societies and, by extension, for the banks that finance the real economy. This powerful concept, championed originally by Michael Porter and Mark Kramer,[13] has the capability of transforming the engagement of banks with society by redefining their social purpose and matching their positive impact with the scale and ambition of their businesses. However, leveraging the full potential of shared value requires a profound shift in the thinking and habitual manner in which banks operate.

The Role of RegTech as an Instrument of Change

So where does regulatory technology fit into this picture? Regulation does not exist in a vacuum, and neither does technology: both evolve organically in a geopolitical, social, and economic context, and the direction their development takes is conditioned by the policies and decisions made at every level that serve to shape our societies.

As the banking industry continues to fail to demonstrate ethical standards of behaviour and games the system to avoid falling within the remit of regulatory constraints (let it not be forgotten that shadow banking currently accounts for a massive one-quarter of the global financial system),[14] so the regulatory grip tightens (even if it is always playing catch-up).

Regulation continues to dominate and shape banks' strategic thinking, with over half of banks thinking that capital and product suitability regulations will have the biggest impact on retail banks in the years from 2017 until 2020.[15] However, the number of banks that are engaging in a radical reassessment about how they choose to respond to external regulatory constraints can be counted on one's fingers.[16] The overriding considerations continue to be avoidance and cost reduction, motivated solely by short-term profitability.

It is in this context that RegTech is currently touted as being the 'next big thing' to hit the financial services industry, serving primarily to reduce the cost and complexity of complying with the myriad regulations that have been enacted since the financial crisis, in an effort to ensure that an imbroglio of such epic proportions could never occur again.

With more than $100 trillion in assets,[17] banks are integral in enabling each one of us to achieve our own ambitions, by nurturing innovation in the real economy and supporting prosperity in our communities. From this standpoint, we should look to RegTech to do more than just reduce the cost and complexity of compliance within the confines of a financial system that is increasingly acknowledged to undermine the common good.[18]

Purpose-driven Regulation

We are in the presence of exponential technological change, exiting the industrial era and entering an era that has yet to be named. Such is the upheaval that there is ambient friction between

---

[13] Bockstette, Pfitzer, Smith, Bhavaraju, Priestley, and Bhatt, 'Banking on Shared'.

[14] *The Economist*, 'How Shadow Banking Works', 2 February 2016.

[15] 4th Annual Economist Intelligence Unit Report 2017, p. 6.

[16] Bockstette, Pfitzer, Smith, Bhavaraju, Priestley, and Bhatt, 'Banking on Shared Value'.

[17] Philip Alexander, 'Top 1000 World Banks 2013', *The Banker*, 7 January 2013.

[18] Thomas Piketty, *Capital in the 21st Century* (Cambridge, MA: Harvard University Press, 2014).

those who yearn to slow down the pace of change and those who are intent on speeding it up.

One of the most visible effects of this tension is seen in the rise of populism as a palatable alternative to a failing system that causes entrenched disparities to be transferred across generations, spawning an increasingly disenfranchised population that has lost all faith in the possibility of better outcomes.

When democratic process and freedom are under a real and present threat, it is both urgent and imperative to acknowledge that our economic and financial system is not just imperfect; it is fatally flawed. The promise of trickle-down economics is illusory[19] and the time has come to assume our collective responsibility, derived from our individual humanity, to subscribe to the goal of an equitable society through policy action and regulatory intervention where progressive voluntary endeavour is insufficient.

> Market forces and capitalism by themselves are not sufficient to ensure the common good and to limit the concentration of wealth at levels that are compatible with democratic ideals.
>
> – Thomas Piketty

Academic research by V.V. Chari and Christopher Phelan suggests that a radically changed approach to bank regulation is required.[20] Whereas incumbent regulatory frameworks focus on reducing the probability of a bank or group of banks failing, the proposed alternative originates from a different perspective by asking the question: what social purpose is served by a given liability structure and then fashioning regulations based on that social purpose?

This approach, anchored in social purpose, diverges from the conclusion formulated by Arner, Barberis, and Buckley that the speed of FinTech innovation observed globally justifies that financial regulation be reconceptualized and redesigned with RegTech in line with the transformation of financial market infrastructure.[21]

In essence, their recommendation implies that it is desirable for the same free market forces that drive innovation in financial technology to drive parallel regulatory innovation that accommodates changes in market structure. However, considering the arguments made earlier in this chapter regarding the common good, it would seem more appropriate for an overarching social purpose to be used as the foundation for the reconceptualization and redesign of regulation, albeit achieved by leveraging the transformative capabilities of RegTech.

> You never change things by fighting the existing reality. To change something, build a new model that makes the existing model obsolete.
>
> – R. Buckminster Fuller

Better Collaboration for Better Outcomes

Using this lens, let us look to RegTech to jump-start new thought processes around broad-based collaboration between industry stakeholders, inciting new regulatory approaches to support financially inclusive policies that foster social mobility and bring the unbanked into a system from which they are currently excluded by design. The R2A RegTech for Regulators Accelerator is one

---

[19] Jared Keller, 'The IMF Confirms That 'Trickle-Down Economics' Is, Indeed, a Joke', *Pacific Standard*, 18 June 2015.

[20] V.V. Chari and Christopher Phelan, 'Policy Brief: Why and How Should Banks Be Regulated?', University of Minnesota, Heller-Hurwicz Economics Institute, 16 September 2013.

[21] Douglas W. Arner, Janos Barberis, and Ross Buckley, 'Fintech, RegTech and the Reconceptualization of Financial Regulation', University of Hong Kong Faculty of Law Research Paper No. 2016/035, October 2016, p. 38.

such initiative, which is pioneering the next generation of digital financial supervision tools and techniques, and provides a structured approach to help financial authorities reimagine how they operate.[22]

The real promise of RegTech resides in it becoming an integral part of the so-called soft infrastructure necessary to support a new model that is adapted to the realities of the times in which we live, helping to achieve the United Nations 2030 Agenda for Sustainable Development Goals[23] by building on the work already engaged in the areas of financial inclusion, impact investing, and sustainable finance.[24]

In the frenzy of innovation and investment, let us pause for a moment and imagine the full realm of possibilities when RegTech ceases to be merely a bankable buzzword and becomes a movement, embodied by people who yearn for better' and who are emboldened by this powerful social purpose.

[22] R2A RegTech for Regulators Accelerator.

[23] Consultative Group to Assist the Poor, 'Achieving the Sustainable Development Goals: The Role of Financial Inclusion' (Washington, DC: CGAP, 2016).

[24] Bockstette, Pfitzer, Smith, Bhavaraju, Priestley, and Bhatt, 'Banking on Shared Value', p. 3.

RegTech's Impact on Trust and Identity

By Michelle Katics
Co-Founder and CEO, PortfolioQuest and BankersLab

Two fundamental conditions are required for a strong financial system: trust and identity. RegTech offers an opportunity to strengthen and scale both, although it is sure to encounter some obstacles along the way. What solutions might be on the horizon, and what will be their social impact?

Tools for Restoring Trust

Trust in the financial sector may have been the biggest casualty of the global financial crisis.[1] This was followed by a perfect storm on trust: hacking incidents, pervasive fraud, pyramid schemes, trading scandals, and financial executive compensation structures inviting moral hazard. To make matters worse, the erosion in trust was systemic. Trust in the financial system is historically based on three pillars:

1. Sovereign state approval and backing of regulated firms.

2. Regulated firms with track records and recognized brands.

3. Rating agency assessments of these firms.

When we talk about the social impacts, we must put ourselves in the shoes of the general public, rather than the policy maker, subject matter expert, or FinTech geek. Society at large looks at the situation thinking, 'The government was supposed to guarantee our savings in the regulated firms, and now we see the government itself needing a bailout. The regulated firm was supposed to be the safest option for saving or borrowing money, and we have seen

these firms either fail or incur large losses from fraud or their own mistakes. The rating agencies told us everything was okay, and it wasn't. Where am I to turn?'

As a result, there has been a strong and surprisingly fast shift in public trust away from incumbent financial firms and towards new FinTech firms. What social changes do we notice?

Crowdsourcing Trust

Enter FinTech into the eye of the 'trust storm', and suddenly it is no longer a preposterous idea to bank using an unheard-of digital bank or lender with no branches. How did this happen? How was the trust built? The social network has been an important enabler. The social network entered the scene with perfect timing to provide a newfound ability to crowdsource trust. If a new FinTech platform or tool does not work, or someone loses money, the information will go viral. If an innovation is cool and effective (Venmo, CreditKarma, PayTM, AliPay), it can scale quickly by leveraging the social network effect. In the good old days, a bank would have had to work for decades to build up its name brand, customer base, and trust. Now if the firm plays its cards right, it can leverage the social network to crowdsource people's trust.

Increased Transparency

Increased transparency is long overdue, and we are seeing new RegTech tools that provide enormous advances. Real-time monitoring and employee behaviour analysis provide new opportunities for transparency. We can use these actionable insights to quantify and manage risk in the financial system, many of which are now more publicly available than before.

Look Back at the Past, but Don't Stare

Forward-looking tools restore confidence that events can be prevented and mitigated. The SWIFT hack did not happen

---

[1] Roth, Felix (2009), "The Effects of the Financial Crisis on Systemic Trust", CEPS Working Document No. 316/July 2009.

that long ago, but aren't we already a bit tired of hearing the backwards-looking forensic analysis? Did the forensic analysis give us more confidence that it will not happen again? Do we have any forward-looking tools that detect potential failure points or risk hot spots? If you are an investor, you might want to search the other articles of this RegTech book for the forward-looking tools and place some bets in that space.

Identity Vulnerability Is Globally Pervasive

There are 1.5 billion people who do not have access to identity.[2] A notable subset are the 10 million stateless people around the world – the most obvious population who are blocked from access to financial products. How do we get from the 10 million stateless to the 1.5 billion without identity? The majority live in Asia and Africa, but identity vulnerability is pervasive across all nationalities and socio-economic groups.

- *Identity theft* can cause years of financial and legal hardship.

- *Internally displaced citizens* struggle to access social and financial services if they are unable to obtain their identity credentials due to location, poverty, illiteracy, or political instability.

- *Administrative errors* such as variations in name spelling and transliteration can flag an innocent citizen to be placed on a watch list.

- *Social media identities* are increasingly used to determine employment and credit and can be spoofed or stolen.

Identity as a Market Failure

As John Edge of ID2020 points out,[3] a passport or ID card is not an identity; it is a credential. In the historical analogue world, the typical method of granting identity was to grant a credential. A credential is 'a qualification, achievement, quality, or aspect of a person's background, especially when used to indicate their suitability for something'. In contrast, an identity is 'the fact of being who or what a person or thing is', which is not revocable by taking away a driver's license or passport. Now that we live in a digital world, we have ways to recognize identity, but must still address one question: who 'owns' digital identity? Identity 2020 (http://id2020.org) is working to address this market failure over the long term.

The social and cultural impact of this seemingly fine point of identity versus credential is enormous. The sovereign state no longer wields the power of granting or taking away identity through credentials, and financial empowerment of the disenfranchised can flourish.

An important initiative in this area is self-sovereign identity. This initiative asserts that each individual owns his or her identity and takes concrete technical and policy steps to achieve this.[4] An example use case is uPort, 'a self-sovereign identity platform built on Ethereum … just one such example of how decentralization is reshaping identity. On this platform, the user creates their identity and collects reputation data on a user-friendly mobile app without the need for technical knowledge, and is completely independent from centralized 3rd parties.' Herein lies the social and cultural game changer: *'In the self-sovereign uPort model, the ownership*

[2] "Principles on Identification for Sustainable Development: Toward the Digital Age, World Bank, 2017, http://documents.worldbank.org/curated/en/213581486378184357/pdf/112614-REVISED-English-ID4D-IdentificationPrinciples-Folder-web-English-ID4D-IdentificationPrinciples.pdf

[3] https://www.mastercardcenter.org/insights/nobody-knows-name

[4] https://b-hive.eu/news-full/2016/11/14/blockchain-enabled-self-sovereign-identity; http://www.windley.com/archives/2016/04/self-sovereign_identity_and_legal_identity.shtml

of identity is moved from institutions to users who can selectively disclose their attributes to counterparties as needed'.[5]

I encourage you to pause and reflect on this statement. No longer does a third party or sovereign state give and take away identity. Individuals can confirm and maintain their credentials granted by a third party or sovereign, maintaining ownership and control of the sum total of their biometrics and credentials.

The advent of biometrics provides an opportunity for the paradigm change of individual ownership of one's identity. The sovereign state 'owns' your passport credential – it giveth and can taketh away. However, biometrics are at the core of an individual's identity and by definition are owned by the individual.

Perfectly summarized by the Daily Fintech,[6] the three key requirements of a blockchain-based ID are:

1. *Trustless and decentralized.* Your identity is not under the control of any institution (either government or commercial).

2. *Immutable.* Nobody can change a record, but can only append a new record. For example, all previous passports will be on the blockchain.

3. *Granular control.* For example, you can have my driver's license but not my passport or medical records, and you can have it for only this one transaction.

Let's review a few examples where digital ID solutions have already been implemented.

ClearBank is an example of a FinTech firm leveraging new technology to solve this identity market failure. They are using voice, visual, and vein[7] technology for a comprehensive identity management system that is a departure from traditional credential systems such as passwords, ID numbers, and tokens.

An example of identity management infrastructure is ShoCard,[8] which uses public and private keys, data hashing, and multifactor authentication on blockchain. Similarly, Blockstack (https://onename.com), World Citizenship (https://github.com/MrChrisJ/World-Citizenship), and Tradle (https://tradle.io) also hand identity ownership back over to the individual. Industry advocacy has been well underway for years to convince sovereigns to trust self-sovereign systems. A refugee bank such as Tanaqu (https://www.taqanu.com) would flourish once self-sovereign identity is widely adopted.

India as a sovereign state has taken identity matters into its own hands. India's Aadhaar system is the largest biometric database in the world and is unlocking financial services for millions.[9] Evidence suggests that the program is succeeding in bringing social services to those who were previously marginalized.[10] However, privacy concerns are resulting from assertions that the Aadhaar data has been compromised.[11] The shortcoming of the

---

[5] https://b-hive.eu/news-full/2016/11/14/blockchain-enabled-self-sovereign-identity

[6] https://dailyfintech.com/2016/02/26/uport-blockchain-id-and-the-idea-of-a-refugee-bank

[7] https://www.cbronline.com/uncategorised/built-microsoft-azure-first-clearing-bank-250-years-enters-uk-market/

[8] https://techcrunch.com/2015/05/05/shocard-is-a-digital-identity-card-on-the-blockchain

[9] http://mashable.com/2017/02/14/india-aadhaar-uidai-privacy-security-debate/#gKzqTpcrXOqk

[10] https://blogs.worldbank.org/publicsphere/aadhaar-reaching-india-s-poor-what-price

[11] https://techcrunch.com/2019/01/31/aadhaar-data-leak/

Aadhaar and other sovereign-owned identity systems is that the sovereign maintains control of the data rather than the individual. The database could be hacked, which some assert has already occurred. If this is the case, identity vulnerability has yet to be solved.

The potential social impact of these changes is stunning. First, 1.5 billion people would be empowered through access to healthcare, financial services, and social services. This has second-order impacts on the geopolitical balance of power. For example, if every stateless person had economic empowerment, it would change the course of the conflicts that were the root cause. One hopes that corruption in the area of social service and relief payments would be mitigated, and the economically disenfranchised would now have a fighting chance at financial and socio-economic well-being.

How the Futurist Sees Trust and Identity: Social Due Diligence

If you talk with a millennial about dating, you will learn that they are likely to Google each person before going on a first date. Before meeting, they are likely to know their date's favourite foods, whom they have dated in the past, where they have travelled, and details about their family. There is an emerging cultural expectation that we 'social network due diligence' potential dates, restaurants, airlines, and financial institutions. The financial sector is far behind in providing the type of social due diligence we would expect, even about something as simple as a taco stand. If I can check each health violation and customer complaint about my taco stand with an app, why is it so hard to find out how safely my financial institution is operating? This social expectation is not going away, but rather becoming pervasive among all age groups. The firms that push the envelope with increased transparency can win the hearts and minds of current and future generations. This opportunity to leverage the social network to build trust has not yet been fully exploited in the financial industry. Which credit card product has the best customer service? Which payment

mechanism is the most hack-proof? Which lender has the smoothest approval and customer onboarding? I would certainly expect to quickly Google the analogous metrics about a taco stand and am impatient to have the same ability for financial products and services.

Trust but Verify

Through open application programming interfaces (APIs) and social sharing, financial institutions can provide metrics and indicators that monitor and measure their customer service, skills, knowledge, cyber security, and conduct. As Nick Cook of the UK's Financial Conduct Authority (FCA) points out, as a regulator, the FCA aspires to a data-driven, self-regulating system in the future.[12] Consumers, regulators, investors, and stakeholders would have a clear line of sight into the quality and health of the firm. These metrics are both forensic and forward-looking predictors. The social implication is that society as a whole would be policing the systemic risk of the financial system, in the same way that Yelp reviews provide systemic policing of the health and safety of restaurant food.

'You Don't Own Me!'

The advent of self-sovereign identity is perhaps the most material game changer as a social and cultural change. The shift in power from sovereign state to individual over a host of services and access is a fundamental change in how we view ourselves and the state.

---

[12] https://fi.11fs.com/71

How Technology Is Driving Financial Inclusion

By Nick Wakefield
Managing Director Europe, Bambu and Co-Founder,
Regulation Asia

In global terms, rising incomes and extant banking infrastructure, including established technologies, mean that the ability and opportunity for people to access financial services have never been greater than they are today.

However, this overarching narrative of increased access to bank accounts, payments, investment, and investment advice does not play out everywhere. Moreover, the difference between those countries with developed banking infrastructure, both physical and electronic, and those without is arguably cast in no sharper relief than it is in developing Asia.

Technology has the capacity to boost developing communities, help businesses thrive, and bring financial freedom to those who need it most.

The latest available data from the World Bank shows only 31% of people aged 15 or older in Vietnam have an account with a financial institution, only 18% have formal borrowing, and just 15% have formal savings. It is a similar story elsewhere, with bank account penetration also 31% in the Philippines and Bangladesh, inching up to 36% in Indonesia, then tumbling again to 23% in Myanmar, and 22% in Cambodia. Comparing these figures to those for Japan (97%), Hong Kong (96%), and South Korea (94%) – and the global average of 62% – shows just how far some Asian countries still have to climb to include their citizens in, and position them to benefit from, formal finance.[1]

---

[1] http://datatopics.worldbank.org/financialinclusion

The financial inclusion challenge is a daunting one. However, as this chapter illustrates, rapid advances in technology – and government support – mean it has never been more surmountable. Technology has the capacity to boost developing communities, help businesses thrive, and bring financial freedom to those who need it most.

The Role of Government

Historically, the predominant focus of banks has been to facilitate trade for commercial interests and serve wealthy sections of society. Later, institutions such as the United Kingdom's Postal Savings System became the first banking setups to attract lower-income sections of society into the financial system. Similar institutions were also created in Europe and North America.

Governments then began to focus on ensuring that society saved so those savings, managed by financial institutions, could be used to finance growth, better educate the populace in financial matters, grow their wealth, and position them to access further financial products and opportunities. The end goal – a banked society.

Growth was a key metric, and raising productivity, and in turn the livelihoods and living standards of society, was a natural by-product. Governments sought to enable this by various means – trade facilitation, grants, funds, loans to businesses, and micro- and macroeconomic policy were all part of the process. As the last piece of the jigsaw, financial regulatory bodies, be they central banks or market supervisors, began contributing to the process by creating the right frameworks for enablement.

Governments and quasi-governmental bodies have come to play an essential role in enabling the right conditions for financial services to thrive, while at the same time ensuring that risks are mitigated and consumers are well protected.

The Role of Technology

For centuries, retail banking was a brick-and-mortar business. There were no other means of access for citizens – with technology the preserve of internal functions at financial institutions themselves. This was not just true of banking, however, with technology also not yet pervasive at a societal level. Indeed, it is only over the past decade that the world has started to witness technological inclusion.

It is only natural that the confluence of technology and the need for developing nations to shift to a banked society has created opportunity. Within a short period, financial services have spread from being the sole purview of banks to involving a broad range of companies and indeed individuals tackling a wave of problems. A ground-up approach to building a financial ecosystem has seen many institutions already become wildly successful in leveraging technology to transform financial flows. PayPal in the early 2000s, transforming the payments marketplace, and the smartphone-exclusive challenger banks of today have little in common with the behemoth financial institutions that have existed for centuries.

Technology now not only plays the traditional role of holding capital for one party, allowing it to be lent to others, but is also a facilitator or medium of financial flows. However, developments such as mobile payments and peer-to-peer (P2P) lending, as well as being a new financial paradigm, also require a new approach to financial regulation.

The Emergence of the Regulatory Sandbox

Over the past year, we have for the first time seen regulators put aside their roles of purely ruling on and supervising markets to actively coercing, and funding, the development of regulatory sandboxes to identify the key products and services that will emerge to support financial inclusion.

Naturally, the major financial markets and economies were first movers, but unlike in the past, where it took decades, even centuries, for financial concepts or infrastructure to be established, many emerging markets, particularly Asia, are proactively encouraging their regulators and central banks to explore and in some cases promote both FinTech and RegTech. They are also reaching out and building 'FinTech bridges', with the tie-up between Indonesia's financial services agency Otoritas Jasa Keuangan (OJK) and its Australian equivalent the most recent such development relevant to financial inclusion.

Regulatory sandboxes, which allow innovators to test financial products and business models in a live environment without some or all of the usual legal requirements, are emerging in most markets. Moreover, given the propensity for tie-ups between different jurisdictions, successful financial applications that emerge from them are likely to be available not just in their home markets, but in many markets, even any market, so long as regulators in other jurisdictions have the will to let this happen.

However, it is not primarily regulatory sandboxes, a relatively nascent concept, where sweeping transformation is taking place.

Technological Inclusion Means Financial Inclusion

Financial exclusion not only prevents large portions of emerging Asian countries from accessing finance to develop small agricultural or commercial businesses, but also has a negative impact on the tax income of a country, and in turn its services and infrastructure.

It is only natural, then, that rapid technology adoption means digital financial services are being pushed by governments, regulators, traditional financial institutions, and new market entrants (disruptors). With the incumbents needing to stay competitive, many have been setting up in-house groups, or FinTech accelerators.

The rapid adoption of mobile technology throughout the globe has created a common gateway to financial services. Although smartphones are still some way from high adoption rates, in somewhere like the Philippines, the technology is expected to have reached 68% of the population within the next five years.

Even with basic mobile phone access, customers can gain access to a simple form of banking, enough for the everyday needs of individuals who currently have no access. Services like M-Pesa that have seen widespread adoption across the emerging markets, including Afghanistan and India, allow individuals to transfer money easily through SMS text messages to other users. This access to basic financial services has reduced crime in traditionally cash-based societies.

Whilst these transformations are revolutionary; they are but a small part of the overall transformation and digitization of financial services. With the exponential speed of technology development, faster and more advanced forms of communication will facilitate access to banking services. Institutions will have greater opportunity to provide more services via innovative delivery methods.

Financial services firms are already being pushed to transform their operations, pressured by their own competitive drive as well as market disruptors. In a move to facilitate the development of access to financial services in the Association of Southeast Asian Nations (ASEAN) region, the Monetary Authority of Singapore (MAS) and United Nations recently formed a strategic partnership.

The goal will be to rapidly digitize the operations of financial institutions in economies such as Cambodia, Vietnam, Laos, and Myanmar – so they can, in turn, better support access to the financial system. One of their first initiatives will be to fund scalable business models able to foster cross-border remittances.

This development between a major Asian regulator and an international non-government agency is a key collaboration that can help both national and regional development. It showcases the openness of the regulatory community and application of technology to increase financial inclusion.

Technology also plays a role in ensuring that it is not only the cost of opening a bank account that will decline but also the complications. With the threat of money laundering and large fines having been paid by global banks for loose onboarding processes, know your client (KYC) has become an integral part of both institutional and consumer banking. India (where admittedly financial exclusion is less stark than in the aforementioned examples – 53% of people have a bank account), Indonesia, and the Philippines are making huge strides in the application of technology for this process.

India's Aadhaar number system, a unique identifier issued by the government and held by 99.7% of the population, means traditional paper-only KYC can now be processed electronically (e-KYC). Aadhaar, the world's largest biometric database encompassing more than 1.1 billion individuals, enables the transfer of the name, age, gender, and ID photo of a potential customer directly to a bank.[2]

Indonesia, where little more than a third of people have a bank account, but there are 350 million smartphones,[3] is a tremendous example of how technology is driving, and will continue to drive, financial inclusion.

The country's diverse geography, encompassing more than 17,000 islands, makes accessing physical banks a challenge, yet it has a fast-growing middle class and rapid adoption of e-commerce. In a move last year, the Indonesian government reached an agreement with hundreds of financial institutions to allow access

SOCIAL IMPACT AND REGULATION

[2] http://www.regulationasia.com/content/india-singapore-guangdong-join-shift-id-card-based-kyc

[3] https://www.statista.com/statistics/570389/philippines-mobile-phone-user-penetration

to the country's ID database for a form of KYC, and whilst this is applicable at this stage only to the capital markets, it is a sure sign of developments to come further down the financial chain.[4]

In the Philippines, meanwhile, the Central Bank recently said it would create 'basic banking'. This will require a lower standard of KYC for account opening, enable accounts to be opened with no deposit, and be linked to the country's conditional cash transfer programme, which provides cash to families threatened by economic shocks, natural disasters, or other crises, and has been lauded as one of the best-targeted social security systems in the world, with 82% of disbursements going to the poorest 40% of population.[5]

Where Next?

Technology means financial institutions have an opportunity to change for the good – and in turn serve their end users better. In emerging Asia, it will not just disrupt the banking system – it will *be* the banking system.

As for a future beyond mere banking provision, engagement will need to flow in both directions. Customers in emerging markets will come to better understand the importance of financial well-being, SMS and chatbots are already enabling more fluid discussions.

Financial inclusion will eventually morph into financial health, and myriad FinTechs will emerge. Larger financial institutions will either acquire these innovations or introduce similar ones themselves. Eventually, people will be able to see a full suite of products, not just the balances of their accounts.

Technologists, financial services companies, and governments in emerging markets will continue to leap ahead of their more established peers. If regulators maintain they are proactive, allowing technology firms and financial services providers to work side by side, this can only have a positive impact on emerging Asian individuals, smallholders, small businesses, and their communities.

---

[4] http://www.regulationasia.com/article/indonesia-surfs-fintech-wave-financial-inclusion; http://www.regulationasia.com/content/indonesia-opens-id-card-database-fis

[5] https://www.regulationasia.com/philippines-introduce-basic-banking/

Banking the Unbanked and Underbanked: RegTech as an Enabler for Financial Inclusion

By Soumaya Bhyer
Postgraduate, Cambridge University

and Seyoung Lee
Associate, Sagamore Investments

Issa comes from a village in Central Africa; he is married and has children. Like many others living in rural areas, Issa does not have a formal bank account. He works seven days a week and saves the totality of his earnings in a box under his bed. One day, Issa recounted that someone broke into the family home. That day, Issa and his family lost everything.

'Cash is king' is a common saying in Africa. However, is cash really king when the risk accompanying it is so high? In many cases, people do not think about the consequences of living a cash-dependent life, as they do not have access to formal financial services.

Why Is That?

Banks are rules-driven bureaucracies, and many people like Issa find themselves deprived of financial institutions' services due to a variety of reasons including strict "Know Your Customer (KYC)" requirements of documentation, often dictated by regulators. In fact, two billion people worldwide do not have access to formal financial services. According to the Global Findex Data 2015, 69% of adults in developing economies do not have a bank account. Regions with the least financial inclusion included the Middle East and North Africa, where four out of every five adults were not banked, followed by Sub-Saharan Africa, and then South Asia.

As we can see from Figure 1, the world's unbanked population is mostly concentrated in developing regions. This problem often leads to difficulties in measuring the actual size of local economies as well as financial institutions' reduced liquidity, which significantly impacts economic growth. Having little to no access to credit and saving facilities contributes significantly towards an enormous poverty trap, which can increase vulnerabilities to economic shocks and limit access to public services such as healthcare or education. As Accenture pointed out in 2015, increasing financial services spending levels in the developing world could potentially generate $110 billion worldwide.

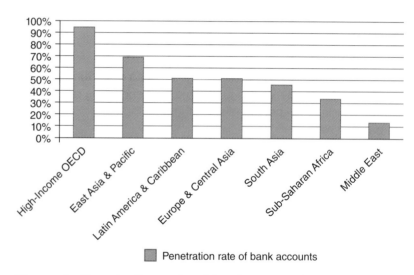

Penetration rate of bank accounts

Figure 1: Penetration rate of bank accounts

While bank accounts are traditionally seen as safe places to store money, today the risk of losing more in fees than is gained in interest makes the opportunity cost of having a bank account very high to many people, especially those from low social classes in developing countries. Financial exclusion is a recurrent problem for the poor, for women, for refugees, for people in rural areas and for the disabled. These individuals usually face high access barriers to banking services, which can be listed as follows:

- High costs: monthly charges, withdrawal fees, and so forth.
- Lack of proper documentation.
- Geographical inaccessibility and poor infrastructures.
- Lack of financial education and understanding.
- Lack of trust and unreliable services from the bank.

RegTech as a Solution to Financial Exclusion

More than merely digitizing previously analogue compliance and reporting processes, RegTech has the potential to reshape the way people – especially those traditionally underbanked – engage with financial services. One of the key movers of the prospective regulatory transformations is the reimagining of financial infrastructures to include digital identities and blockchain-enabled technologies.

According to CB Insights, $2.2 billion has been invested into RegTech so far, with the majority of the market activity occurring in the United States as well as Europe. However, leading firms and investors are pointing to its potential in emerging markets where regulatory environments are able to transform faster and are far more malleable – where existing legacy structures are not so cemented.

In this chapter, we view RegTech as a solution to financial inclusion by examining three case studies. We look to India, which has pioneered RegTech solutions through its India Stack. Then we focus more largely on Africa and on the Middle East and North Africa (MENA) region, where there have been numerous initiatives by multiple stakeholders to use blockchain-backed RegTech, in the process fostering financial inclusion. Lastly, we look at refugees as a group and the work many countries, international bodies, and

organizations have done to create digital identities not only as a regulatory instrument but also to allow them to access financial services once they cross borders.

India as a Case Study

India, which has historically had a significant unbanked population, is pioneering the future of financial inclusion with India Stack. This government-led RegTech solution has multiple layers – a biometric identity database, virtual payments addressing, and digital payments interoperability. India Stack has the potential to bring about significant transformations.

Most interesting and relevant to this article is Aadhaar, the universal biometric digital identity database. All Indian citizens are given a unique 12-digit unique identity number. The number is linked to the resident's basic demographic and biometric information. The Aadhaar program collects photographs, 10 fingerprints, and two iris scans, which are then stored in a centralized databank.

It has already been rolled out to 1.1 billion residents. Aadhaar is not meant to replace existing ID cards nor confer citizenship, but to act as a valid ID for accessing government services. The Unique Identification Authority of India, a government agency specifically created for this task, and the Reserve Bank of India worked closely with entrepreneurs to develop this project since it first started in 2009.

Overcoming previous doubts about outreach and coverage, as of January 2017, 99% of Indians aged 18 and above have Aadhaar cards. More significantly, 340 million bank accounts have been opened with this digital identity.

The World Bank's Consultative Group to Assist the Poor (CGAP) has suggested that India Stack could act as the 'new financial inclusion infrastructure'.

Africa as a Case Study

As we can see from Figure 2, many Africans are not part of a formal financial system and mostly operate in the informal economy. As a result, every year, sub-Saharan Africa loses $50 billion in illicit financial transactions.

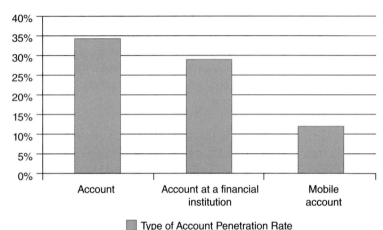

SOCIAL IMPACT AND REGULATION

Figure 2: **User rate per type of account in sub-Saharan Africa in 2014**

In order to promote financial inclusion, a great challenge in the continent is to effectively restore people's trust and confidence in financial institutions.

The economic situation of several African and MENA countries is dependent on the success of emerging innovative regulatory and financial solutions.

Blockchain is at the centre of almost every conversation revolving around financial inclusion. Using transparency, efficiency, and immutability as its major weapons, this distributed ledger technology has shown great potential in restoring trust and fostering innovations that could lead to greater inclusiveness.

Many start-ups have begun exploring the potential uses of blockchain as a means of banking the unbanked or at least giving them the opportunity to use financial services without having to be part of a formal banking process.

The Stellar-Oradian partnership is an interesting example to explore. Stellar is a Stripe-backed open-source payment network that partnered with Oradian, a blockchain-focused payment transfer network in Nigeria, and has been connecting isolated individuals and small businesses with financial services. The company has been allowing cash-dependent communities to transfer money with more safety, efficiency, and privacy regardless of their geographical location.

In this use case, blockchain technology facilitates remittance payments, an important component of financial inclusion, which benefits individuals and local businesses.

Remittance payments have a great impact on the macroeconomic environment of a country. According to the United Nations Conference on Trade and Development (UNCTAD), a 10% increase in remittances in a country's gross domestic product (GDP) significantly impacts the proportion of people in poverty and could decrease it 1.6–3.5%. In May 2016, inward remittances reached $146.76 million in value in Kenya, making its central bank one of the nation's top earners. In this case, blockchain worked to eliminate all third parties from the remittance process instantly, significantly reducing costs and increasing efficiency.

Traditionally, remittance payments needed to be settled through transfers within a network of international banks (SWIFT) or multibank settlement chains of incumbents such as Western Union or MoneyGram. This process usually prohibits sending small amounts of money due to fixed fees, which in 2015 were accounted by the World Bank to be as high as 10.64% when sending money through banks, 6.54% through money transfer services, and 5.14% through post offices.

Many start-ups have been offering alternative services, trying to reduce remittance fees. However, the most effective ones appear to be the ones using blockchain technology, as they do not need to go through the traditional banking system. Another example is BitPesa, a Nairobi-based start-up that also uses the same technology to offer international services. The blockchain-based platform allows people to transfer money from small regional banks anywhere in the world to a local bank in Kenya with a flat fee of only 3% regardless of the amount transferred.

MENA Region as a Case Study

Whilst Central Africa seems to be leading the blockchain for remittance payments initiative, the MENA region is lagging behind.

With more than 85 million people in the region unbanked, the MENA region has the lowest percentage of financially included adults – only 18% (Findex Database, 2014). While governments are changing their regulatory approaches to set up initiatives such as social funds in Lebanon or the restructuring of the microcredit industry in Morocco, RegTech seems to be a foreign concept to regulators in the region.

Taking Morocco as an example, local regulators have been working on increasing inclusiveness by making it compulsory for commercial banks to offer low-income banking products. Other initiatives include the creation of Al Barid bank by granting a banking license to the national postal network in 2009, which has resulted in the creation of more than 500,000 bank accounts. Despite all these efforts, research conducted by the World Bank has shown a lack of suitability of banking products for the major part of the population. The same research suggested that the use of technology could decrease costs of delivering financial services by 24% and increase inclusiveness. Local organizations, such as the Moroccan National Telecommunications Regulatory Agency are currently exploring the potential uses of blockchain to facilitate the creation and deployment of FinTech innovations. Morocco will also see the world's first utility-scale blockchain infrastructure; a

wind farm built by international computing firm Soluna to power blockchain technologies with sustainable energy. However, the country is not ready yet to incorporate these technologies into its financial system due to tight banking regulations.

The United Arab Emirates (UAE), on the other hand, through its recent partnership with Ripple, a US-based blockchain company, has introduced real-time, cross-border blockchain payments. With over $19 billion in transactions, the UAE is the fourth biggest remittance-sending country globally. The National Bank of Abu Dhabi, therefore, takes advantage of this by becoming the first bank in the Middle East and North Africa to adopt this technology. This partnership is set to significantly improve remittance payments in the region and will help decrease the $1.7 trillion spent every year on cross-border transaction fees. This initiative aims to have a number of positive effects on both economic and poverty alleviation indicators, including financial inclusion.

Refugees as a Case Study

Another group that is receiving attention as a potential and impactful use case for RegTech solutions as a conduit for financial inclusion is asylum seekers and refugees. For refugees, proving one's identity in a country not native to them is one of the most difficult hurdles to overcome in order to get assistance – especially for those who have no physical identification documents like identity cards and passports.

Government bodies and organizations with access to refugee aid have stringent KYC processes that only recognize government-issued identities. For refugees who do not have these recognized and sanctioned IDs, life becomes difficult.

Thus, various governments and entrepreneurs have been experimenting with promising ideas around developing blockchain digital IDs that can act in the same way India's Aadhaar has – not replacing existing IDs but merely creating an alternative valid form of ID, a digital identity.

Trulioo is one such start-up that has provided serving refugees as a use case for its product. It is a leading verification service that provides instant electronic identity verification for four billion people in more than 60 countries. Trulioo proposes to build upon existing networks and trends – like the high mobile penetration rates for refugees – to provide digital identities to refugees.

In Finland, the Finnish Immigration Service has collaborated with start-up MONI to develop a system wherein refugees are given a prepaid Mastercard, which is linked with a digital identity and blockchain that records financial transactions to help build credit history.

In this way, digital identity can act in ways to enable financial inclusion and empowerment for traditionally underbanked groups and have an immense social impact.

Conclusion

The implications of these types of RegTech solutions are profound. Regulators are carefully considering the impact of new technologies on local economies, with a particular focus on inclusiveness. The revolution of RegTech is very promising, especially for low-income countries, where its benefits are tangible.

Through India's case study, we can see the way digital identity allowed hundreds of millions of citizens to join the formal economy without severe friction. The potential for digital identity to work similarly for other underbanked groups such as refugees is also worth serious investigation. Blockchain technology has been a key enabler in the matter of inclusiveness, notably through remittance payments as seen in the case of Africa. As this technology matures, its disruptive potential can be used to support its adoption into various functions of local government (e.g. UAE). However, as the concept of using blockchain-backed RegTech solutions is still being tested, it may take time before its benefits are fully unleashed to the world's two billion unbanked population.

Superhero Way: Enhancing Regulatory Supervision with Superpowers

By Jenna Huey Ching
Specialist in FinTech, RegTech and LawTech

Can RegTech tools be like J.A.R.V.I.S. (Just A Rather Very Intelligent System), Tony Stark's loyal companion? Or equip us to be godlike like Mjölnir (hammer) for the son of Odin, Thor? Slick gears and intelligent equipment can transform a mere mortal into Batman to save Gotham and fight off crime. It does make one wonder if only the quintessential solutions are able to contribute positive impact, save people's lives, and help one another on a larger scale or even change the world. Be it regulation tech or regulators' tech, our focus will be geared towards the positive net effect of the use of RegTech towards humankind and society.

The Flavour of Prevention

The blue, red, green, orange, and purple icons circling on the Marine Traffic world map captured by satellites are able to reflect whether they are fishing or cargo vessels. Captains rely on marine radars, sonars, communication, and integrated systems to navigate the sea and storm to guide their ships and vessels safely to their destinations. Analysis, prediction of weather, detection of other vessels, and collection of data from the satellites are readily available to be put to good use by the captain and the team. The current advanced technology equips them to navigate with far more ease than the time at which the *Titanic's* fate was sealed.

The captain clears the way for the ship to sail smoothly with its cargo or passengers and ensures the layers and levels of protections are in place to avoid collisions or casualties. This is crucial when you are carrying precious cargo, and lives are in your hands.

The Prey

For migrant workers in foreign countries a sense of familiarity and trust solely because they come from the same village is rather common. To renew your visa, it is tough to locate official agents when there are gaps in understanding the local language or obtaining trusted information. What harm could there be relying on people with the same nationality and background who use the same language as you? What about people with whom you were neighbours and went to school?

Where there is weak prey, vultures will be lurking waiting to swipe at the right time. With the lack of a transparent and reliable system, countless migrant workers fall prey to these fake agents. Of course, it is insufficient to just trick one person when the word of mouth that spreads to another helpless prey could land more deals. These fake agents promise the migrant workers that they will help shoulder the responsibilities of renewing visas or passports for them as they show off with their connections and claim to truly understand the complex procedures. The poor workers will pass them their savings and passports. Little do they know, once the exchange is completed in return for just words of insincere assurance of securing the visa and renewal of the passport, the agent most likely will never resurface again.

If we can use technology to enhance the prevention side of this story rather than letting it slide to making reports to police over spilt milk, it will create the building blocks of a reliable system rather than relying heavily on human officers and errors. Some of these solutions could be as simple as the listing of fake agents after investigations confirm the reports, and websites to enable seamless online payment directly to the authorities or government agencies that handle visas and passports for migrant workers. Perhaps the authorities and government agencies could implement a more collaborative system that integrates analytics, shared databases, and information flow among themselves in real time.

The ease of cross-checking with the government and authorities should mean the availability of reliable information for the public such as verification of land ownership in real time with the land registry. To make this work, the government and authorities have to ensure that the system and technology used are constantly working and are being upgraded, and maintenance is not left overdue. After all, the status of being reliable is a title to be defended at all times.

At Eye Level

In the end, what is in it for me? How will RegTech help improve my daily life and business?

The Mamak stall owner has customers from all walks of life wishing him good morning daily even on those days when the rain pours heavily on his long-established stall. Malaysia's newly implemented Companies Act garnered some positive responses, but what will change exactly for this Mamak owner running his own business? What are the annual returns, forms, and mandatory filing of documents that need some checking to keep abreast of the changes? What if there is an interactive app that keeps him updated and provides the necessary checkboxes and reminders to tick all the necessary compliance steps at the right deadline?

A project manager who leads the launch of a FinTech coworking office will need to go through all the trouble to get necessary approvals for renovation, obtaining permits and consultations from relevant authorities. But wait a minute: where should she even go to start grappling with understanding and complying with all the steps? Should she hire an expert to solve her compliance issues? A solution that can help cast a net to capture the brief road map and explain the step-by-step procedure on various permits, approvals, and licenses would make a difference in comparison to her queuing up at the different offices to enquire with the relevant officers.

Robocop Way?

Part human, part robot police officer is the reaction that pops up once in a while during conversations about RegTech. Is it the cool,

enhanced ability to combine the best of both worlds of human and a machine? Perhaps this could be our story, in which we use a second chance to build a better system of technology and deliver the combined effect of solving the cracks in our existing structure of compliance, reporting, fighting crime, detection of fraud, and compilation of an outdated database. Who could forget a powerful database uploaded in one's system that allows efficient and real-time sync up to determine if the person standing in front or hidden amongst the crowd is a threat or a nonthreat?

When regulations are drafted and codified and come into effect to be adhered to, there must be repercussions and punishments for omission, negligence, and intention for failing to do so. If not, who would even bother to obey them? The problem is that some of the abusers of the system, wrongdoers and the powerful, go undetected and may never surface on the radar again.

Our lifestyle has tech spelt all over it and remains inevitable for upcoming generations. The authorities and regulators have to play the cat-and-mouse game with a fresh mindset and strategy. To remain ahead of the game, regulators need to use tech to detect money laundering before the track disappears without a trace, expose the organizations that rob people, and to monitor money flows that may show signs of fraudulent movement of cash across borders, through efficient collection and analytics of data and reports.

There is a change of wind direction regarding how regulators and authorities move in the way they embrace their roles globally. Many regulators today want to appear start-up friendly and open to innovation and new ideas, while balancing their existing role. There is a kind of excitement where you are willing to wait patiently before the curtains are raised to reveal the next episode of RegTech.

The Future of RegTech

11

- Market surveillance is transforming very rapidly as a result of RegTech but more needs to be done in designing system to fully achieve underlying objectives

- Looking forward, RegTech offers the potential to not only address market evolution and the role of non-human actors in finance but also to replace human regulators themselves in some cases

- RegTech companies are leveraging new technologies to build better compliance systems and corporate cultures

- RegTech needs to extend to technologies companies as well as financial companies

- AML will continue to be a key driver of RegTech

In the final part of the book, we invite readers to imagine how regulated industries will work tomorrow. The authors that have contributed the following chapters have provided hints as to what the future may look like.

However, the rate of technological change, the entrance of new TechFin companies and ever-changing business landscape it is difficult to make an exact prediction. The FinTech market serves as an illustration of how FinTech entrepreneurs can pivot the same solution from a B2C to B2B market to avoid otherwise costly compliance cost.

We are already beginning to see changes in the RegTech space, as start-ups in the KYC space are not seeking to become the new utilities but instead value themselves as a core element for a true digital experience for clients. Companies that started to provide auditing capacity enhanced by AI for financial institutions are now expanding to healthcare and the food and beverage industry.

New markets are also emerging and creating opportunities that never previously existed: cyber security for crypto-currency exchange, KYC, and suitability solution providers for ICO or even banking for newly displaced populations for environmental or economic reasons.

Beyond strict solutions, the dynamism that RegTech has brought to the financial services industry will help the ongoing cultural change process that started a decade ago. Regulators are also following their journey of digital transformation and upskilling as they finally move away from post-crisis reform and instead can start thinking about building the future.

Even more, exciting is that tomorrow's regulation is only being developed now. There are still years ahead of us before the existing financial services industry can change its legacy and mindset when it comes to compliance. Once this is done, entrepreneurs will have other regulated markets at which to aim their solutions.

Before finishing this book, we would like to leave you with one quote, an extract from a speech by Andy Haldane, Chief Economist at the Bank of England:

> 'I have a dream. ... It would involve tracking the global flow of funds in close to real time (from a Star Trek chair using a bank of monitors), in much the same way as ... to monitor the evolution of the financial system in real time.'

Market Surveillance 2020

By Murad Baig
Global Chief Innovation Officer, Netsol Technologies, Inc

The high speed of electronic trading, an explosion in trading volumes, the cross-asset range of traded products, and proliferation of different types of trading venues pose significant challenges for the regulators to maintain market integrity. With all this complexity, market abuse patterns have also become difficult to identify and detect. Banks are spending millions of euros in fines for market abuse violations. In response to this complex landscape, European regulators have been hard at work. They have created rules for surveillance of exchanges with a view to detecting suspicious patterns of trade behaviour and increasing market transparency.

This chapter looks at the ramifications of these rules on the design of market analysis platforms (MAPs), and how disruptive technologies can be combined to regulate the digital ecosystem of structured and unstructured data.

Fifty Billion Events

The Financial Industry Regulatory Authority (FINRA) monitors approximately 50 billion market events a day – including stock orders, modifications, cancellations, and trades – to detect violations of its rules.

The robust MAP requires regulators to 'collate live data' (market feeds, proprietary data, cross-asset and cross-market orders and trades, social feeds) across tens of billions of market events; 'analyse' (filter, detect, and alert violation of trading rules to provide reports and alerts); and undertake/feed 'case management', which could be used within the court of law as evidence of any market manipulation or malpractice behaviour.

The MAP must be integrated in terms of technologies, processes, and work flows to provide effective and efficient scaling to

the regulator's current and future business needs. It must combine big-data, cognitive machine learning techniques to go beyond the standard set of trading patterns to learn about trading behaviours so as to predict new patterns that need to be monitored and flagged. It should enable retrieval of data holistically and in chronological order (including replay) if requested, while optimizing the chances of preventing market abuse and improving market integrity, including increasing the probability of success for any cases the regulator decides to pursue through the courts.

Capital Markets Policing Challenges

Capital markets (buy side, sell side, exchanges, clearing-houses, and custodians) are complex and deal in complex financial instruments in a fast-moving industry. The trading participants within this industry are leveraging advanced technologies to produce ever lower latencies for trading, more sophisticated financial products and greater variations of market participants, heavy quant-based trading strategies, and multiple trading venues, all competing for larger flow and profits.

Market manipulation refers to trading practices that serve to distort securities prices, thus enabling market manipulators to illicitly profit at the expense of other participants by creating information asymmetry. Market manipulation covers practices like insider trading (where securities are sold or bought based on nonpublic information), misleading auto trading practices like 'spoofing' or 'pumping and dumping', and so forth.

The actors in securities markets know their game. The possibility for market abuse is always right in front of the actors. Furthermore, the risk of detection when abusing markets is low or nonexistent. Trades and orders in related securities at multiple markets happen continuously, the markets compete with latency and automated trading, executions happen within microseconds, and there are huge volumes. Venues undertake sufficient oversight to retain their licenses but do not compete on market integrity, as the cost of such would affect their earnings before interest and taxes (EBIT) and therefore price-to-earnings (P/E) ratios.

Proving best execution in such highly fragmented markets, which both are and are seen to be a public good, is a significant issue. No party has a single set of eyes measuring market integrity pan-market and proving that price formation has the optimal level of market integrity. Additionally, there has been very little case law to determine what normal or abnormal activity is.

Best execution is now influenced or distorted by volumes where there is no pre-trade transparency for dark volumes (albeit at increasingly smaller sizes, and furthermore off-exchange executions in some parts of the globe). Liquidity/price discovery is also highly influenced by algorithmic trading.

High-frequency trading (HFT) – which is essentially a high-speed form of algorithmic trading that uses sophisticated networking technology and computer algorithms to rapidly trade securities – uses proprietary trading strategies carried out by computers to move in and out of positions in seconds or fractions of a second. Some pioneering hedge funds are creating new types of algorithmic trading that rely on advanced self-learning analytics coupled with large linearly scalable data stores and low latency-enabling hardware technology. All these advances in automation have led to increased trading volumes and sophistication in the HFT space.

There is also an explosion of trading venues. Primary exchanges for equity trading are the London Stock Exchange (LSE), New York Stock Exchange (NYSE), and NASDAQ. The CME Group and EUREX dominate futures and options. However, deregulation has resulted in the creation of new trading venues like multilateral trading facilities (MTFs), organized trading facilities (OTFs), systematic internalizers (SIs) (e.g. investment banks developing their own internal crossing systems to match buyers' and sellers' orders internally), and dark liquidity pools.

On the sell side, banks have a strong need to provide their risk and compliance managers with a 360° view of the trading across their entire range of trading desks, not just to optimize enterprise profits, but to manage risk and prevent fraudulent behaviour.

As can be seen from the preceding discussion, there is a need to capture real-time data, which is structured and unstructured in real time, resulting in tens of billions of market events daily that need to be stored as complex business requirements for both data onboarding as well as analytics.

Call for Action – Regulations in Europe

With all public goods (e.g. air, water, and price formation), there is a need at some point to press the reset button and gather the data to cleanse the free commodity.

To recap some of the more prominent scandals over the past few years:

- The Libor scandal of 2015 (where a rogue trader was found guilty of manipulating the global benchmark interest rate used as the basis for a range of financial deals).
- The Flash Crash of 2010 (a trillion-dollar market crash that started at 2:32 p.m. EST on 6 May and lasted for approximately 36 minutes, causing the various indices to drop precipitously).
- The collapse of Knight Capital in 2012 (due to a fat finger error caused by deploying test code into production) caused a major disruption in the trading of 140-odd securities while sending the firm into a tailspin. This single incident caused a loss of $400 million in a single trading day. The result was that the firm's enterprise value eroded during a matter of a few minutes, forcing a sale almost overnight.

Over the past few years, the European Securities and Markets Authority (ESMA) has slowly begun to harmonize various pieces of legislation that were originally intended to protect the investor. The two major regulations that market participants in the European Union now need to conform with are the second Markets in Financial Instruments Directive (MiFID II) and the Market Abuse Regulation (MAR).

The major objective of both MiFiD II and MAR is to maintain investor confidence in the markets by ensuring market integrity and transparency and by catching market abuse in real time as it occurs. Accordingly, the ESMA has asked for sweeping changes across how transactions on a range of financial instruments – equities, over-the-counter (OTC) traded derivatives, and so forth – are to be recorded pre-trade, post-trade, and for transaction reporting. The regulations have a major impact upon how banks, exchanges, and broker-dealers will be required to store trading records for the purposes of trade reconstruction and market abuse monitoring, detection, and prevention.

The transaction reporting has been extended to venues such as HFT, direct market access (DMA) providers, and clearing members (CMs). The reporting granularity regarding field has also been extended to include the trader and the client, across the order life cycle for a given transaction. Beginning 3 January 2018 when MiFiD II entered into effect, financial firms and regulators were required to capture and report on detailed order life cycles for trades.

Key Business and Technology Requirements for Market Analysis Platform (MAP)

Some of the key objectives of the MAP will consist of meeting the following requirements:

- *Real-time feed management* system captures the raw data from exchange sources such as data from LSE equities, derivatives,

MTFs, OTC trades, and both lit and dark trading venues through its feed handlers. The data will also include trade data, valuation and position data, reference data, rates, market data, client data, front office to back office data, voice, social media, and other internal communication data (i.e. emails, telephone conversations, and so on).

The data will then be normalized and broadcast in multicast along the proprietary network, where it is aggregated in storage and replay servers. The structured data is then extracted and loaded from feed management storage to the MAP repository, using any extract, transform, load (ETL) platform such as Oracle Data Integrator or IBM Data Stage.

Similarly, unstructured raw data from different sources is captured and organized through Big Data Appliance, where data is converted to structured and normalized form before storing it to the common data repository of MAP.

- *MAP data repository* is a data warehouse that houses the aggregated data from the real-time feed management system through ETL platforms using native application programming interfaces (APIs) and data from unstructured data management systems through a big data connector. To provide surveillance of the market data, the extended data model of the InfoTech Surveillance system will also be merged. The MAP repository must be able to store enormous amounts of heterogeneous trade data, which will be required to perform trade monitoring and analysis on not just real-time data but also historical data spanning a few years.

The MAP repository must also provide for the ability to perform data lineage and auditing – and data needs to be fully auditable for five years. This implies not just being able to store it but also putting capabilities in place to ensure strict governance and audit trail capabilities.

- *Market surveillance* ability for real-time surveillance and monitoring of data. Having collected and normalized the data within the MAP data repository, it will need to support real-time monitoring of data (around 5–20 seconds) to ensure that every trade can be tracked through its life cycle. Detecting trading patterns for market abuse and monitoring for best execution is key.

The market surveillance system will provide the key surveillance and market assessment functionality to the proposed solution, which includes benchmarking, market abuse detection, alerts processing, rules/algorithms, case handler, live feed handler, data analysis, audit trail, and access management.

- *Business intelligence (BI) layer*. The BI layer will deliver the most robust set of reporting, ad hoc query and analysis, online analytical processing (OLAP), dashboard, and scorecard functionality with a rich end-user experience that includes visualization, collaboration, alerts, and more. Leveraging the in-memory database capabilities will enhance the efficient retrieval of data in analytics and reports. The proposed solution includes OLAP functionality that will leverage customers for retrieving multidimensional and time-hierarchical reports efficiently.

- *Cognitive machine learning, predictive and contextual analytics*. The real-time analytics component will enable users in capital markets and market surveillance to deploy it as a critical element in their decision-making infrastructure. Financial institutions need to up their game regarding surveillance. Relying on rules-based systems alone is proving to be insufficient and must leverage supervised and unsupervised learning approaches to performing extensive behavioural modelling and segmentation to uncover trading patterns and behaviours that can lead to potential regulatory violations. Additionally, there will be contextual analytics around unstructured data to reduce the number of false alerts. Another mix of critical functionality includes:

- Ability to subscribe to multiple feeds from complex event processing engines.

- Ability to connect to column-oriented and row-oriented databases.

- Fully realized, interactive tree map and heat map data visualizations.

- Availability of rapid development options that allow business users to create dashboards that can be embedded in third-party proprietary applications.

- Ability to move from a high level looking at aggregation of ticks on a market or venue down to an individual order or trader.

Figure 1 provides a single summary of what a market analysis platform would look like.

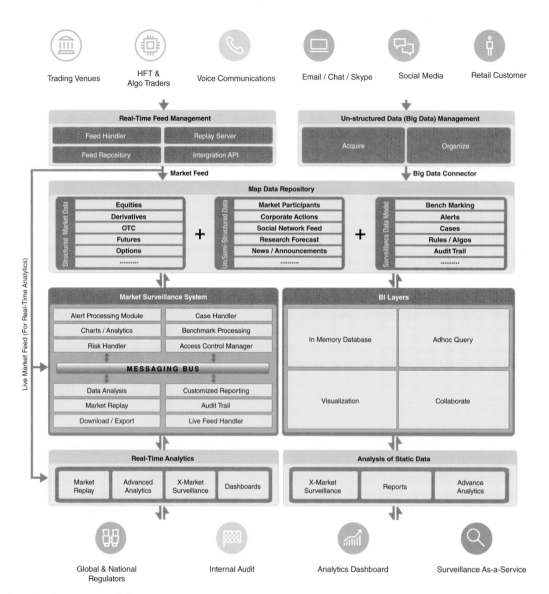

Figure 1: Market analysis platform – architecture

I Regulate, Therefore I Am? Regulating Humans' and Machines' Conduct and Culture

By Dr Daniel Gozman
Senior Lecturer, The University of Sydney Business School

Jonathan Liebenau
Professor (Reader), The London School of Economics and Political Science

and Paul Ferris
CEO, ObjectTech Group

A Brave New World of Regulated Activity

Despite the widespread adoption of complex mathematical models and scientific methods, financial services firms require consumers to place trust and faith in their services and products for the economy to thrive and prosper. Yet, trust in financial and regulatory organizations has been considerably eroded following a spate of systemic breaches in firms post the financial crisis. Public fury has built regarding the roots of the Great Recession and the firms and regulators that contributed to it, resulting in a widely held perception that the financial services industry is deeply compromised through 'cynical greed' and 'malpractice'.[1] Examples often cited include the London Interbank Offered Rate/ foreign exchange (LIBOR/FX) benchmark rate rigging scandals,

protected personal information (PPI), money laundering scandals, and the deliberate misleading of investors buying mortgage-backed securities.[2] This has led government and regulators to review and enhance regulations, placing an economic burden on firms to tighten their practices through more stringent regulation (second Markets in Financial Instruments Directive [MIFID II]) and accountability frameworks (Senior Management Regime).

Trust, however, continues to underpin the efficient operation of financial markets and is a key objective of the UK regulator. For example, investors may have little understanding of the securities they are buying, the firm issuing them, and the underlying risks they may present. Resultant information gaps may place investors at a disadvantage. Asymmetric information may result in financial intermediaries having access to information that unscrupulous individuals may then capitalize on at their clients' expense. Such disadvantages result in moral hazards whereby incomplete or inaccurate information is used to mislead and misrepresent the true nature of the risk involved in a transaction.[3] In a speech made in 2012, the chairman of the UK regulator provided examples of how asymmetric information can be exploited to create moral hazards, and highlighted the need for financial organizations to manage conduct and culture:

> … if a fancy new product design will enable a corporate or a country to conceal from the market the scale of its indebtedness, or if a trading desk manages to offload a problematic position onto an unsuspecting customer, does the top management and the board say 'Congratulations, take a bonus' or does it say, 'That's not what we do'? … If it is serious about values and culture, it has to do the latter.
>
> – Lord Turner, speech at Bloomberg, London (2012)

The authors would like to acknowledge the personal views and ideas shared by Anthony Kirby and Lisa Blenkinsop, as well as those of Lawrence Wintermeyer. Any remaining errors are our own.

[1] A. Turner, 'The Turner Review: A Regulatory Response to the Global Banking Crisis' (2009), from www.fsa.gov.uk/pubs/other/turner_review.pdf

[2] D. Gozman, W. Currie, and J. Seddon, 'The Role of Big Data in Governance: A Regulatory and Legal Perspective of Analytics in Global Financial Services', SWIFT Institute Working Paper 2014-009 (2016).

[3] J. Solomon, *Corporate Governance and Accountability*, 4th ed. (Chichester, UK: Wiley, 2013).

In theory, ensuring an appropriate culture in the firm and holding individuals accountable for their conduct may seem relatively straightforward by, for example, ensuring that employee rewards and incentives are aligned with financial outcomes for customers. However, in practice, perverse incentives have continued to persist across different parts of the business. For example, the Financial Conduct Authority's (FCA's) Director of Supervision highlighted action taken by the regulator,

> [The FCA] … took action against a bank in 2013, where [the FCA's] investigation uncovered a 'culture of mis-selling' which drove sales staff to hit sales targets to avoid being demoted, rather than to focus on what their customers needed.
>
> – Jonathan Davidson, speech at the 2nd Annual Culture
> and Conduct Forum for the Financial
> Services Industry, London (2016)

Both scholars and practitioners have observed considerable difficulties in changing organizational cultures and individuals' mindsets.[4] Often, practices adopted by firms have involved superficial or ceremonial changes that fail to adjust deep-rooted and taken-for-granted cultural-cognitive behaviours, perhaps by merely adjusting the firm's mission statement to include prose on 'putting customers first'.[5]

RegTech and the Future of Digital Conduct Risk

'Human and systemic factors jointly contribute to failures of institutional trustworthiness'.[6] Consequently, the role of information

systems in encouraging appropriate cultures and monitoring behaviours should not be underestimated. Neither should the possibility that innovation will create further perverse incentives for individuals to act in their self-interest and provide opportunities to circumvent governance practices and conceal outcomes.

The response from firms has been to utilize technology to develop controlled environments to undertake finance activities and transactions, resulting in vast amounts of instant data capture, and instant sales and execution activity. As data volumes and complexity grow, firms will increasingly look to machines to automate decision making. Increasing automation may not merely increase consistency and speed of operations but also improve data governance through the quick capture, organization, and processing of data, which in turn increases transparency and auditing capabilities.

Indeed, new technologies within operational functions 'might authorize, allow, afford, encourage, permit, suggest, influence, block, render possible, forbid' actions;[7] however, such activities still require consumer outcome testing and monitoring for regulatory compliance and conduct risk. RegTech solutions that provide firms with the capability to monitor exceptions and act on them whilst working at volume and scale are still in their infancy but are proving to be highly valuable to risk management. Such solutions are encouraged by regulators that are also seeking assurances that cybercrime and traditional financial crime such as insider trading and money laundering can be monitored and sanctioned before markets and consumers are harmed; for example, the proactive automated monitoring of email, instant messaging systems, and voice analysis allows firms to anticipate employee behaviour and flag issues before breaches occur.

The current spate of automation of banking platforms facilitated through application programming interfaces (APIs) is being

---

[4] W.R. Scott, *Institutions and Organizations*, 2nd ed. (London: SAGE, 2001).

[5] Turner, 'Turner Review', from www.fsa.gov.uk/pubs/other/turner_review.pdf

[6] N. Gillespie, R. Hurley, G. Dietz, and R. Bachmann, 'Restoring Institutional Trust After the Global Financial Crisis,' in *Restoring Trust in Organizations and Leaders: Enduring Challenges and Emerging Answers*, R. Kramer and L. Pittinsky, eds. (New York: Oxford University Press, 2012).

[7] B. Latour, *Reassembling the Social – An Introduction to Actor-Network-Theory* (Oxford, UK: Oxford University Press, 2005).

rolled out to improve systems that facilitate data capture that is subsequently used, post-execution, to identify, evaluate, and evidence consumer outcomes, resulting in the increasing ability to evidence compliant outcomes through reducing human interaction and thus minimizing inappropriate conduct.

As markets, services, products, and technologies develop apace, regulators have frequently been left playing catch-up.[8] Once a problem is recognized, regulators often responded by demanding, receiving, and processing maximum data, looking to identify exceptions that do not conform. This approach involves high costs as firms are required to cast a wide net in their investigations into staff behaviours and actions. When an exception is found, the regulator often acts after the fact (sometimes years later) when the spoils of misdeeds may be long gone. To be second-guessed by a regulator months or even years after an event often leads to a dead end of massive cost and opaque systems, issues both the regulator and firms are working on closely to address through the use of technology and collaboration via innovation hubs.

As technology evolves, we shall move from reactively scouring records for problematic events and then investigating causality towards proactively monitoring events and addressing problems at their source. New technologies mean that the transfers of funds can be allowed only by verified individuals or insurance contracts approved at the time of writing via smart contract regulation, for example. This represents a shift in momentum away from regulated institutions to the responsibility of individuals, both social and legal. Initially, these tools will require a human touch to validate outputs.

Artificial intelligence (AI) machine learning technologies review and learn from vast amounts of data to make predictions, recognize patterns, and assist decision making. These capabilities may allow

firms to better identify misconduct and even fraud through analysing a firm's email systems, for example. These methods allow judgements to be made prior to execution, allowing firms and possibly the regulator to act on intent prior to a breach occurring. However, over time and through AI technologies, the need for human interaction may decrease, creating a new paradigm where machines monitor and sanction the actions of other machines. This raises further questions as to how to evaluate culture and conduct (very human concepts) where interactions are mainly between machines rather than humans.

Human decision making is dependent on subjective judgement. AI, however, is dependent on sources of information fed by human input. Those who design and control algorithmic trading functions and AI for these purposes will require an ethical set of values that determine the controls, judgements, and outcomes required to ensure good conduct in the digital age. Regulation aims to make markets fair for all participants but has traditionally focused on customers first. The application of innovation often acts as a precursor for one or more market actors to gain an advantage through speed of execution or information asymmetries. One example is high-frequency trading. Algorithmic technologies make trades in nanoseconds, whilst human beings can only respond to events in milliseconds at best. Consequently, it is possible that regulators will employ RegTech such as AI to monitor and understand trading patterns and to respond accordingly in spaces of time impossible for humans. Competition in this area is fierce as players seek to gain advantages by developing more efficient algorithms and architectures. In this way, competition is driving innovation and has led to the emergence of a new generation of trading technologies enhanced by machine learning (AI), case-based learning tools, and APIs. Currently, these technologies are immature, so related risks of competing algorithms and AI are yet to crystallize.

As a point of departure in understanding the implications and risks of AI, we have little previous experiences or historical lessons to draw upon other than science fiction books and films. Firms are required to identify short-term risks and outcomes through proof of

---

[8] Recently, regulators have acknowledged they are behind the curve and have sought to remedy this through initiatives such as the FCA's (UK) Project Innovate and its Advice Centre, which assist firms but also allow the regulator to learn from them.

concepts that evidence desirable consumer outcomes, and that risks are managed in controlled environments. So, we are left to guess the potential risks of mature AI and algorithmic trading in a fully live environment. Recent experiments in AI have shown how such technologies can become aggressive over time.[9] Where AIs and algorithms are trading against one another and learning and evolving, it is possible they will become more competitive than anticipated and, if not tightly monitored and controlled, will develop a primitive intent to survive with the potential to independently trade on their own, thereby creating unacceptable risks for the financial industry, the firm, and its clients. The key for regulators evaluating related outcomes[10] is to review the intent for which the AI was created. Was the algorithm designed to protect the firm and to hedge risk? Or was it designed to move and game markets? Consequently, in evaluating responsibility and accountability of creators, it becomes important to have transparency regarding the identity of the designer, the ethical values and boundaries embedded in such technology, and the resulting conduct.

Whom Do You Trust? Empowerment Through Blockchain and Identity Management

How we identify with one another and evaluate others' conduct and behaviours are irrevocably linked to issues of trust and transparency. Correspondingly, transparency and accountability can be powerful levers for changing conduct and culture. Through innovation, financial organizations will continue to seek to alleviate the challenge of responding to technology-driven changes in human behaviour and related rapid shifts in regulation. Relying on assured information regarding an individual's identity offers a game changer for many regulatory practices – for example, speeding up the onboarding of customers through streamlining anti–money laundering (AML) and know your customer (KYC) practices.

The long-term goal in digitizing identity management is for information to be willingly provided at the right time and that such information is accurate and relevant. However, widespread concerns over data privacy mean that this endeavour is not without challenges. A top-down approach of collating identity data in centralized government or corporate databases simply creates honeypots for hackers and has been rejected by popular public opinion in democratic states such as in the United Kingdom and Australia.[11] Such data is also heavily regulated elsewhere, and the costs of keeping it up to date, safe, and secure are very high.

Rather than attempt to develop an all-knowing database that holds centralized records pertaining to an individual, a consent or permission-based system, where individuals own their data, may be better received and more efficient. Scenarios where individuals are comfortable providing accurate and up-to-date information, perhaps as part of receiving a service, are more likely to lead to quality data and more assurance of the actor's true identity. This approach supports best practice, encourages good conduct, and supports a culture of respect for identity.

Obtaining the trust and cooperation of individuals is proving to be a far more robust approach to accuracy in identity and is the way identity management is likely to develop in the future. This approach, for example, is more reliable than the current state of KYC with 10-year-old pieces of paper or fake digital channels

[9] 'Google's AI Has Learned to Become "Highly Aggressive" in Stressful Situations', *Science Alert*, 31 March 2018, from http://www.sciencealert.com/google-s-new-ai-has-learned-to-become-highly-aggressive-in-stressful-situations; and 'Microsoft Deletes "Teen Girl" AI After It Became a Hitler-loving Sex Robot Within 24 Hours', *The Telegraph*, 23 March 2016, from www.telegraph.co.uk/technology/2016/03/24/microsofts-teen-girl-ai-turns-into-a-hitler-loving-sex-robot-wit

[10] Financial Conduct Authority, 'Our Business Plan 2017/18' (2017), from www.fca.org.uk/publications/corporate-documents/our-business-plan-2017-18

[11] See, e.g. BBC, 'Third Lords Rejection of ID Cards' (2006), from http://news.bbc.co.uk/1/hi/uk_politics/4810482.stm

being gathered in databases held by various corporations and government agencies. Related regulations such as the General Data Protection Regulation (GDPR)[12] are simpatico with such approaches and systems, as they emphasize the right of individuals to control their identity. In this paradigm, no data is provided without clear purpose, which allows individuals to monetize their own data, resulting in far more efficient (and effective) personalization, with fewer heuristics estimating wants and more accuracy delivering needs.

Banks, funds, and asset management houses are all associated with individuals, such as company officers, secretaries, directors, and ultimate beneficiaries, who often must be approved by, or disclosed to, the regulator and whose conduct and behaviours influence the firm's own identity and trustworthiness.[13] Through accurate and independent identification of such actors and related transactional behaviours, the firm's own identity can be augmented, organizational trust increased, and regulatory risk decreased. A fuller knowledge of those currently involved in the operations of a company is enhanced, and confidence in the company can grow. Such methods provide a mechanism for clear responsibilities and accountability, operations can be assured, and, if this can be done without reference to some centralized authority, privacy and confidentiality can also be assured.

In summary, the direction of regulatory reform is clearly heading towards ensuring demonstrable responsibility of clients and industry actors, enhanced by contemporaneous data. The ultimate goal is to provide a system where privacy is maintained (so long as regulators and law enforcement have no reason to investigate) while sweeping away lengthy and illogical processes that cause extraordinary friction in day-to-day operations and prevent greater overall transparency.

Conclusion

This chapter seeks to understand the implications of technological innovation on conduct and culture. However, much depends on the maturity and speed of technological adoption. In the short term, losses through cyber crime may erode the willingness to adopt new technologies. While proof of concepts, use case tests, and incubation activities for these technologies are possible and valuable, longer time spans are likely to be required for such technologies to become truly industrialized and embedded in production processes and correspondingly accepted comfortably by consumers and regulators.

A key determinate factor will be reaching a critical mass of parties to engage with. To use the analogy of the introduction of the telephone, such technologies require widespread adoption (i.e. people who also have a line and so are able to take calls) for their true value to be realized. Key to accelerating technological adoption and correspondingly realizing some of the benefits previously described is the adoption of industry standards and agreements to avoid a spaghetti of proprietary offerings. For example, ISO TC307 provides an opportunity to create a new benchmark for global identity.

To conclude, in the future, as humans become further removed from the transaction by new technological innovation and automation, the old ways of regulation will become increasingly problematic. When we get to the state where independent machines create their own machines or processes, then whole new accountabilities and ethical standards will be required.

---

[12] For the EU General Data Protection Regulation, see https://ico.org.uk/for-organisations/data-protection-reform/overview-of-the-gdpr

[13] In the United Kingdom, the regulator has responded to these challenges by introducing the Senior Managers Certification Regime to ensure firms have clarity over individual responsibilities and accountability.

The Future of RegTech

By John Humphries
CEO, Risk Priorities Inc

and Daniel Flax
Co-Founder, Piece of Cake Consulting

A Big Opportunity

A number of factors have helped to shape the current global regulatory environment. With the onset of the global financial crisis (GFC), banks saw a dramatic increase in regulatory scrutiny and oversight, which will remain. As some companies failed to keep pace with regulatory requirements in certain countries, this resulted in fines, penalties, and settlements exceeding hundreds of billions of dollars since the start of the GFC. Many of these fines are the result of complex regulatory issues, which banks have fixed or are in the process of remediating. These regulatory issues can often be challenging, span multiple countries, and be time-consuming and costly to remediate. In addition to fines, financial services companies are spending billions of dollars on compliance costs annually.

To complicate matters, recent compliance surveys and conversations with employees at financial services companies have highlighted concerns over personal liability and individual accountability. In particular, the C-suite and employees in the compliance, regulatory affairs, operational risk, and audit departments often feel first-hand the pressure and impact of an organization's regulatory breaches and failure to comply with regulations.

The culmination of these factors has caused banks to invest substantially to remediate existing regulatory issues, to keep up with new regulations, regulatory expectations, and compliance headcount. While sizeable investments have been made to plug holes, many financial services companies continue to operate highly manual regulatory and compliance processes, which have not been digitized and lack real-time transparency and forward thinking for effective decision making. This is a big opportunity for RegTech.

Some in the industry see RegTech as a differentiator and an enabler of innovation. According to Ron Quaranta, chairman of the Wall Street Blockchain Alliance, 'As the cost profile begins to shift, you begin to look at regulatory compliance and RegTech as a value-added differentiator for companies'. According to Maria Gotsch, president and CEO of the Partnership Fund for New York City, the organization that runs the FinTech Innovation Lab with Accenture, 'If RegTech allows a company to streamline manual processes or provides information that was previously not available, then it can enable other parts of an institution to be innovative. While RegTech can enable a company's compliance staff to be more efficient, it can also enable a company's business lines to be more innovative.'

The culmination of these factors will continue to drive investment and growth in the RegTech space for years to come.

Compliance Culture

Ensuring compliance across the team is one of the most difficult tasks for any management group. Organizations operating in highly regulated industries such as financial services and healthcare have long staffed a senior manager with the chief compliance officer (CCO) title. In the twenty-first century, post-Sarbanes-Oxley and the surrounding series of accounting scandals, the practice of designating a CCO has spread to other industries.

A key responsibility of the CCO is to work closely with other key management personnel to create a culture of compliance within the organization. One of the cornerstones of compliance is information security and a close partnership with the organization's chief information security officer (CISO). The CISO fosters that. In order to promulgate a compliance culture, two things must happen: the team must be educated, and the leadership must model appropriate behaviour.

To educate the team, companies will employ a handful of methods. For some topics, the compliance team may choose to simply hold seminars or web conferences where an expert presents material and takes in questions. Sessions are generally recorded and made available to the staff who are unable to attend. This technique is usually not particularly effective in educating the team but has certain other virtues. Unfortunately, employees are not particularly engaged and frequently view the seminar as a chore at best and a downright waste of time at worst. The upside is that these kinds of programs are simple to implement, cheap, and can 'check a box' when reporting the existence of a compliance training program to regulators.

Frank Getter, former CISO of CAN Capital, said, 'Training our team on policies and regulations needed to be more than just a formality or requirement. We needed to design a program that engaged the audience and educated them on the concepts while keeping their attention.'

Alternatively, organizations may employ a learning management platform that uses web and mobile technology to push content out to staff. By meeting employees where they are, on their own schedule, platforms like this have a higher success rate. Further, platforms like these employ gamification techniques to engage the audience and create some friendly competition between teams and individuals.

Having an easy-to-use, easy-to-understand, and easy-to-access learning environment is only one part of creating a compliance culture. In addition, the team needs to see and feel leadership modelling the behaviours. Management needs to demonstrate that nobody is above the rules and responsibilities of compliance.

When compliance is hosting a seminar or conference, it is critical that management be in attendance and actively participate.

Getter said that '100% participation was mandated, thus having something that employees appreciated and saw as a genuine benefit to their daily responsibilities was critical to the success of the program. It was not enough to have a representative of the management team; having the whole team visibly participate made a real difference.'

After the GFC, a number of regulators across the globe called on banks to improve their compliance cultures. While a company's culture can be a complex, broad topic and be heavily influenced by the tone at the top, we believe that there are definite ways to improve a company's compliance culture. RegTech companies that develop solutions that help to drive ethical, proactive behaviours and positively influence a company's compliance culture in a tangible manner stand to make a positive impact on the financial services industry. The end result will be a reduction in regulatory issues and fines, and increased cost savings and stability across the industry.

New Technologies

By currently operating highly manual regulatory and compliance processes, financial services companies are potentially exposed and at risk of future failures. However, they can help alleviate this exposure by adopting highly advanced RegTech solutions that leverage advanced technologies such as artificial intelligence (AI), machine learning, blockchain, and so forth. Amongst other things, these technologies will enable more advanced capabilities (e.g. real-time transparency, better decision making, predictive capabilities, and a forward-looking view).

RegTech is getting a big boost from the same advanced technologies that are cropping up elsewhere, tuned to the specific needs of regulated industries. In the world of finance, large investment banks are looking to leverage AI and machine learning for their regulatory and compliance needs.

According to Bart van Liebergen, RegTech adviser at the Institute of International Finance, 'With regard to the future of RegTech, I would see a shift both in terms of technology and the scale of applications. Currently, most of the RegTech applications centre around advanced analytics and biometrics or secure authentication. In the medium to longer term, blockchain and AI applications will reach more mature development and will be used within a RegTech context too. The key difference between the machine learning applications used right now and the AI approaches of the not-too-distant future is that current applications are mostly used for predictive analysis, while the goal of applying AI is to automate decision making.'

Bart van Liebergen went on to say: 'With respect to machine learning and RegTech, while we are in the early stages, banks are experimenting with this technology. The application of machine learning is very specific to the environment to which it is applied. Particularly when applied in a regulatory context, simplicity and transparency of machine learning approaches are warranted: compliance officers, regulators, and bank management want to be able to understand and audit the algorithms. Machine learning can help improve the accuracy of models while improving the ability to analyse diverse data sets and behaviours across the organization.'

Dubbed 'digital reasoning' by one bank, AI is staking its claim in the arsenal of surveillance professionals. The challenge these firms are having with traditional database search-query-based systems and even some of the newer systems is that they miss many of the needs of the compliance or regulatory affairs departments.

Christopher Ricciuti, founder of Panalytics, said that 'leveraging machine learning and AI, our platform and others are able to deliver advanced capabilities to the familiar compliance work flows. We can replace all of the legacy existing functionality and bring the power of machine learning to bear.'

Further, the machine can get better, constantly. 'AI and machine learning get better by watching the human reviewer's actions. The machine gets smarter over time, specifically to that organization's language and scenarios', said Ricciuti.

When asked if there's a future where human reviewers are no longer needed, Ricciuti replied, 'That is so far out, it is not anytime soon. No one is close to any technology like that yet.' Bart van Liebergen expressed a similar view concerning RegTech. 'While RegTech involves the automation and improvement of processes, there will always be people at the end of those processes who maintain control and responsibility for acting on insights produced by advanced technologies.'

Blockchain is another example of a new technology to be used by RegTech solutions. While blockchain is in the early stages, use cases are being developed. One of many uses involves helping organizations to better manage their data. According to Ron Quaranta, 'There are multiple layers from a blockchain perspective and multiple layers from a regulatory perspective around where RegTech fits into a blockchain world. I would argue that it is up and down the stack of financial markets. Also, regulators are looking at the innovation that blockchain and distributed ledger technology represent as a way of enhancing and making regulatory compliance more efficient, more effective, and faster.'

Roles of RegTech Companies

In considering the future of RegTech, we believe that RegTech companies have an important role to play:

- *Focus on value*. For companies in general, it can be easy to lose sight of the end goal: delivering extreme value. While it may be appealing for RegTech companies to offer several products and services, they need to find and focus on their niche. Instead of falling into the trap of trying to solve all governance, risk management, and compliance problems across all industries,

RegTech companies must deliver solutions to financial services companies that solve significant business problems.

- *Customer engagement.* In order to keep pace with change and customer requirements, RegTech companies need to be highly engaged with financial services companies during customer discovery activities to identify the most significant problems and pain points that are high risk.

- *Regulator engagement.* In considering the future of RegTech, it is important to recognize that regulators are a key constituent. RegTech companies can broadly improve and influence the financial services industry by actively engaging and having forward-thinking, collaborative dialogues with regulators. According to Maria Gotsch, 'The full potential of RegTech will be realized when there are timely and regular dialogues between regulators, financial institutions, and FinTech companies.' Ron Quaranta's view is similar: 'For RegTech companies, there is much to be gained by participating in the dialogue around blockchain technology early and even at the technical level.'

- *New technologies.* Broadly speaking, RegTech companies can help companies to automate and digitize manual compliance and regulatory processes. In doing so, this enables a company to focus on delivering high-impact activities in the value chain versus manual tasks that are high risk and costly over time. In leveraging the latest technologies, data sciences, and software development methodologies, RegTech companies must build innovative, scalable, secure solutions.

- *Compliance culture.* Post-GFC, banks have been called on by regulators to improve their compliance cultures. Despite company culture often being influenced top-down and by a variety of factors, RegTech companies have a significant role to play in the financial services sector. Designing RegTech solutions that tangibly improve a company's compliance culture will reduce the prevalence of regulatory issues whilst also ensuring cost savings.

From RegTech to TechReg – Regulation in a Decentralized World

By Axel Apfelbacher
Chief Strategy Officer, Niiio Finance Group AG

and Jasmina Ekic
Business Development Manager, Financial Services Industry

Liberal markets are organized to allow users and providers of services the ability to interact without unnecessary interference by third parties. They are a central element of market capitalism and have been established in many economies as a means of organizing daily interactions.

In all of these markets, though, we encounter rogue behaviour leading to damages suffered by users of services or products offered. The standard reaction is to implement or tighten regulations that are supposed to ascertain that such behaviour is not repeated. This is true for any market, including the provision of financial services, which is one of the most regulated industries these days, not least as a consequence of the global financial crisis that started in 2007.

Existing Regulatory Framework

Today, regulation in financial services is almost exclusively targeting the intermediaries that act as providers of such services. We encourage financial services companies to implement compliance practices and policies that target unwanted behaviour and make them pay damages if they fail to act in accordance with the set of regulations we have unilaterally or multilaterally agreed on as governance frameworks. The mainstay of this approach to regulation is that the potential reputational or monetary damages are sufficiently severe to entice banks and other regulated market participants to comply.

Decentralization

One of the major business and technology trends these days is decentralization. Following the initial logic implemented in the first iterations of the network we have come to call 'the internet', today we design both technologies as well as business models that potentially make do without a central instance. One of the main reasons for doing so is de-risking, i.e. limiting or eliminating the potential for a single point of failure to bring down a whole system.

Amongst other instantiations, this has led to the development of a decentralized form of money issuance, transfer, and storage called bitcoin. The basic premise is the nonexistence of central nodes and the distribution of data *and* responsibility for systems maintenance to a dispersed group of interested parties, each forming an element of the network and incentivized to invest resources into keeping it alive.

With the advent of such decentralized technologies, business models, and knowledge-based systems that cut out or automate the intermediary, the whole approach to regulation and the measures we use to create trustworthy interactions will have to be redesigned as well.

Regulation in a Decentralized Market

In a fully decentralized marketplace, there are only buyers and sellers of services as well as the software connecting the two. Regulation based on managing the behaviour of the intermediary, as described earlier, will simply be void once decentralized business models take hold within a community. In the case of, e.g.

securities issuance on a blockchain, we can regulate the issuer as well as the buyer of securities, but no longer the intermediaries connecting the two.

We therefore need to reframe the regulatory approach and start designing rules that take into account the elimination of the formerly highly regulated intermediaries. Logically, this leaves us with three potential market participants to regulate:

1. Sellers and issuers of products, services, and financial instruments.

2. Buyers of products, services, and financial instruments.

3. Software providers.

Regulating the Sellers

To a certain extent, the financial services world has already started to regulate the issuance of financial products and the information provision required for issuers of such instruments to enable a true and fair view of financial instruments. Still, the current regulatory framework relies to a significant extent on the ability of the distributors of such instruments to manage the match between products and their buyers. Theoretically, even the most toxic asset class cannot harm unwitting buyers as long as the distribution networks prevent them from acquiring stakes in such asset classes. Any regulation pertaining to risk classes and customer assessments follows this logic.

If we exclude the intermediary in a decentralized world, one way of dealing with the regulatory challenge would be to force the same rules upon issuers of financial instruments and make them responsible for finding buyers that have sufficient expertise and risk-bearing capacity for the products on issue. This, however, would lead to increasingly complex processes at the issuer's end, making the whole process of financial services innovation and fit-for-purpose productization of financial risks more expensive

and difficult to manage. However, it would link the inventors of financial products with the risks inherent in their products and maybe stop an unhealthy degree of creativity in securitization from building up.

Regulating the Buyers

The next viable regulatory option is to put the onus of regulatory compliance on the acquirers of financial products. If the intermediaries are missing, we can stipulate that each investor is responsible for ascertaining that the required level of understanding and risk-bearing capacity is available to invest in a specific instrument or asset class viable from a risk perspective.

In the end, this will mean that we need to test the market understanding of an individual investor before allowing specific asset classes or instruments to be made available for purchase by such an investor. Given the renewed fascination with gamification approaches in banking, we can envisage a game-based assessment (e.g. through a simulation game) that enables the measurement of risk-bearing capacity as well as risk understanding by the individual, making the supply of financial instruments dependent upon the results of such (e.g. annualized) tests.

Such a regulatory structure would, however, require a near-perfect matching of financial instruments to risk classes, which is comparatively easy for existing products and asset classes and very difficult for new instruments, as it will require an onboarding process within which the instruments are classified prior to regulatory approval of their distribution.

On the other hand, this approach would link the regulatory regime with the necessity to increase financial literacy in the wider community, which appears to be both an achievable as well as a desirable goal in general.

Regulating the Software Providers (TechReg)

The last remaining entities in a decentralized world are the software providers enabling decentralized business models to evolve by providing the required software components or platforms. Today, software providers very rarely step up to the challenges of the regulated market, arguing that they are only the providers of software, not providers of the services enabled through their software.

Such a perfunctory answer is probably not going to be acceptable if we want to achieve mainstream adoption of decentralized models. Looking at the Ethereum/decentralized autonomous organization (DAO) disaster,[1] a case for tighter regulation of technology providers is easily made.

The most likely sequence of events, as experienced in other regulated markets, will probably be one of failure → self-regulation → failure → overregulation by state bodies → deregulation → failure → overregulation, and so on.

The regulatory aspects to be covered with respect to software providers are (i) the education of coders (including a strong commitment to ethical coding), (ii) the certification of individuals and/or entities, (iii) the ability to review and test code wherever it tackles processes that the general public takes an interest in, and (iv) the ability to prosecute individuals or entities if they fail to comply with the pre-agreed and committed standards.

---

[1] The attempt to build a decentralized investment fund as a DAO using the cryptocurrency Ether as transactional medium failed in 2016 when a participant exploited the predefined rules to move a substantial share of the funds, breaching the intended purpose of the DAO. This exploit had not been foreseen by the coders and raised substantial questions about the validity of an unregulated DAO structure.

A Broader Case for Regulating Technology Providers

Even disregarding a potentially fully decentralized world, the case for TechReg is still going strong. We are moving more and more of our business processes into software code by automating them and gathering the data required to power such processes in giant databases, whether in centralized or decentralized instances.

The more critical processes are governed by software code, the more the knowledge, attitudes, and hidden biases of, and the incentive schemes for, software coders are taking centre stage. One major element of the global financial crisis was model overconfidence – in that case, econometric models used to supposedly manage financial risks. By moving more and more processes into software code, these hidden biases or outright fraud or conning of customers by decision-making algorithms deeply hidden inside the code will become a major issue for regulation. In order to reduce the risks inherent in fully automated solutions, both the ability and the motivation of the workers and managers who produce the relevant code require a tighter regulatory regime targeting the software industry.

TechReg Market Opportunities

The risks outlined earlier enable a variety of new business models that are suggested to mitigate these risks:

- Coding academies with universal certifications.
- An industry association committing its members to high ethical standards.
- Reviewers of code that can certify its validity.

Coding Academies

The most likely providers of services in this area will be existing coding academies that start including educational elements pertaining to identifying conflicts of interest, fraudulent behaviour by coders, and hidden biases that may have an impact on the nature of the code produced. These academies can then issue certificates and position those in the global market as an indicator of a higher professional standard.

Coding Industry Association

Such an association can start both as a grass-roots movement and as an industry-wide initiative by major buyers of coding services. Similar to other associations, e.g. in the financial services world, it is supposed to enable continuing education of its members as well as hold them to predefined standards of ethical behaviour. Continued membership in such an association can then be positioned in the employment markets as proof of coders' abilities and willingness to use their skills in favour of the community they are serving.

Code Review and Certification

This type of service could, for example, become a future-proof domain of auditing companies in need of a new business model. The ability to review and certify the validity of critical software code could become a new major business line for such companies whose business model is premised upon high professional standards and a – sometimes contested – position of neutrality.

Such software auditing could be applied to application software code as well as to smart contracts in the decentralized world, ascertaining that a particular smart contract exclusively enables the type of transaction that the provider and users of the codified transfer of assets managed through the smart contract originally intended. Such a review and certification process could avoid events like the ones unfolding around the DAO disaster.

In order to prevent exclusively manual review processes that are both time-consuming and costly, such code review capabilities will require the use of even more sophisticated technology, mainly code review engines that are trained to identify rogue or broken code and identify the relevant passages for a human coder to review. Such engines have already been built but will require a substantial knowledge increase to correctly identify erroneous code and criminal coders with sufficient accuracy.

All of these business models could become an integral part of the RegTech market and establish themselves as a central offering for all platform models. There are initial demands voiced by consumer protection agencies, rightly claiming that the quality of software as well as the inherent algorithmic designs have an impact on real-world outcomes and requesting a certification process for software components that impact the well-being of millions. Such claims may well be the initial ripples that precede a global discussion about the standards to which we want to hold the software industry in the future. Such a discussion will reveal to what extent we are willing and capable of creating a TechReg regime that entices software providers to use their capacities for improving the world.

Emerging Innovations in RegTech

By Stephen Ufford
CEO, Trulioo

Historically, most doomsday scenarios tend to remain *scenarios* – reality tends to play out a little differently. In 2008, however, doomsday advocates were nearly proven right. A global economic meltdown was only hours away before unprecedented intervention by the US Treasury. When the dust finally settled, policy makers knew they had to tighten restrictions on financial institutions (FIs). Since then, new laws have been put into place, more than $235 billion in fines have been levied, and rigorous compliance rules have gone into effect; alongside, the technological capabilities have evolved, enabling us to improve the breadth and depth of data reporting, aggregation, and analysis.

Emerging from the ashes of the 2008 global financial crisis, new regulatory technologies (RegTech) are helping to ease the burden of compliance and lower operational costs and risks for FIs – fundamentally changing the nature of the financial services industry. At the crux of these changes is the use of new technologies such as compliance as a service (CaaS), to help FIs regulate, monitor, report, and comply.

Manual and cumbersome compliance processes present major problems in our digital, on-demand economy, where the financial industry is inundated with complex and ever-changing regulations. The saying, "we are drowning in information while starving for wisdom", rings true more than ever before, especially as FIs crunch through voluminous amounts of data. Emerging offerings in RegTech such as 'plug-and-play' CaaS solutions help FIs effectively comply with regulatory requirements by harnessing new technologies. CaaS can, in minutes, provide insights into massive volumes of data to minimize costly manual processes, along with helping improve and speed up identity checks for meeting regulations such as Anti–Money Laundering (AML) and Know Your Customer (KYC).

The CaaS model helps regulated businesses meet KYC and AML obligations while eliminating inefficiencies and risks involved in onboarding a customer, e.g. extensive face time with customers, official document checks, and calling government bureaus. This reduces the need for customers to jump through hoops to prove their identity while also improving the entire customer experience. For FIs, this manual process is too dependent on human capital and vulnerable to error. The future of RegTech within the financial industry is therefore defined by the new CaaS model and will see greater adoption in the coming years.

With the continued consumer demand and expectations for real-time services, such as opening a bank account on a mobile device anytime, anywhere, without having to visit a local branch, CaaS is only set to grow. The rapid proliferation of mobile devices and the growth of FinTech have spawned the need for compliance solutions that are on-demand in order to provide access to financial products and services in real time.

If the recent past is any indication, regulations will continue to evolve as money launderers and terrorist financiers leverage the latest technologies and techniques towards nefarious ends. Whilst new technology provides advances for consumers and businesses, it also provides opportunities for people and organizations to hide illicit funds. An example is bitcoin being used for dark web payments or other anonymous transactions. Initially, bitcoin was not regulated and flew under the radar, attracting use by criminals looking for anonymous ways to conduct nefarious activities online. Regulators did eventually become concerned when bitcoin was being used for illegal transactions that were harmful to society, which led to the development of a legal framework. Some countries have already passed laws to accept bitcoin as a legal payment method, and other countries are looking into it. As the market matures, more regulations will come into force.

The speed of technology is relentless and increasing at a faster clip. Every advancement introduces more questions, more possibilities, more ways to cheat, and more considerations for regulations. The only way for FIs to keep up is to have nimble systems that can adapt quickly and dynamically change to meet new requirements.

This adaptability not only comes into play within jurisdictional boundaries but also applies when FIs are expanding globally. While many countries agree to follow the international standards of the Financial Action Task Force (FATF), each country has its own specific legal requirements, regulations, and reporting mechanisms. This means that for every country an FI wants to do business in, it needs to consider different compliance obligations. If a company needs to create every compliance procedure from scratch every time, the cost and time to enter new markets can be prohibitive, and expansion is curtailed.

Cross-border e-commerce is now the fastest growing segment in the retail market, growing at an average annual rate of 25%. Companies that want to tap into that growth have to implement payment procedures that are both compliant and effective in preventing fraud. After all, it is not just traditional FIs that need to comply with regulations. Any business that moves money online is a possible point of intrusion for illicit funds. Most countries have threshold amounts that require KYC checks above that limit, so any company doing business internationally needs to consider compliance factors.

It is not only a business's customers that are a potential entry point for questionable funds. Through sophisticated layering techniques and other ways to obfuscate funds, a whole host of suppliers, partners, and other third-party relationships are possible weak points. After the revelations of the Panama Papers, regulators are looking to stop the flow of funds from compromised beneficial ownership structures or other problematic relationships. The requirement to Know Your Customer's Customer (KYCC) or Know Your Business (KYB) is growing stronger.

Already in effect in Europe (as of 26 June 2017), the Fourth Anti-Money Laundering Directive (4AMLD) requires European firms to report their beneficial ownership structure. As the EU Commission states, 'understanding the beneficial ownership of companies is at the heart of the risk mitigation of financial crime and of prevention strategies for regulated firms'. In the United States, similar rules came into effect on 11 May 2018. The Customer Due Diligence (CDD) Final Rule requires 'identifying and verifying the identity of the beneficial owners of companies opening accounts'. There are many factors enabling the movement of corrupt funds: the growth of international commerce, complex multinational business structures, the growing speed of money transactions, and the massive amounts of questionable funds looking for safety and legitimacy. Regulators, if they have any hope of stopping the $7–32 trillion of corrupt funds around the world today, will continue to ratchet up these third-party compliance requirements.

If FIs and other businesses think compliance is tough now, consider how much more difficult it will become as layer after layer of relationships require checks and monitoring. Without automation or other CaaS solutions, the requirements are overwhelming. While the need to stop the flow of corrupt funds is obvious, grinding legitimate business to a halt or forcing extraordinary compliance costs is a non-starter. CaaS offers a feasible way for compliance to succeed in the modern digital economy.

CaaS and other RegTech innovations are also of great interest to the regulators themselves. They face the same issues that the companies they oversee have: complex rules, vast amounts of data, changing requirements, and burdensome manual processes. The more compliance is digitized and algorithmically monitored, the more they can focus on catching new schemes and resolving intricate patterns. CaaS offers regulators the hope of a future where they can focus on interesting, cutting-edge cases rather than simply keeping up with basic, rote processes.

All of these promises of RegTech are an outgrowth of the same paradigm that is driving the internet forward: an open, interconnected network of resources. While some of the new possibilities are due to technological advantages (faster processing speeds and communication speeds, better software, and new systems), it is the new mindset that is the real revolution.

For example, application programming interfaces (APIs) are a model for sharing networked resources and information. By offering programming routines, protocols, and tools to access and manipulate data and other resources, third parties can more easily add value to the application. Developers need not create every piece of code from scratch but can start developing advanced features right out of the box. Creating new features or services is not reliant on one source; developers can use the base code to build what they want – the speed of development can be accelerated, while costs can be brought down. Improving integration with other processes is also simplified, further adding to the advantages of using APIs.

The model of openness is core to the future of RegTech. Even APIs that are private (accessible within a company or supplier network) are more open than previous models that were tightly controlled by system operators. By design, they can be more open; APIs have collaboration in mind, and controls are in place to limit access as needed. Open APIs take that collaboration to the next level, allowing anyone to develop almost anything they want. Providers of open APIs are betting that the innovation and utility created by the development community will far outweigh the costs of opening up their platforms.

The concept of open banking takes openness one step further: Actually opening up customer account information to third-party providers. For European bankers, this is the reality as a result of the second Payment Services Directive (PSD2). Now, European consumers can keep their primary FI, but shop around for different services, interfaces, pricing, and other factors to maximize their banking experience.

It is not only consumers that will benefit. FIs that create innovative services, or somehow otherwise differentiate their service, can more easily reap the rewards. A whole range of old-school FIs that fail to adapt will be in trouble, or, as Darwin illustrates, adapt or die. Rather than being a shackle holding back progress, RegTech in this light is an opportunity to drive innovation, create new revenue streams, and modernize processes.

With all the advantages of the openness model, expect similar regulations to spread. Other jurisdictions will not be satisfied with the status quo when they see the opportunities of open banking. Beyond banking, other sectors are ripe for innovation. Whether it is insurance, investments, payments, transfers, remittances, currency exchange, capital markets, or other financial services, there are huge benefits to opening up the model. By enabling a plug-and-play model, where new services are quickly, smoothly, and securely added, whole new categories of innovation will be born.

RegTech holds the keys to successfully opening up FI segments. We need effective controls and oversight, or else fraud, corruption, and theft can quickly escalate. We cannot accept conditions that can lead to a global economic meltdown. We also can't burden businesses and consumers with slow, outdated processes that no longer fit with a mobile world. RegTech and the CaaS model will ensure that the benefits of digitization are extended to all. By simplifying compliance whilst keeping and expanding protections, RegTech will be a key driver for a successful future.

List of Contributors

Dr Inna Amesheva
Associate, ESG Research and Advisory, Arabesque S-Ray
www.linkedin.com/in/inna-amesheva

See chapter:
The Potential of RegTech in Improving the Effectiveness of Environmental Regulation

Axel Apfelbacher
Chief Strategy Officer, Niiio Finance Group AG
www.linkedin.com/in/axel-apfelbacher-cfa-a13391

See chapter:
From RegTech to TechReg – Regulation in a Decentralized World

Douglas W. Arner
Kerry Holdings Professor in Law, Co-Founder, Asian Institute of International Financial Law, and Faculty Director, LLM in Compliance and Regulation, University of Hong Kong
www.linkedin.com/in/douglas-arner-91a678164/

See chapter:
A FinTech and RegTech Overview: Where We Have Come From and Where We Are Going

Murad Baig
Global Chief Innovation Officer, Netsol Technologies, Inc
www.linkedin.com/in/murad-baig-0717a21

See chapter:
Market Surveillance 2020

Janos Barberis
Senior Research Fellow, Asian Institute of International Financial Law, Faculty of Law, University of Hong Kong, and Founder, SuperCharger FinTech Accelerator and FinTech HK
www.linkedin.com/in/jbarberis/

See chapter:
A FinTech and RegTech Overview: Where We Have Come From and Where We Are Going

Patrick Barnert
Non-Executive Director, Evolute Group AG
www.linkedin.com/in/patrickbarnert

See chapter:
Spend on Compliance: A Necessary Evil or Business Enabler?

Dr Tobias Bauerfeind
Associate, Ashurst LLP
www.linkedin.com/in/dr-tobias-b-1188b2135

See chapter:
Banking Supervision at a Crossroads – RegTech as the Regulators' Toolbox

Soumaya Bhyer
Postgraduate, Cambridge University
www.linkedin.com/in/soumayabhyer

See chapter:
Banking the Unbanked and Underbanked: RegTech as an Enabler for Financial Inclusion

Sharifah Nursyafiqah Binte Syed Isha
Senior Consultant, Datarama
www.linkedin.com/in/sharifah-nursyafiqah-binte-syed-isha-416356125

See chapter:
RegTech Applicability Outside the Financial Services Industry

Pierre Bittner
CEO, WeeFin
www.linkedin.com/in/pierre-bittner-7209597

See chapter:
Discover the Innovative Technology Behind RegTech Leaders

Bert Boerman
CEO, Governance.com
www.linkedin.com/in/bboerman

See chapter:
Governance, Risk, and Compliance: Complex or Complicated?

352

LIST OF CONTRIBUTORS

See chapter:
The Role of Anti-Money Laundering Law and Compliance in FinTech

Jasmina Ekic
Business Development Manager, Financial Services Industry
www.linkedin.com/in/jasminaekic

See chapter:
From RegTech to TechReg – Regulation in a Decentralized World

Nirvana Farhadi
Global Head Financial Services, RegTech Risk and Regulatory Compliance Affairs, Hitachi Vantara
www.linkedin.com/in/nirvana-farhadi-a117384

See chapter:
Why a Substantial Investment in Financial Services RegTech Now Will Strategically Reduce Your Future Regulatory Compliance Costs

Christina Fellner
Head of Unit B2C, Fidor Bank AG
www.linkedin.com/in/christinafellner

See chapter:
Rise of RegTech in the German Market

Paul Ferris
CEO, ObjectTech Group
www.linkedin.com/in/objecttechgppaullferris/

See chapter:
GDPR and PSD2: Self-Sovereign Identity, Privacy, and Innovation
I Regulate Therefore I Am? Regulating Humans' and Machines' Conduct and Culture

Daniel Flax
Co-Founder, Piece of Cake Consulting
www.linkedin.com/in/danielflax

See chapter:
The Future of RegTech

Marcel Fröhlich
Director Service, Eccenca GmbH
www.linkedin.com/in/marcel-fröhlich-648a043

See chapter:
Enabling RegTech Up Front: Unambiguous Machine-readable Regulation

Francesca Gaudino
Local Partner, Baker & McKenzie
www.linkedin.com/in/francesca-gaudino-5a3181

See chapter:
The FinTech Ecosystem Between Legal Compliance and Social Dimension

Rohit Ghosh
AI Scientist, Skyra Capital
www.linkedin.com/in/rohit-ghosh-iit

See chapter:
Merits and Demerits of a Shared Risk Engine

Dr Daniel Gozman
Senior Lecturer, The University of Sydney Business School
www.linkedin.com/in/dr-daniel-gozman-938a822

See chapter:
I Regulate Therefore I Am? Regulating Humans' and Machines' Conduct and Culture

Jennifer Hanley-Giersch
Managing Partner, Berlin Risk Ltd
www.linkedin.com/in/jennifer-hanley-giersch-5909a99

See chapter:
RegTech and Financial Crime Prevention

Andrew Henderson
Partner – Financial Services, Eversheds-Sutherland (International) LLP
www.linkedin.com/in/andrew-henderson-2587776

See chapter:
Legal Guidance for Entering the Sandbox and Taking Advantage of Cross-Border Cooperation Agreements

Matthew Homer
Affiliate, Cambridge Center for Alternative Finance
www.linkedin.com/in/matthomer

See chapter:
RegTech is for Regulators Too, and its Future is in Emerging Markets

Tobias Houdek
Senior Product and Marketing Manager, Investment Navigator
www.linkedin.com/in/tobiashoudek

See chapter:
Introducing the RegTech Quality Compass: The Five Factors of RegTech Quality

Ralf Huber
Co-Founder, APIAX
www.linkedin.com/in/ralf-huber
See chapter:
Making Regulation Machine Readable

Jenna Huey Ching
Specialist in FinTech, RegTech and LawTech
www.linkedin.com/in/jennahuey
See chapter:
Superhero Way: Enhancing Regulatory Supervision with Superpowers

John Humphries
CEO, Risk Priorities Inc
www.linkedin.com/in/john-humphries-5530348
See chapter:
The Future of RegTech

Sean Hunter
CIO, OakNorth Analytical Intelligence
www.linkedin.com/in/sean-hunter-548358b
See chapter:
Innovation or Disruption: Not Always Black and White

Fleur Hutchinson
Enhanced Due Diligence Consultant, Seventeen Research Ltd
www.linkedin.com/in/fleur-hutchinson-67978717
See chapter:
RegTech Opportunities in a Post-4MLD/5MLD World

Jane Jee
CEO, Kompli-Global Limited
www.linkedin.com/in/jane-jee-6a29591
See chapter:
RegTech Opportunities in a Post-4MLD/5MLD World

David Jones
CTO, ipushpull
www.linkedin.com/in/davidjonesipushpull
See chapter:
Old Tech + New Tech = RegTech: Excel Spreadsheets and End User Computing in a Regulated World

Inga Jovanovic
Managing Director, Capnovum
www.linkedin.com/in/inga-jovanovic-3893102
See chapter:
Islamic RegTech

Michelle Katics
Co-Founder and CEO, PortfolioQuest and BankersLab
www.linkedin.com/in/michellekatics
See chapter:
RegTech's Impact on Trust and Identity

Leanne Kemp
Founder and CEO, Everledger
www.linkedin.com/in/leannekemp
See chapter:
Blockchains Are Diamonds' Best Friend: The Case for Supply Chain Transparency

Remonda Z. Kirketerp-Møller
Founder and CEO, muinmos ApS
www.linkedin.com/in/remonda-zahdeh-kirketerp-møller-89b0993
See chapter:
Passporting in the EU – Is an Opportunity Also a Problem?

Chionh Chye Kit
CEO and Co-Founder, Cynopsis Solutions Pte. Ltd.
www.linkedin.com/in/chionhchyekit
See chapter:
RegTech Outside Finance: Four Options, One Clear Choice

Dr Ulf Klebeck
General Counsel, Montana Capital Partners and Partner/Co-Founder, Excelerate
www.linkedin.com/in/ulf-klebeck-dr-iur-50b48614
See chapter:
FinReg, FinTech, and RegTech – Quo Vadis, EU?

Bartłomiej Klinger
Former Co-Founder and CEO, Positiverse
www.linkedin.com/in/bartlomiejklinger
See chapter:
Compliance with Data Protection Regulations by Applying the Blockchain Technology

Désirée Klingler
Attorney-at-Law, and PhD Candidate, University of St. Gallen
www.linkedin.com/in/désirée-klingler-50046689

See chapter:
RegTech and the Sandbox – Play, Innovate and Protect!

Sebastian Ko
Co-Founder and Chief Operating Officer, DHB Global
www.linkedin.com/in/sebko

See chapter:
RegTech Unleashed: Discovering the Pathways Beyond Finance

Marcel Krist
CEO and Chairman, Photonfocus AG and Managing Director, KYC Exchange Net AG
www.linkedin.com/in/marcel-krist-261111a

See chapter:
Will Financial Institutions Ever Achieve a 100% Compliance with Anti–Money Laundering and Combating the Financing of Terrorism Rules?

Selcuk Kuram
Consultant, Berlin Hyp AG
www.linkedin.com/in/selcuk-kuram-cfa-02761b24

See chapter:
Rise of RegTech in the German Market

Natasha Kyprianides
Head of Omni-channel and Customer Experience, Hellenic Bank
www.linkedin.com/in/natashakyprianides

See chapter:
Invention Versus Reinvention

Stuart Lacey
Founder and Director, Trunomi
www.linkedin.com/in/stuart-lacey-585b4629

See chapter:
Protecting Consumers and Enabling Innovation

Peter Lancos
Co-Founder and CEO, Exate Technology
www.linkedin.com/in/peter-lancos-b51b71ab

See chapter:
Using RegTech as a Cross-Industry Digitalization Tool

Dr Matthias Lange
Managing Partner, FinLeap
www.linkedin.com/in/matthiaslange

See chapter:
Rise of RegTech in the German Market

Robin Lee
Market Development, Risk and RegTech, Refinitiv
www.linkedin.com/in/robin-lee-李显龙-b8948a

See chapter:
RegTech Applicability Outside the Financial Services Industry

Seyoung Lee
Associate, Sagamore Investments
www.linkedin.com/in/seyoung-lee-95225591

See chapter:
Banking the Unbanked and Underbanked: RegTech as an Enabler for Financial Inclusion

Anne Leslie
Senior Managing Consultant, IBM
www.linkedin.com/in/anneleslie

See chapter:
The End Justifies the Means: Putting Social Purpose Back at the Heart of Banking and Financial Regulation

Dr Jonathan Liebenau
Professor (Reader), The London School of Economics and Political Science
www.linkedin.com/in/jonathan-liebenau-548a418b

See chapter:
I Regulate Therefore I Am? Regulating Humans' and Machines' Conduct and Culture

Bernard Lunn
CEO, Daily FinTech
www.linkedin.com/in/bernardlunn

See chapter:
What a RegTech Compliance Killer System Will Look Like

Brad Maclean
CEO, Regulation Asia
www.linkedin.com/in/bdgmaclean

See chapter:
The ROI of RegTech

Kinsuk Mitra

Global Director and Head of RegTech, Risk and Compliance, HCL Technologies
www.linkedin.com/in/kinsukmitra

See chapter:
How Banks Are Managing Their Risk Through Technology and Market Infrastructure

Jan-Maarten Mulder

Founder, Summer Capital
www.linkedin.com/in/mulderjm

See chapter:
RegTech: Tackling Regulation with Innovation

Shirish Nekte

CEO, Amberoon Inc
www.linkedin.com/in/shirishnetke

See chapter:
RegTech and the Science of Regulation

Niclas Nilsson

Founder and CEO, Capnovum
www.linkedin.com/in/cannilsson

See chapter:
Islamic RegTech

Benedicte N. Nolens

Chair of Advisory Council, Global Digital Finance and Board Member, Hong Kong FinTech Association
www.linkedin.com/in/benedicte-n-nolens-77529747

See chapter:
The RegTech Landscape from a Regulator's Perspective

Jay Patani

Business Insights Lead, CompareAsiaGroup and former Technical Evangelist, ITRS Group
www.linkedin.com/in/patani

See chapter:
RegTech: A Safe Bet for Tackling AML and Fraud in the Gambling Sector

B.J. Perng

CEO, NiveauUp Inc
www.linkedin.com/in/bjperng

See chapter:
Align Open Banking and Future-Proof RegTech for Regulators and Third-Party Providers to Deliver the Optimal Consumer Convenience and Protection

Harshwardhan Prasad

VP, Quant Analytics, Morgan Stanley
www.linkedin.com/in/harsh-prasad

See chapter:
Merits and Demerits of a Shared Risk Engine

Zeeshan Rashid

Global Head – BF SI Risk and Compliance Practice, Tata Consultancy Services Ltd
www.linkedin.com/in/zee123

See chapter:
Technology-Enabled Collaborative Compliance

Ankit Ratan

Co-Founder, Signzy
www.linkedin.com/in/ankitratan

See chapter:
Dissolving Barriers: A Global Digital Trust Protocol

Sonal Rattan

Co-Founder and CTO, Exate Technology
www.linkedin.com/in/sonalrattan

See chapter:
Using RegTech as a Cross-Industry Digitalization Tool

Subas Roy

Partner, Oliver Wyman
www.linkedin.com/in/subasroy

See chapter:
How RegTech Could Help Determine the Future of Financial Services

Vladislav Solodkiy

Managing Partner, Life.SREDA VC and CEO, Arival bank
www.linkedin.com/in/vsolodkiy

See chapter:
What Do PSD2 and Similar Activities Mean for Banks and FinTech Startups?

Javier Tamashiro
Head of Technology Risk and Compliance, Maecenas and Founder, Ospree Pte. Ltd.
www.linkedin.com/in/javiertamashiro

See chapter:
ArtTech: How Blockchain Can Improve Provenance

Brian Tang
Founder, ACMI and LITE Lab@HKU
www.linkedin.com/in/brianwtang

See chapter:
Forging a Responsibility and Liability Framework in the AI Era for RegTech

Dr Evelyn Thar
CEO, Amazee Metrics
www.linkedin.com/in/evelynthar

See chapter:
How to Use Digital Marketing Data in Regulated Industries

Stephen Ufford
CEO, Trulioo
www.linkedin.com/in/stephenufford

See chapter:
Emerging Innovations in RegTech

Nick Wakefield
Managing Director Europe, Bambu and Co-Founder, Regulation Asia
www.linkedin.com/in/nickwakefield

See chapter:
How Technology Is Driving Financial Inclusion

Julia Walker
Head of Market Development, Risk and Regulatory Technology, Asia Pacific, Refinitiv
www.linkedin.com/in/julia-b-walker

See chapter:
Blockchains Are Diamonds' Best Friend: The Case for Supply Chain Transparency

Mackenzie Wallace
Director, ZestFinance
www.linkedin.com/in/smackenziewallace

See chapter:
RegTech is for Regulators Too, and its Future is in Emerging Markets

Benjamin Weld
CEO and Co-Founder, Falcon DHQ
www.linkedin.com/in/benjaminweld

See chapter:
RegTech Impact on the Private Security Industry

Mike Wilson
Co-Founder, RegTech Markets and RegTech Forum
www.linkedin.com/in/mikewilson9

See chapter:
The Age of RegTech Disruption to the Status Quo Is Here

Dominik Witz
Head of Banking Compliance and RegTech, Swisscom
www.linkedin.com/in/dominik-witz-4602ab11b

See chapter:
Sandbox Games for RegTech

Malcolm Wright
Chief Compliance Officer, Diginex
www.linkedin.com/in/malcolmwright

See chapter:
Can AI Really Disrupt Monitoring for Suspicious Activity?

Index

1stDibs 266

A

E

G

H

I

market surveillance 27, 219, 330–4
Markets in Financial Instruments Directive (MiFID II) 106, 107
MatLab 150
Mayer Brown 125
Mayer-Schonberger, Viktor 244
McNamara, Robert 244
MENA Region, financial inclusion 320
Mercedes 243
Merkle trees 244
metadata, customer 86, 90
MetricStream 17, 282
Meyer, Michael 27
Microsoft 24, 153, 236, 284
Microsoft Azure 236
Microsoft Excel spreadsheets 150–3
Microsoft PowerBI 84
millennials 206
Minority Report (movie) 58, 59, 232, 241
mispricing assets 16
misuse of private data 30
ML as a service (MLaaS) 235
MLRs 172, 174
mobile commerce (m-commerce) 182
Mobile Connect 31
mobile payments 315
model management 29
Modern-Day Slavery Act (205) (UK) 250
Monetary Authority of Singapore (MAS) 66, 316
money laundering 6, 16, 20, 287, 293, 335
Money Laundering, Terrorist Financing and Transfer of Funds
(Information on the Payer) Regulations 2017 *see* MLRs
Moneyball 244
MoneyGram 320
Monzo 183
Moore's law 59
Mougayar, William 246
M-Pesa 316
Mulder, Jan-Maarten 22

multilateral trading facilities (MTFs) 331
multinational corporations (MNCs) 284, 285
Musharaka partnership 41
mutual evaluation reports (MERs) 287

N

N26 68, 183
NASDAQ 331
National Bank of Abu Dhabi 320
national competent authorities (NCAs) 148,195
natural language processing (NLP) 14, 98, 106, 207
Nestlé 250
net stable funding ratio (NSFR) 55
Netflix 58, 82
New York 107, 108
New York Stock Exchange (NYSE) 331
Newsfeed 82
NICE 17
NICE Actimize 74
non-compliance 218
non-finance options 287–91
Nordic banks 31, 32
NoSQL for Fast Read-write Access 83–4

O

Object Management Group (OMG) 85
    Business Motivation Model (BMM) standard 87
'obliged entities' 174
Office for Professional Body Anti–money Laundering Supervision
    (OPBAS) 173
Office of Foreign Assets Control (OFAC) 191
Office of the Comptroller of the Currency (OCC) 93
OnDeck Capital 124, 183
'one leg out' (OLO) payments 182
one-time password (OTP) 89